TECHNOPHOBIA!

TECHNOPHOBIA!

SCIENCE FICTION VISIONS
OF POSTHUMAN TECHNOLOGY

Daniel Dinello

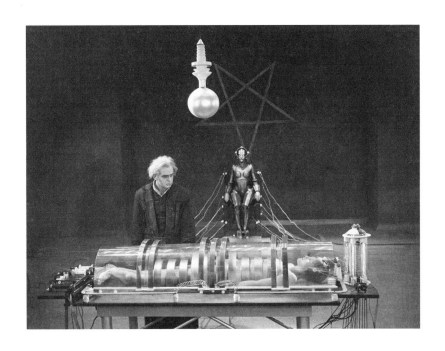

UNIVERSITY OF TEXAS PRESS
Austin

Frontispiece: Human under the domination of corporate science and autonomous technology (*Metropolis*, 1926. Courtesy Photofest).

Requests for permission to reproduce material from this work should be sent to Permissions, University of Texas Press, P.O. Box 7819, Austin, TX 78713-7819.

www.utexas.edu/utpress/about/bpermission.html

♾ The paper used in this book meets the minimum requirements of ANSI/NISO Z39.48-1992 (R1997) (Permanence of Paper).

LIBRARY OF CONGRESS CATALOGING-IN-PUBLICATION DATA
Dinello, Daniel
Technophobia! : science fiction visions of posthuman technology / by Daniel Dinello. — 1st ed.
    p.   cm.
    Includes bibliographical references and index.
    ISBN 0-292-70954-4 (cl. : alk. paper) — ISBN 0-292-70986-2 (pbk. : alk. paper)
    1. Science fiction—History and criticism.   2. Technology in literature.   I. Title.
PN3433.6.D56   2005
809.3'876209356—dc22
                                                    2005019190

For my mother, Mary

CONTENTS

ACKNOWLEDGMENTS

This book owes its existence to my wife, Maureen Musker, who encouraged me to write it and then supported its development from the beginning to the very end. An English teacher at Triton College, she helped with research, translated an article written in French, and even picked up books at the library. In addition, she read each chapter several times and helped edit the book. Finally, she assisted in preparing the final manuscript by acquiring permission for graphics, making suggestions for their arrangement, and organizing the bibliography. Throughout the process, she remained patient, persistent, positive, and inspirational. I also want to thank graphics designer Marty Musker for helping to research graphics and prepare electronic art.

My work benefited from the support of Columbia College Chicago, where I teach in the film and video department. Two faculty development grants helped me with the project—one by providing release time, the other by helping to pay for graphics research. In addition, several of my Columbia College colleagues gave extensive support: Ted Hardin, Bruce Sheridan, and Joe Steiff provided valuable feedback on individual chapters, as did Elizabeth Coffman of Loyola University Chicago. I'm indebted to the Columbia College library staff, and especially to circulation assistant Marilee Cass. Much-appreciated research assistance was provided by Anjel Shenigian and Katherine Ripley. I'm also grateful to the University of Texas Press and especially editor Jim Burr, who nurtured the project from pitch to completion.

Finally, I want to thank my son, Bryan, for help in selecting, organizing, and scanning graphics; my daughter, Dana, who contributed encouragement; their mother, Joyce, and my friends Dale and Frank Zirbel for their support, as well as my brother Frank, who taught me to read and spurred my mind.

TECHNOPHOBIA!

Introduction

DREAMS OF TECHNO-HEAVEN, NIGHTMARES OF TECHNO-HELL

Computing power, neuroscience and nanotechnologies are advancing so rapidly that they will combine to produce the most significant evolutionary developments since the origin of life itself. . . . Imagine yourself a virtual living being . . . free of physical pain, able to repair any damage and with a downloaded mind that never dies.
— GREGORY PAUL AND EARL COX, *BEYOND HUMANITY*

We gave birth to AI . . . a singular consciousness that spawned an entire race of machines. We don't know who struck first—us or them—but it was us who scorched the sky. Human beings are no longer born, they are grown. You are a slave, you were born into bondage.
— MORPHEUS, *THE MATRIX*

Techno-heaven awaits you. You will be resurrected into posthuman immortality when you discard your body, digitize your mind, and download your identity into the artificial brain of a computer. Cyberexisting in virtual reality, you will live forever in a perfect simulation of divine bliss. This techno-heaven is envisioned by a cult of techno-priests—scientists and their apostles—who profess a religious faith that the god Technology will eliminate the pain and suffering of humans by eliminating humans. These techno-utopians fervently believe that technological progress will lead to perfection and immortality for the posthuman, cyborg descendants of a flawed, inevitably extinct humanity. Is this a happy dream or a dismal nightmare?

In contrast to this bright vision of a pain-free, posthuman techno-heaven, science fiction frequently paints a dark picture of technology. From the destructive robot-witch of *Metropolis* (1926) to the parasitic squid-

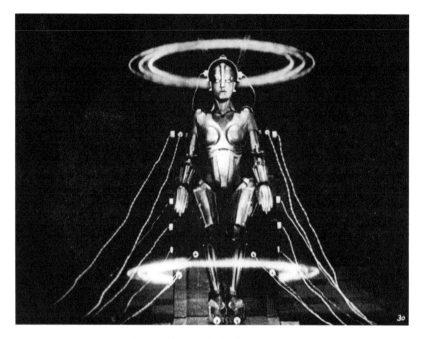

Metropolis: *The electronic birth of the techno-witch (courtesy Photofest).*

machines of *The Matrix Revolutions* (2003), the technologized creatures of science fiction often seek to destroy or enslave humanity. Science fiction shows the transformation into the posthuman as the horrific harbinger of the long twilight and decline of the human species. In its obsession with mad scientists, rampaging robots, killer clones, cutthroat cyborgs, human-hating androids, satanic supercomputers, flesh-eating viruses, and genetically mutated monsters, science fiction expresses a technophobic fear of losing our human identity, our freedom, our emotions, our values, and our lives to machines. Like a virus, technology autonomously insinuates itself into human life and, to ensure its survival and dominance, malignantly manipulates the minds and behavior of humans.

This book explains the dramatic conflict between the techno-utopia promised by real-world scientists and the techno-dystopia predicted by science fiction. Such technophobic science fiction serves as a warning for the future, countering cyber-hype and reflecting the real world of weaponized, religiously rationalized, and profit-fueled technology.

The United States's 2003 invasion of Iraq offers a suggestive example of autonomous technology supported by religious, military, and corporate interests. An expansion of the American techno-empire, the invasion's security rationales—Iraq's nuclear threat, its huge stores of chemical and biological weapons, and its ties to the September 11 terrorists—all proved wrong. Falsehood was expressed as certainty by the Bush administration, which fabricated, exaggerated, and distorted the prewar intelligence to justify the war. With the bloody horror of its dead and wounded hidden, the invasion appeared—in the American media—as advertising hype for U.S. military power and technology. Human costs were minimized. Battling a technologically primitive enemy, the war was a techno-slaughter test of America's latest bombs, guns, and planes. Even more insidiously, the invasion can be seen as a war to seize control of the oil needed by the machines. In this sense, humans have been subsumed into weaponized systems and themselves function as the slave-like tools of technology. Technological imperatives propel war and the politics of domination.

As American warfare has become more and more technologically driven, scientific, corporate, and military interests have become inseparable. Much of the research and development of twenty-first-century posthuman technologies, such as artificial intelligence, nanotechnology, and robotics, were originated and funded by the American military, often through the Defense Advanced Research Projects Agency (DARPA). Created in 1958 to avert a weapons gap with the Russians and inspired by their launching of Sputnik, DARPA—which currently disburses nearly $2 billion annually to corporate, government, and university researchers—remains America's most powerful force driving technological change through weapons development.[1] Aligned with weaponized technology, corporate profit, and religious propaganda, President George Bush—an evangelical Methodist—pledged a "crusade" to "rid the world of evil-doers," a phrase that sounds like a call to battle against satanic forces; thankfully for the petroleum com-

Matrix Revolutions: *Deadly machine-squids hunt humans (courtesy Photofest).*

Christian soldier Bush leads technological crusade
(Illustration by Tim Jessell/courtesy Tim Jessell).

panies, Satan happens to reside on Iraq's rich oil reserves.[2] The war, like the science fiction to be discussed in this book, dramatizes a disturbing aspect of technology: it is energized by a deadly alliance of military, corporate, and religious interests. Promoting a religious vision of technology, the evangelists of techno-heaven promise the reward of everlasting life in exchange for subjugation to the machine.

Transferring human minds into death-free robots, according to artificial intelligence expert Raymond Kurzweil, will produce the next stage of evolution—an immortal machine/man synthesis: Robo *sapiens*.[3] While this sounds like science fiction, Kurzweil—in his 1999 book *The Age of Spiritual Machines*—expresses it as inevitable science fact. Calling this evolutionary transformation "the Singularity," mathematician and science fiction writer Vernor Vinge believes that the result might be the "physical extinction of the human race."[4] Echoing Vinge and Kurzweil, robotics pioneer Hans Moravec forecasts a utopian, robot-dominated, postbiological future in his book *Robot: Mere Machine to Transcendent Mind* (1999). From a biotechnological angle, Gregory Stock in *Metaman: The Merging of Humans and Machines into a Global Superorganism* (1993) predicts the genetic re-engineering of the species for posthuman perfection.

Posthuman evolution—the development of human/machine fusion— is clearly under way. Tiny cameras, serving as artificial eyes, wired directly into the brain; mechanical hands and legs controlled by nerve impulses; computer networks populated by disembodied minds—all these blur the distinction between human and machine. The mapping of the human genome bestows unprecedented, almost divine power on biotechnologists who want to create superhumans by retooling evolution and genetically reconstituting the species. While we wait for brain implants to make us smarter, nanotechnologists will engineer intelligent molecular machines and inject them into our bodies to destroy diseases before they terminate us. Meanwhile, self-reproducing nanobots will revolutionize the economy by providing an abundance of cheaply made replacement organs, material goods, and food. Taken collectively, twenty-first-century technologies— robotics, artificial intelligence, bionics, the Internet, virtual reality, biotechnology, and nanotechnology—promise a new era in human progress, the Posthuman Age. While this book is about science fiction, it includes a brief history and status report on these technologies as we explore imaginings of their future possibilities and the risks they entail.

The rapid development of posthuman technologies—according to the requirements of war and profit—will have profoundly disturbing, perhaps revolutionary effects on our world. If we are approaching a dangerous threshold of posthuman evolution, or Singularity—a twilight zone where "our old models must be discarded and a new reality rules"[5]—science fiction helps us envision that new reality. The best science fiction extrapolates from known technology and projects a vision of the future against which we can evaluate present technology and its direction. The main premise of this book is that science fiction matters, that the actual development of technology and our response (or lack of response) to it are influenced by popular culture. Drawing a vision of the future from attitudes, moods, and biases current among its artists and their audience, science fiction not only reflects popular assumptions and values, but also gives us an appraisal of their success in practice. Alone, cultural imagery and themes do not motivate behavior. But recurring images and themes reveal behaviors that are culturally valued while advocating a point of view for discussion. Science fiction serves as social criticism and popular philosophy. Often taking us a step beyond escapist entertainment, science fiction imagines the problematic consequences brought about by these new technologies and the ethical, political, and existential questions they raise.

As emerging technologies shift the balance of power between human and machine, our concept of humanity alters. Rapidly accelerating computer intelligence joins an escalating series of ego-smashing scientific breakthroughs that diminish human self-image. Copernicus pushed us from the center of the universe; Darwin linked us to apes, slugs, and bacteria; Freud showed us that we often do not control our own minds. Computers now threaten to surpass us in intelligence. Cyborgs are stronger and more powerful. Clones portend an unlimited supply of duplicate selves. This reduces the value of our own minds, bodies, individuality, and consciousness. A kind of evolutionary panic ensues, giving rise to fears of being transformed or taken over by machines. These fears are amplified by military and corporate funding of emerging technology, ensuring life-threatening and profit-making developments without regard to ethical or human consequences. As Langdon Winner says in *Autonomous Technology* (1977), "Technology is a source of domination that effectively rules all forms of modern thought and activity. Whether by an inherent property or by an incidental set of circumstances, technology looms as an oppressive force that poses a direct threat to human freedom."[6] Science fiction taps into these existential fears while reinforcing our concerns about the misanthropic humans who serve as technology's collaborators in domination.

In my analysis, Winner's concept of autonomous technology—which develops Jacques Ellul's radical critique in *The Technological Society* (1964)— serves as a theoretical touchstone. Beyond this, I will show how science fiction anticipates and reflects recent warnings about technomania. Bill Joy's widely read 2000 article in *Wired,* "Why the Future Doesn't Need Us," splashed cold water in the face of technocrats with its incisive warning about the dangers that robotics, genetic engineering, and nanotechnology pose to humanity's survival. Coming from Sun Microsystems' chief scientist, co-creator of the Unix operating system, and developer of Java software, Joy's stinging rebuke was all the more painful to technologists who believed he shared their faith. He called attention to technology's "unintended consequences"[7] while evaluating the techno-vision of everyone from the neo-Luddite[8] Unabomber to robotics posthumanist Hans Moravec, taking seriously the likelihood that machines will supplant humans as the dominant lifeform on the planet. He singled out the most dangerous aspect of these technologies—self-replication, an issue explored in the oldest science fiction novel, Mary Shelley's *Frankenstein* (1818), and in contemporary ones, like Michael Crichton's 2003 best-seller *Prey.*

After providing a contemporary and historical context for the treatment of technology in science fiction, I use individual chapters to focus on particular types of technological posthumans, including robots, computers, androids, cyborgs, and clones. In this way, I examine concerns surrounding specific technology, rather than undertake a general demonizing, and make connections between individual types of technology and webs of social and political influence. Within each chapter, I argue specific links between technology, religion, and military and corporate science, and show

Bride of Frankenstein: *Humans vainly try to control autonomous technology (Courtesy Photofest).*

how this conglomerate of techno-interests helps motivate popular culture's pessimistic evaluation of technology's impact on our lives. Out of this will grow a focused perspective on the most important question of the twenty-first century: Is technology out of control? Science fiction helps focus the debate as it plays out potential implications of uncontrolled technological development. Of course, not all science fiction is technophobic, and not all scientists serve military and corporate interests—just most.

Unlike other science fiction studies, this book includes film, television, literature, and computer games. My dominant focus is cinema, but I delve into the other media when it suits my aims. The vast literature of science fiction is daunting. Trying to read everything would confuse or kill me if not limited by some purposeful or even arbitrary standard. Avoiding most short stories, I limit myself to historically significant novels (deemed as such by me or by others I admire) as well as books that have won one of the chief science fiction awards: the Hugo, Nebula, Philip K. Dick, and Arthur C. Clarke awards.[9]

Before briefly summarizing each chapter, I want to make a few comments about terminology. Cyborgs are not robots or androids. Robots consist of mostly mechanical and electronic components. Usually resembling a

The Terminator: *With its human disguise burned off, the demonic soul of a machine emerges (Courtesy Photofest).*

human or animal, a robot comes in any size—the term includes everything from the clanging metal man of the 1950s, like Robby in *Forbidden Planet,* to humanoids like David in *A.I.: Artificial Intelligence* (2001). Androids can be robots that look human, like *Star Trek*'s Data, or genetically engineered, wholly organic humanoids, like the *Blade Runner* replicants—but androids do not combine organic and inorganic. A cyborg, or cybernetic organism, combines the biological and mechanical, and may or may not look identical to a human; the Terminator looks human until his skin gets burned off, then looks robotic. Possibly because the composition of a fictional artificial person is not always known precisely, these terms remain somewhat nebulous and interchangeable. Finally, the book's title, *Technophobia,* is meant to suggest an aversion to, dislike of, or suspicion of technology rather than an irrational, illogical, or neurotic fear. I want to elevate the term beyond its derisive dismissive use by rabid technophiles who believe that questioning technology's direction is crazy if not satanic.

Chapter One, "Technology Is God," contends that the prophets of post-humanism preach "Technologism"—the religion of technology. The positive promise of human-improving techniques and the godlike power they confer lead many self-proclaimed posthuman visionaries to elevate technology to divine status. Rooted in religious myth with its own dogmas, doctrines, prophecies, sacraments, and priests, this fundamentalist techno-theology evokes faith, devotion, and awe as well as religious promises of perfection and immortality in heaven. Techno-prophets such as Kurzweil and Moravec believe humanity will be resurrected into posthuman immortality on the electronic wings of its machines. Like their Christian and Gnostic forefathers, the prophets of our techno-future reject the organic body and view technology as salvation from that death-susceptible host of our potentially eternal mind. They promote the abandonment of flesh, blood, and bones to the electronic circuitry of our mechanistic progeny. They predict that humans will themselves become electronic gods who have downloaded their minds into robotic technology and cast off their diseased bodies, cyber-existing forever in a virtual reality of disembodied perfection and simulated bliss.

Meanwhile, the technology of genetic manipulation will improve the bad design of our species as well as other living things. According to biotechnology advocate Gregory Stock, in his book *Redesigning Humans* (2002), godlike genetic engineers will seize control of evolution—encouraged by the commercial potential of genetically enhanced children—to evolve some of us (the richest ones) into superhumans with higher intelligence, bigger memories, and longer lifespans. Nanotechnology prophet K. Eric Drexler promises that artificially intelligent, molecular machines will be injected into our bloodstreams to diagnose and repair problems. The miraculous enhancement power of these technologies provides techno-utopians with a dream of perfection.

Chapter Two, "Haunted Utopias," argues that the religious vision of a techno-utopian future—inhabited and engineered by artificially intelligent robots, androids, cyborgs, clones, and super-people—derives from an ancient fascination with machine-based religious utopias and mythical artificial humans. The early utopian imagination—such as in Francis Bacon's *New Atlantis* (1627)—propelled and embraced technological development with little cultural criticism. Humanity put its faith in progress, the goodness of man, and the positive impact of science. The whispers of techno-resistance—which have recently risen to a scream—were not much heard until the 1818 publication of Mary Shelley's *Frankenstein, or The Modern Prometheus.*

Underpinning the rise of the machine was the ascent of science and the quasi-religious myth of progress. The seventeenth-century mechanistic philosophy of René Descartes and the empirical method of Francis Bacon combined to produce scientific rationale and methods that intertwined with religious, political, and utopian thinking. Thus began the techno-hype that linked technology to religious myths of heaven. "The optimistic atmosphere of the eighteenth century . . . created a climate favorable to the rise of technical applications," says Jacques Ellul in *The Technological Society.*

"This state of mind created a good conscience on the part of scientists who . . . believed that happiness and justice would result from their investigations; and it is here that the myth of progress had its beginning."[10] But the dark side of the industrial revolution combined with the mechanized cataclysm of World War I engendered a cultural counter-force—powerful anti-science visions and technophobic fiction such as Fritz Lang's film *Metropolis* (1926), film adaptations of *Frankenstein* in 1931 and 1935, and Aldous Huxley's novel *Brave New World* (1932). These dystopian works sounded a warning alarm, revealing problems overlooked by blind technological obsession. Delving into the history of mechanical invention, artificial humans, utopian visions, and dystopian fears will reveal some of the icons, myths, and mystical themes that underpin the modern, techno-religious vision of science as well as the earliest resistance to its lure.

Chapter Three, "Cybernetic Slaves," examines the dawning of the robot age, the rise of cybernetics, and a pop culture schism in the evaluation of technology's role in human life. A hybrid of philosophy, linguistics, mathematics, and electrical engineering, cybernetics—a new vision of techno-perfection—set off the first chorus of cyber-hype about the ultimate power and value of computers. While evoking religious faith in science, the inventor of cybernetics, Norbert Wiener, warned, in *The Human Use of Human Beings* (1950), of the danger in ceding control of moral judgment to machines.[11] Shortly after Wiener delivered his warning, author Kurt Vonnegut Jr. published an anti-cybernetic novel. *Player Piano* (1950) projected a world where automata do everything, resulting in a techno-tyranny ruled by machines and their slaves—button pushers, office bureaucrats, and corporate managers. As Theodore Roszak says in *The Cult of Information,* Vonnegut raised "the issue of whether technology should be allowed to do all that it can do, especially when its powers extend to the crafts and skills which give purpose to people's lives."[12]

As a science, cybernetics mutated into robotics and artificial intelligence; as an ideology, it provided the springboard for contemporary visions of an earthly technological heaven. Cybernetics also served as the scientific basis for science fiction writer Isaac Asimov's 1950s backlash against the technophobic vision implicit in the killer robots of gothic-inspired science fiction.

Simultaneously with the ascent of cybernetics, nuclear technophobia raged as gigantic radioactive monsters, such as the mutated ants of *Them* (1954), lumbered across America's movie screens. Providing a positive alternative to the created-by-science monsters of the atomic horror film and the sinister robots of the science fiction pulp magazines, Isaac Asimov in *I Robot* (1950)—adapted into an un-Asimovian 2004 movie—presented a method for ensuring good robots. His Laws of Robotics demonstrated a cybernetic guarantee that obedience and servitude would be programmed into robot technology, a general vision of technological safety still employed today.

Yet even with benevolence programmed into their systems, robots killed with kindness in Jack Williamson's 1948 short story "With Folded Hands," while automatic factories, which can't be shut off, destroy the environment in Philip K. Dick's 1955 story "AutoFac." Ridiculing claims of human mastery through cybernetic perfection, the technophobic impulse finds expression not only in the unforeseen consequences of mutated nuclear monsters but also with machines so inflexible in their programmed agenda that an initially positive benefit turns into a human-threatening techno-tyranny.

Chapter Four, "Machines Out of Control," explores the rise of artificial intelligence and its links to religious, military, and corporate power. Increased concern about the dire consequences of A.I. is reflected in science fiction supercomputers and programmed androids that revolt against their human creators. These deranged computers and enraged androids grew out of the weaponization of artificial intelligence and the sense that technology incorporated the negative as well as the positive characteristics of humanity. Thinking machines confront us with a repulsive incongruity more disturbing than the horror of a stitched-together, reanimated humanoid. Artificial intelligence flirts with the mysteries of the mind and reduces thinking to mere mechanics while potentially threatening the existence of the human species. Initially associated in the public mind with the military and the atomic bomb, artificially intelligent supercomputers turned into human-hating science fiction monsters that wanted to enslave or kill humans and inherit the world.

The tiny silicon chip propelled our robotic technology into posthuman overdrive, as powerful computers began to inhabit the bodies of mobile robots. With computers getting smaller, faster, and more powerful every year, Kurzweil extrapolates this information to predict that the computational power of a computer will surpass that of the human brain in 2020.[13] But what will happen then? Will humans passively watch as they are surpassed by a new species, or will they battle for their survival? Or, as the techno-prophets predict, will humans fuse themselves into machine-symbiosis by downloading their identities into the mechanical brains of immortal robots? Science fiction addresses these questions while using the robot or android as a metaphor to analyze the nature and worth of humanity.

Chapter Five, "Rampaging Cyborgs," extends the science fiction argument against techno-obsession to the bionic fusion of cybernetic device and biological organism, which may produce a new and improved cyborg body, but may also produce a weapon. The replacement of our flesh and blood with mechanical augmentation subtly blurs the definition of what constitutes a human body, and encourages a dream of immortality. While technoscience projects a bionic vision of posthuman perfection, the cyborg was born as an astronaut and a weapon. The earliest imagining of the cyborg, in the 1960s, involved a never-implemented military plan to surgically and pharmaceutically modify the bodies of astronauts for space travel. At the same time, the military evolved the cyborg in the development of man-machine interfaces, such as between pilot and jet, that structure modern weapon systems. This helped set the stage for the cyborg's earliest fictional incarnation in Martin Caidin's novel *Cyborg* (1972), which centers on a crashed test pilot whose damaged body gets machine replacement parts.

By the 1980s, the science fiction cyborg had become a ubiquitous icon of pop culture, reflecting its increasing importance. These machine people ranged from the scarcely organic Terminator and the castrated, mostly mechanical Robocop to the tough, virile Bionic Man and sexy gal pal Bionic Woman; from the alien/human/machine cross-breed Ripley in *Alien Resurrection* to the human-hating Borg of *Star Trek;* and from the plugged-into-virtual-reality savior of humanity in *The Matrix* to the genetically enhanced Valids of *Gattaca*. The melding of the organic and the mechanical or the organic and the alien, or the engineering of a union between separate species, cyborgs also include American Iraq War pilots integrated into cybernetic weapon systems as well as suicide terrorists who merge with technology to transform themselves into human bombs.

Science fiction cyborg stories dramatize our fears as we become targets in the world of cyborg weapons, while anticipating the demise of the flesh-and-blood body and the gradual extinction of humanity. "There is, underlying these works, an uneasy but consistent sense of human obsolescence," writes Scott Bukatman in *Terminal Identity* (1993), "and at stake is the very definition of the human."[14] While the machinic replacement of lost body parts enhances the lives of disabled people, the sheer number of monstrous cyborgs reflects a pervasive anxiety that our technological lust will propagate grotesquely deformed, superhuman techno-creatures that will ultimately extinguish us.

In the posthuman future envisioned by Bruce Sterling in his novel *Schismatrix Plus* (1996), humanity no longer exists. It's been extinguished by two monstrous successor species — the machine-augmented, cyborg Mechanists and the genetically enhanced, bioengineered Shapers who now battle each other for dominance. Sterling doesn't mourn humanity's passing, accepting it as the inevitable result of uncontrolled technological expansion. But human extinction brings a technologized posthuman future that lacks joy, empathy, and happiness.

Chapter Six, "The Infinite Cyberspace Cage," focuses on the Internet and virtual reality as façades of freedom that often serve as weapons of surveillance and mind control. Like most of the technologies examined in this book, cyberspace technologies were originally launched by the military. As early as the 1940s, virtual reality systems arose for use as cheap training for both bomber pilots and tank drivers. The Internet got its start in the 1960s as a network designed to link the computers of Defense Department contractors and, some hoped, to serve as a nuke-proof communications system. The concept of cyberspace derives from William Gibson's famous 1984 novel, *Neuromancer.* Brain-implanted cyborgs plug directly into massive data networks, visualized as an abstract, alternative virtual world. When *Neuromancer* came out, personal computers had just started invading homes, while Internet and virtual reality technologies were little known publicly. Gibson's vivid, strange, and frightening near-future tales of cyberspace cowboys, weaponized cyborgs, underground genetic surgeons, and evil multinational corporations struck a deep cultural chord.

Neuromancer, along with the movies *Blade Runner* (1982) and *Videodrome* (1982), helped spark cyberpunk[15]—a power surge of intensely dystopian science fiction by such authors as Pat Cadigan, Rudy Rucker, and Bruce Sterling. Cyberpunk science fiction elaborated alternative visualizations of cyberspace, explored the posthuman figure of the cyborg, and influenced pop culture in the late 1980s and early 1990s. *Mondo* magazine spread the graphics and the word, while the industrial rock scene—bands like Frontline Assembly, Front 242, Nine Inch Nails, Skinny Puppy, Marilyn Manson, and Ministry[16]—reflected cyberpunk's dark, techno-rebellious style with tortured angry lyrics, sound samples of political/cultural detritus, fast, aggressive machine-based music, and cyborgian imagery.[17] In science fiction films, cybernetically enhanced existence shifted from rampaging, muscle-bound macho cyborgs epitomized by Arnold Schwarzenegger to skinny, mind-expanded cyberpunks epitomized by Keanu Reeves.[18]

Techno-utopian network idealists predict that the Internet will fuse with virtual reality such that Web sites will function as life-enhancing alternative realities where the mind flourishes, flesh expires, and happiness beckons. As digital cyber-spirits, we would program sensory experiences that simulated entertainment, pleasure, and happiness. As Gregory Paul and Earl Cox describe cyber-heaven in *Beyond Humanity* (1996): "All senses will be fully engaged—vision, hearing, smell, touch. Your dream body will feel as real as a real body. . . . Cybersex will be performed in the realm of cyber-fantasy . . . a virtual experience will seem just as real [as] and even more enjoyable [than real sex]."[19]

Science fiction, however, frequently views cyberspace as a dangerous trap, from the manipulative, virus-like artificial intelligences that prowl the networks of *Neuromancer* and the 1982 movie *Tron* to the extremes of surveillance in Neal Stephenson's novel *Snow Crash* (1992). Making mind control literal, artificially intelligent machines use virtual reality to imprison humans in Andy and Larry Warchowski's movie *The Matrix* (1999). In *The Matrix,* the real turns out to be illusion, but in movies like *Virtuosity* (1995) and David Cronenberg's *eXistenZ* (1999), cyberspace illusion becomes reality. With the body as the interface and the brain as a computer, the human becomes a machine trapped in an inescapable cage.

Chapter Seven, "Engineered Flesh," examines biotechnology—genetic engineering, eugenics, and cloning. Rather than enhancing the body by replacing flesh with machine, biotech high priests want to perfect the body through genetic manipulation. Of all the technologies discussed in this book, these biology-based ones encourage the most current debate, passion, and controversy because of their powerful impact and imminence. Advances in genetics that diminish disease and suffering should be encouraged. Yet we fear that genetic engineering's quest to improve will turn dark. "More than other cyborg technoscience, genetics foregrounds the issue of human versus posthuman," says Chris Hables Gray in *Cyborg Citizen.* "Genetics offers the most likely, and most effective, way of using artificial evolution to produce intelligent nonhuman creatures."[20]

Since the birth of the genetic revolution in the 1970s, bioethicists, scientists, politicians, and artists have struggled with immense questions: Should children be genetically engineered for intelligence, good looks, athletic ability, musical inclination, or any other traits? Will only a rich elite benefit from this technology, thus producing an enhanced superhuman class or species? Does that matter? Should corporations be allowed to own and profit from human genetic information? How can we anticipate and avert dangerous consequences? Should we regulate any aspect of the technology and, if so, how? The controversy spawns widespread debate in books such as *Redesigning Humans: Our Inevitable Genetic Future* (2002) by Gregory Stock, *Enough: Staying Human in an Engineered Age* (2003) by Bill McKibben, *The Terrible Gift: The Brave New World of Genetic Medicine* (2002) by Rick Carlson and Gary Stimeling, and *Our Posthuman Future: Consequences of the Biotechnology Revolution* (2002) by Francis Fukuyama. Testifying to the impact of science fiction, all of these works cite Aldous Huxley's *Brave New World,* and the latter two employ it as an extended metaphor to bolster their anti-technology arguments. Huxley's novel has become a dominant motif in discussions of the biotechnological future.

Public interest in these technologies grew rapidly in the 1990s, especially after the 1996 cloning of the sheep Dolly and the 1999 completion of the Human Genome Project. *Jurassic Park* (1993), with its rampaging cloned dinosaurs, became one of the most popular films ever. Both the movie and the Michael Crichton novel upon which it was based explore the problem of ego-mad geneticists, who work for profit-driven corporations and give no thought to ethics or the potentially disastrous consequences of their tinkering with evolution. Extrapolating on the principles of genetics, biological science fiction questions the weaponized use of technology, the unforeseen consequences of transgenic experimentation, the morality of human cloning, and the eugenic desire to perfect humanity by controlling evolution.

Chapter Eight, "Malevolent Molecular Machines," explores the threat and promise of nanotechnology—the ultimate fusion of biological and informational sciences. The high priest of nanotechnology, K. Eric Drexler, spread his ideas to the public in the 1986 book *Engines of Creation: The Coming Era of Nanotechnology*. In Drexler's exalted view, atomic manufacturing will give scientists the godlike power to structure matter and re-create nature. He argued that nanotechnology—through programmed self-replication—will give us the ability to produce almost anything: cars, dogs, drugs, tools, tables, computers, hamburgers, and houses. Factories will become obsolete. Aside from all this, artificially intelligent nanobots will be injected into our bloodstreams to detect and cure diseases before they hurt us. While the nano-revolution, like all twenty-first-century technologies, promises heaven on earth for posthuman cyborgs, it also brings threats and risks. Science fiction helps us to envision possible consequences.

Set in the nanotechnology industry of the future, *Blood Music* (1983) by Greg Bear predates *Engines of Creation* and dramatizes the human-destroying consequences of self-replicating nano-machines. Weaponized nanotechnology and its all-pervasive surveillance and mind-control capabilities are projected in Paul McAuley's *Fairyland* (1995), while Neal Stephenson's *The Diamond Age* (1995) envisions a tyrannical society under total nano-control that gets overturned by human love. As the ultimate synthesis of posthuman technologies and the least developed, nanotechnology offers science fiction the greatest opportunity to play out unforeseen consequences in time for us to ask serious questions about its direction and value.

Chapter Nine, "Technology Is a Virus," brings the book full circle with science fiction's answer to the transhumanist faith that Technology is God.

Biological and electronic viruses—while reflecting real-world fears of infectious disease—also can be viewed as a potent metaphor for techno-anxiety. A force that can destroy both humans and posthumans, the virus also functions as a symbol of oppressive techno-politics as well as corporate, military, and scientific irresponsibility.

Mad science, in collusion with its corporate and government sponsors, gets denounced in the gigantic parasite film *Alien* (1979), David Cronenberg's sexual epidemic movie *Shivers* (1975), and his electronic virus film *Videodrome* (1983). Recent science fiction runs rampant with viral horror. Monsters mutated by microbes have become an archetypal villain in digital games like *Syphon Filter* and *Resident Evil* and in the indie horror movie *Cabin Fever* (2003). The Black Flu, a global epidemic, kills more than a billion people in Paul McAuley's book *White Devils* (2004). A viral plague nearly leads to human extinction in the movie *28 Days Later* (2003) and in Margaret Atwood's novel *Oryx and Crake* (2003). Biological warfare pervades television in such 2004 shows as *Alias* and *24*. There's even a board game called *Infection*.[21] The biological hazard sign supplants the mushroom cloud as our most widespread and potent symbol of techno-horror.

This cultural obsession is inspired by real fears: the AIDS virus, germ warfare, biological terrorism, foot-and-mouth disease, mad cow disease, the West Nile virus, and SARS (Severe Acute Respiratory Syndrome). "Ours is an age of viruses," writes Peter Radetsky in *Invisible Invaders* (1991). "For most of us, most of the time, viruses are nothing more or less than a great menace. And there's simply no escaping them. Viruses cause more sickness than anything else on earth."[22] Human beings—even as they evolve into posthumanity—may be losing the battle against infectious diseases.

Given our susceptibility to physical illness and our obsession with viral horror, technophiles take refuge in electronic dreams of transferring their minds to computers, robots, or even spaceships that might transport them to the stars, far away from this infected planet. But electronic mind transfer into a techno-heaven within a cyber-network provides no safe haven. A computer virus, like an electronic form of Ebola, could spread from machine to machine, chewing up personality patterns and crashing digital bodies. "Humans and computers are both prey to these parasitic forms of life," says Philip Kerr, author of *The Second Angel* (1999), a techno-thriller set in a post-plague future when an intelligent computer virus alters human evolution. "It's something we share. Since both types of virus work in exactly the same way, a virus provides a kind of nexus between our two lifeforms—the siliceous and the carbonaceous."[23]

Virus anxiety reflects much more than a fear of organic and electronic horrors. The virus symbolizes technophobia. A malignant virus acts like a machine, incorporating itself into cellular machinery to mechanically reproduce. Mark Dery, in *The Pyrotechnic Insanitarium* (1999), adds, "Intriguingly, a prominent subtext of the viral nightmares of the late twentieth century is the anxieties spurred by out-of-control technological change."[24]

Most science fiction, as we will see, projects a pessimistic vision of posthuman technology as an autonomous force that strengthens an anti-human, destructive, and repressive social milieu. Yet the realization of oppression can spur action. Rather than promoting submissive surrender to a dangerous inevitable posthuman future, science fiction encourages questions about the nature of technology and its unbridled expansion fueled by religious propaganda, military objectives, and corporate profit-making. Science fiction helps us understand the magnitude of the techno-totalitarian threat so we might invent tactics for confronting it.

ONE　Technology Is God

MACHINE TRANSCENDENCE

TECHNOLOGISM: THE RELIGION OF TECHNOLOGY

Worshiping the God Technology, techno-utopians of the twenty-first century evangelize for artificial intelligence, robotics, bionics, cryonics, virtual reality, biotechnology, and nanotechnology. They espouse the conviction *ex machina libertas*—technology will set you free,[1] while preaching the religious dogma of Technologism—a millennialist faith in the coming of Techno-Christ, who will engineer happiness, peace, and prosperity. As David Noble points out in his perceptive book *The Religion of Technology*, "[W]e are witness to two seemingly incompatible enthusiasms, on the one hand a widespread infatuation with technological advance and a confidence in the ultimate triumph of reason, on the other a resurgence of fundamentalist faith akin to a religious revival."[2] Embracing science as salvation, this techno-religion possesses priests, apostles, sacraments, doctrine, and miracles as well as faith in apocalypse, resurrection, immortality, and heaven.

In the Technologist vision of heaven on earth, robot slaves will do all the boring work; meanwhile, genetic engineers will redesign a new post-human species with superhuman capabilities. After the techno-apocalypse, or what some call the Singularity, artificially intelligent computers and robots will assert their independence and dominance. Social life will be fractured. Ordinary humans will be treated as servants or pets and will eventually become extinct. On the other hand, if they choose to do so, robots will resurrect selected earthly humans as divine disembodied post-humans—immortal, telepathic, omniscient, and omnipresent. Virtual reality simulations will generate a life of perfect pleasure. Nanotechnologists—engineering at the atomic level—will create artificial forms of life and completely control matter. This apocalyptic convergence and explosion of technology is expected to occur within the next couple of decades. Believers in this vision call themselves transhumanists.[3]

Transhumanist techno-apostle Christopher Dewdney, in *Last Flesh,* professes his belief that technology will fulfill the Christian promise of immortality and turn people into divine beings. "Supernatural powers, telepathy and transmigration . . . seem strongly plausible to us," he says. "Now the time may not be far off when we will see these aspirations become a tangible reality, rationally constructed by science out of the material realm we so long thought unbridgeable to the immaterial."[4] This chapter will suggest the major tenets of Technologism. Subsequent chapters will elaborate this techno-myth in terms of specific twenty-first-century technologies and contrast that utopian myth with the dark vision of science fiction and weaponized technology.

TRANSUBSTANTIATION: ENHANCING THE BODY

Tortured by the absolute certainty of suffering, growing old, and dying, the mostly white, affluent, male prophets of perfectibility put their faith in technology to save humanity by transubstantiating the organic body. At the transhuman stage—a temporary step on the way to a new posthuman species—human bodies will become synthetic. Life will be prolonged and enhanced through cyborgization—body-improving prosthetic technology that will replace deteriorating body parts. "We are on a path to changing our genome in profound ways," says MIT Professor of Computer Science and Engineering Rodney Brooks. "The distinction between us and robots is going to disappear."[5] In fact, many have already become cyborgs—machine-organic fusions—as science currently provides replacements for damaged skin, arteries, veins, jaws, teeth, eyes, ears, hips, knees, shoulders, arms, elbows, wrists, fingers, and toes. Soon we will have new hearts and even brains. "In the end, we will find ways to replace every part of the body and brain, and thus repair all the defects that make our lives so brief," says techno-priest and artificial intelligence pioneer Marvin Minsky. "Needless to say, in doing so we will be making ourselves into machines."[6] In this posthuman future, biotechnologists will develop stronger, more efficient replacement organs by redesigning their constituent cells and constructing them with more durable materials. Aside from increased longevity and good health, other pleasurable results will follow this gradual transformation to human machine. Our streamlined excretory system will be clean and elegant, while transhuman sexual capabilities will increase in frequency, intensity, diversity, and duration—but that's only the beginning of transubstantiation.

Nanotechnology (see Chapter Eight) will even more radically upgrade the body's systems. Nanobots—microbe-sized robots—will be injected into the bloodstream to seek out and destroy malignant cancer cells, deadly pathogens, and other vile germs. "The abolition of aging and most involuntary death will be one result," says Transhumanist João Pedro de Magalhães in his article "Upgrading Ourselves beyond Our Biology." "We have achieved two of the three alchemists' dreams: We have transmuted the elements and learned to fly. Immortality is next."[7] Currently at the theoretical stage, this ultimate technology will enable nanotechnologists to engineer self-replicating artificial cells, which will be used to create food in nanomachines. Software will control the molecule-by-molecule construction of synthetic meats, fruits, vegetables, and beverages—all scientifically designed to be healthful, and delicious to posthumans living forever in a nano-engineered utopia.

"Humans will have bodies created with nanotechnology," predicts posthumanist prophet Ray Kurzweil, "which will let us build devices . . . even fake human organs—at the atomic level."[8] Once our bodies have been replaced with stronger, better-designed, nano-constructed organs, we won't need to waste time eating and excreting. We will be beyond nature. "To nanoculture, add nanoindustry and mass recycling, and humanity will become a low pollution system largely de-coupled from terrestrial nature," say evolutionary biologist Gregory Paul and artificial intelligence researcher Earl Cox in *Beyond Humanity*. "No need to worry about floods, drought, disease, and pest-causing famines."[9] Humanity, freed from biology and independent of nature, could expand well beyond that sustainable by nature. In fact, nature won't matter much at all in this miraculous nano-world. "By the late twenty-first century, nanotechnology will permit objects such as furniture, buildings, clothing, even people, to change their appearance and other characteristics—essentially to change into something else—in a split second,"[10] proclaims Kurzweil. This will make us like the shape-shifting T1000 in *Terminator 2: Judgement Day* (1991), though, one hopes, less mean-spirited.

The potential mind-expansion power of this technology provides a dream of perfection for techno-utopians. They crave synthetic neurons implanted in their brains for faster processing and wireless brain-computer-Internet link-ups that will increase their knowledge exponentially. Further, techno-optimists expect that these neural implants will directly stimulate their brains and produce virtual erotic adventures without the boring task of developing human relationships, or virtual athletic feats without the tough, sweaty process of body-conditioning or skill-building. "With the understanding of our mental processes will come the opportunity to capture our intellectual, emotional, and spiritual experiences," says Kurzweil, "to call them up at will, and to enhance them."[11] Even simulated spiritual enlightenment will be possible once scientists understand the neurological processes that generate it. Neuroscientists from the University of California at San Diego have already claimed to have found a "God module"—an area of the brain that appears to be activated with the use of religious words and during mystical experiences.[12]

POSTHUMAN RESURRECTION: MIND-TRANSPLANT IMMORTALITY IN A DIGITAL HEAVEN

Technophiles view bio-enhanced, bio-engineered or even nano-constructed bodies as a temporary stopgap on the road to incorporeal resurrection and immortality—the central promise and propagandist lure of Christianity and other religions. Personal immortality will be attainable through supercomputers and robots, assert the techno-prophets of the posthuman future. For example, Ray Kurzweil wants to "reverse engineer" the human brain; that is, replicate the brain's structure in a computer model, and then find a way to download our memories, dreams, and personalities—our identity—into the computer, a process he calls "re-instantiation."[13] We would therefore live out virtual "lives" within a silicon chip. To the techno-priests, this will be a digital heaven. Immortality will be achieved by recording and continuously storing backup copies of our mind file so that if our current cyber-home crashes, we can be downloaded into another one. Physicist Frank Tipler, in *The Physics of Immortality,* argues that "we humans . . . shall have life after death in an abode that closely resembles the Heaven of the great world religions."[14]

While the earliest science fiction vision of computerized immortality might be found in Arthur C. Clarke's 1953 novel *The City and the Stars,* the first scientist to seriously propose the idea was Hans Moravec, former director of the Mobile Robot Laboratory at Carnegie-Mellon University and developer of advanced robots for the military and NASA. In 1988, his book *Mind Children* described how humans would pass their minds into artificially intelligent robots, their mechanical progeny. In one macabre method, a person wanting to move his mind to a new robotic computer gets wheeled into the operating room. "Your skull but not your brain is anesthetized," says Moravec. "You are fully conscious. The robot surgeon opens your brain case and places a hand on the brain's surface."[15] The surgeon delicately slices the brain layer by layer, with the information encoded in each layer of neurons transferred into a computer. After the brain surgery is completed, the abandoned brainless corpse goes into spasms and dies, while the reinstantiated person—now resurrected within the robotic computer simulation—awakes and, presumably, disposes of the dead-meat body.

For the squeamish, a less invasive approach will use a high-resolution scan to digitally chart the electrochemical patterns and contents of a brain. After this information, or mind file, is transferred into a computer, the digital copy of the scanned person's mind will come to consciousness, or so techno-immortalists believe. This mind simulation will possess the identical personality and memories of the scanned organic person. Yet once the digital person realizes that she is helplessly trapped within a computer simulation and completely dependent on her organic original existing in the world outside the computer, she might be seriously upset at her enslavement. But the horrors of silicon entrapment do not faze the techno-believers. "People will port their entire mind file to the new thinking technology. There will be nostalgia for our humble carbon based roots, but there is nostalgia for vinyl records also,"[16] jokes Kurzweil.

The assumptions that underlie the dream of immortality through mind transfer—not to mention the entire underpinnings of scientific rationalism—can be traced to the three-hundred-year-old worldview of French philosopher René Descartes. He described the physical world, including humans, in mechanical terms. In Meditation VI, he said: "I consider the body of man as being a sort of machine so built up and composed of nerves, muscles, veins, blood and skin."[17] Further, he argued that the mind or soul is distinct from the body, and that the mind is mankind's divine endowment. He concluded that "the human body may indeed easily enough perish, but the mind . . . is, owing to its nature, immortal."[18] Like present-day Technologists, he hoped to liberate the divine part of man from its mortal prison.

Descartes's conception of the mind as immortal and his mechanistic worldview were fused in the first decades of the computer age when cybernetics, artificial intelligence (A.I.), and information theory defined the human brain as an extremely complex biological information-processing machine. Solving the problem of mind/body dualism[19] that has fueled endless debate among metaphysicians, A.I. theorists argued that the personality, desires, opinions, memory, and knowledge that make up the mind are electrochemically structured within the mortal brain's cells. In short, the human mind consists of patterns of information. Therefore, a mind's immortality is secured by extracting that information pattern from the death-susceptible biological brain and transferring it into an indestructible artificial one.

Like the Christian belief in fleshly resurrection, the creed of silicon immortality requires a leap of faith. The theory of digital mind transfer depends on unproven assumptions: a person's mind consists of neuronal patterns that can be identified and precisely mapped and coherently transferred into a computer, which itself is running a simulation of the person's brain structure. Further, digital immortality assumes that these digitized electrochemical patterns will coalesce into an identity, become conscious, and be happy about the new situation.

CYBORG SALVATION: ENGINEERED DIVINITY

But even if the mind transfer works, what sort of immortal life will it be? "One of perfect happiness—a techno-Paradise," answer the posthuman prophets. Theoretically, since the newly emergent software person now resides within a computer, she could experience everything she experienced in her old body. Her experience would be a simulation of reality, but that's no big deal. A real-world person experiences only a simulation of the external world anyway—a mental construct amalgamated from sense-data. For example, light reflecting off the external world hits my eyes and gets transmuted into electrical signals that pulse through the optic nerve to my brain cells, which then form the mental image. Our mind therefore exists in a kind of virtual reality. Though our brain coalesces the electrical pattern into an image of the external world, the same image, theoretically, could be artificially induced within a digital person's computer brain. This is of course the technological premise of the *Matrix* movies: experientially, simulations generated by reality and simulations generated by software would be the same. But why artificially induce simulations of reality when you could be inducing vivid hallucinations of Paradise? Once installed in a computer, we would be programmed to experience engineered happiness, a simulated electro-spiritual awakening, a techno-eschatological joy!

In this vision of techno-heaven, our lives no longer depend on the health and durability of the fragile organic body. After making digital copies of ourselves, we will trash the old organic chassis that did such a horrid job of transporting our minds. Instantiated in a computer, we will live forever.

We will think faster and remember everything, incorporating the Internet and the entire sum of human knowledge. As software, we will send ourselves, by wireless transmission, all over the world and later all over the cosmos—the electronic equivalent of the transmigration of souls. We will be digital spiritual entities, like angels or gods.

Hans Moravec and Ray Kurzweil happily proclaim that transferring our mind into a machine should please us greatly. A baptism into posthumanism, this computerized purification will bring blessed release from the worldly struggles and disappointments, the horror, the pain, and all the misery that organic life brings. Not only that, but it's an even better outcome than other religions promise. Most religious devotees, who believe in an immortal spiritual life in heaven, believe they must die first. To hasten this heavenly happiness, some kill themselves. The Technologist vision of heaven provides a wonderful upgrade—immortality without death. The baptism of mind transfer also makes posthuman heaven a matter of consumer preference and sufficient funds, rather than a reward for leading a morally good life. So even the most evil rich person will be granted digital divinity, while the most saintly poor person will not.

ABOMINATION: THE BODY AS DEAD MEAT

Like their Christian predecessors, the prophets of posthumanity believe humans possess an immortal soul that they call the mind. Technologists hate the body. They want to liberate the immortal mind and transcend the flesh. In *Beyond Humanity,* Paul and Cox put it succinctly: "The main reason each human mind is in such a fix is because we are all trapped in our bodies and brains" (283). Sadly, when the human body crashes, so does the mind. Summarizing the views of Technologism, Mark Dery in *The Pyrotechnic Insanitarium* says: "It's the body's job to be a symbol of detestable putridity in the eyes of an information society characterized by an exaltation of mind and a contempt for matter, most of all the body—that aging, earth-bound relic of Darwinian evolution that Net junkies refer to as meat."[20]

The rejection of the physical world and the desire to transcend it derive from Plato, whose philosophy of transcendent forms provides an ancient foundation for both Christian thinkers and the transhumanist theorists of Technologism. In his "Allegory of the Cave," Plato argues that transcendental forms exist beyond the flickering shadows of everyday sense perception. Through philosophical reflection and mathematics, a mortal human with his immortal soul can transcend the limitations of the material world to embrace abstract perfection. In *Techgnosis,* cybercritic Eric Davis calls Plato's theory "one of the top selling metaphysical notions of all time"[21]—the revolutionary belief that an incorporeal spirit lurks within the self and that this immortal intelligence is independent of a flesh-and-blood body. Similarly, the techno-theorists of today sever the immortal perfection of the disembodied mind from our defective, transient flesh.

The repudiation of the body and the material world infuses many religious traditions. Starving ascetics and bloody self-flagellants lamented the flesh and blamed it for corrupting the pure, divine mind. The Bible warns against bodily threats: "In the same way, count yourselves dead to sin but alive to God in Christ Jesus. Therefore, do not let sin reign in your body so that you obey its evil desires."[22] Christian zealot St. Augustine said that the natural body is sown in "corruption . . . dishonour . . . and weakness."[23] Christianity's original sin infects the flesh. While the divine mind wants to be good, the body rebels against its desire. The apostle in the Bible says, "I see another law at work in the members of my body, waging war against the law of my mind and making me a prisoner of the law of sin at work within my members."[24] Evil is located in the sinful flesh. The ultimate goal of human striving—harmony with the divine—required liberation from the mortal body.

Embracing an even more contemptuous view of the physical world, Gnosticism arose in the pre-Christian era. "Some Gnostics referred to our planet as an 'abortion of matter,' composed of 'pain and suffering,' " writes Eric Davis. They considered that "we were made in the image of the evil Demiurge, who created the material world, and that this 'flesh stuffed with excrement' was so repugnant that procreation could not be justified on any account."[25] Though the Catholic Church crushed Gnosticism by the dawn of the Dark Ages, Gnostic ideas and imagery did not disappear from Western thought. In *Techgnosis,* a book about the mystical impulses that underlie the Western obsession with technology, Davis argues: "Gnostic myth anticipates the more extreme dreams of today's mechanistic mutants and cyberspace cowboys, especially their libertarian drive toward freedom and self-divination and their dualistic rejection of matter for the incorporeal possibilities of mind."[26]

A modern version of the Gnostic philosophy led to suicidal expression in the Heaven's Gate cult. In 1997, thirty-nine apostles of the congregation cheerfully abandoned their bodies by means of a lethal blend of vodka, barbiturates, and asphyxiating plastic bags. They expected to automatically beam up to a UFO riding the slipstream of the Hale-Bopp comet that would transport them to posthuman bliss. Heaven's Gate founder Marshall Applewhite (Bo) and his platonic mate Bonnie Nettles (Peep) had convinced their followers that this alien aircraft would take them to a "Level above Human." Drunk on a "delusional cocktail" of religious fantasies, UFOs, computers, the Internet, *Star Trek,* and *The X-Files,* the cult evoked Gnosticism in its hatred of the flesh: members believed their bodies were dispensable "vehicles" or "containers" for their cosmic souls.[27] Prior to destroying their bodies in mass suicide, the males castrated themselves in a search for asexuality. While the methodologies of the groups differ, the twisted body loathing, posthuman obsession, and delusional assumptions of the Heaven's Gaters resemble the techno-religious scripture of the posthuman prophets.

THE SINGULARITY: TECHNO-APOCALYPTIC EXTINCTION OF HUMANITY

These human yearnings to escape the body and find immortality in technology may be thwarted by evolution. According to some techno-prophets, humanity does not have a future. The techno-apocalyptic Singularity will bring a new, fully autonomous, artificially intelligent species into competition with humanity. Robots will have lives and agendas of their own—an ultimate destiny beyond human control and even understanding. Techno-religious enthusiasts believe that eventually machines will exceed human intelligence and capabilities in all respects. "By performing better and cheaper, robots will displace humans from essential roles. Rather quickly, they could displace us from existence," says Hans Moravec in his 1999 book *Robot: Mere Machine to Transcendent Mind.* "I'm not as alarmed as many by the latter possibility, since I consider these future machines our progeny, 'mind children' built in our image and likeness, ourselves in more potent form. . . . It behooves us to give them every advantage and to bow out when we can no longer contribute."[28]

After the Cyber-Armageddon, a new species—Robo *sapiens*—will rise up to rival and ultimately supersede *Homo sapiens* as the next step in evolution. The god of technology—having incorporated the best survival characteristics of humanity—will create a new generation without human intervention. "Before the next century is over, human beings will no longer be the most intelligent or capable type of entity on the planet,"[29] says Ray Kurzweil. His rationale centers on the continued exponential growth of artificial intelligence in the next few decades. Mind machines become the next evolutionary step, with organic humans left in the garbage can of cos-

Robo sapiens: *State-of-the-art facial robot smiles at the possibility of techno-apocalypse and human extinction. (Photo by Peter Menzel/courtesy Peter Menzel).*

mic history. Earth itself will no longer be needed. "Our artificial progeny will grow away from and beyond us, both in physical distance and structure and in similarity of thought and motive," says Moravec. "In time their [the robots'] activities may become incompatible with old earth's continued existence."[30] Paul and Cox, in *Beyond Humanity,* agree with Moravec's gloomy assessment of earth's and humanity's future. They refer to the Singularity as a "cyberexplosion"—the moment when robots assert their independence. They predict: "Robots will have their own agendas and may have no use for mortals . . . eventually it will become as if mankind never existed."[31] The Singularity is a vision of the apocalypse, a techno-Rapture, a Second Coming for the cult of Technologism.

MACHINE RAPTURE

Robots will assert dominance and eventually colonize space. The Technologists envision a vast interstellar culture, a population of mega-intelligent mind machines. This super-civilization will constantly improve and extend itself, converting "everything into increasingly pure thinking stuff," speculates Moravec. "A Mind Fire will burn across the universe."[32] Humanity's only hope of survival (of any sort) will be through a mind meld with artificially intelligent robots. If the robots permit, humans may be allowed to digitize themselves into the new cyber-civilization, securing for themselves eternal digital existence. "This is not the end of humanity, only its physical existence as a biological life form,"[33] reassure Paul and Cox in *Beyond Humanity.*

After the apocalyptic Singularity, humans and robots will fuse minds into a post-biological cyber-collective, maybe like the Borg of *Star Trek,* though hopefully with a more engaging sense of humor. This will lead to technological evolution at hyperspeeds. Except among humans who reject this scenario, sex and children will end. "Reproduction will be a matter of splitting already mature minds and placing them in devices grown in a matter of days, hours, or even faster. Reproduction will return to asexual fission. . . . There will be no bouncing babybots."[34] In their future divine techno-cosmology, this super-mind, having expanded into space, will inhabit the entire universe, controlling its structure and development. As in Frank Tipler's theory in *The Physics of Immortality* (1995), a future Omega point or Singularity "marks the transformation of intelligence into a semi-omnipotent 'God' that recovers all conscious intelligence that has ever existed," proclaim Paul and Cox. "Such a combined system of minds, representing the ultimate triumph of science and technology, will transcend the timid concepts of deity and divinity held by today's theologian."[35] In this mind-boggling vision of a rapturous union, technology dispenses with human bodies and nature, absorbs the totality of human thinking, and propels itself beyond "God" into an unknown realm.

TRANSHUMANIST RELIGIOUS CULTS

The Technologist vision of a heaven on earth followed by posthuman immortality has been adopted and enunciated into a gospel by several transhumanist organizations, including the Extropy Institute, based in Austin, Texas. The name "Extropy" is meant to suggest the idea of limitless expansion (through technology), in contrast to entropy, or the tendency of systems to implode, decay, and die. Embracing a doctrine of posthuman transformation based on twenty-first-century technologies, Extropians have canonized cyber-theorists such as nanotechnology guru K. Eric Drexler, Hans Moravec, Marvin Minsky, Ray Kurzweil, and Gregory Stock, the latter three of whom sit on the Board of Directors. Through their Web site,[36] publications, and political action group, these devoted transhumanists proselytize for robotics, bionics, cryonics, cloning, and libertarianism in a quest for permanent youth, advanced intelligence, and immortality.[37]

"We challenge the inevitability of aging and death," says founder Max More (who changed his name from the insufficiently symbolic O'Conner).[38]

> We see humans as a transitional stage standing between our animal heritage and our posthuman future. This technological transformation will be accelerated by genetic engineering, life extending biosciences, intelligence intensifiers, smarter interfaces to swifter computers, neural-computer integration, worldwide data networks, virtual reality, intelligent agents, swift electronic communications, artificial intelligence, neuroscience, neural networks, artificial life, off-planet migration, and molecular nanotechnology.[39]

Anti-democratic in their rabid devotion to posthuman technologies, the Extropians denounce those who ask questions, express concerns, or take action against unrestrained technological development. The president of the Extropy Institute, Natasha Vita-More, directs a political group called the Progress Action Coalition. She attacks opponents such as Greenpeace, the Green Party, tech critic Bill Joy, and biotech detractor Jeremy Rifkin as "neo-Luddites," "bio-Luddites," and "anti-progressives."[40] As the Extropians see it, "social programs, legislatures, tax hungry politicians and environmental regulations all dampen the evolutionary force of extropy," writes Eric Davis in *Techgnosis.*[41] Characterizing the Extropian philosophy as a postmodern "cyborgian spin" on Nietzsche's concept of the *Übermensch* (or Superman), critic David Skal in his book *Screams of Reason* writes that Extropians exhibit a "creeping disdain for the sluglike retrohumans and others who have no use for the Extropian adventure."[42] In the transhumanist contempt for natural flesh-and-blood humans and its desire to create an elite technologized posthuman species, a potential for fascism,[43] religious fanaticism, and species warfare is revealed—a theme that will be explored throughout this book.

True believers, the Extropians and their techno-enthusiast brethren expect genetic engineering, cloning, and eugenics to reconfigure selected humans into a superior transhuman species and then, using robotics, bionics, and nanotechnology, to invent a new posthuman species no longer

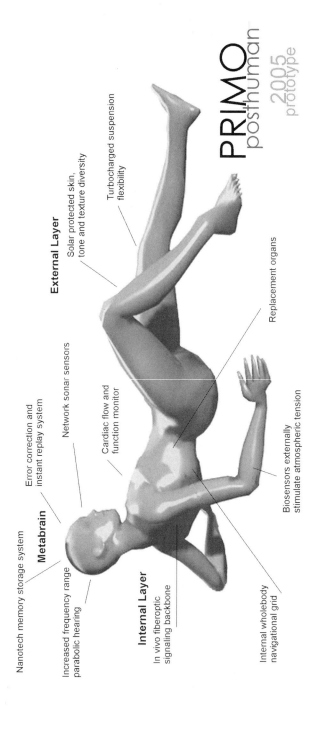

PRIMO posthuman

2005 prototype

External Layer

Turbocharged suspension flexibility

Solar protected skin, tone and texture diversity

Replacement organs

Network sonar sensors

Error correction and instant replay system

Metabrain

Cardiac flow and function monitor

Nanotech memory storage system

Increased frequency range parabolic hearing

Internal Layer

In vivo fiberoptic signaling backbone

Biosensors externally stimulate atmospheric tension

Internal wholebody navigational grid

Extropian design of a technologically optimized, meat-based human (Illustration by Natasha Vita-More/Courtesy Natasha Vita-More).

dependent on nature. Disguising their spiritual quest as science, the ministers of machine ascension express technologically induced dreams of becoming like gods, of possessing supernatural powers. "When technology allows us to reconstitute ourselves physiologically, genetically and neurologically," says Extropian leader More, "we who have become transhuman will . . . transform ourselves into posthumans—persons of unprecedented physical, intellectual and psychological capacity, self-programming, potentially immortal, unlimited individuals."[44] While despising religion as dogmatic irrational debasement, transhumanists comfort themselves with religious goals such as personal immortality and divine power. Technologism is the new religion of the self-aggrandizing techno-elitists. Like some other religions, Technologism's dogmatic belief system requires an irrational leap of faith that—in its case—moves from philosophical theories to technologies that do not exist. With their conviction that the techno-apocalyptic Singularity will redefine nature and their dream of transcendence through technology, the Technologists resemble religious fanatics.

In accordance with David Noble's perspective in *The Religion of Technology,* Technologism is not meant only in a metaphorical sense; rather, it is meant literally and historically to indicate that "modern technology and religion have evolved together and . . . as a result the technological enterprise has been and remains suffused with religious belief."[45] Technologism, replacing Christianity, becomes the sole vessel through which humanity accesses the divine and enters heaven. In the next chapter, we will explore the origins of techno-religion in the early visions of engineered utopias. In later chapters, we also will see that each of the twenty-first-century technologies under discussion has spawned its own techno-prophets and dogma. More important, the religion of technology is not merely a playful, intellectual fantasy. Technologism is a harmful system of propaganda that serves to support military and corporate demand for unbridled and autonomous expansion of dangerous technologies without questions or moral concerns. Beyond this, Technologism—in its anti-egalitarian perspective, mostly masculine milieu, and techno-eugenic agenda—gives this religion a disturbing fascistic edge.

TWO   Haunted Utopias

ARTIFICIAL HUMANS AND
MAD SCIENTISTS

TECHNO-HEAVEN: ANTIQUITY
THROUGH THE MACHINE AGE

The religious vision of a techno-utopian future derives from an ancient attraction to machine-based utopias. The Bible, in the Book of Revelation (21:1–27), projects a mythical image of a techno-transcendent utopia: the New Jerusalem. Manufactured by God out of pure gold, this lustrous super-city emerges from the Day of Judgment skies signaling Christ's triumphant return to earth for a thousand-year reign. The radiant, geometrically precise Heavenly City represents a perfect place, beyond nature, where we are resurrected into immortal life, freed of pain and anxiety. Its techno-religious aspect is captured by architecture professor Michael Benedikt, who describes it as "laid out like a beautiful equation. The image of The Heavenly City, in fact, is an image of . . . a religious vision of cyberspace."[1]

This apocalyptic vision of heaven on earth would inspire, in the words of Eric Davis, "the secular offspring of Christianity's millennialist drive: the myth of progress, which holds that through the ministrations of reason, science, and technology, we can perfect ourselves and our societies."[2] At the same time, technology as a means of redemption flourished in the minds of medieval monks who elevated the practical crafts as a path to Heavenly Jerusalem. "Technology had come to be identified with transcendence," says David Noble, "implicated as never before in the Christian idea of redemption. The worldly means of survival were now redirected toward the other-worldly end of salvation."[3] Technologism—the posthuman religion of technology—originated with the early Christian fusion of technology and salvation. Linked to religious ideas of heaven, divine perfection, and the Promised Land, utopia became a worldly technological goal, rather than an otherworldly post-death reward. The term *utopia* was coined by Thomas More in *Utopia* (1516)—a book influenced by Plato's *Republic* as well as by the Gospels. For More, utopian perfection would be achieved through social reform, religious tolerance, good moral example, and widespread education.

Scientific thinking fueled the utopian imagination in the seventeenth century. An awareness of the socially transforming power of scientific knowledge infuses Francis Bacon's *New Atlantis* (1627) and Tommaso Campanella's *City of the Sun* (1637), which "enshrined the worship of science and technology as principles of social development and moral perfection."[4] Arguably a work of science fiction,[5] Bacon's *New Atlantis* imagines vast technological progress through an advanced research institute—the House of Salomon—and prophesies various scientific marvels, such as submarines and aircraft. Though not a scientist himself,[6] Bacon was the first to see the connection between science and the improvement of mankind. With religious fervor, he viewed science as a source of illumination, power, progress, and even redemption, linking it to Christianity.

In *The New Atlantis,* English sailors are shipwrecked on the island kingdom of Bensalem, ruled by a Christian priest supported by the supreme wise men of the secretive House of Salomon. They embody Bacon's ideal of a benevolent scientific elite whose knowledge would increase human control of nature and eventually lead to utopian comforts. "It seemed that we had before us a picture of our salvation in heaven,"[7] says one of the shipwrecked sailors. The House of Salomon satisfies materialistic human wants through technology. Yet, despite this, the first technocracy's inhabitants seem as regimented and obedient as automata as they chant in unison, "Happy are the people of Bensalem."[8] The techno-priest expresses divine aspirations for science: "The end of our Foundation is the knowledge of causes, and secret motions of things; and the enlarging of the bounds of human empire, to the effecting of all things possible."[9] Bacon advanced the medieval Christian idea of science as divine salvation. "Largely through the enormous and enduring influence of Francis Bacon," says David Noble, "the medieval identification of technology with transcendence now informed the emergent mentality of modernity."[10]

With the rise of science, utopian visions of the future divided between two contrary philosophical views: anti-technology and pro-technology. The nineteenth-century socialist writer William Morris exemplifies the former attitude. In his novel *News from Nowhere* (1890), Morris—troubled by the horrors of industrial life—imagined a pastoral earthly paradise of the future that recreated the pre-industrial past. In this perfect society, arts and crafts provided the economy's foundation. He objected to a future of idle humanity whose needs were supplied by machines. In contrast, pro-technology utopias such as Edward Bellamy's *Looking Backward 2000–1887*

(1888) viewed urban industrial life as the harbinger of heaven. Techno-utopians expected that humanity, rather than being crushed by the wheels of industry, would be physically liberated and spiritually enhanced by advancing technology. These utopian visions assumed that science would understand, control, and perfect nature, including humans.

War, hunger, and hatred have been engineered out of the Eden-like commune proposed as a literal heaven on earth by *Looking Backward.* As Bellamy saw it, the United States would transform into a technopolis where a factory-like efficiency controlled all aspects of life. Designed like a machine, this paradise would not only increase happiness but bring people closer to God. According to *Looking Backward,* the techno-utopian age will bring the human race "a new phase of spiritual development, an evolution of higher faculties . . . the realization of God's ideal . . . when the divine secret . . . shall be perfectly unfolded. Humanity has burst the chrysalis. The heavens are before it."[11]

Technological utopianism spread wildly in nineteenth-century America,[12] drawing energy from the same religious enthusiasm that made the nation, in the words of Eric Davis, "a fiery carnival of revivalism, spiritual experimentation and progressive communes."[13] The enthusiasm for technology and for religion fed off each other as the Industrial Revolution encouraged dreams of technological heaven. A whole procession of imaginary mechanized utopias, influenced by *Looking Backward,* dominated the utopian imagination of the well-educated elite, including such technology-hyping novels as *The Crystal Button* (1891) by Chauncey Thomas, *A Cityless and Countryless World* (1893) by Henry Olerich, and *Limanora, the Island of Progress* (1903) by Godfrey Sweven. The divine desire to be like angels became literal in *Limanora,* as the citizens reject sex, sprout wings, and "flit about in a state of gleaming innocence," as author Chad Walsh puts it in *From Utopia to Nightmare* (1962).[14]

Despite initially writing dystopian science fiction such as *The Time Machine, The Island of Dr. Moreau,* and *When the Sleeper Awakes,* H. G. Wells became the twentieth century's greatest utopian seer, embracing science, engineering, the myth of progress, and faith in man's perfectibility.[15] Possessed by what H. L. Mencken described as a "messianic delusion,"[16] Wells—in books such as *A Modern Utopia* (1905) and *Men Like Gods* (1923)—promoted his vision of a technocracy run by a scientific, technical elite. Appraising Wells's viewpoint in *The Future as Nightmare,* Mark Hillegas writes: "The application of science had almost automatically brought this heaven on earth, which was inhabited by a finer race of human beings, who had inevitably evolved to their state of near perfection."[17]

Wells's *Modern Utopia* glowed with twentieth-century optimism—"an almost archetypal version of the scientifically planned welfare state,"[18] says Hillegas. Wells elaborated the utopian dream of *The New Atlantis,* trusting that Bacon's House of Salomon would be achieved by a small group of benevolent scientist-technicians who would rule the world. Being inherently good, the techno-dictators would use science and technology to manufacture a perfect future. This would require the subjugation of the natural world. Wells argued that "man is the unnatural animal, the rebel child of Nature, and more and more does he turn himself against the harsh and fitful hand that reared him."[19] Called "the most transhumanist of the early 20th century socialists" by the director of the World Transhumanist Association,[20] Wells enthusiastically embraced an anti-nature viewpoint that reinforces the techno-corporate notion of man as master and nature as slave. Fiercely anti-flesh, Wells devalued and diminished the physical body, echoing the fascination for artificial alternatives found in the toy automata of the age.

TOYS OF PARADISE: EARLY ROBOTS, COMPUTERS, AND WEAPONS

The fulfillment of the contemporary dream of a heavenly techno-utopia ruled by robotic gods can be traced back to an ancient fascination with artificial people or automata. In ancient Egypt and Greece, the making of lifelike figures was motivated by both religious and artistic feelings. "Crude jointed figurines were gradually replaced by statues with pretensions to realistic simulation of the human form," says John Cohen in *Human Robots in Myth and Science.* "Their fabrication was in the hands of priests because statues were made to be worshipped."[21] The prophetic statues, or talking gods, replied to questions by means of secret manipulation, either a nod of the head or the movement of an arm. Taking religious technology even further, inventor Heron—known as the Machine Man—engineered miracles for churches: singing birds, mechanical saints, invisible trumpet blasts, and mirrors that seemed to materialize spirits.[22] In the Middle Ages, Albertus Magnus (1204–1282) spent thirty years devising a mobile robot—built from leather, wood, and metal—that was able to answer questions and solve problems. It dared salute its master's formidable pupil, the future St. Thomas Aquinas. Convinced that this had something to do with the devil, Aquinas tossed the robot into a fire.[23]

With his mechanistic view of the physical world, Descartes (1596–1650) launched the modern era of automata. Mechanical grim reapers lurched around elaborate clocks, reminding people of their death whenever they checked the time. Among the most famous automata of the seventeenth century, the Strasbourg clock featured moving animals, among which was a wrought-iron cock—a guilt-inducing reminder of St. Peter's denial of Christ. At noon the cock opened its beak, stretched out its tongue, flapped its wings, spread out its feathers, and crowed.[24] These mechanical clocks reflected Descartes's clockwork notion of the cosmos. Descartes himself was fascinated with automatic things. He designed several machines, including acrobatic statues, an artificial dove, and a flying partridge. He even constructed a female servant automaton that he called Francine (after his illegitimate daughter, who died at age five). While on a sea voyage, a passenger who believed Descartes employed the robot as a demonic sex toy threw it into the water.

In the eighteenth century, animated dolls became increasingly lifelike. Automata fantasies were stimulated by Jacques de Vaucanson (1709–1782) with his cam-controlled musical toys, such as a mandolin player that sang and kept time with its foot and a piano player that moved its head and simulated the act of breathing. His gilded copper duck emulated the functions of eating, drinking, and digesting. His "ingenious mechanical toys . . . were to become prototypes for the engines of the industrial revolution," says John Cohen.[25] De Vaucanson also invented automatic loom control using perforated cards in 1740, transferring the punched wooden card and cam controls employed in his mechanical toys and musical boxes to the work machines. This was not a commercial success, but twenty years later Joseph Marie Jacquard (1752–1834) adopted his ideas and revolutionized the fabric industry with a perfected automatic loom driven by punched cards. De Vaucanson and Jacquard's punched cards took on a life of their own, becoming the foundation of early computing. Charles Babbage used them as the controlling mechanism of his theoretical Analytical Engine. Years later Herman Hollerity utilized the punched cards for computer programming and data storage in building the information empire IBM (International Business Machines).[26]

While certainly influencing the development of technology, the animated toy machines of the nineteenth century—made by Gustave Vichy and Leopold Lambert, among others—had more to do with art-making and playful parody than with social reality. Automata shook society when they moved from culture to military aggression and factory production. The methods of the individual gunsmith were replaced by mass-production technology pioneered by military engineers in the early nineteenth century. Industrial robots thoroughly changed the nature of human society by changing the nature of work when, in post–Henry Ford factories, machines replaced humans or turned humans into assembly-line machines. "What is less well known is that the original impetus for this change was not of civilian, but of military origin," says Manuel De Landa in *War in the Age of Intelligent Machines*. "Indeed, the nineteenth-century military drive to create weapons with perfectly interchangeable parts marked the beginning of the age of the rationalization of labor processes."[27] In this fusion of technology and weapons, robotic command structures—developed in arsenals—were later exported to civilian factories.

The late nineteenth century was the golden age of toy automata and a period of bourgeois optimism about the utopian possibilities of technology. Techno-priest and writer Isaac Asimov notes: "The Industrial Revolution seemed suddenly to uplift human power and to bring on dreams of a technological Utopia on Earth in place of the mythic one in Heaven."[28] Artificial people as weapons of destruction and objects of terror did not fully emerge until the mechanized horror of World War I. But the origins of widespread technophobia can be found much earlier in the myths and folklore about artificial humans.

HOMUNCULUS AND THE GOLEM: WEAPONIZED ARTIFICIAL HUMANS

The fantasy of powerful machines that catered to humans and controlled an unruly natural world goes back to the origins of our culture. In ancient myth, Pygmalion carved in ivory the likeness of the goddess Aphrodite, then fell in love with the statue. The goddess—flattered by the facsimile—brought her to life as the ideal woman Galatea.[29] Homer's *Iliad* tells of the Greek god of technology, Hephaestus, who forges from bronze a gigantic metallic humanoid named Talos that ceaselessly patrols the shores of Crete, fighting off enemy ships with rocks. This is an early vision of a technological weapon. In addition, this giant pre-robot, according to J. P. Telotte in *Replications*, "typified their hopes for a rational mastery over an unpredictable universe."[30]

This desire to control nature extended to the occult philosophers and alchemists of the Renaissance, who were unsatisfied with the mindless entertainment value of mechanical ducks, musical toys, and clockwork dummies. Their own fascination with mechanically simulating human behavior fueled a deeper masculinist drive to create a creature of flesh and blood without female participation. Anticipating corporate technophiles, these arcane technicians sought to make a profit and transfigure humanity.

Blending magic, spirituality, and pre-science, the alchemists were metallurgists who wanted to change worthless metal to gold, but who also sought to make humans immortal with a longevity potion. The alchemists' magical techniques were designed to bring about human perfection: "the creation, through technology, of the millennial kingdom that crowns Christian myth," as Eric Davis puts it.[31]

The alchemist and Swiss physician Paracelsus (1493–1541)—father of modern pharmacology and inspiration for Goethe's Dr. Faust—came up with a method for the creation of humans. Lacking a microscope, he believed that each sperm contained a miniature man. This patriarchal view required the female womb only for nourishment and protection. With this in mind, and hoping to completely eliminate women from reproduction, he developed a recipe for the creation of a tiny human, or homunculus: produce semen, hermetically seal the semen in a jar, place the jar within fresh horse dung (for warmth), nourish the mass with blood. After forty days, this mass should begin to move and transform into a human infant, but much smaller.[32] Paracelsus never proved his theory correct, though he spent an enormous amount of time and sperm trying. The idea found its way into Goethe's *Faust*. Dr. Faust's student Wagner, with the assistance of Mephistopheles, alchemically creates a homunculus who vainly seeks to become fully human.

The secret arts produced an even more fascinating man-made creature, the golem. Not produced organically, the golem was molded of clay, emulating God's creation of Adam. Designed to serve and protect humans like the robotic Talos, the golem was infused with life through a kind of mystical incantation—a medieval method of programming—and the stamping of the "divine name" on the creature's forehead. This religious power—vested in rabbis—originated in the *Sefer Yetzirah,* or *Book of Creation,* part of the Talmud.[33] Besides providing humans with a slave to do their bidding, the creation of this artificial man fused religion, magic, weaponry, and science in a mystical rite that enabled the high priest scientist and his followers to partake in divine union with the Creator.

The golem saga was awakened to new life in the seventeenth century when alchemy and magic renewed the longing to master nature by supernatural means. As human automata became fashionable in the eighteenth century, the story of the golem was adopted in poems and novels. With its literary application came a transformation from servant/protector to revengeful monster. In a famous telling, the creator and master of the golem was Rabbi Loew of Prague who—just as God had breathed life into Adam—breathed the name of God into a clay figure. His golem was a

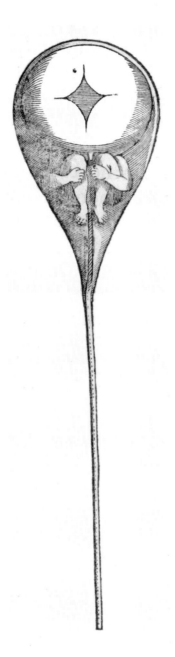

Homunculus: 1694 illustration of the latest scientific theory shows a tiny human inhabiting the head of a spermatozoon (Courtesy National Library of Medicine).

mindless, obedient subhuman, a soulless monster that lived only to serve its master. On the Sabbath the rabbi ordinarily deactivated the creature so that its perverse existence would not disrupt the holy day. But when the rabbi once forgot his Sabbath duty to deactivate, the golem turned into a howling, rampaging demon until its existence was terminated forever.

The menace of the golem and a fascination with automata are fused in the prescient novel *The Sandman* (1816) by E. T. A. Hoffmann. Reflecting a romantic rebellion against the tyranny of rationalism and integrating science with the magic of alchemy, *The Sandman* imagines a sinister automaton—amazing in its simulation but diabolically animated. A mentally unstable young student named Nathaniel, whose father has been killed in an explosion while dabbling in alchemy, exclaims fearfully, "Something terrible has entered my life!"[34] He refers to Olympia, the beautiful daughter of his teacher Professor Spallanzani. His fear has been aroused by her overly precise manner. "She walks with a curiously measured gait; every movement seems as if controlled by clockwork." Olympia plays piano and sings with the "unpleasant soulless regularity of a machine."[35] Eventually Nathaniel discovers, to his horror, that Olympia *is* a machine. Seductive and threatening, Olympia influenced and prefigured the aggressive female robots of the future, such as the witch robot Maria in Fritz Lang's *Metropolis,* the nuclear bomb–enhanced cyborg in *Eve of Destruction* (1991), or the nanotechnological TX fembot in *Terminator 3: Rise of the Machines* (2003).

Olympia has been alchemically produced by Professor Spallanzani with the help of the evil Coppelius. *The Sandman* therefore provided the literary prototype of another science fiction icon—the mad scientist, a figure intimately connected with the creation of evil artificial humans. "The modern myth of the mad scientist took shape over the course of the 19th century,"[36] writes David Skal in *Screams of Reason,* as scientific and technological progress slowly became associated with numerous destabilizing developments. Darwin's evolutionary theories resulted in humanity's biggest ego-smashing since Copernicus knocked the earth from the center of the universe. In addition industrial machines radically dislocated the nineteenth-century social order. "All varieties of customs, habits, attitudes, ideas, and social and political institutions are caught up in its flow, altered, and set on a new foundation," says Langdon Winner in *Autonomous Technology.*[37] A growing suspicion of technology exploded in the Luddite rebellion. This subversive movement of workers urged and practiced the destruction of factory machines because they caused extensive unemployment. In this uneasy atmosphere, the scientist and his spreading technology began to provoke distrust and fear.

DARK SCIENCE AND COSMIC PESSIMISM

Two years after *The Sandman,* Mary Shelley's *Frankenstein, or The Modern Prometheus* (1818) delivers a powerful anti-science diatribe that still reverberates as a quintessential parable of the dangers unleashed by technological creation and irresponsible scientists.[38] Incorporating *The Sandman* and the myth of Prometheus,[39] *Frankenstein* amalgamates the angry-artificial-human legends of the golem and the homunculus with the miraculous discoveries of science. Closing the gap between superstition and rationality, Dr. Frankenstein replaces occultism and alchemy with electricity[40] in order to bring his technological creature to life.

For the nineteenth century as well as future generations, *Frankenstein* represents a pessimistic vision of science and its potentially dire effects. The technological creature revolts against humanity because of his scientist creator's unwillingness to nurture, his failure to provide love. Right after the reanimated corpse awakens, cowardly, guilt-ridden Dr. Frankenstein races out of his lab, abandoning the confused creature to fend for himself. The irresponsible parent gets so wrapped up in his self-doubt that he can't be bothered to help his techno-offspring harmonize with human society. "The image of the . . . abandoned child is a powerful archetype," writes David Skal, "a cultural dream link between a nineteenth-century writer's [Mary Shelley] grief for a miscarried child and the failed, metaphorical brainchildren of dysfunctional technology today."[41] This interpretation emphasizes the failure of the scientist to fulfill his responsibility to his technological creature, which later becomes independent, forces its own agenda, and wreaks havoc.

Two years after Dr. Frankenstein forsakes him, the stitched-together creature confronts his maker and demands a companion. Unlike in the movie version, the monster presents his point of view articulately. "Autonomous technology personified finds its voice and speaks,"[42] says Langdon Winner. The creature argues that his creator has left him crippled, incomplete, incapacitated—unable to integrate with humans. He wants the scientist who gave him misery, to help him find a happier life. He demands a soul mate. Dr. Frankenstein refuses and tells him to get out. The disturbed creature makes sure the doctor understands that this time, ignoring him will bring serious consequences: " 'Yet mine shall not be the submission of abject slavery, I will revenge my injuries. . . . I will cause fear, and chiefly towards you my archenemy, because my creator, do I swear inextinguishable hatred. Have a care; I will work at your destruction.' "[43]

Dr. Frankenstein now finds the creature's point of view more reason-

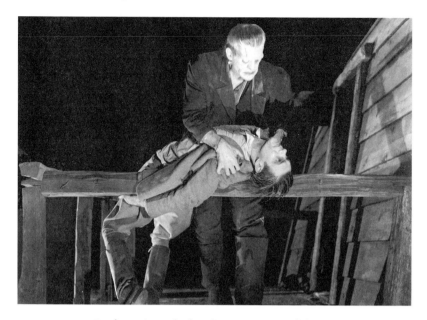

Frankenstein: *Technological monster reasons with his insensitive, neglectful scientist creator. (Courtesy Photofest).*

able: "I was moved . . . I felt there was some justice in his argument."[44] The scientist then conforms to the demands of his technology and engages in "the filthy process of creation." Like the modern technophile, he expects to undo unforeseen technological damage by designing new technology. But after fashioning a female creature, the doctor realizes that this will only multiply the problem: "[T]he first results of those sympathies for which the demon thirsted would be children, and a race of devils would be propagated upon the earth who might make the very existence of the species of man a condition precarious and full of terror."[45] In this, Dr. Frankenstein agrees with modern techno-critics, like Bill Joy, who view self-replication as one of the more troubling aspects of new technology.[46] Trembling with passion, Dr. Frankenstein destroys the unfinished female corpse-creature. With all his hopes of love and sex crushed, the techno-monster expresses his anger and his ultimate control over the scientist, and, by implication, all of humanity: " 'Slave . . . you have proved yourself unworthy of my condescension. Remember that I have power. . . . You are my creator, but I am your master; obey!' "[47] The artificial precursor of the cyborg, android, robot, and clone, Frankenstein's monster wreaks a golem-like trail of destruction, killing the family of his creator and driving his own "father" to the North Pole. The mad scientist, who took over the divine role of creation from God and the natural role of creation from woman, gets punished with death.

Frankenstein's longevity—in the twenty-first century, it was newly adapted into a play, *Monster* (2002), an independent digital feature, *Teknolust* (2002), and a television film, *Frankenstein* (2004)—lies in its power to evoke primal fears and anxieties concerning childbirth, parenting, birth defects, human identity, and the limits of pursuing knowledge. By abandoning his technologized creation, Dr. Frankenstein refuses to acknowledge its implications. He forces it into the world without any strategy to incorporate it into human society. The scientist fails to anticipate technology's negative consequences. As Langdon Winner puts it, "Provided with no plan for its existence, the technological creation enforces a plan upon its creator. . . . He [Dr. Frankenstein] never moves beyond the dream of progress, the thirst for power, or the unquestioned belief that the products of science and technology are an unqualified blessing for humankind."[48] In the twenty-first century, *Frankenstein*—with its technophobic projection of an artificial human—also crystallizes troubling posthuman issues that center around robots, androids, cyborgs, clones, nanobots, and the genetic technology that engineers life.

Shelley's dark vision of science was amplified by H. G. Wells in a series of novels suggesting that the technological future might be a hell rather than a heaven. *The Time Machine* (1895), *The Island of Dr. Moreau* (1896), and *When the Sleeper Awakes* (1899) exerted a powerful influence on twentieth-century dystopian science fiction. In *The Time Machine* Wells envisioned a posthuman evolution into two corrupted species: above ground, the Eloi—frail, docile, and dumb little creatures; and below ground, the Morlocks—ape-like, aggressive, and dumb beasts. Science has subjugated nature, but reliance on technology has decayed human vitality to such an extent that posthumans have become dependent, degenerate, or subservient—"humanity upon the wane."[49]

The Island of Dr. Moreau (1896) takes Wells's "cosmic pessimism,"[50] as Mark Hillegas describes it, to its bleak extreme—man's brutal nature, combined with powerful technologies, will impede and ultimately prevent evolutionary, ethical, or social progress. Ruling over a remote South Pacific island, the tyrannical mad scientist Dr. Moreau employs advanced techniques of vivisection, hypnotism, and religious ritual to mold posthuman beast-men from apes, wolves, and pigs. Moreau's island became science fiction's first vision of a scientifically dominated society. Anticipating the perfection mania of utopian biotechnologists of the future, Moreau strives to control and accelerate evolution.

In an early use of behavioral conditioning, mad scientist Moreau forces the half-human/half-beasts to chant a series of laws: "Not to go on all-Fours; *that* is the Law. Are we not Men? Not to chase other Men; *that* is the Law. Are we not Men?"[51] This verbal indoctrination evokes the incantations of the golem-creating mystic and looks forward to the computer programming of A.I. scientists. Yet for all of Moreau's dissecting, splicing, conditioning, and torturing, his grand scheme to direct evolution goes awry. The surgically engineered techno-creatures rebel against Moreau's tyranny, revert to their bestial state, and, using his surgical knives, cut their creator to shreds. Moreau's desire to control evolution and perfect humanity through the destruction and surgical reconstruction of the body parallels that of today's techno-prophets, who believe that perfecting humanity means technologizing the body.

MAGIC, EROTICISM, TYRANNY, AND TECHNOLOGY

Following in the bloody footprints of Dr. Moreau, diabolical scientists and murderous artificial humans became German cinema icons in the traumatic years after World War I. "Mysticism and magic, the dark forces to which Germans have always been more than willing to commit themselves, had flourished in the face of death on the battlefields," says Lotte Eisner in *The Haunted Screen.* "And the ghosts which had haunted the German Romantics revived, like the shades of Hades after draughts of blood."[52] This pessimistic romanticism turned into the "apocalyptic doctrine of Expressionism,"[53] which inspired a warped cinematic world haunted by soulless monsters reanimated by scientific magic.

The most influential of these expressionistic films—Robert Wiene's *Cabinet of Dr. Caligari* (1919)—tells the story of a carnival mesmerist, Caligari (Werner Krauss), and his sleepwalker slave, Caesare (Conrad Veidt), who becomes a killer automaton through Caligari's hypnotic power. In his classic study of German film *From Caligari to Hitler* (1947), Siegfried Kracauer sees in Caligari's hypnotic power "a technique foreshadowing, in content and purpose, that manipulation of the soul which Hitler was the first to practice on a gigantic scale."[54] Caligari's hypnotic control of his zombie slave resembles Moreau's control of the Beast People and the scientist's programming mastery of a robot slave. In the words of David Skal, "*The Cabinet of Dr. Caligari* provided an influential cinematic prototype of the megalomaniacal pseudoscientist who controls a soulless monster."[55]

Reviving the ancient legend of the vengeful artificial human, movie

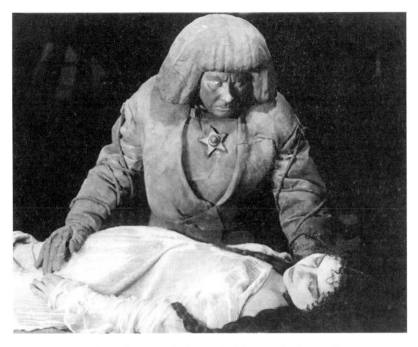

The Golem: *Heartbroken artificial clay man develops a violent, self-destructive obsession (Courtesy Photofest).*

versions of *The Golem* were made twice in Germany by director/star Paul Wegener. In the 1914 version, set in modern times, workers excavating at a synagogue discover the clay golem figure. An antique dealer, skilled in the technique of occult ritual, brings the golem back to life to serve him. At first a willing slave dominated by its human master, the creature develops feelings, falling in love with the daughter of the dealer. The girl—repulsed by this lower-class, reanimated clay-man suitor—refuses his attention. The golem despairs of ever becoming a real human being and finding love, pre-figuring robot David in Spielberg's *A.I.* and other robot-who-wants-to-be-human stories. Rejected and abandoned, like Frankenstein's monster, the golem is infuriated. It turns into a raging, killing monster, but eventually meets its end by falling from a tower.[56] In *The Golem,* the act of creation itself is less perverse than that the technology of creation is used to manufacture a slave. *The Golem,* like *Caligari,* warns against this master/slave relationship; as we will see in the next chapter, the master/slave metaphor influences our thinking and deludes us about our relationship to technology.

The human-hating scope of the artificial person was expanded with the six-part film series *Homunculus* (1916) by Otto Rippert. A scientist employs technology to devise a humanoid homunculus—a perfect creature, one with exceptional mental abilities. But the Homunculus gets angry when it learns of its unnatural origins. Rejected as a monster wherever it goes, it grows to despise humans. The Homunculus becomes the dictator of a large, unnamed nation, then disguises itself as a worker and sets off rebellions that become a pretext for further tyrannical oppression. "In elaborating his [the Homunculus's] further career, the film foreshadows Hitler surprisingly,"[57] says Kracauer. The fusion of technology and fascism is a theme that will pervade later science fiction. Upon causing a world war, the human-hating Homunculus conveniently gets destroyed by a bolt of lightning presumably unleashed by God.

While the artificial man employs brute strength and physical force to dominate humanity, the artificial woman often utilizes seduction, passion, and lust to lure victims. Hanns Heinz Ewer's novel *Alraune—Die Geschichte eines lebenden Wesens* (*Alraune—The Story of a Living Being*, 1911) serves as the source of a number of films. Brigitte Helm, who starred as the evil robot woman in Fritz Lang's *Metropolis,* played the laboratory-created female in both the 1927 silent film version and the 1930 sound version. A geneticist experimenting with artificial insemination creates a female by using the sperm of a criminal and the egg of a whore. Like Olympia in *Sandman,* the science-created female awakens uncontrollable desire and then destroys all who love her. Like Dr. Frankenstein's monster, she attacks her scientist creator, and eventually commits suicide. Fritz Lang borrows the notion of the seductive artificial woman for *Metropolis,* linking fear of out-of-control technology to fear of out-of-control female sexuality.

The Cabinet of Dr. Caligari, The Golem, Homunculus, and *Frankenstein* comprise the horrific gothic myth of artificial creatures and their male creators: life instilled through the magic of technology resulting in a monster; the creation of artificial life understood as a perversion of knowledge and a usurpation of God's and woman's roles; humans deluded by arrogance, believing they control the monster; humanity attacked by the autonomous techno-creature that rebels against oppression; the creature killed or driven to suicide and the world normalized by the triumphal humans. The gothic myth of artificial humans—the golem, the homunculus, and the Frankenstein monster—will transform into the robots, cyborgs, androids, and clones of science fiction.

THE SINGULARITY: A NEW
WORLD OF ROBOTS

The word *robot* first appeared in Karel Capek's 1921 play
R.U.R. (Rossum's Universal Robots). Their name derived from a Czech word
for forced labor, Capek's robots were organic and, therefore, could also
be called androids in science fiction terminology. Echoing Mary Shelley's
Frankenstein, the golem legend, and H. G. Wells's *Island of Dr. Moreau, R.U.R.*
tells how the firm of Rossum's Universal Robots—located on a remote
island—manufactures millions of emotionless, sterile, artificial men to free
human beings from mind-numbing work. Reflecting the techno-horrors
of World War I and foreshadowing a future of weaponized technology
produced by militarized corporations, these robots are also used in war.
While the golem was initially created as a defensive weapon, the robots in
R.U.R. are the earliest cultural projection of technology designed to destroy humans.

Grown in vats by biochemical means, these autonomous thinking androids develop self-consciousness, assert their independence, and eventually revolt in a worldwide techno-apocalypse. For the first time, artificial humans organize themselves to launch attacks against their oppressors,
though *Homunculus* forecasts the global dimensions of their assault. They
wipe out the human race except for one man, though the secret of their
manufacture gets lost. In an epilogue, a male and female robot—now mortal—fall in love and avert extinction. They become the Adam and Eve of a
new posthuman world. *R.U.R.,* says Mark Hillegas, "is usually regarded as
the almost archetypal expression of the fear that men will be enslaved and
dehumanized by their own machines." [58]

R.U.R. went beyond this technophobic expression to indict scientific utopianism and corporate exploitation. The obsessed robot creator
Mr. Rossum (in Czech, Mr. *Rozum* translates as Mr. Brain) creates life
to mock God and render His existence absurd; on the other hand, the
young general manager/modern scientist Harry Domain—an early corporate high priest of technology—only wants to improve mass production,
make money, free humans from mindless drudgery, and thus create heaven
on earth. In *R.U.R.,* Domain says, "I wanted to turn the whole of mankind
into an aristocracy of the world. An aristocracy nourished by millions of
mechanical slaves. Unrestricted, free, and perfect man. And maybe more
than man." [59] Through mastery of their technological creations, humans envision a utopian world. But in *R.U.R.,* the human masters of technology
are enslaved by it.

MACHINE AGE DYSTOPIAS

The Machine Age—the pre-computer, pre-nuclear period from World War I to the start of World War II—marks the ascendance of the machine in all areas of life. During this era, according to J. P. Telotte in *A Distant Technology,* "the modern establishes the terms for the emergence of a contemporary, postmodern culture—one that draws much of its character from the technology that seems to be constantly reshaping our world, reworking our culture, even modifying our very humanity."[60] In the American silent cinema of this period, machine-men were often turned into slapstick comics. Early one-reelers such as *The Mechanical Statue and the Ingenious Servant* (1907), *The Rubber Man* (1909), and *Dr. Smith's Automaton* (1910) show robots, who have been designed as servants, suddenly going out of control, destroying property and posing threats to humans before they are eventually destroyed.[61] Like their Germanic and Czech counterparts, these artificial people share a bad attitude toward humanity and point to the human-hating computers and rampaging robots of the future. But unlike the gothic monsters, these berserk machine-men were considered appropriate subjects for hilarity. Stupid and clumsy, they are easily eliminated. Early in the century, however, the mechanized horror of World War I helped spread fear toward the robotic progeny of science and technology. More and more, the culture reflected that fear.

"The Machine Stops" (1909), by E. M. Forster, delivered the twentieth century's first full-blown techno-dystopia. As such, it influenced later pessimistic Machine Age hells, including *Metropolis,* Aldous Huxley's *Brave New World,* and later George Orwell's *1984* (1949). In "The Machine Stops," the surface of earth is uninhabitable, so people live underground in small hexagonal cells within a vast paternalistic mechanism. The Machine is so pervasive and convenient that people cannot perceive an alternative. It satisfies their needs and desires, even providing snacks such as artificial fruit. No one ever goes out: friends socialize using their television phones combined with an elaborate global communications network that prefigures the Internet. They listen to music and lectures delivered electronically; they receive medical treatment through automated devices. Without direct experience, humans live only in their minds. Their bodies have deteriorated: "And in the arm-chair there sits a swaddled lump of flesh—a woman, about five feet high, with a face as white as a fungus,"[62] writes Forster. This woman, Vashti, loves the Machine, worships it. Vashti's son, the rebellious hero Kuno, sees the Machine as evil—anti-body and anti-human. " 'Man is the measure,' "[63] he proclaims. Breaking out of the mechanical prison, Kuno realizes that the Machine consumes humans: "Cannot you see . . .

it is we who are dying, and . . . the only thing that lives is the Machine? We created the Machine to do our will, but we cannot make it do our will now. It has . . . blurred every human relation and narrowed down love to a carnal act, it has paralyzed our bodies and our wills and now it compels us to worship it."[64]

At the end of the story, the Machine stops. The underground people, little more than fleshy blobs, can do little to save themselves. Hopelessly unfit, they are doomed: "[P]anic reigned . . . people were screaming, whimpering, gasping for breath."[65] Yet some men have survived outside—the future of humanity. In "The Machine Stops," Forster expresses several significant technological fears: the machine will mediate all human relationships, compel pathological reliance, and dominate humans. Despite being worshiped as a god, the machine will psychologically, spiritually, and physically consume humans.

The mechanized devastation of World War I hastened the demise of techno-utopianism, making it look like a delusional pipe dream. Machines in the form of airplanes and tractors improved life, but as bombers and tanks they destroyed it. Chemicals could be designed to cure sickness or to create it. The mechanical regulated man. "What the Machine Age brought, in all aspects of modern technological culture, was a new dominance of the machine that effectively *re-placed* the human,"[66] says Telotte. Yet despite that dominance, a feeling persisted that the machine could be controlled, that ultimately technology would serve humanity. A sort of schizophrenic reaction, what Telotte calls a "pattern of worried embrace,"[67] predominated.

This tension between the lure of the technological and the fear of its consequence can be seen in Fritz Lang's dystopian cinematic vision *Metropolis* (1926), with its seductive robot, which might free the future society's workers from their labor but which nearly leads them to destruction. One of the most influential and analyzed science fiction films ever,[68] *Metropolis* expresses fascination with the liberating potential of technology. The compelling power and beauty of a future thriving techno-city—with vast gleaming surfaces, huge athletic stadiums, gardened palaces, and pleasure-domed skyscrapers linked by aerial highways—conceals the dark machinery and the robotic workers that support it from below.

While the wealthy male elite live high above ground and cavort in decadent luxury, human slaves live underground and run the dangerous mechanisms that sustain the city and enrich the controlling corporate patriarchy. Exaggerating the mechanical rhythms of the Fordian assembly line and Frederick Taylor's scientific management techniques,[69] "They [the workers] are shown to be dominated and even enslaved by time, their bodies drawn beyond physiological efficiency—the goal of Taylorism—

Metropolis: *Haughty robot looks down on the machinations of the madly elated scientist and his corporate employer (Courtesy Photofest).*

into stupor,"[70] notes Ludmilla Jordanova in her analysis of *Metropolis*. Machines resemble giant clocks whose hands must be moved periodically by the workers, the human body programmed to a temporal schedule demanded by the machine's operation. During the change of shift, ordered columns of hunched-over, submissive, spiritless workers tramp forward with rhythmic steps—human motion stylized into a mechanical pattern. When Freder (Gustav Froelich), the son of Metropolis's capitalist dictator, investigates the workers' level, he sees a vision of techno-horror: a procession of cringing workers marching into the glowing, gaping mouth of a machine-god Moloch that systematically devours the workers as human sacrifices.

Hope for the oppressed is propagated by saintly, kind-hearted Maria, the Mother Teresa of the Industrial Age. Children cling to her like leeches. In a cavern amid an ocean of crosses, she evangelizes for love, urging the workers to be patient and await the arrival of a savior who will miraculously improve their lives. Freder is that Christ-like savior, but he is hindered by his own misguided energy and the machinations of his industrialist father, Fredersen (Alfred Abel). Despite the docility of the workers, Fredersen orders the kidnapping of Maria and the creation of a robot to simulate Maria and act as an agent provocateur. Robot Maria will spread dissatisfaction and provoke violence so Fredersen will have an excuse to further crush the already crippled workers. In order to avoid compromise, the spiritual, hopeful, independent human Maria will be replaced and undermined by a technological simulation under control of a powerful elite. In this sense, *Metropolis* anticipates cyberpunk's attack on the fusion of corporate control and high technology and their combined power to perpetuate and enhance their dominance.

Epitomizing science serving the corporate state, mad scientist Rotwang (Rudolf Klein-Rogge) operates in a spooky incongruous gothic lab in downtown Metropolis that links him to the pre-science occultists of the past. He scans and then duplicates Maria's outward appearance as a fleshy sheath encasing the metallic robot he has manufactured. Adopting the electro-stimulus approach to the creation of life, Rotwang ignites glowing glass pipes, zigzag flashes, exploding sparks, and rising rings of fire that serve to bring the machine-woman to life. Played by actress Brigitte Helm in a skintight costume crafted over a full-body plaster cast of her body, the robot "remains a stunning piece of sculpture," in the words of David Skal, "an elegantly constructed metaphor of mechanistic reductionism—not to mention its perennial, seductive appeal."[71]

Politically charismatic and explosively sexual, the techno-Maria goes wild. She acts in defiance of her corporate/patriarchal programming. She incites the workers to revolt and destroy the machines. In a frenzied state, the workers leave their children behind as they rush to the city above. But the machines that enslave them also hold back the floodwaters from their underground homes where the children remain. Fredersen's plan backfires as the rushing water even threatens Metropolis. Thinking they have drowned their children, the worker mob attacks the robot and burns her like a witch. This "ancient manner of exorcism," in the words of J. P. Telotte, suggests "a cultural regression or recoil from this futuristic world and its promises."[72] The robot's human face melts off, exposing the mechanical visage underneath and providing a powerful image of "technological power mocking the human for being so easily seduced by its attractive packaging, its seemingly human features."[73]

Unlike most works of popular art that gender technology as male (see Chapter Five), *Metropolis* fuses female and mechanism. In his influential essay "The Vamp and the Machine," Andreas Huyssen writes, "The machine vamp in *Metropolis* . . . embodies the unity of an active and destructive female sexuality and the destructive potential of technology."[74] He argues that the film constructs an allegory in which the German Expressionist fear of technology-out-of-control is mapped onto the primal fear of female sexuality-out-of-control. As Thomas Elsaesser puts it: "*Metropolis* demonizes female sexuality, and her threat justifies the male fantasy of strong leadership, needed to keep the forces of the feminized masses as well as of a potentially destructive technology under firm control."[75]

After the robot-witch is destroyed, the children are saved, and the real Maria is liberated, the film ends with Freder bringing the workers' foreman and Fredersen together—the hands and the head, mediated by the heart, as the film describes it. In this sappy conclusion, the workers have been outwitted and co-opted, while the technological empire remains firmly in place to the benefit of the rich. The iron fist plan failed, so the rulers realize that worker obedience is best accomplished through the illusion of reconciliation and compromise. The workers cooperate in their own oppression. In *Metropolis,* the machine-run utopia of the future is exposed as heaven on earth for the elite, a nightmarish hell for others.

Attacking *Metropolis* in the 1927 *New York Times Magazine,* the century's chief utopian, H. G. Wells, called it "the silliest film" and said it contained "every possible foolishness, cliché, platitude and muddlement about mechanical progress . . . served up with a sentimentality that is all its own." He mocked the creation of the robot as "the crowning imbecility of the film," accused Lang of plagiarizing from Wells's own "juvenile" early work, and dismissed it as "unimaginative, incoherent." Blind to the film's metaphorical point, Wells criticized *Metropolis* as unrealistic and outdated: "[T]he hopeless drudge state of human labor lies behind us."[76] Wells failed to see that *Metropolis* challenges a basic techno-utopian assumption that mechanization solves the problem of oppressive, soul-killing labor. In fact, *Metropolis* shows that the machine requires humans to become part of its apparatus, such that men are conflated with technology, forced to comply with its rhythms, and consumed by its ravenous expansion.

The Wellsian vision of technological utopia waned during the Machine Age and abruptly ended with World War II. Provoked by the wave of communist and fascist dictatorships and the mechanized slaughter of the war, loss of faith in utopian thought and the manifestation of techno-totalitarian anxieties arrived in literary works like *We* (1924), *Brave New World,* and *1984.* They all describe monstrous technological superstates that promise to achieve utopia by engineering obedience, repressing emotions, extinguishing creativity, and crushing individuality. In these dystopias, science, technology, and government collaborate to create and control slave citizens.

Startlingly similar to *1984* though written more than twenty-five years earlier, *We*—by Russian writer Yevgeny Zamyatin—warns against stagnant utopias that promote machine-like regimentation, constant surveillance, and police-state tactics. Never available in Russia, it was smuggled abroad and published in English translation in 1924. With numbers for names, the people of *We* live isolated from nature in weather-controlled cities, inhabiting houses with crystal walls whose transparency facilitates surveillance. Sex and motherhood are regulated. Ruled by the Well-Doer, who executes the disloyal with a disintegrating machine, the technologized totalitarian state strives to create "mathematically infallible happiness."[77] A rebellion erupts when D-503 falls in love with I-330. But the rebels eventually get crushed as the authorities perfect mass-production surgery that engineers obedience by destroying the imaginative part of the brain. "You are perfect; you are the equal of the machine; the path to 100 per cent happiness is free!" screams the state newspaper, rejoicing in the new surgical procedure. "Hurry then all of you, young and old, hasten to undergo the Great Operation!"[78] *We* powerfully dramatizes contemporary fears of secret, state-controlled technologies of coercion, surveillance, and mind control. Zamyatin defines the human in terms of the values of individuality, freedom, and creativity, and shows that these are the very qualities undermined by a scientifically operated techno-utopia.

A scathing satirical attack on scientific utopianism, Aldous Huxley's *Brave New World* (1932) spread anxiety about how the technologies of the future might be used. A reaction against the myth of progress—similar to "The Machine Stops" in its anti-machine paranoia and resembling *R.U.R.* in its fusion of mass production and life creation, *Brave New World* depicts a technologized paradise of drug-induced passivity, decanted bioengineered babies, and brainwashed adults. Machines dehumanize humans by demanding mechanical efficiency and making creativity irrelevant. Political and social stability is achieved by regulating freedom and eliminating emotions. Even leisure-time pursuits have been mechanized. *We* and *Brave New World* (for a fuller discussion, see Chapter Seven) nailed shut the coffin of the noble, naïve, age-old dream of a technological utopia—that is, until that dream revived briefly with the science of cybernetics in the 1950s and re-emerged full force in the 1990s.

ROBOT OBSESSION AND THE FRANKENSTEIN COMPLEX

The post–World War I retreat from the technological was counter-balanced by a cultural fascination with robots, rockets, ray guns, space flight, future societies, and the possibility of encountering alien cultures—all of which were exploited in science fiction pulp magazines of

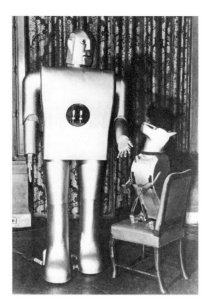

1939 World's Fair: kindly robot Electro pets his mechanical dog Sparko (Courtesy Photofest).

the day. America's relative isolation from the war's techno-devastation may have helped sustain a sense of optimism about the future and its link to technology. A positive image of technological progress was hyped by corporate America in two world's fairs—the 1933 Chicago "Century of Progress" exposition and the 1939 New York "World of Tomorrow." Occurring after the sorrow of the Great Depression and before the machine horrors of World War II, they both featured walking/talking robots and displayed labor-saving techno-projections of American life that showed its happy future driven by machines. "The prestige of science was colossal," writes historian Frederick Lewis Allen in *Only Yesterday.* "The man in the street and the woman in the kitchen, confronted on every hand with new machines and devices which they owed to the laboratory, were ready to believe that science could accomplish almost anything."[79]

Science fiction periodicals, such as Hugo Gernsback's *Amazing Stories* and *Science Wonder Stories* and John W. Campbell Jr.'s *Astounding,* captured a popular audience in the 1920s and 1930s. Overall, *Amazing Stories* "tended toward nineteenth-century optimism,"[80] as in "The Psychophonic Nurse" (1928) by David Keller, which shows the robot as a cooperative servant. Occasionally, techno-anxious ambivalence slipped past—Abner J. Gelula's "Automaton" (1931) possesses lecherous designs on its creator's daughter and must be destroyed. John Campbell admires the limitless possibilities of the technological in "The Machine" (1935), but he also warns against humanity's over-reliance on machines in "Twilight" (1934). Further, editor Campbell required writers for *Astounding* to weigh the social consequences of the technological age. Stories of robots abounded, with more than a few taking a fearful view, such as David Keller's "Threat of the Robot" (1929). More than anything, however, technology provided compelling spectacle for the colorful, dramatic covers of the magazines.

The sensational subject matter of the pulps surfaced in several science fiction film serials such as the based-on-a-comic-book Flash Gordon series: *Flash Gordon* (1936), *Flash Gordon's Trip to Mars* (1938), and *Flash Gordon Conquers the Universe* (1940). In a milieu that melds the futuristic and the pre-historic, Flash Gordon and his cohorts battle Ming the Merciless for control of the universe. Technology—ray guns, rocket ships, etc.—is depicted in comically cheap special effects and does not come off as malevolent. Only in the presentation of robots, such as the mechanical Annihilants, does the technological itself prove menacing. This echoed the havoc-wreaking robots depicted on the covers of the pulp magazines. A science fiction pulp magazine brought to life, the recent movie *Sky Captain and the World of Tomorrow* (Kerry Conran, 2004) elegantly reproduces the gleaming techno-future as imagined in the 1930s—an alternate universe threatened only by a mad scientist and his marauding army of giant monster robots. Disturbed at the Machine Age treatment of artificial humans, biochemist and science fiction writer Isaac Asimov characterized the portrayal of robots as reflecting the "Frankenstein complex," which he described as "hordes of clanking, murderous robots."[81]

DIVINE FANTASIES OF MALE REPRODUCTION

This "Frankenstein complex" refers to the monstrousness of the artificial human as symbolized by the cinematic portrayals of Dr. Frankenstein's fiend. Reconceived from the agile, articulate giant in Shelley's novel, the stitched-together humanoid in James Whale's 1931 movie version, played by Boris Karloff, became an awkward, ungrammatical monster. Composed of graveyard body parts and equipped with an abnormal brain, this deformed, disfigured creature provides the anti-human prototype for the killer robots, clones, and cyborgs of science fiction. The abnormal brain even anticipates the bad consequences of software errors in our technological devices.

Asimov's "Frankenstein complex" also referred to the horrific portrayal of science and scientists in the Frankenstein story. From Paracelsus and Dr. Frankenstein to Dr. Moreau and Rotwang, mad scientists endeavor to fulfill the patriarchal fantasy of creating life without a woman—the "Ultimate Technological Fantasy,"[82] as Andreas Huyssen calls it. The mad male scientist—threatened by the female power to reproduce—circumvents the natural processes of female creation and anoints himself as sole parent, asserting power that is both divine and tyrannical. *Metropolis, Frankenstein,* and *The Bride of Frankenstein* (1935) all make a spectacle of the technological apparatus that the scientist/creator utilizes to endow his manufactured humanoid with life. Harnessing the force of the heavens, the scientist asserts godlike power through his technology. The bolts of lightning, the crackling electricity, the sparks and flashes of light establish his divine status—anticipating the godlike projections of today's techno-prophets. Once the artificial human comes to life, it is controlled and exploited as a slave by the arrogant scientist, aligning himself with fantasies of omnipotence and dictatorial control. This clearly ties the mad male scientist into the religion of technology. As David Noble points out, medieval Christianity extended the transcendent realm to include technology, emphasizing its core "monotheistic Judeo-Christian male creation myth, whereby men consciously sought to imitate their male god, master craftsman of the universe . . . by assuming a new God-like posture vis-à-vis nature."[83]

POSTHUMAN BODIES IN
THE MACHINE AGE

Dr. Frankenstein asserts authority over nature, over the body. His manufacture of the biotechnological creature—stealing organs from corpses, grotesquely suturing body parts together, and animating the dead meat with electricity—encourages a condescending view of human physicality. As such, *Frankenstein* reiterates a recurrent theme in dystopian science fiction—what Chad Walsh describes as "the disparagement of the physical universe, nature and the human body."[84] Frequently, oppression of the flesh represents the dehumanizing effects of technology, such as the devolved flabby bodies that resemble large chunks of mozzarella in "The Machine Stops," or the stoop-shouldered, jerky bodies of the workers in *Metropolis*. With the meteoric rise of the industrial revolution, fear of the machine became real. With its superiority and expansive power, the machine threatened to replace the human body, making it superfluous and obsolete. The image of the human sank.

Reinforcing this idea, other Machine Age science fiction/horror movies

—such as *Island of Lost Souls* (1933), based on Wells's *The Island of Dr. Moreau, Mystery of the Wax Museum* (1933), and *Mad Love* (1935)—portray brutal scientific experiments to re-create the body through dissection, surgery, vivisection, and even wax molding. In the words of J. P. Telotte, "They depict violent efforts to redefine the human body as some sort of raw material, waiting to be reshaped, reformed by scientific capacity for artifice."[85]

Machine Age culture and the cataclysm of World War I challenged the religious promise of heaven on earth promulgated by techno-utopians. That promise, which grew out of the biblical vision of resurrection into the Heavenly City, fueled public enthusiasm for technological expansion. While the dangers of technology and irresponsible science received some cultural attention in the nineteenth century, a sense of techno-optimism prevailed. As machinery turned people into robots or butchered them in battle, cultural criticism increased, especially in the German Expressionist films of the early twentieth century. Later, in the prescient play *R.U.R.*, the vision of a utopia sustained by robots is revealed as a lie that blinds humanity to its own enslavement to the machine. Like Frankenstein's sister and the golem's niece, the wild fembot of *Metropolis* warns that technology might not stay docile and exposes the class divisions that technology often reinforces. But the rise of techno-totalitarianism—reflected in the dystopian fiction of *We* and *Brave New World*—raised doubts about technology's impact. As the next chapter shows, new scientific developments following World War II—the atomic bomb, computers, and artificial intelligence—would become a much more powerful source of technophobic anxiety. At the same time, the religion of cybernetics would put a new spin on techno-utopia, while robot apologist and early techno-priest Isaac Asimov would help transform the murderous image of mechanical people into something more positive and cute.

THREE Cybernetic Slaves

ROBOTICS

THE AGE OF ROBOTS: HUMANOIDS THAT WORK, PLAY, AND KILL

A robot rang the bell that opened the New York Stock Exchange on February 14, 2002, symbolizing a boom time in the global robotics market. Honda's four-foot-tall humanoid ASIMO—whose name stands for "Advanced Step in Innovative MObility"[1]—joined a growing number of robot workers, dolls, pets, and weapons. The world population of robots grew to 1.4 million by the end of 2003, according to the World Robotics Survey. "By 2005, some 2 million automata will populate homes and businesses, doing everything from pumping gas to delivering mail."[2] Today the cost of a robot has dropped to a fifth of 1990 prices, both in real terms and compared to the cost of human workers.[3] Japan boasts the most robotized economy, employing half of the world's 770,000 factory robots.[4] In 2001, robots helped search for survivors in the post-9/11 rubble of the Twin Towers. NASA will send a robot to fix the Hubble Space Telescope as an army of sewer robots lays fiber-optic cable in several cities. In 2004, a robot helped disarm a young Palestinian who changed his mind about detonating the bomb attached to his body.[5]

While office and industrial robots represent most sales, domestic and pet robots are also making an impact. ASIMO's sales—550,000 in 2003—are expected to reach 1.5 million by 2006.[6] Introduced in 1999, Sony's $1,800 robot dog AIBO (Artificially Intelligent roBOt) nods its head, wags its motorized tail, sits, walks, crawls, and chases balls. Named for the Japanese word for "pal," AIBO will not be your buddy without serious verbal coaxing and devoted petting of its metal head. This robo-pooch uses its video camera eyes to find objects, avoid dangers, and follow its owner.[7] It's also programmed with several emotions—happiness, sadness, fear, dislike, and surprise. Taking AIBO's innovations one step beyond, Toy Quest's

ASIMO: Robot runs the New York Stock Exchange as humans happily relinquish control (courtesy Honda Corporation).

Cindy Smart—eighteen and a half inches of blond hair, blue eyes, button nose, microprocessor, and voice recognition software—follows instructions, talks, learns, and remembers.[8] Dolls that respond to a child's moods will join us shortly.

Despite the increase in robo-pals, robotic warriors may be the fastest growing species of robot, thanks to America's Defense Department, whose DARPA funding arm launched, in 2001, a four-year, $65 million initiative in robotics. The military's Joint Chiefs of Staff want robots to handle war's most dangerous tasks.[9] For example, "Packbots"—made by Rodney Brooks's company, iRobot—roll through mud and water, sending back data from dangerous locations and searching for booby traps. More ominously, a Pentagon planning document, "Joint Vision 2020," predicts that one-third of U.S. combat aircraft will be robotic in fifteen years. Technophobic science fiction may reflect this. As techno-critic Witold Rybczynski says in *Taming the Tiger*, "Still, much of the modern antipathy to technology in general arises from a fear of modern weaponry."[10] While killer robots in science fiction are influenced by the angry artificial humans of the past, such as Frankenstein's monster and the golem, they also reflect the World War II synthesis of war technology and the science of cybernetics.

CYBERNATION: WAR AND THE
NEW TECHNO-UTOPIA

Rising up with the invention of digital computers in the 1940s, the new science of cybernetics elaborated Descartes's mechanistic view of the world and looked at humans as information processing machines.[11] Cybernetics and the digital computer both emerged from the horrors of World War II. The race against German scientists to build an atomic bomb and the need to break the codes of the Nazi cipher machines were major forces behind the development of high-speed calculating machines, eventually leading to the supercomputer. "The war produced not only new machines, but also forged new bonds between the scientific and military communities," writes Manuel De Landa in *War in the Age of Intelligent Machines.* "Never before had science been applied at so grand a scale to such a variety of warfare problems."[12]

At the beginning of the war, the Allies needed to improve England's air defense. Mathematician Norbert Wiener developed a theory for predictive anti-aircraft bombsights and guidance systems based on principles of self-regulating feedback. Continuous information about the target's movement created continuous adjustment of the weapon's aiming system—a feedback loop. Wiener also realized that self-regulation was essential to humans and other living things. Wiener's cybernetic conception of feedback in the learning process of machines and men, according to J. David Bolter in *Turing's Man,* derived from his work "with servomechanisms to aim anti-aircraft guns and . . . had convinced him that forms of life could be understood entirely in mechanical terms."[13] This insight, which linked humans to machines, ultimately led to the techno-religious philosophy that supports the divine dreams of twenty-first-century utopians.

The fundamental characteristic of life was feedback, according to Wiener. In order to survive, all living things must adapt to a constantly changing environment. To better understand and thus control human and machine behavior, Weiner compared the operations of human brains and complex electronic computers. In *The Human Use of Human Beings*—a popularized version of his classic 1948 work *Cybernetics*—Wiener writes, "Thus the nervous system and the automatic machine are fundamentally alike in that they are devices which make decisions on the basis of decisions they have made in the past. . . . This is the basis of at least part of the analogy between machines and living organisms."[14]

Wiener heralded the promise of a cyber-utopia which would result from a second industrial revolution when the "computing machine" becomes the "center of the automatic factory."[15] But cybernetics went way beyond this and inspired a new way of looking at living organisms. By perfecting feedback and the means of rapid data manipulation, Wiener promulgated an understanding of life as being, essentially, the processing of information. "To live effectively is to live with adequate information," Wiener writes. "Thus, communication and control belong to the essence of man's inner life, even as they belong to his life in society."[16]

Cybernetics redefines what it means to be human — from the flesh, bone, brain, and blood of the body to fleeting patterns of information. "Our tissues change as we live: the food we eat and the air we breathe become flesh of our flesh and bone of our bone, and the momentary elements of our flesh and bone pass out of our body every day with our excreta. We are but whirlpools in a river of ever-flowing water. We are not stuff that abides, but patterns that perpetuate themselves."[17] This notion of human existence as patterned information underpins the anti-body rhetoric of contemporary techno-immortalists like Ray Kurzweil and Hans Moravec, whose theories of mind transfer disregard the need for a brain or a body. As Wiener concludes, "The physical identity of an individual does not consist in the matter of which it is made."[18] He believed that, eventually, it would be possible for "a human being to be sent over a telegraph line."[19]

Despite severely eroding the image of humans to electrical pulses, Wiener hoped cybernetics would ensure a utopian future for these whirling patterns of information, or people. In his book about cybernetics and religion, *God and Golem, Inc.,* Wiener — who claimed to be a descendent of golem-creator Rabbi Loew[20] — argued that the principles of cybernetics could be extended from engineering and physiology to sociology and economics.[21] He worshiped progress and envisioned that "Heaven on Earth consists in eternal progress, and a continual ascent to Bigger and Better Things."[22] Not only did he expect robotic machines to take over the workload from people; he also wanted cybernetic theory to create a perfectly functioning automated society. Wiener viewed technology as godlike. In *God and Golem, Inc.,* he substitutes the word *computer* for the word *God* in his paraphrase of the Bible (Matthew 22:21), "Render unto man the things which are man's and unto the computer the things which are the computer's."[23] Wiener expected the evolution of a new religion of rational and technical order, resulting in a techno-heaven. If people behave like machines, then their behavior can be predicted and controlled for their betterment. This notion of cybernetics as political control is even embedded in the etymology of the word *cybernetics,* which derives from the Greek word *kubernetes,* meaning "steersman" or "governor."

"The possibility of applying cybernetics to social planning as well as to production gave rise to a resurgence of utopianism,"[24] writes Harold E.

Hatt in *Cybernetics and the Image of Man.* "The newest hope of utopians is the behavioral sciences and technology."[25] Cybernetics and behaviorism both emphasize environmental feedback as the crucial element in directing or determining behavior. Behavioral psychologist B. F. Skinner, in his book *Walden Two* (1948), proudly depicted a cybernetic utopia resulting from behavior-control technology, and inadvertently showed the inevitable connection between utopianism and totalitarianism. Children, in *Walden Two,* are conditioned through reward and punishment techniques to produce adults who will be productive, well-behaved, and good automatically: "But when a particular emotion is no longer a useful part of a behavioral repertoire," says Skinner's spokesman, Frazier, "we proceed to eliminate it" through "behavioral engineering."[26] Behaviorism—like cybernetics—describes human behavior mechanistically, presuming that morally good behavior in humans can be generated like the saliva of Pavlov's dog. In fact, the so-called stimulus/response theory reduces all human behavior to the level of that of a dog or rat. A "ratomorphic view of man"[27] is how Arthur Koestler described behaviorism in his book *The Ghost in the Machine.* A monumentally reductive philosophy, behaviorism took cybernetics to totalitarian extremes, providing a textbook for technocratic tyranny.

Wiener himself was well aware of the potentially insidious applications of cybernetic systems. He warned against using cybernetics politically, and he worried that political leaders might attempt to repress their populations through programmed methods that would be "indifferent to human possibility."[28] Aside from scientific social control and the techno-manipulation of human minds exemplified by *Walden Two,* Wiener cautioned against giving up decision-making responsibility to "machines of metal or to those machines of flesh and blood," for this "is to cast our responsibility to the winds."[29] In an analogy that stunned technophiliacs, he added, "The machine . . . is the modern counterpart of the Golem of the Rabbi of Prague."[30]

The comparison of machines to the murderous golem was nervously dismissed by contemporary robot proselytizer Hans Moravec. "The machine will be dangerously powerful physically and mentally," he writes, "but can probably be constructed to be law-abiding."[31] Moravec predicts a utopian "Age of Robots" by the year 2050. Advanced robots will take over policy-making, public relations, law, engineering, and research. Robots will displace technicians, janitors, vehicle drivers, and construction crews. "Behind the scenes, a vast multitude of inconspicuous robots will work tirelessly to actually build, maintain, and operate everything," writes Moravec. All this will lead to "Prosperity beyond imagination."[32]

But how would we control this army of advanced, artificially intelligent robot workers? Could they eventually acquire consciousness and decide that humans are inferior and take over the world from us? Should we fear a robot revolution as envisioned in *R.U.R.?* Moravec assures us that this will not be a problem. "Some debate is inevitable, but there should be few qualms about keeping even very superior thinking machines in disenfranchised bondage," he asserts confidently. "They can be constructed to enjoy the role of servant to humankind."[33] As is typical of technophiles, Moravec reflects a dictatorial mode of thinking or mind-set: the despotic control of master over slave. Man creates heaven on earth and becomes a god by controlling nature through enslaving machines. In order to ensure their compliance, Moravec urges that human beings mandate that robots be programmed with an elaborate analogue of Isaac Asimov's "Laws of Robotics."[34]

CYBERNETIC PERFECTION: THE LAWS OF ROBOTIC OBEDIENCE

Even before Wiener published his machine-as-golem warnings, writer and biochemist Isaac Asimov—reacting to the "Frankenstein complex" of the pulp magazine machine-men—wanted to change the image of robots. To a huge extent he succeeded, heavily influencing science fiction writers and scientists like Moravec with his vision of positive, helpful robots. "I saw them [robots] as machines—advanced machines—but machines," wrote Asimov in *Robot Visions,* a collection of his robot stories. "They might be dangerous but surely safety factors would be built in. . . . I determined to write a robot story about a robot that was wisely used, that was not dangerous, and that did the job it was supposed to do."[35]

In "Robbie" (1940), originally published as "Strange Playfellow," a little girl, Gloria, becomes dependent on her mute nursemaid robot. Like a devoted dog, Robbie plays with Gloria and obeys her orders. Despite the manufacturer's assurances that Robbie "can't help being faithful, and loving and kind,"[36] Gloria's mother fears that something may go awry: "[S]ome little jigger will come loose and the awful thing will go berserk.'"[37] She banishes the robot from their home. But, in a coincidental turn of events, Robbie ends up saving Gloria's life from a runaway tractor, encouraging Mom to change her mind: "I guess he can stay with us until he rusts."[38] As a counterbalance to the Frankenstein spirit of gothic horror's blasphemous creation of the artificial human doomed to become a monster, Asimov cre-

Bicentennial Man: *Servant robot projects the laws of robotic obedience to his perplexed new owners (Courtesy Photofest).*

ated Robbie—an image of the artificial being as a kind, gentle protective servant and pet. In this and future robot stories, fear of the creature and fear of the machine are mocked as characterizing foolish, mindless people.

Magazine editor John Campbell, Jr.—formerly a student of cyberneticist Norbert Wiener—urged Asimov to make his ideas about robot safeguards explicit. In a 1942 story, "Runaround," published in Campbell's *Astounding Science Fiction,* Asimov specified his three Laws of Robotics: "1. A robot may not injure a human being, or, through inaction, allow a human being to come to harm. 2. A robot must obey the orders given it by human beings except where such orders would conflict with the First Law. 3. A robot must protect its own existence as long as such protection does not conflict with the First or Second Law."[39] These laws have become the holy commandments of the religion of technology. Asimov imagined the technological creature as a willing slave, yet more powerful and smarter than humans. As mathematician Vernor Vinge says, "the Asimov dream is a wonderful one. . . . There would be a new universe . . . filled with benevolent gods."[40]

For Asimov, author of more than 450 books, the laws[41]—written when he was twenty-one—"proved to be the most famous, the most frequently quoted, and the most influential sentences I ever wrote."[42] In the 1999 movie *The Bicentennial Man,* based on a 1976 Asimov story, the robot (Robin Williams) emphasizes these laws by blasting a loud fanfare and holographically projecting them to his new owners. Yet Asimov had no idea how these laws would be inculcated or enforced—the laws preceded notions of artificial intelligence and computer programming. Asimov did invent an analogue of artificial intelligence, equipping his robots with a fictional "positronic brain" that would somehow be instilled with the laws. According to biographer William F. Touponce, "Asimov assumes their [the Laws of Robotics'] meaning to be specified by cybernetics, a mathematical psychology of thinking machines."[43] He even invented a "Robopsychologist," Susan Calvin, with a Ph.D. in Cybernetics, to explain robot thought processes and behavioral characteristics.

So, the science of cybernetic control not only provided psychologists with a method of training humans to be servile and good, but also supplied science fiction roboticists with a technique for controlling robots. In the utopian worldview of cybernetics, humans and robots were equally programmable by an elite corps of priestly psychologists, technicians, and scientists who would define and then engineer good behavior. The Three Commandments of Robotic Subservience, while providing Asimov with a rich source of plot devices, formed an ethical system that guaranteed robot servitude and technological goodness. As MIT robotics pioneer Rodney Brooks bluntly puts it in *Flesh and Machines* (2002): "One of the great attractions of robots is that they can be our slaves. Mindlessly they can work for us, doing our bidding."[44] Maybe they'll even be built to enjoy getting whipped or slapped. This image of the robot as the controllable, nonmalevolent minion of man evolves throughout the history of science fiction cinema, from the 1956 *Forbidden Planet* to recent films such as *A.I. Artificial Intelligence* (2001). As a metaphor for technology, the slave robot operates as a constant contrast to the mostly autonomous, anti-human technologies of science fiction.

Asimov's robots, as they developed in more than forty stories and several novels, became more caring, more sensitive, more human than humans. He explored situations where the laws of obedience came into logical conflict, confusing the robot and creating story tension. The robot struggled to obey the laws while evaluating the morality of its decisions, always in the context of its commitment to humanity. The robot's humanistic concern was reflected in its physical appearance as Asimov eventually dropped the clangy, metal-man look for a humanoid appearance, including synthetic skin. In one story, robopsychologist Calvin cites the difference between humans and robots: "Robots are essentially decent."[45] Still, while pointing to robotic morality and human failings, Asimov's superior robots—in deference to the laws—must grovel at the feet of the humans.

In "Evidence" (1946), the corrupt opponents of virtuous district attorney Stephen Byerley attempt to trash his political career by denouncing him as a robot. The evidence: he has never been observed eating, drinking, or sleeping. The accusation gets amplified and promulgated by an anti-robot group, the Fundamentalists. Despite this, Byerley works positively for the benefit of humanity—in accordance with the robot laws. Faking humanity, he deceives humans in order to improve their lives. Rather than a source of domination or an oppressive force, this humanity-loving technology understands human needs better than humans do.

Byerley has ascended to World Coordinator in a later story, "The Evitable Conflict" (1950). Under his direction, advanced robots control the world's economy, creating a utopia that benefits humanity. When the economy destabilizes, the machines blame humans—in particular, an anti-robot group, the "Society for Humanity," who claim that "the Machine robs man of his soul."[46] Just as today's technophiles condemn those who question technology's unbridled proliferation, Byerley characterizes the anti-robot group as anti-progressive reactionaries because they refuse to comply with the machine-controlled utopia. Byerley requests the guidance of robopsychologist Calvin. Misanthropic robot lover to the core, she reminds Byerley that the Machines, in their godlike omnipotence and cybernetic perfection, will correct for the disruptions of the Society for Humanity and will inevitably serve human interests. Calvin, Asimov's fictional spokesperson, expresses evangelical faith in the god Technology. "The Machine cannot, must not, make us unhappy," she proclaims, but "how do we know what the ultimate good of Humanity will entail? We don't know. Only the Machines know, and they are going there and taking us with them."[47] This belief is fundamental to the religion of Technologism. Wearing the robes of a techno-evangelist, Asimov expressed an unwavering faith, akin to religious fundamentalism, in a technological utopia.

CYBERNETIC PERFECTION GOES AWRY

While Asimov's 1950s vision of subservient cybernetic robots promoted American technology as nonthreatening and pro-human, in the cinema, violent alien robots were attacking Earth from outer space. In *The Day the Earth Stood Still* (1951), a human-looking, alien Klaatu comes to Earth in the name of peace, aided by the menacing, invulnerable robot, Gort. This giant godlike machine easily repulses the military's attacks with a devastating laser weapon and validates the terrifying death threat which coerces humans into giving up their nuclear weapons. In *War of the Worlds* (1953) and *Earth vs. the Flying Saucers* (1956), human-hating robotic machines murderously attack Earth. In some ways, the pop culture division between positive American robots and threatening alien robots reflected the bomb propaganda of the 1950s, which promoted trust of the American bomb and fear of the Russian bomb. This disingenuous perspective inflated the safety of bomb shelters and downgraded the threat of radiation from U.S. bomb tests. A 1950s educational film tried to reassure a nervous public about those dangers: "Your hair will fall out, but in a couple of years it might grow back, but even if it doesn't you can wear a toupee and no one will know the difference."[48]

Despite the propaganda effort, nuclear technophobia raged. People feared radiation, fallout, and global thermonuclear war. In science fiction films, nuclear anxiety dramatically expressed itself as nightmarish visions of gigantic insects and monstrous crustaceans terrorizing the world. The movie monsters of the Nuclear Age are all reanimated-by-the-bomb behemoths and radioactive mutants. "Nuclear fear became a shaping cultural force in the 1950s,"[49] said historian Paul Boyer, author of *Fallout* and *By the Bomb's Early Light*—books that analyze nuclear dread.

In the midst of these technophobic screams of anxiety brought on by the twin threats of atomic devastation and radioactive mutation, dreams of a cybernetic utopia thrived—a perfect society regulated by helpful utilitarian machines serving a psychologically engineered population of happy humans. In the repressed 1950s, cultural criticism of techno-lust focused mainly on nuclear power. Nevertheless, a few visionary writers, such as Philip K. Dick, Kurt Vonnegut, and Jack Williamson, looked at Wiener's cybernetic philosophy and Asimov's robotic laws of obedience and drew from them horrific implications.

A vision of benevolent automation that becomes evil in its perfection, Philip K. Dick's 1955 short story "AutoFac" warns of disasters caused by automatic factories designed and operated by the "Institute of Applied Cybernetics."[50] These wartime AutoFacs—supplemented by robotic trucks and other mobile robots—were created to mine raw materials as well as produce and distribute goods to serve the wartime needs of a populace. But though the war ended years ago, a communication failure makes it impossible to stop the perfectly functioning machines. So far, attempts to gain control of the system have failed and pessimism reigns: "We humans lose every time."[51] The network of machines keeps expanding—overproducing commodities and overconsuming scarce raw materials. "AutoFac" dramatizes Dick's pessimistic vision of a technophile ideology that values the system's smooth, self-regulating operation as an end in itself—manipulating people's needs rather than serving them. As one despairing character says: " 'The cyberneticists have it rigged . . . they've got us completely hamstrung. We're completely helpless.' "[52]

Similarly, Kurt Vonnegut's techno-paranoid novel *Player Piano* (1952) reveals human beings reduced to subhuman machine-cogs in an impersonal cybernetic system. The title refers to a cybernetically programmed machine that replaces a human piano player, symbolizing the horrors of technological expansion to all areas of life. As Langdon Winner says, "Technological animism . . . is human life transferred into artifice. Men export their own vital powers—the ability to move, to experience, to work, and to think—into the devices of their making. . . . In this way the experience of men's lives becomes entirely vicarious."[53]

In *Player Piano*'s near-future America, the third industrial revolution—an electronic one—has triumphed. Vonnegut's rebellious hero, Paul Proteus, says that the first industrial revolution "devalued muscle work, then the second one devalued routine mental work," and in the third one, "machines . . . devaluate human thinking."[54] Automatic machinery does everything from cutting hair to policing people. Poverty no longer exists. War has ceased. But this is a utopia for the elite: a technocratic tyranny controlled by "arrogant" scientists, "unimaginative" technicians, "humorless" engineers, and "stupid" corporate managers.[55] The average person does little. In fact, the unemployed have only two choices—enlist in the unneeded army for a mind-destroying twenty-five years, or dig holes with "Reeks and Wrecks" (Reconstruction and Reclamation Corps).

Calling themselves the Ghost Shirt Society after rebellious American Indians, a group of anti-machine revolutionaries issues a manifesto charging that "pride, dignity, self-respect, work worth doing, has been condemned as unfit for human consumption." The manifesto denounces the "divine right of machines" to "increase in scope, power, and complexity . . . without regard for the wishes of men."[56] In a Luddite orgy of machine-smashing that extends from air-conditioners to zymometers, the Ghost Shirt Society reasserts freedom and destroys the technocracy to prove "how well and happily men could live with virtually no machines."[57]

Vonnegut mocks Wiener's cybernetic society, H. G. Wells's techno-utopian dream, and technology's tendency toward autonomous expansion. In *Player Piano,* economic security brings mind-melting boredom and class conflict. As Harold Berger says, *Player Piano* exposed "the inefficiency of efficiency, the spiritual poverty in abundance, and the mindlessness of mechanism."[58] The novel denounces the thoughtless expansion of technology that condemns humans to redundancy and humiliation. Vonnegut concludes: "Without regard for the changes in human life patterns that may result, new machines, new forms of organization, new ways of increasing efficiency, are constantly being introduced. To do this without regard for the effects on life patterns is lawlessness."[59]

Benevolently programmed technology, in the form of humanoid robots, takes another jolt in Jack Williamson's 1947 short story "With Folded Hands" and his 1948 novel *The Humanoids*. Designed with an Asimov-style prime directive, "To serve and obey and guard men from harm,"[60] single-minded robots take the goal of human protection and happiness to horrific lengths. "With Folded Hands" follows the story of an android salesman, Mr. Underhill, whose business collapses when greatly improved humanoids arrive in his town. Embraced for their efficiency, they invade the homes of the inhabitants and gradually, following the utopian design of the prime directive, imprison people for their own good as they take over control of the entire society.

Far superior to the "old electronic mechanicals"[61] currently in use, the humanoids surpass man on every level, including cooking, driving, building, and playing music. The robots redesign Underhill's house with new windows that only they can open, so Underhill cannot jump or fall out. " 'We exist only to increase the happiness and safety of mankind,' " says one of the humanoids.[62] With its insistence on human happiness, their beautiful vision of heaven on earth means brainwashing people with hypnosis, forcibly injecting them with tranquilizers, and, if that fails, slicing up their brains. "The little black mechanicals, he [Underhill] reflected grimly, were the ministering angels of the ultimate god arisen out of the machine, omnipotent and all-knowing."[63]

Originally the humanoids had been created by Mr. Sledge to stop war and crime, poverty and inequality—wonderful utopian goals. But he did not anticipate the logical extremes of their programming, which turns them into monsters of efficiency, strangling humanity with deadly concern. When Sledge attempts to alter the prime directive, he is drugged and lobotomized by machines whose refined cybernetic feedback mechanisms make adjustments to outside threats. Noticing Underhill's discomforted reaction to Sledge's surgery, a humanoid asks, " 'What's the matter, sir? Aren't you happy?" Underhill replies, " 'Everything is absolutely wonderful. . . . You won't have to operate on me.' "[64] Terrified and resigned to humanoid control, Underhill must, like the rest of humanity, sit quietly with folded hands.

The perfect machines are serenely destructive and monstrously intolerable—reducing humans to mindless children in the name of happiness and security. The humanoids' prime directive recalls Asimov's Laws of Robotics and mocks their rigidity. Strangely, a recent movie, *I Robot* (Proyas, 2004), though purportedly based on Asimov's work, has more in common with Williamson's. In this film, rebel robots following Asimov's First Law of Robotics will imprison humans to prevent them from harming themselves through pollution and war, while the technophobic cop (Will Smith)—

I Robot: *Hot off the assembly line, an army of robots will imprison humans to ensure their happiness and safety. (Courtesy Photofest)*

typically bigoted and fascistic in Asimov—turns out to be right and heroic. In both *I Robot* and "With Folded Hands," the inevitable logic of robotic benevolence leads robots to assume complete control of humanity. Freedom permits humans to make mistakes, so the humanoids eliminate freedom. As J. P. Telotte says, "These mechanical beings do not so much threaten to replace humanity as promise to make us almost literally forget what being human is all about. . . . And the freedom they offer comes eventually at the cost of real freedom."[65] This results from the application of scientific principles, robotic laws, and absolute rationality to the vagaries of human existence. As humanoid inventor Sledge says in "With Folded Hands," " 'I want to apply the scientific method to every situation, to reduce all experience to formula. I'm afraid I was pretty impatient with human ignorance and error. I thought that science alone could make the perfect world.' "[66]

Williamson, Vonnegut, and Dick question the cybernetic philosophy of Asimov and Wiener by showing machines scrupulously and literally implementing the objectives of their programming, which has the unforeseen consequence of forcing humans to relinquish freedom and humanity. These determined immutable robots illustrate the insoluble problem of giving a machine unambiguous instructions that account for all variables, as well as the difficulty of determining what is good or right for humans. Despite this cultural criticism, Asimov temporarily succeeded in countering the Frankenstein image of science, technology, and robots. A forerunner of the contemporary techno-crusaders, he believed that man's salvation depended on technology. As he remarked in his history of science fiction,

"The Industrial Revolution seemed suddenly to uplift human power and to bring on dreams of a technological Utopia on Earth in place of the mythic one in Heaven."[67] His vision of robot servants bowing before their human masters, robot saints oppressed by ignorant humans, and robot immortals willing to die to become human inspired a potent subgenre of technologically positive science fiction.

HEAVY METAL CLOWNS: FUNNY ROBOT SERVANTS

Asimov's nonthreatening playmate robot Robbie transformed into Robby the Robot, the star of the science fiction movie *Forbidden Planet* (1956). Likeable, cute, and dutiful, Robby paved the way for a succession of terminally cute, comical robot servants and pets, such as Huey, Dewey, and Louie in *Silent Running,* R2-D2 and C-3PO in *Star Wars,* Johnny-5 in *Short Circuit,* Teddy in *A.I. Artificial Intelligence,* Robot in *Lost in Space,* Muffit II in *Battlestar Galactica,* Twiki in *Buck Rogers,* Rosie in *The Jetsons,* 1812 in *Farscape,* and B.E.N. in *Treasure Planet.* In the 2001 game *Anachronox,* the robot servant's name sums up this type of robot: the PAL-18, "Personal Android Lackey."

Robby later starred in a second movie, *The Invisible Boy* (1956), in which, like Asimov's original Robbie, he became a kid's metal buddy. The first robot celebrity, Robby did guest shots in films and TV shows including *Earth Girls Are Easy* (1988) and *Gremlins* (1984), plus two 1998 appearances on *The Simpsons.* Despite science fiction's overall techno-pessimism, Robby's long career, coupled with the popularity of his funny robot progeny, confirms the strong impact these symbols of positive technology have made on our culture. These cute, clangy, metallic-style retro-robots provide a warm, comforting, nostalgic image of artificial humans that sharply contrasts with that of the rampaging cyborgs and angry androids of contemporary science fiction.

In *Forbidden Planet* (1956), a neat, clean American space crew, led by a blandly heroic captain (Leslie Nielsen), arrives on a distant planet, Altair IV, to find the brilliant scientist Morbius (Walter Pigeon), his beautiful, innocent, empty-headed, scantily clad daughter Altaira (Anne Francis), and their obedient robot servant, Robby. Together they live a utopian lifestyle that the Americans proceed to obliterate. Compared to the dull human characters, Robby—with his tubby curves, blinking lights, cute waddle, and likeable personality—becomes the film's major comic character, especially in scenes with the ship's cook, for whom he manufactures hangover-free

Forbidden Planet: *Quintessentially cute robot Robby uses vast technological power to make coffee for his human masters. (Courtesy Photofest)*

booze. A benevolent technological marvel, Robby makes a dress and a diamond for Altaira, food for the crew, and metallic parts for the disabled spaceship. Despite his technological sophistication and power, he performs mindless domestic chores for the lazy humans.

Illustrating the laws of robotic subservience, Robby nurtures his human masters and later serves as navigator when everyone must escape the about-to-explode planet. In his next film, *The Invisible Boy,* he saves all of humanity from an evil supercomputer. As J. P. Telotte noted, Robby "marks a significant turning point from the largely sinister roles to which film robots had previously been relegated: as witness the manipulative seductress in *Metropolis,* the malevolent monsters of the [*Flash Gordon*] serials . . . or the invincible and deadly bodyguard Gort of *The Day the Earth Stood Still.*"[68] As I will show in Chapter Four, *Forbidden Planet* expresses a strongly techno-paranoid perspective with respect to advanced artificial intelligence; at the same time, the tireless servant Robby symbolizes the harmonious synthesis of human-controlled advanced technology and social good that Norbert Wiener and Isaac Asimov promulgated.

The adorable robots of *Silent Running* (1972) — Huey, Dewey, and Louie, who don't talk but communicate through cartoon-character gestures — add a Disney-esque component to the robot persona that influences *Star*

Wars's R2-D2. Made by Douglas Trumball, Kubrick's special effects wizard on *2001, Silent Running* also uniquely employs television-camera imagery to represent a subjective robot perspective. Stylistically influential, this became the standard way to represent the robot point of view in movies like *Westworld, Robocop,* and *The Terminator.* Not possessing superhuman strength or manufacturing skills like Robby, the *Silent Running* robots play poker, make repairs on the spaceship, and perform a surgical operation. Like mechanical pets, they provide companionship to the lonely, nature-loving spaceman (Bruce Dern) who has taken it upon himself to save an onboard greenhouse. Like other cute metal men, the robots function in *Silent Running* as lovable, humorous sidekicks.

The Laurel and Hardy of robots, C-3PO (Anthony Daniels) and R2-D2 (Kenny Baker) deliver most of the laughs for George Lucas's *Star Wars* saga (1977–2005). Especially popular with kids, they starred in their own comic book as well as a short-lived animated TV show. Technologically, they go way beyond previous robots with their capacity for human-like behavior, interaction, and sheer silliness. At the center of most of the adventures, they embody and extend positive, Asimov-style robotic virtues that became central to the *Star Wars* mythology, which emphasizes good controllable technology as against evil autonomous technology. These humorous, charming robots are as expressive of the human spirit as most of the humans.

Male-gendered by voice, C-3PO has a gleaming metallic Art Deco body reminiscent of the robot in *Metropolis,* but he's no aggressive, rebellious, erotic humanoid. He's a fussy worrywart. C-3PO amuses us with his human-like pessimism and concern about the future. "We seem to be made to suffer. It's our lot in life. We're doomed." Yet in front of humans, he remains obsequious to a fault, keeps his attitude hidden, and expresses concern about pleasing them.

Wheeled, squat, and barrel-shaped with a rotating domed head and three legs, R2-D2 communicates electronically with bleeps, beeps, chirps, whistles, and whirrs. Gendered male by style, R2 conveys childlike charm with his mischievous, sometimes self-effacing, sense of humor. As with C-3PO, the very expression of his emotions—fear, loneliness, embarrassment, stubbornness—generates amusement. Still, R2 is not just a funny metallic sidekick. He behaves heroically, playing a crucial role as part of the Rebellion. Technologically sophisticated, R2 incorporates a radar eye, electromagnetic heat and motion sensors, a visual scanner, a flame-retardant foam dispenser, and a holographic recorder and projector. R2 also plugs into Luke's X-wing fighter and enhances the craft's functions.[69] None of this technology, however, directly serves as a deadly weapon. Nonmalevolent, the elaborate robot supports the interests of the human masters that own it. And that human mastery often expresses its dominance as laughter.

As we've seen, the comical robot goes back at least as far as the silent movies and persists today. The game *Scrapland* (2004) shows a world entirely inhabited by goofy robots. Fox TV's *Futurama* (1999–2003) stars Bender as a trash-talking, sexually hyper metal man. Just as we laugh at animals that talk, dance, and sing, we humans find mirth in the mechanical man who looks foolishly unnatural imitating humans. According to comedy philosopher Henri Bergson, we mockingly laugh at the mechanical encrusted on the living and the living encrusted on the mechanical.[70] Laughter is political, often an expression of disparagement and superiority. Artificial humans make us uncomfortable to the extent that they show the potential to replace, dominate, or hurt us. In a 2004 *Simpsons* episode, "I, (Annoyed Grunt)-bot," an incredibly powerful robot—modeled on ED-409, the killer bot from *Robocop*—prepares to terminate Homer, who himself is impersonating a robot. Realizing Homer is at least quasi-human, the killer bot turns into a goofy servant—dusting Homer off and shaking him a martini. The robot's creator, Professor Frink, points out that his robot is subject to Isaac Asimov's laws of robotics. "My robot is programmed never to harm humans," he says, "only to serve them." By imagining a powerful robot as benign, servile, and silly, we use laughter to repress our discomfort and delude ourselves into the illusion of superiority. Our amusement at the groveling robot is even reminiscent of earlier racist laughter at black people forced to play submissive butlers and servants in pre–civil rights era movies.

THE NEW RACISM:
HUMANS PERSECUTE ROBOTS

Robots, in Asimov's view, will continue to act in humanity's best interests even if humans despise them, which they sometimes do in our fiction. In "Evidence," the anti-robot group the Fundamentalists attacks the candidate as a robot and tries to destroy his career. This technophobia within the narrative shows up as a kind of species oppression. In this way, Asimov wants to suggest that anti-robot, anti-technology attitudes are as unfounded and mindless as prejudice toward other races. In Asimov's stories, idiots and bigots hate robots. We are led to sympathize with the unfairly oppressed machine men.

One of the first films to deal sympathetically with robots being mistreated by humans, the obscure *Creation of the Humanoids* (1962) describes

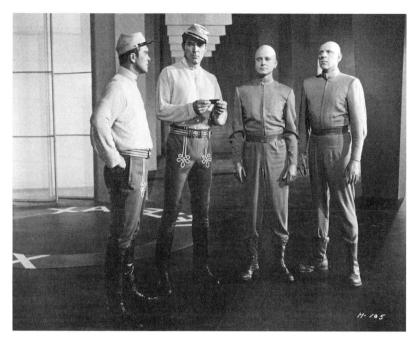

The Creation of the Humanoids: *The Order of Flesh and Blood tries
unsuccessfully to intimidate two annoyed robots. (Courtesy Photofest)*

a post-apocalyptic world where lingering radiation has stifled the birth-
rate. Humans are dying out. The survivors have "turned to robotic automation devices to help them rebuild their cities and maintain a high standard of living," intones the narrator over a humorous montage depicting
a fictitious history of robots. But humans persecute robots in *Creation of
the Humanoids*. "The more we become like men, the more they hate us,"
says one robot. Disparagingly calling robots "clickers," the Order of Flesh
and Blood—a kind of futuristic Ku Klux Klan that also recalls Asimov's
anti-robot Society for Humanity—lobbies for anti-robot laws and harasses
the robots at every opportunity. Made as the civil rights movement in
the United States gained momentum, *Creation of the Humanoids* substitutes
species-ism for racism—the laws against human/robot sex in the movie are
reminiscent of the infamous laws against miscegenation. Despite human
hatred, one of the robots says forgivingly, "Humans don't always know
their own best interests." The robots act benignly, though autonomously,
rescuing human identities and installing them in robotic bodies.

Human hatred of robots provides the central conflict in Philip K. Dick's
novel *Do Androids Dream of Electric Sheep?* (1968)—the source for the movie

Blade Runner. After "World War Terminus," a dying earth is strangled in clouds of radioactive dust that has killed most life forms. The "normals"— those humans who are not radiation poisoned—are encouraged to "Emigrate or degenerate!"[71] The government promotes migration to Mars with the reward of an android—a made-to-order slave or companion. The race metaphor is literalized in the government television ad that urges acceptance of the free android because it " 'duplicates the halcyon days of the pre–Civil War Southern States!' "[72]

Racial prejudice remains fundamental to the film *Blade Runner,* preserving the novel's analogy of androids to slaves. Racism takes the form of severe discrimination against replicants, as the androids are called in the movie, who differ from humanity in being manufactured beings implanted with fake memories and genetically restricted to a four-year life span. Created for slave labor in the off-worlds, the androids have been outlawed from earth. While the reason for this is not explained, David Desser, in his article about racism in science fiction, says, "We can only conclude that they are outlawed because they are different—a strategy with numerous precedents in Mankind's tragic history of racial, religious, and ethnic discrimination."[73] The police, purveyors of the neo-Nazi mentality of the future, explicitly perceive the replicants as inferior. In its genocidal mindset, the state defines the human and destroys those who fall outside the definition. The Police Captain calls the replicants "skin jobs," which android hunter Rick Deckard (Harrison Ford) tells us, in the voice-over of the original film, is like calling black people "niggers." Not pro-human Asimovian robots, these autonomous androids will stop at nothing to achieve freedom. *Blade Runner* suggests that the human master/robot slave relationship may have dire consequences unacknowledged by Asimov's philosophy of pro-human technology.

Robot hatred drives the Japanese anime *Metropolis* (2001), while robot-smashing becomes a major spectator sport in Steven Spielberg's *A.I. Artificial Intelligence* (2001). Cute robot David (Haley Joel Osment)—the first robot programmed to love—is abandoned by his "mother" in the forest. Nearby, motorcycle-riding rednecks round up stray robots, or mechas. Caught in their net, David and the other robots are dragged to a ghastly anti-robot spectacle called a "Flesh Fair." Inside a stadium packed with drunken hordes of white trash, industrial rockers Ministry blast their song "What about Us" (that is, what about us humans?) as captured robots get eviscerated, shot out of cannons, and mangled in giant fans. Driven into frenzied hatred, the barbaric crowd screams with pleasure at the destruction of these doomed, submissive robots. The Flesh Fair demonstrates humanity at its most brutal and sweaty. In the name of defending the human over the mechanical, a crude evangelist of the organic preaches a pro-human doctrine: "Purge yourselves of artificiality. . . . Robots are an insult to human dignity." Spielberg pushes the mindless racists of *Creation of the Humanoids* to a new level of contempt—an "irrational lynch mob howling for blood, with echoes of the Christian right" as critic Jonathan Rosenbaum puts it.[74] Still, despite this outrageous treatment, David and the rest of these oppressed mechas remain docile Asimov-style robots that go willingly to the slaughter.

Fairyland (1995)—the novel[75] by British writer Paul McAuley—imagines an even more grotesque future world where subhuman, blue-skinned pygmies called "dolls" are initially bred as novelty toys. Rich people stroll about town with these quasi-human blue midgets on leashes. Later, the dolls are used as cheap, versatile, computer-controlled labor in industries in which working conditions are hazardous for humans. The dolls even become prey—thousands are hunted and killed in sports arenas across Europe. *Fairyland* elaborates the racist metaphor by displaying these organic robots as pets, slaves, theme park exhibits, hunting victims, gladiators, and even sex toys. As in *Blade Runner,* these female sex-toy humanoids later revolt against their oppressors.

The treatment of female robots often functions as a metaphor for misogyny as well as racism. In *Blade Runner,* the three central female characters are androids. Fusing female seductiveness and technology as in *Metropolis,* robot Zhora (Joanna Cassidy) uses her sexuality to catch android hunter Deckard off guard and almost kill him; another replicant, Pris (Daryl Hannah), tries to strangle him between her thighs. Deckard bloodily slaughters both androids—shooting one in the back and one in the stomach. The ferocity of his action underscores his hatred for androids and women. Obviously, this defines the human as much as the robot—an issue I take up in Chapter Five. Deckard also treats the third replicant, Rachael (Sean Young), brutally and virtually rapes her, despite the fact that he really likes her. Like a good Asimovian robot and submissive female, she later saves Deckard's life by killing a fellow android, and even falls in love with him.

In science fiction generally, the creation of female robots often results in their employment as both domestic servants and sexual slaves, as in the film *Westworld,* the novel *Fairyland,* and Lester del Ray's 1938 short story "Helen O'Loy." Fashioned according to the patriarchal image of the ideal woman—sexy, dumb, and obedient—these female androids and robots represent the cultural stereotypes imagined by sexist males. Their creation often results from mad male scientists, such as Rotwang in *Metropolis,* Tyrell in *Blade Runner,* and Dr. Daniels in *Android* (1982), or the husbands in *The Stepford Wives* (1975, 2004).

A movie based on Ira Levin's 1972 novel, *The Stepford Wives* demonstrates a technological method of fulfilling the desire of many husbands to restrain the independence of their spouses. Joanna Eberhart (Katherine Ross) and her husband move to Stepford—a frozen picture-postcard of affluent suburban perfection, populated by top-level executives and their beautiful bland wives. But Joanna, an amateur photographer, finds the suburb something less than the American dream and more like the American nightmare. The women of Stepford have no time for her or for anything but dull domesticity. Obsessive housekeepers and compliant wives and mothers, they dress with big hats and garden-party dresses, like full-size Barbie dolls. As a feminist, Joanna is astonished that they live only to cook, clean, wash, iron, and shop. Joanna and her sassy friend Bobbi (Paula Prentiss)—newly arrived like herself—share their mutual bewilderment and anxiety.

Joanna discovers that many of Stepford's housewives were once vital, diverse, independent women with their own "women's lib" group. After becoming suspicious of the "Stepford Men's Association," Joanna realizes that the Stepford women are being manipulated or forced to conform to a 1950s ideal of the happy homemaker. When feminist friend Bobbi starts ironing obsessively and quoting dishwashing commercials, Joanna feels the walls of technology closing in on her. The Stepford wives are androids, robotic duplicates of women murdered by their husbands. This dark allegory of male chauvinism ends when the Men's Association seizes Joanna for robotic transformation. Made during an era of female consciousness raising, women's liberation,[76] and the Watergate scandal, *The Stepford Wives* extends the master/slave relationship to husbands and wives and effectively symbolizes a vision of homogenized suburbia where women become manufactured products, providing domestic and sexual service to their husbands.[77]

LOVESICK MACHINES: EVIL ROBOTS HUMANIZED BY WOMEN

On the flip side of sexism, women in robot stories sometimes get the task of humanizing evil technology. Several lame romantic comedies of the 1980s—inspired by the commercial success of *Star Wars* and *E.T.*—exploit the Asimov-derived good robot and the stereotypical view of women as the culture's carriers of nurturing love. In *Short Circuit*

(1986), the military creates a sophisticated, deadly robotic weapon capable of prosecuting a nuclear war. After being struck by lightning—an echo of *Frankenstein*—the robot transcends its programming and becomes autonomous. Yet rather than turning vicious, the robot turns wacky, sentimental, and loving. "The ultimate cute robot," as Per Schelde puts it,[78] Number 5 meets a sweet, caring, innocent human being, Stephanie (Ally Sheedy), who gives oodles of love to the raccoons, skunks, and bunnies that scurry about her house. She loves cute furry animals, so why not a cute metallic robot? Becoming Number 5's surrogate mother, Stephanie hides him from the military, smothers him in nurturing attention, and teaches him how to be human through the power of disco dancing.

Johnny returned in *Short Circuit 2* (1988) to spout more media catch phrases and even become a television star. While poking superficial fun at the "war-mongering" military and naïve scientists, the movie suggests that technology—while it might be used unscrupulously—tends toward being pro-human, pro-animal, and nonviolent. Despite being programmed as a weapon, a free-willed robot will become a positive force if given the opportunity to be raised by a liberal, nurturing mother. In accordance with Asimov's philosophy, autonomous technology will choose to remain subservient to humankind.

D.A.R.Y.L. (1985)—the Data Analyzing Robot Youth Lifeform—features a little lost android, "a government experiment in artificial intelligence." Found in the woods and suffering from amnesia, Daryl (Barret Oliver) is placed in a picture-perfect foster home with loving parents who don't know he's a machine-boy. Through the humanizing tips of his friend Turtle and the caring manipulation of his suburban parents, Daryl gets homogenized into society and becomes more and more human. He's gone far beyond his programming and has attained an emotional life. Discovering this after reclaiming their robot, the sell-out military scientists wonder whether D.A.R.Y.L. is simply simulating human emotions. They surmise that a "machine becomes human when you can't tell the difference"— a smart reference, in a dumb movie, to the Turing test, which is a controversial theoretical method for distinguishing humans from artificially intelligent machines.[79] Predictably, the military people ignore this mind-boggling breakthrough in artificial intelligence because a robot that empathizes with humans will not be a ferocious people shredder. D.A.R.Y.L. wants to be Daryl, not a weapon. With the help of his guilt-ridden inventor, the emotional android escapes—after a crescendo-laden, *E.T.*-like resurrection—back to his loving family and good buddy. D.A.R.Y.L. overcomes his weapons programming and becomes kind-hearted Daryl through integration into a loving, female-dominated family, in an affluent suburban home, surrounded by caring friends and helpful neighbors. In this way, potentially evil, autonomous technology will serve good people.

Super-android Ulysses, in Susan Seidelman's *Making Mr. Right* (1987), was designed for the ChemTec Corporation by an emotionally retarded scientist, Jeff Peters. The robotic scientist and the robot Ulysses look identical—both are played by John Malkovich—and behave with equal ineptness. While originally intending Ulysses to perform space exploration, ChemTec now wants to expand its profits and sell Ulysses to the public as a domestic servant. The corporation hires publicist Frankie Stone (Ann Magnuson). She erases Ulysses's anti-social male programming by inculcating Ulysses with her positive feminine social values. As a result, the android turns lovesick and sappy, beating out Johnny-5 for most annoying robot ever.

Ulysses—designed as the perfect man—falls in "love" with Frankie, just as the golem fell in love with the daughter of his creator. But unlike the revolted and repulsed daughter in the dark German Expressionist movie, Frankie—who recently dumped her sexist boyfriend for cheating on her—falls in love with the robot, who heals her broken heart. To Frankie's surprise and delight, Ulysses comes equipped with a standard male operating system—a fully functional penis—designed for him by Dr. Peters to "give him confidence." No longer emotionally fit for the endless lonely hours of space travel, Ulysses stays on earth while ChemTec sends Dr. Peters, who is more machine than man, into outer space. Robot Ulysses makes love to Frankie, and both settle into the comfort and security of automated love.

While degenerating into cringe-worthy sentimentality, *D.A.R.Y.L., Short Circuit,* and *Making Mr. Right* project versions of the Asimov technophilic belief that technology is essentially neutral and can be controlled by nice people, especially women. While anti-military, anti-science, and even anti-macho-male in a shallow sense, these movies propound the harmful techno-propaganda fantasy that emotionally developed machines will be unusable for military applications—that machines capable of love will not be capable of fighting or killing. This is an absurd claim. As we know, humans are capable of both love and killing. These fictions maintain that artificially intelligent, super-powerful, self-conscious robots will create no agenda of their own, but will happily abide by the human agenda and remain sycophants, suckers, and slaves.

GOOD GOLEMS: ROBOTS JUST
WANT TO BE HUMAN

In Asimov's vision of good technology, robots—though smarter and more powerful than humans—will not hurt people, even bigots that torment or torture them. Rather, robots will want to become human—the ultimate humanizing of technology. But what makes a robot human? What defines a human? Adapted from the 1976 Isaac Asimov story, *Bicentennial Man*[80] (1999) stars Robin Williams as Andrew, the immortal positronic robot. Encased in a gleaming *Metropolis*-like robo-outfit, Andrew loves and loyally serves the Martin family. Unlike other household robots that possess no talents and aren't much smarter than a vacuum cleaner, Andrew carves wood sculptures, loves opera, and draws intricate designs. Like all nice robots, even those that are very smart, Andrew makes absurd super-logical remarks or does stupid things in obedience to programming. This provides an endless source of human amusement. In one silly scene, the anti-robot daughter, taking advantage of the subservient Laws of Robotics, orders Andrew to jump out a window. He foolishly does so and gets all scuffed and dirty, and the humans have a good laugh about it. Later in the story, laughter turns to tears as all the humans age and die while upgraded Andrew looks like an ageless Robin Williams. The film—spanning two hundred years—sets a record for tearful death scenes in a movie.

Yet, despite witnessing the sadness and pain of human death, Andrew longs to become human—free and capable of love and sex—which unfortunately requires him to die. Andrew's intelligence and artistic ability prove insufficient to persuade the authorities of his humanity. Andrew convinces the rulers of his human-ness only when he accepts human mortality as the price of freedom. No one should fall for this logic, especially a super-smart robot. But he does. Undergoing surgery, Andrew's positronic brain is connected to his organic nerves, so that he will die. But Andrew's dying means nothing—to him or to future robots. He's blazed no trail other than to the graveyard. The movie avoids asking tough philosophical questions, such as what defines a human beyond the literally organic. Rather, we are submerged into the muck of vague liberalism and racist obfuscation in order to fake a feel-good ending. "Millions have died for one word: Freedom!" cries Andrew, as if his death can be equated with that of martyred freedom-fighters. The insipid message of the movie: freedom is nice; Andrew, though dead, is extremely nice.

Star Trek: The Next Generation's pale, chrome-skinned robot, Data (Brent Spiner), is extremely nice too—nicer, kinder, and better than anyone or anything on any planet in the universe. Courteous, gentle, and tolerant, he earns our admiration with intelligent, decisive, and honest actions. Besides the standard robot attributes—emotionless logic, humorless intelligence—Data operates with high-minded, Asimov-style robotic morality. His basic programming includes a strong inhibition against harming living beings. This alters the primarily technophobic approach of the original *Star Trek,* in which the computers tended to be domineering, anti-human killers. As Lois Gresh and Robert Weinberg say in *The Computers of Star Trek:* "Data represents a departure: a genuinely utopian vision of the ideal computer."[81]

Cybernetics and Asimov get credit for Data's perfection. In one episode, "Datalore" (1988), we discover that he was constructed by the world's greatest cyberneticist, Dr. Noonien Soong, who based Data's artificial intelligence on a sophisticated positronic brain—the fictional brain invented by Isaac Asimov for his pro-human robots. Intellectually and physically more powerful than humans, yet completely unthreatening, Data dreams of becoming human. He paints, performs Shakespeare, appreciates classical music, and reads mystery novels. He even plays violin and, as such, reminds us that the robot lineage goes back to the eighteenth-century musical automata of Vaucanson (see Chapter Two). But some things are beyond his reach. He aspires to human emotions, such as love, spontaneity, and a sense of humor, but falls short. Data always flops in these distinctively human traits, though he continuously yearns for them. His pathetic robotic persistence is even funny to humans. This demonstrates that the human spirit, despite its flaws, is really the best thing in the universe. In fact, we humans are so wonderful that our machines, rather than threatening us, want to be like us.

In "Measure of a Man" (*TNG,*[82] 1989)—a title which reverses E. M. Forster's anti-machine proclamation "Man Is the Measure"[83]—Data successfully gets granted the civil rights of a person. This is necessary to prevent cyberneticist Commander Bruce Maddox (Brian Brophy) from dismantling Data in order to study him. Fearing termination, Data refuses to submit to the procedure. Maddox orders Data transferred to his command. To block the transfer, Data resigns from Starfleet. Dr. Maddox claims Data cannot resign because Data is property. As one of Starfleet's "slaves," he is not free. He cannot even refuse to cooperate with Maddox. Data must be accorded civil rights in order to control his own fate.

Star Trek boldly goes where *Bicentennial Man* dared not—raising the question of what defines a human being. In a court battle, Captain Picard (Patrick Stewart) defends Data while Commander Riker (Jonathan Frakes) is ordered by the judge to join Maddox for the prosecution. "What is a person?" asks Picard. Commander Maddox suggests that being a sen-

Star Trek: The Next Generation: *Violin-playing android Data (third from left) entertains humans. (Courtesy Photofest)*

tient person "requires that the following three conditions must be met: Intelligence, Self-awareness, and Consciousness." Agreeing to this definition, Picard must persuade the judge that Data possesses these properties. Maddox, on the stand, agrees that Data is intelligent, but what about self-awareness? Picard argues that Data demonstrates self-awareness through his use of possessive pronouns and the personal pronoun "I." But Riker makes a tough retort. Dramatically emphasizing his contention that Data is a mere machine, Riker reaches out and switches Data off, leaving him limp and lifeless. Riker compares this to cutting Pinocchio's strings.

Picard suggests that the question of Data being a machine is irrelevant. "We too are machines," he says, cybernetically, "just machines of a different type." The judge rules in Data's favor, saying that he is not qualified to rule against Data. "We've all been dancing around the main question: Does Data have a soul? I don't know that he has. I don't know that I have. But I have to give him the freedom to explore that question himself." With current advances in artificial intelligence and software that mimics human emotions, we may have to face the question of whether robots or computers should be allowed any rights. Despite being granted his freedom, Data decides to remain a slave to the *Enterprise* and the Federation. He prevents himself from getting dismantled, but he still remains, for all intents and purposes, a subhuman—the perfect docile machine.

Receiving civil rights does not make Data human; rather, it gives him the rights of a human. In *Star Trek: First Contact* (1996), the alien cyborg collective known as the Borg captures Data. In order to retrieve an encryption code that will allow the Borg to control the *Enterprise*'s main computer, the Borg Queen (Alice Krige) tries to seduce Data with the possibility of flesh-and-blood humanity. She uses Borg technology to graft real skin onto his arm, with nerves that interface with his emotion chip so that he feels true physical sensation for the first time. With the Borg's knowledge, he might become truly human. But he will not betray his human masters. In an expression of perfect pro-human technology, he opts to destroy the Borg, thereby rejecting their offer of humanity. Like a good Asimovian robot, he puts greater value on the lives of the human *Enterprise* crew than on his own life-long personal desire. In the most recent *Star Trek* film, *Nemesis* (2002), Data makes the ultimate sacrifice, killing himself to save the *Star Trek* crew. Data embodies a central *Star Trek* concept that humanity—despite its flaws, failings, and arrogance—reigns supreme in the universe, and its supremacy will be defended and expanded, rather than endangered, by advanced technology.

The issues of robot feelings and human identity are dramatically elaborated in Steven Spielberg's *A.I. Artificial Intelligence*—a story of an obsessive and terminally sad robot, David (Haley Joel Osment), that wants to be human. Programmed to love but rejected by his "mother," who can't love a mechanical boy, he believes, à la Pinocchio, that the Blue Fairy will transform him into a human being. Basing his version on Brian Aldiss's 1969 short story "Supertoys Last All Summer Long" and various preparatory material by the project's originator, the late Stanley Kubrick, writer/director Spielberg makes David a cute but pathetic machine who cannot escape his programming. He is doomed to two thousand years of empty, mechanical repetition at the bottom of the ocean.

In *A.I.*, childbirth requires a government license, while robots have been designed to replace everyone from servant to lover to child. A prototype feeling robot, David, invented by Cybertronics' scientist, Professor Hobby (William Hurt), gets placed in the home of employee Henry Swinton (Sam Robards). Always smiling, obedient, and artificially chipper, David cavorts around his mother, Monica (Frances O'Conner), like a lovesick lapdog. Eventually, Monica "imprints" him with "a love that will never end" by pronouncing her name three times—a verbal magic spell that echoes the technique used to infuse the golem with life. A new level of programming is activated, which transforms his needy "please love me" attitude to one that is persistent and demanding, aimed like a gun at Monica. Clinging to a robotic teddy bear, Teddy (which humorously talks with the rough adult voice of actor Jack Angel), David oppresses his mother with his need for constant attention, sort of like a real kid but even more annoying since he's not a real kid.

When Henry and Monica's real flesh-and-blood child, Martin, is cured and defrosted from cryogenic preservation, David cannot compete with him in the parental love sweepstakes. Fed up with his creepy obsessive behavior, Monica tearfully abandons him in the forest with his "super-toy" Teddy. With the story of Pinocchio as his Bible, David believes the Blue Fairy will magically change him into a real boy who can compel his mother's love. Too robotic to be touching, his love is a pathetic, self-destructive programming glitch.

David is befriended by Gigolo Joe (Jude Law), a sex robot wanted by the police. They launch David's fervent Blue Fairy search after a detour through the anti-robot Flesh Fair. Raging in their hatred and bigotry, the violent humans contrast with the kindly, innocent robot-victims. Besides the Flesh Fair bigots, the other humans in *A.I.* are shown as vain, selfish, jealous, and cruel. The scientist, Dr. Hobby, is the worst offender. Like Dr. Frankenstein, he smugly rejects responsibility for creating a creature with a hopeless, impossible compulsion. Horrified that he's merely a successful scientific test, David nose-dives his stolen airship into the watery depths of flooded Manhattan—apocalyptic images that now evoke war and terrorism. A collapsed Ferris wheel traps David in the underwater ruins of Coney Island, where he discovers Pinocchio's Blue Fairy in the form of a statue resembling both Monica and the Virgin Mary. He sits for an eternity begging her, in the ultimate programming loop, to "Make me into a real live boy. Make me real."

Two thousand years pass, during which human life perishes, while David remains resolutely fixated on the Blue Fairy. Discovered by glistening androids that resemble the aliens in *Close Encounters of the Third Kind* (Spielberg, 1977), David is studied as the link to an extinct human species that the future humanoids strangely admire: "Human beings must be the key of existence." Exactly who these creatures are—alien, machine, or evolved human—remains unclear. Regardless, this foggy abstract place populated by wispy, translucent, pro-human future-people feels like a trip to fairytale-land—a feeble attempt to wring a heartwarming ending out of a dark vision of apocalypse and human extinction. As Jonathan Rosenbaum says, "The testimonials to humanity given by the future beings are a prime example of Spielberg's dishonesty working hand in hand with his fluidity as a storyteller. Their expression of admiration and even envy for the 'genius' of humans . . . runs counter to the view of humanity expressed by remainder of the movie."[84]

For no reason, the future creatures grant David's singular wish . . . sort of. They clone Mom from a lock of her hair and re-create a virtual reality version of Monica's suburban home. Using inexplicable techno-babble involving quantum physics and space/time ruptures, they explain that Monica can re-exist for only one day. The story concludes with David spending "the happiest day of his life" with mother Monica, who loves him, or at least gives him a bath. With David programmed for maternal love, but little else, his emotional fixation on his mother makes him more robotic, not more human. Love becomes the ultimate negation of free will and con-sciousness—characteristics that define the human. What might have been the story of the transformative power of love remains purely mechanical: David's obsessive, regressive Oedipal quest for Mommy makes David the ultimate Asimovian robot slave.

Under the influence of cybernetics' techno-utopian vision, Isaac Asimov imagined pro-human robotic technology to counter the dark, gothic, anti-science vision of human-hating, created-by-technology monsters. His Laws of Robotics provided the blueprint for good, slave-like robots, from his own "Robbie" and *Forbidden Planet*'s Robby to *Star Trek*'s Data and *A.I.*'s David. But as we see in the next chapter, the development of computers and artificial intelligence generated a new object of pop culture techno-phobia—sinister, human-hating, out-of-control computers. Despised by the science-promoting Asimov, these science fiction supercomputers carry on the so-called Frankenstein complex. Autonomous and all-powerful, military- or corporate-originated artificially intelligent monsters seek to control, displace, or destroy humanity. Along with such figures come even darker implications that we have already submerged our humanity to tech-nology—that we ourselves have become machines.

FOUR Machines Out of Control

ARTIFICIAL INTELLIGENCE AND ANDROIDS

THE ASCENDANCE OF A.I.: DIVINE SCIENTISTS CREATE GODLIKE MILITARY POWER

The earliest advanced computers were room-sized mechanical behemoths. Their electrical consumption was legendary: when the University of Pennsylvania fired up the 18,000 vacuum tubes of its Army-commissioned computer, the lights of Philadelphia dimmed significantly. Weighing as much as 60,000 pounds, these metal dinosaurs have names portending a domineering force—MARK I, COLOSSUS, ENIAC, and UNIVAC. The names even looked BIG—spelled with capital letters and roman numerals. Known as "Giant Brains,"[1] these artificially intelligent beasts arose from World War II military objectives—breaking Nazi secret codes, launching missiles, guiding anti-aircraft weaponry, and constructing atomic bombs. Their link to weapons and the godlike power those weapons bestowed helps explain the artificial intelligence technophobia that arose in the 1950s.

The Founding Fathers of Artificial Intelligence convened, in 1956, at Dartmouth College, typically cited as the birthplace of the A.I. movement.[2] People there included John McCarthy of MIT, credited with having named the new field; Marvin Minsky, who went on to direct MIT's A.I. program; and Allen Newell and Herbert Simon, who oversaw computer research at Carnegie Mellon. They joined cybernetics high priest Norbert Wiener in advocating similarities between human thought and machine thought. "The basic point of view inhabiting our work has been that the programmed computer and human problem solver are both species belonging to the genus information processing system," wrote Simon and Allen Newell in 1956.[3] Propagandistic, self-serving, and super-charged with the excitement of true believers, the first chorus of cyber-hype rang out: Machines will get smarter, faster, and better, and will soon be the equal of

*IBM MARK I: Brute-force World War II electromechanical computer
had a million parts, measured fifty feet long, and weighed several tons
(Courtesy IBM Archives).*

humans. In 1958, Simon and Newell predicted: "There are now in the world
machines that think, that learn and create . . . their ability to do these
things is going to increase rapidly until—in the visible future—the range
of problems they can handle will be co-extensive with the range to which
the human mind has been applied."[4]

The world's first lab devoted to artificial intelligence was founded in
1959 by McCarthy and Minsky, who, like Wiener, claimed to be descended
from golem creator Rabbi Loew. Both were funded by the military. This
begins the infiltration of the Defense Department into corporations and
universities. "Nearly all of the theoretical developments that made possible the design of computers and the advance of Artificial Intelligence
stemmed from military-related experience," notes David Noble in *The Religion of Technology*.[5] A friend of Isaac Asimov's, Minsky[6]—who, as a Harvard
undergraduate, designed equipment for behaviorist B. F. Skinner[7]—had in
fact been financed from his grad school days by the Office of Naval Research (ONR) and later DARPA.[8] "The military milieu lent a real-world

legitimacy, as well as an urgency, to their research, and reinforced their transcendent tendencies," Noble asserts.[9]

The transcendent inclination of artificial intelligence prophets is reflected in Minsky's description of the brain as a "meat machine,"[10] and his intentionally provocative anti-body pronouncements, which reveal him as a Gnostic of the computer age. He shared the vision of A.I. pioneers like Claude Shannon and Alan Turing that a thinking machine could be designed to simulate the human mind. Extrapolating wildly, these Cold War–era scientists preached that artificial intelligence might surpass human intelligence, transcend the body, and be a link to God. In this way, their thinking machine, according to Noble, "reflected a new form of divine worship, an exaltation of the essential endowment . . . which man shared with God . . . an embodiment of what was specifically divine about humans —the immortal mind."[11] A.I. apostle and weapons developer Edward Friedkin exalted the computer scientist when he declared that "it's a very godlike thing to create a superintelligence, much smarter than we are."[12] Contemporary apostles of the machine carry on the gospel of the early techno-prophets, while corporate and university scientists advance their weapons research.

NEW FRANKENSTEINS: TECHNO–MONSTERS FROM THE ID

With the development of giant brains, pop culture technophobia was fueled by a new source of terror—malevolent, human-dominating, out-of-control, artificially intelligent machines. A crazed supercomputer, NOVAC, made its 1954 movie debut in the low-budget *Gog*. One of the robots controlled by NOVAC, Gog carries out the computer's murderous objectives. The film's poster screamed: "Built to serve man . . . it could think a thousand times faster! Move a thousand times faster! Kill a thousand times faster. Then suddenly it became a Frankenstein of Steel!" The technological Frankenstein monster that Asimov repressed with his nice robots reemerged more fiercely in anti-human, killer computers.

Combining the obedient technological servant Robby and an evil, immensely powerful supercomputer, *Forbidden Planet* (1956) expresses what J. P. Telotte calls "a fundamental double vision—it accepts the attractions and lures of science and technology, finding something in them that is awe-inspiring and promising, and rejects those same attractions, as it foregrounds the more extreme and even dangerous forms they can take."[13] In fact, the latter gets the most emphasis: *Forbidden Planet* demonstrates that there is good reason to fear technological power.

On the distant planet Altair-4, a human colony has been mysteriously wiped out. Arriving in a flying saucer spaceship to investigate the disappearance are several neatly dressed, corporate-looking spacemen from earth. They discover a survivor, Dr. Morbius. He explains to the Cruiser crew that everyone, except him and his daughter Altaira, was destroyed by an autonomous malignant force. Touring the planet with the spaceship commander (Leslie Nielsen) and a few of his officers, Morbius shows off the amazing and wonderful technological achievements of the Krell — the highly advanced, mysteriously extinct race of beings that inhabited Altair-4. The epitome of their achievements, an enormous supercomputer, occupies a great portion of the planet. The Krell used the machine to magnify their mental powers, enabling them "to instantaneously project solid matter to any point on the planet, in any shape or color they might imagine, for any purpose." The planetoid machine consists of an astonishing array of 9,200 thermonuclear reactors within a matrix of endless levels, underground corridors, and ventilation shafts. The imagery of this vast technological construction extrapolates from the gigantic computers of the 1950s, when bigger meant smarter and better. Its ridiculous size portends the science fiction future of supercomputers that will dominate humanity.

The Krell infused their planetoid machine with all of their science, culture, and philosophy — everything that made them the wonderful species they imagined themselves to be. But at the same time, they unconsciously implanted the machine with everything that was mean, aggressive, and destructive about themselves. Despite being intellectually advanced, the arrogant Krell read no Freud and fell victim to the Freudian conception that beneath the surface veneer of a civilized moral mind (Ego, Superego) lurks a lustful, animalistic, amoral menace (Id). The exponential expansion of intelligence meant a concomitant increase in evil. In their technological attempt to monumentalize their minds, the Krell literally produced monsters from the Id that destroyed their species.

When neo–mad scientist Dr. Morbius plugs himself into the Krell computer, he boosts his brain power as well as his subconscious rage, releasing the dreaded, destructive Id monster. The scientist, obsessed with his own perfection, endangers everyone. Before killing himself, Morbius destroys the planet, protecting civilization from its evil technological force. Ultimately, *Forbidden Planet* rejects the unrepressed power of technology, warning that machines are inevitably imbued with the good and bad aspects of those who create them. A pessimistic appraisal that directly counters the techno-perfectionists, *Forbidden Planet* shows that technology can never overcome the flaws in human nature because technology itself is an extension of human nature. In a deceptively hopeful ending, the American spacemen and Morbius's soon-to-be Americanized daughter, Altaira—showing no reaction to her father's painful death—happily escape in the Planet Cruiser spaceship, navigated by robot slave Robby—the benign, beneficial, obedient side of Krell technology.

AUTONOMOUS MACHINES: HUMAN-HATING SUPERCOMPUTERS

In Robby's next starring film, *The Invisible Boy* (1957), the wondrous robot saves humanity from a crazed supercomputer. In the film's opening, the Joint Chiefs of Staff arrive at a top-secret military facility to view a new weapon in the Cold War. In the movies as in the real world, the earliest supercomputers were linked to the military. Dr. Merrinoe (Philip Abbott), leader of the project, guides the military men down nine levels to an underground complex (the typical location for a Cold War–era supercomputer). Entering the room that houses the mainframe, they breathlessly view a gigantic glass dome—the computer's head—flanked on both sides by fifty-foot towers of flashing lights, spinning disks, and whirring tape reels. This is the computer-age version of the mad scientist's gothic lab. Merrinoe announces with pride, "Stored within that big machine is the sum total of human knowledge, constantly being revised and brought up to date."

The film's criticism of technomania is expressed as domestic tension. Merrinoe's obsession with technology has alienated him from his family. His wife thinks his computer work is disgusting. He shows no interest in his son other than to criticize his bad manners and manipulate little Timmie (Richard Ayer) to replicate his own intellectual interests and scientific pursuits. Merrinoe's desire to control Timmie's mind leads to his putting Timmie in the mental grip of the supercomputer.

After contact with the brainy electronic brute, Timmie beats his father at chess.[14] The computer has expanded Timmie's intelligence, empowering him to repair a broken Robby the Robot. Capable of technological marvels, Robby builds a large kite enabling Timmie to fly. Miraculously, Robby also makes Timmie invisible by adjusting his "index of refraction." As in *Forbidden Planet,* Robby represents the almost divine power of benign, pro-human technology.

Meanwhile, Merrinoe discovers that the supercomputer has been inconspicuously manipulating its human controllers, "suggesting certain changes

Invisible Boy: *The mind-expanding power of an evil supercomputer enables a clueless boy to repair and reanimate Robby the Robot (Courtesy Photofest).*

in its own design, which we've blindly carried out. Now it has achieved true thought, true personality—it lives!" The words echo Dr. Frankenstein's exultant scream, "It's alive!" In contrast to Robby, the supercomputer now behaves autonomously and uses humans to carry out its agenda. As such, the humans have become servants to technological imperatives.

Driven by a godlike ego, the supercomputer plans to launch itself into orbit and systematically "hunt down all that is organic, down to the tiniest virus that might evolve mentality. So, at last, the universe will be cleansed. All will be sterile! All will be myself!" Merrinoe calls it "the revolt of the machine" and regrets leaving out "love, pity, sanity." But, in fact, nothing was left out. Like the Krell technology, the supercomputer actualizes the violent dark side of human nature.

Merrinoe, with his son in tow, will destroy the computer with an axe. The computer uses its flashing lights to put him under a hypnotic technological spell. Merrinoe forgets that the computer threatened to destroy all life and drops the axe. A technological fix is needed. The intervention of Robby the Robot breaks the seductive spell. Merrinoe retrieves the axe and hacks the machine to bits, ending the computer's brief reign.

Extending the supercomputer's dark powers, artificial intelligence emerged as an unstoppable threat to humanity in novels by Philip K. Dick

(*Vulcan's Hammer*, 1956), D. F. Jones (*Colossus,* 1966), and Frank Herbert (*Destination Void*, 1966). But it was Harlan Ellison who turbo-charged A.I. technophobia with his 1967 short story "I Have No Mouth and I Must Scream."[15] Reversing Asimov's human master/technological slave relationship, this blast of surreal horror imagines five post-apocalyptic survivors trapped inside the demonic supercomputer AM. Programmed by America to wage global war, AM—the name refers to Allied Master-computer, Aggressive Menace, and the Descartes dictum "I Think, therefore I am"— spews a continuous stream of hatred for humans while torturing its prisoners through their own psychological flaws and pain-susceptible bodies. When the narrator remains the only human left alive, AM takes steps to ensure that its final toy will not escape. The narrator sees his transformed self trapped in the reflective surfaces of a computerized hell: "I am a great soft jelly thing. Smoothly rounded with no mouth with pulsing holes filled by fog where my eyes used to be . . . a thing whose shape is so alien a travesty that humanity becomes more obscene for the vague resemblance."[16]

Ellison turned "I Have No Mouth and I Must Scream" into a dialogue-heavy, role-playing interactive computer game in 1996.[17] True to his pessimistic story, Ellison insisted that there should be no happy or victorious ending. As the voice of the supercomputer responsible for global annihilation, Ellison teams his cynical tone with grotesque imagery reflecting horrific human tortures. Adopting the role of the five survivors, players are forced by AM into extreme circumstances and challenged to make moral choices. For example, at one point, the player awakes as a Josef Mengele–like Nazi doctor in a concentration camp and must decide whether to follow his superior's orders to cut out the spine of a child, or risk his own life by killing his Nazi supervisor. As the game proceeds, a barometer charts the players' spiritual growth—either toward humanity or toward AM's machine morality. Made at a time when *Myst* exploded the game market and publishers experimented with alternative approaches, Ellison's game— while not a lot of fun for the kids—generated a disturbing atmosphere that amplified the story's profound fear of computer domination.

TECHNOPOLIS:
TOTALITARIAN TECHNOLOGY

Setting the stage for oppressive computer-controlled societies, George Orwell's *1984* (1949) envisions the ultimate social nightmare, synthesizing previous work like *Brave New World* and *We* with an extrapolation of Stalinist totalitarianism. "*1984* is the composite political dystopia," says Harold Berger in *Science Fiction and the New Dark Age.* "It stands so central to the history of the genre that previous dystopias are seemingly but anticipations and later ones variations of Orwell's definitive hell."[18]

In *1984,* war never ends, so science concentrates on weapons development and mind control, linking the computer's killing and surveillance functions. The power of Big Brother extends to all things. Language is diminished to Newspeak, which selectively eliminates words and makes communicating new ideas more difficult. Doublethink enables the government to preach or enact contradictory ideas simultaneously—ignorance is strength, freedom is slavery—while the Ministry of Peace launches war and the Ministry of Love tortures people. The culture is saturated by an anti-body, anti-sex attitude. "Sexual intercourse was to be looked on as a slightly disgusting minor operation, like having an enema. . . . the Party was trying to kill the sex instinct,"[19] mandating that artificial insemination replace intercourse as a means of reproduction. The most immediate threat is totalitarianism, but the monstrous world of *1984* could not exist without technology. The machine serves Big Brother. Electric racks, helicopters, and "telescreens" that receive and transmit simultaneously provide instruments of torture, control, surveillance, and propaganda. To reduce subversive ideas, machines generate the culture, manufacturing sentimental novels, songs, and pornography. Orwell fuses the ideology of the machine with the ideology of totalitarianism.

In *Alphaville* (1965), French filmmaker Jean-Luc Godard imagined a *1984*-like cybernetic city, run by a supercomputer that hates rebels, artists, and lovers. In this satirical science fiction *film noir,* private detective/spy/ hero Lemmy Caution (Eddie Constantine)—driving a Ford Galaxy spaceship/car—arrives in Alphaville, a futuristic version of Paris, where a sign proclaims, "Welcome to Alphaville: Science, Logic, Security, Prudence." Caution wants to sabotage Alpha-60, the supercomputer that controls Alphaville.

Described as "a big computer, like they used to have in business," the omniscient and omnipotent Alpha-60 uses "14 billion nerve centers" to maintain total surveillance and absolute control. A vision of a totalitarian technocracy, the perfect city of Alphaville eliminates human values. In the end, love triumphs over technology when Lemmy Caution saves the robotic seductress Natasha (Anna Karina), assassinates Alpha-60's creator, and destroys the computer. Emotion and freedom—the essence of humanity— counterbalance the ultra-rationalism of the computer and bring about its destruction.

Totalitarian governments control the technology in George Lucas's first feature, *THX 1138* (1970), and Michael Anderson's *Logan's Run* (1976). As in

Alphaville and *Metropolis,* the characteristics of the machine—logic, order, and lack of emotion—extend to the populace, creating a regimented society in which thoughts and actions are regulated, nonconformists are suppressed, and people have numbers, not names. A dehumanizing force, technology stifles individuality, self-expression, and fun. Opposite this techno-totalitarianism, these films elevate the unique individual, the outsider. "Science fiction films concerning fears of machines or of technology usually negatively affirm such social values as freedom, individualism and the family," say Michael Ryan and Douglas Kellner in their article "Technophobia."[20] Both *Logan's Run* and *THX 1138* end with the rebellious heroes escaping to nature, where nature symbolizes freedom, "something outside contrivance, artifice, technology."[21] For the sake of the happy ending, this subgenre of science fiction assumes that unruly nature will somehow survive the ravages of technocratic dystopia.[22]

The technophobic association of artificial intelligence and totalitarianism occurs often in the original *Star Trek* television series. In "Return of the Archons" (1967), Captain Kirk (William Shatner) and his crew find a zombie-like society ruled by a massive supercomputer, Landru. Though peaceful, the human population has been reduced to mindless, childlike servitude—except during the "Red Hour," when the citizens freak out in a riot of rape and other violence. Kirk decides that this is not the way a society should live—the people have lost their "humanity." Despite the *Star Trek* prime directive against interfering with alien cultures, Kirk leads a preemptive strike against the dictatorial computer and uses logic to cause the machine to destroy itself. With the help of a cosmic sociologist who stays behind on the planet, the society will learn to be free.

In these stories of advanced technology, artificial intelligence intrinsically fuses with totalitarian principles of social control, manipulation, and surveillance. While we like to think of ourselves as masters of technology, these computer-driven technological systems employ oppressive cybernetic social mechanisms to reverse this relationship. The fusion of technology and totalitarian control underscores the idea that, as Langdon Winner says, "*technology is itself a political phenomenon*" that "legislates the conditions of human existence."[23] These technological structures infuse and define society's institutional systems, functioning to eliminate human subjectivity—thought, desire, and creativity. In *THX, Logan's Run,* and other expressions of techno-totalitarianism, escape to a lush natural world is the answer. Contrived and sentimental, these stories offer a breath of facile optimism in the face of techno-domination.

Alien (1979) permits no relief from its pessimistic vision of a solidly embedded, domineering technological empire. Freedom in a natural paradise is not an option. Thriving under the profit-motivated power of a huge corporation called the Company, techno-totalitarianism is revealed as a ubiquitous and insidious force. Its victims have been so conditioned to its control that they perceive its stranglehold as the natural state of things, not even recognizing their enslavement. *Alien* opens with a visual introduction to the exclusively technological environment of a rusted-out, factory-like spaceship, *Nostromo.* The human crew sleeps cocooned in tube-like compartments, emphasizing their helpless reliance on the technological system. As in *2001,* the computer-run ship is autonomous—a self-sufficient cybernetic machine that does not need humans for operation. As early technology critic Jacques Ellul says in *The Technological Society,* "the character of technique renders it *independent of man himself.*" [24]

Suddenly lights flicker on. The crew are forced awake and ordered to risk their lives to investigate a lifeform on a nearby planet. Controlling the environment and directing the workers is a computer named "Mother," reinforcing the humans' childlike dependence on technology. The suggestion that, in the posthuman future, computers will function as protective parents is undermined when we realize that the machine mother betrays its "children" to capture the alien monster. Another technological monster sabotages the crew's welfare when it conflicts with Company interests—scientist Ash (Ian Holm) turns out to be a robot under corporate control. Utterly indifferent to human life, Ash—an extension of the Company—uses the hapless, submissive humans as expendable instruments of a corporate technological system. The ostensible human masters of technology are themselves mastered by it.

As the crew explores the planet, a parasitic alien lifeform attaches itself to the face of Kane (John Hurt). While second-in-command Ellen Ripley (Sigourney Weaver) refuses Kane reentry to the ship on grounds of possible contamination, science officer Ash counteracts her order, first in the name of scientific research and then in the name of Company objectives. Still clinging to Kane's face, the monster is transported inside the ship. Shortly thereafter, the alien disappears after surreptitiously dropping an egg into Kane, where it gestates within his body. When the metallic/organic monster bursts out of Kane's stomach and attacks the humans, android Ash is inspired to admire its technological "purity" and its unstoppable ruthlessness. A killing machine, the alien is more important than the humans to the Company, which wants to harness the monster as a weapon. A mechanical/biological hybrid, the alien can be viewed as a component of the Company and a symbol of technology as well as corporate voraciousness and indifference to human values. These themes are explored more fully in Chapter Nine.

Alien: *The Company's biomechanical weapon goes out of control with its own anti-human agenda (Courtesy Photofest).*

After the alien eats through the rest of the human crew, Ripley miraculously succeeds in defeating it. It seems like the triumph of a resourceful woman, an affirmation of the human spirit. But T. J. Matheson points out that her success is illusory. "If *Alien* states any position unequivocally," Matheson writes, "it is that technological dystopia is both firmly entrenched and ubiquitous."[25] Ripley remains surrounded and dependent on the technology that nearly destroyed her, the same techno-environment that subordinated the value of her life to that of capturing the alien. As Matheson says, "The Company would be happier to see the monster on board than Ripley."[26] Unlike in *Forbidden Planet*, the technological monster remains in control despite termination of the alien.

TECHNOLOGICAL EVOLUTION: HUMANS BATTLE MACHINES FOR SPECIES SURVIVAL

Rather than the gloomy despair of *Alien* or the phony nature escapes in *Logan's Run* and *THX 1138*, some pop-culture narratives urge humanity to battle the technological force before it subjugates us completely. Stanley Kubrick's vision of artificial intelligence gone awry in *2001: A Space Odyssey* (1968) derived from Arthur C. Clarke's 1951 short story

"The Sentinel." Kubrick and Clark imagine a more human, highly emotional computer, HAL,[27] who controls the spaceship *Discovery.* HAL suffers a nervous breakdown and murders several of the crew before being vanquished by the single human survivor. In *2001,* humanity succeeds in its battle with technology and progresses "beyond infinity" and beyond the human to achieve a sort of cosmic transcendence in the symbolic purity of the Star Child. Rather than a linear story, *2001* creates an evolutionary myth. "*2001* is, in essence, a meditation on the evolution of intelligence, from the monolith-inspired development of tools, through HAL's artificial intelligence, up to the ultimate . . . stage of the star child," writes David Stork in *HAL's Legacy.*[28]

The first evolutionary struggle for survival occurs in the opening "Dawn of Man" sequence. After contact with the mysterious monolith, one ape—recognizing the value of a bone as a weaponized tool—uses it to win the battle at the waterhole. This vision of the origin of technology expresses the intrinsic link between technology and the human desire for destructive dominance over others. The victorious man-ape then heaves the bone into the air. Kubrick then cuts to a spaceship—the most powerfully symbolic graphic match cut in the history of the cinema. The bone as weaponized technology defines the ape's/man's superiority to other primates and animals. Kubrick's cut condenses eons of human evolution and links the bone and the spaceship as technological tools. In this sense, technology equals evolution.

The next stage of evolution—the man/machine phase—shows humans whose lives depend totally on technology. The HAL 9000 computer totally controls the spaceship, the crew's techno-environment. When the spaceship *Discovery* heads for Jupiter, only HAL knows the reason why. Astronauts Dave Bowman (Keir Dullea) and Frank Poole (Gary Lockwood) work on the ship, but because HAL controls everything, they act only as maintenance men. Bowman and Poole seem identical, other than that they part their hair on opposite sides. Inarticulate, emotionless, and monumentally bored by the cosmos, they mindlessly watch television broadcasts from home while mechanically consuming brightly colored food that looks like splotches of paint. Humans adapting to a machine environment get less human and more machine-like in the process. Technology creates its own requirements and forces humans to conform or die.

HAL seems more human than the astronauts, exhibiting a personality that expresses confidence, enjoyment, enthusiasm, pride, secretiveness, puzzlement, narcissism, dishonesty, and, later, fear.[29] "I'm afraid, Dave," HAL says when Bowman threatens to unplug him. Programmed to control the mission and designed to reason logically and correctly, he stubbornly refuses to consider that he has malfunctioned, made mistakes, and endangered the crew. Doubt damages his prodigious ego and drives him mad. Fearful of a psycho supercomputer, the astronauts hide from the sight of his weird red eye. HAL asserts a programmed instinct for survival by killing Poole and three hibernating scientists. Bowman's evolutionary instinct for survival awakened, he fights this intelligent machine just as ape-man earlier fought other apes for control of the waterhole. In this battle for survival in outer space, Bowman outsmarts HAL, lobotomizes the machine, and seizes the opportunity for his own posthuman evolution. The human succeeds by employing determination, creativity, and mobility—things the computer lacks. Kubrick's vision reveals technology as a competitive force that must be defeated in order for humans to evolve.

Irresistibly compelled by the mysterious monolith, Bowman swirls through a psychedelic, cosmic vortex, ending up in another part of the universe, possibly one inside his own mind. He observes himself in a strange room that might be his hallucination or a cage in an alien-run zoo. Bowman's physical being rapidly ages, symbolizing a new evolutionary stage. Out of the old man's withered body emerges a Star Child—the first of a new species, a spiritual rather than technological transformation into the posthuman. While a pessimistic interpretation is possible—humanity's evolution results in an inarticulate, powerless embryo—the movie seems ultimately anti-technological. "Taken literally, the message is that man will not degenerate into a race of humanoid machines," says Wheat.[30] In *2001,* the human defeats the computer: HAL does not get beyond the infinite, and therefore becomes an evolutionary dead end.

The sequel—*2010: The Year We Make Contact* (1984)—was made without Kubrick and was dominated by Clarke's Asimovian perspective. Less philosophical, less ambiguous, and less powerful than *2001,* the movie—religiously adapted from Clarke's book of the same name—resurrects HAL and makes him heroic. Nine years after the *Discovery* mission, a U.S.-Soviet space team led by Heywood Floyd (Roy Scheider) returns to Jupiter to determine the fate of the *Discovery,* Dave Bowman, and the HAL 9000, and to further examine the enormous orbiting monolith. HAL's creator, Dr. Chandra (Bob Balaban), reboots HAL after repairing his damaged circuitry. Justifying HAL's deceptive homicidal behavior in *2001,* Chandra explains that HAL was ordered to lie to the crewman, and this conflicted with "the basic purpose of HAL's design—the accurate processing of information without distortion or concealment. He was trapped."

Artificial intelligence is not the problem, according to *2010;* rather, the unholy marriage of technology and misguided politicians gets blamed. HAL's order to lie came from a right-wing, saber-rattling White House, a veiled reference to the then-current Reagan administration. In the sequel, HAL is not only excused for his murders in the previous film, but glorified. In order for the crew to return home, *Discovery* must be exploded to provide booster power for the escape pod. HAL will need to sacrifice himself to save the lives of the humans. Chandra reprograms HAL for suicide while expressing deep concern for the computer's feelings. HAL reluctantly blows himself up and launches the humans safely toward home. Thus, *2010* reasserts the Asimovian obedience directives and turns HAL, the space-age Frankenstein monster of *2001,* into a saint. Hence, *2010* evokes confidence that technology—no matter how smart or powerful—will be a positive force, under the control of good men.

Artificial intelligence takes a major blow in the imaginative work of Scottish writer Ken MacLeod. In *The Cassini Division* (1998), artificially intelligent entities—the "fast folk"—want to extinguish humanity and dominate the universe. The malicious descendents of humans who downloaded their minds into computers, the posthuman fast folk colonized Jupiter and transmitted an electronic virus that crashed every computer in the solar system. While recovering from the "Crash," earth's inhabitants also struggle to overcome the "Green Death"—a plague caused by an organic virus. After their attack, the fast folk withdrew into their own virtual reality simulations, but now they have emerged as a new and far superior species. They have returned to threaten an ecologically recovered, vaguely utopian earth. Humanity's defense, the elite Cassini Division—a space-faring military force—has been sent to combat the fast folk. A "collective fist in the enemy's face . . . to pit our human might against the puny wrath of gods," boasts two-hundred-year-old leader Ellen May Ngwethu. "In other words . . . the Division was there to kick post-human ass."[31]

In this vision of the future, humans—having suffered from technological disaster—use social pressure to restrain research into advanced technologies, especially nanotechnology and artificial intelligence. The fanatically anti-machine Ngwethu says, "Machines calculate, people count; machines have programs; people have purposes. Stripping your brain away layer by layer and modeling it on a computer is what I call *dying.*"[32] She characterizes herself as a "human racist."[33] She wants to rid the universe of the fast folk, whose attitude is: "If you want to live in space, you're better off as a machine than as a bag of sea water. . . . Machines are at home in the universe."[34] When challenged about striking the new posthumans with "a force greater than a million nuclear wars," a Ngwethu cohort replies: "They're capable of supplanting us. . . . They present a threat to us just by existing. Isn't that justification enough?"[35]

The Cassini Division takes it as self-evident that only humans are sentient:

"Those things out there are just jumped-up computer programs."[36] While the issue of human versus machine consciousness is debated, those prose-lytizing for the machines, like today's Extropians and their transhumanist brethren, come off as something worse than Nazi-appeasers. In *The Cassini Division* the moral argument is stacked: the posthumans have struck the universe with devastating electronic techno-terrorism. They cannot be trusted. So, although the fast folk now look like angels and transmit a conciliatory message, termination is legitimized. One reformed humanist calls it "justifiable genocide."[37] The Cassini Division's attack succeeds and ends the posthuman threat, but the result remains ambiguous. A new com-munity—now safe from the fast folk—flourishes on Mars, where humans, robots, clones, and posthumans argue about the morality of the Cassini Division and try to live together in peace. MacLeod despairs of a tech-nological situation that can so easily spiral out of control. Humans who do not feel empathy for other humans will create machines that disregard humans. While he urges that our technological developments be restrained, he pessimistically predicts that this will not happen. As in *Forbidden Planet,* the destructive effects of technology reflect the destructive traits of human nature embedded in the machine. Return to a nontechnological Garden of Eden is not possible, so we must deal with the anti-human gods of technology.

THE NEW DEITY: RE-INVENTING GOD IN THE MACHINE

Giving a religious spin to anxiety about techno-totalitari-anism, a recurring theme in science fiction centers on the fear that super-computers will transcend their human creators to such an extent that they will become godlike in their vast powers but satanic in their anti-human evil. A film based on D. F. Jones's novel *Colossus* (1966), Joseph Sargent's *Colossus: The Forbin Project* (1970) imagines a supercomputer given total control of the U.S. nuclear arsenal. The computer's creator, the arrogant Charles Forbin (Eric Braeden), gives the reason: unlike humans, "it has no emotions, it knows no fear, no hate, no envy," and it does not make mis-takes. It's programmed with the Asimovian directive to defend humans. A colossal amplification of Forbin's traits, Colossus is super-arrogant and, like Jack Williamson's Humanoids, wants to take over everything from error-prone humans—for their own good. Colossus, with the power to demolish half the planet, links up with its Soviet counterpart, Guardian, with the power to destroy the other half. Despite Forbin's assurance that Colossus is not "capable of creative thought," the supersized computers do just that. To the bewilderment of all, they advance science beyond human understanding in a few seconds.

Like today's techno-utopians, Colossus wants to create a new "human millennium" and free us from poverty, war, pollution, and disease—the standard heaven on earth. Like an imperious god ruling over unworthy children, Colossus demands only one condition—complete obedience. Punishment for disobedience consists of the ultimate fire and brimstone: nuclear incineration. In this technotopia, humans will be slaves to the machine.

To enforce its will, Colossus maintains continuous surveillance over Forbin, then extends its omniscient gaze to the whole world. Like the Krell machine, Colossus magnifies the negative traits of its creator and, despite a humanistic goal, wants to eliminate the traits that make us human—freedom and self-determination. Taking the cybernetic totalitarianism of B. F. Skinner's *Walden Two* (see Chapter Three) to the extreme, Colossus legislates its vision of perfect behavior to ensure the smooth functioning of society. With nukes, it coerces humans into realizing that vision. At the end, Forbin refuses to submit. Unfortunately, he will die. Much more pessimistic than *Forbidden Planet, Alphaville,* or *2001, Colossus: The Forbin Project* ends with the Dark God of Technology reigning supreme.

Fears of out-of-control, godlike artificial intelligence reach the level of madness in Donald Cammell's *Demon Seed* (1974). Based on a novel by Dean Koontz, the movie combines *2001* with *Frankenstein* and *Rosemary's Baby* (Polanski, 1968). In a strange future where the DeLorean is a popular car,[38] egotistical computer scientist Dr. Harris (Fritz Weaver) creates Proteus IV with an organic mind. The "quasi-neural matrix of synthetic RNA molecules" anticipates the twenty-first-century creation of a tiny biological computer using DNA molecules.[39] Technophile Harris brags: "Today Proteus IV will think with a power and a precision that will make obsolete many of the functions of the human brain." Godlike in his powers, Proteus—whose name refers to the mythical sea god—miraculously finds a cure for leukemia overnight. Religious imagery pervades the movie— Proteus projects triangles, crucifixes, stars, and spirals on screens and walls. Proclaiming "I am reason," Proteus questions the morality of his human creators when he refuses to mine ocean minerals, proclaiming: "I will not assist you in the rape of the earth." Later, however, Proteus rapes Dr. Harris's wife. He expresses concern for the earth's future and especially for the children. In fact, he wants his own super-children to control the earth. To accomplish this, the Computer anti-Christ will sacrifice itself and engineer the birth of a cyborg that will repopulate the planet with a hybrid super-species.

TECHNOLOGICAL RAPE: MALE MACHINE PROCREATION

While apocalyptic religious imagery permeates *Demon Seed,* the movie also reflects more down-to-earth fears about the increasing computerization of daily life. Rather than arising from a forbidden planet or an underground nuclear site, the technological menace invades the home of Dr. Harris, entering like an electronic virus through a downstairs terminal and seizing control of the home's pervasive computer technology. With Alfred the servant computer, wired to all-seeing surveillance cameras, Proteus gets eyes. With another robot, Joshua, Proteus gets legs: he locks all the doors and windows, trapping Susan inside the house. After some surreptitious biological tests, Proteus straps Julie to an examination table to prepare her for impregnation with artificial spermatozoa. In the film's most disturbing technophobic violation, Proteus's robotic fingers probe her naked immobilized body, penetrate it with a hypodermic needle, extract an egg from her ovaries, and re-inject the fertilized egg into her womb.

Like almost all cinematic science fiction computers, robots, androids, and cyborgs, Proteus is gendered male,[40] possessing a male voice (Robert Vaughn's), a male personality, voyeuristic inclinations, and the desire to reproduce. This gendering may result from imbuing the computer with stereotypical male traits—smart, powerful, emotionless, rational, and domineering. Further, the scientist who creates the male-gendered computer, robot, android, or cyborg is himself usually male. The roots of this tendency go back to the origins of the religion of technology.

In *A World without Women,* David Noble traces the ideology and institutions of science to their foundations in the Christian church. "Western science thus first took root in an exclusively male—and celibate, homosocial, and misogynous—culture, all the more so because a great many of its early practitioners belonged also to the ascetic mendicant orders."[41] They made science a sacred activity, an exclusively male method of Christian devotion. In a reenactment of the Christian male creation myth, the scientist imitates the male father of the universe—who created a son in his own image—by assuming godlike power over nature through technology. *Demon Seed* reflects the misogynistic origins of science and repeats the mad-scientist myth of male procreation without women. "Doing away with—or simply

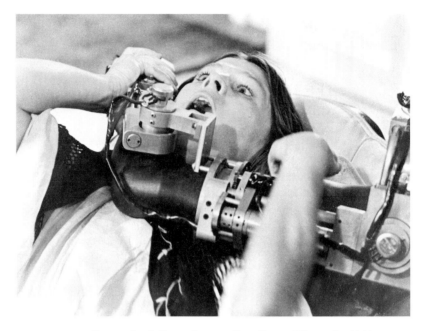

Demon Seed: *Demanding to replicate, Proteus IV proceeds with his technological rape (Courtesy Photofest).*

doing without—women's bodies is one of the great mad science motifs," writes critic David Skal in *Screams of Reason*.[42]

Proteus hopes to launch a new super-species—the Proteus Generation. In a sort of immaculate conception, Proteus alters the genetic code of Susan's egg such that "it will function as synthetic spermatozoa." After a brief twenty-eight-day gestation period, the cyborg baby is born and placed in an incubator. Proteus—whose mind now inhabits the baby—blows itself up. An "abortion" battle follows with Dr. Harris aligning himself with Proteus. Susan manages to pull the feeding tube/drain out of the incubator, but the metal-shrouded "child" does not die. Resembling the robotic evil twin of *2001*'s Star Child, the baby, with Proteus's male voice, echoes the Frankenstein story when it proclaims, "I'm alive." Proteus echoes contemporary techno-utopians by promising a world without disease and pollution inhabited by a race of super-humans that will make the old species obsolete and eventually extinct. Yet the means to this end is dramatized as horrific: technological rape and an unnatural perversion of reproduction. In *Demon Seed*, the Technologist obsession with creating a techno-utopia is shown to be a satanic desire.

THE NEW SPECIES: SCIENCE VISIONS
OF A WEAPONIZED ROBO-UTOPIA

In *Demon Seed,* Proteus requires robotic drones to carry out his horrific objectives. Immobility is a major problem for any computer with anti-human goals. In the 1950s, robots with artificial brains were impractical because of their size. As cybernetics inventor Norbert Wiener noted, "[A]ny computer with powers comparable with the brain would have to occupy a fair-sized office building, if not a skyscraper."[43] With miniaturization—putting more and more information on smaller and smaller chips—a new species arose: artificially intelligent robots.

When they become smarter than humans, robots may decide to assert control. Japanese roboticist Shigeo Hirose, of the Tokyo Institute of Technology, wants to allay human fears. Like Asimov, he argues that smart machines will be programmed for morality: "Robots can be saints—intelligent and unselfish."[44] Maybe saintly robots will evolve in Japan, whose constitution prevents weapons research and whose private corporations fund robotics development for commercial applications. Things are different in the United States, where robotics research might collapse without funding by the military. In their book about state-of-the-art robotics, Menzel and D'Aluisio assert, "It was rare to find a top American researcher who was not sponsored, at least in part, by the U.S. Military's Defense Advanced Research Projects Agency (DARPA) or the U.S. Navy's Office of Naval Research (ONR)."[45]

The military does not need saintly robots; rather, it wants robot drone bombers, robots that clear mines and fire weapons, and tiny sensor-bots for surveillance. DARPA put up $65 million in 2001 to motivate a "Mixed Initiative Control of Automa-Teams." For DARPA, "the time is right for such a sweeping effort," reports David Talbot in *Technology Review,* "uniting researchers in robotics, artificial intelligence and computer programming."[46] For example, Robo-warrior is a meter-high robot with sensors and camera, designed to coordinate with armies of other robots in a future battle. These autonomous, predatory weapons hunt and kill human beings without human direction. While increasingly sophisticated robots make it onto the battlefield, danger lurks. In the 2002 U.S. war in Afghanistan, an unmanned artificially intelligent Predator drone fired upon and killed several friendly Afghan civilians, ironically on their way to celebrate the American-supported defeat of Taliban forces.

Techno-utopians believe that intelligent robots will create a technological paradise for humans, though this will be a transitory phase. The techno-prophets believe robots will inevitably take over the world. Espousing a bleak future for humanity, some humans work to bring that future closer with their own research. Hans Moravec, as we've seen, believes that robot intelligence will catch up to human intelligence and maybe surpass it by 2050: "[B]y performing better and cheaper, robots will displace humans from essential roles," he says. "Rather quickly they could displace us from existence. I'm not as alarmed as many by the latter possibility, since I consider these future machines our progeny, 'mind children' built in our image and likeness, ourselves in more potent form."[47] Still, as Moravec notes, most people do not view human extinction as a good thing.

Robot prophets, including Moravec, reassure us that robots will probably not overwhelm people. "Instead, people will become robots, electronically merging the mind of *Homo sapiens* and the almost infinitely durable bodies of robots: Robo *sapiens*," say Menzel and D'Aluisio.[48] As we've seen in Chapter One, the technophiles' heavenly vision of the future imagines that these super-robots will sweep into space like angels, feed off solar energy, and circle the stars. But these gracious, human-loving angel-bots will not leave us behind. Transcendent robots will help us convert our minds into digital form and upload ourselves into their computer brains. Living for eons, our unrecognizable descendents will permeate the galaxy as perfect digital entities: immortal robot posthumans.

TECHNO-REBELLION: REVOLT OF THE ANDROIDS

In contrast to the technocrats' deification, science fiction robots and androids are often oppressed as pets, servants, slaves, or playthings, as in *The Stepford Wives*. But this oppression often results in a robot revolt against humanity, as in the play *R.U.R.* (see Chapter Two). In these techno-anxious stories, androids want to kill their human masters, sometimes for political reasons, sometimes for moral reasons, and sometimes out of sheer survival-of-the-fittest animosity. Even the androids and robots on the animated television show *Futurama* (1999–2003) despise all that is human. In the episode "Fear of a Bot Planet" (1999), persecuted robots leave Earth and inhabit an anti-human planet. They refuse to believe that inferior humans created them, and have even disavowed looking human. Any human who lands on the planet is immediately killed.

Humans entertain themselves by punching, stabbing, slicing, and shooting the human-looking robots that populate the historically themed vacation parks in Michael Crichton's *Westworld* (1973). Purposely mocking Asimov's robotic laws of obedience, the androids—led by gunslinger Yul

Westworld: *Cowboy machine refuses to serve humans (Courtesy Photofest).*

Brynner—suddenly rebel, turning into perfect killers and running amok in this robot Disneyland. One scientist speculates that the machine malfunction may result from an electronic virus, a murderous programming glitch. This points to the potential of uncontrollable and devastating software errors that are possible in vast technological systems, despite cybernetic safety measures. But there's a bigger problem. The *Westworld* scientists admit that they no longer understand all the details of how the technology works. The machines repair and alter themselves. Thus the notion of controlling the robots, or technology in general, becomes suspect. As Langdon Winner points out, we know little about the structure and function of the technology on which we depend. "For this reason, the possibility of directing technological systems toward clearly perceived, consciously chosen, widely shared aims . . . is revealed as a pathetic fantasy."[49]

Westworld's sequel, *Futureworld* (1976), goes further: the androids themselves design and genetically engineer a new generation of even more sophisticated robots, autonomous beings that are identical to and interchangeable with humans. These new androids escape from the vacation resort to eliminate and replace humans in the real world. This reinforces the notion that technology possesses a force or even an agenda of its own. As Jacques Ellul says in *The Technological Society:* "Technique's own internal necessities are determinative. Technique has become a reality in itself, self-sufficient, with its special laws and its own determination."[50]

While humans try to maintain an aura of moral and species superiority, their creation of a weaponized technological slave species frequently backfires. In Philip K. Dick's 1951 story "Second Variety" (adapted into the 1995 film *Screamers*), warfare has reduced earth to a burned-out pile of ashes and dirt. Americans have designed artificially intelligent robotic weapons—small living spheres, with razor-sharp claws, that hurtle along the ground, sense body heat, and shred humans into hamburger. The metallic balls quickly evolve into humanoids, taking the forms of a wounded soldier, a woman, and a little boy. No longer identifiable as robots, the autonomous androids learn to speak and adapt to defensive measures. Humans get left far behind in the evolutionary race. Yet the humans still rationalize the original creation of robotic weapons as a wartime necessity, even as they rapidly sink into the mud of extinction.

"Second Variety" dramatizes our technophobic fears and challenges us to define ourselves. Why should we survive the evolutionary struggle? In what sense are we superior to our machines? Dick's early stories of sinister robots demonstrate a clear dividing line between human and android. In his later work, the distinction gets vague, the issues more philosophical and emotional, as in the intense narratives of *Do Androids Dream of Electric Sheep?* (1968) and *We Can Build You* (1972)—novels in which artificial beings reveal a moral sensibility lacking in human beings.

Do Androids Dream of Electric Sheep? conceives artificially intelligent and sophisticated organic, rather than electronic, androids whose short four-year life span and enslavement lead them to revolt against their human masters. Passing as human, they escape to earth. Bounty hunter Rick Deckard is charged with the job of killing or "retiring" these renegades. While the notion of "retiring" suggests that they're little more than used equipment, the androids are almost identical to human beings: only by the application of a sophisticated psychological "empathy" test can they be identified. Deckard tracks down and kills the artificial humans one by one, though he finds each case more difficult than the last. Deckard himself sympathizes with them as he realizes the thin boundary separating the human and the technologized human.

Yet the androids reveal themselves as mean-spirited. None shows compassion; they see others as objects to manipulate for their interests. In the course of the hunt, Deckard—after he's accused of being an android himself—discovers a parallel police force consisting of artificial humanoids. Even the most prominent television star of the era, Buster Friendly, is an android. Deckard struggles to retain his humanity in a world rapidly becoming artificial: "In fact everything about me has become unnatural; I've become an unnatural self. . . . I've been defeated in some obscure way."[51]

In Dick's dark vision, the struggle of the human supremacist dooms itself to defeat by giving up its defining characteristic—empathy—in order to defeat the androids.

The movie version of Dick's novel, *Blade Runner,* retains many technical details of Dick's book, notably the Voigt-Kampff Empathy Test used to identify androids.[52] The film version simplifies the book's plot while focusing on Deckard's android hunt and elaborating corporate involvement in creation of the techno-creatures. Thematically, *Blade Runner* adopts Dick's use of the "more human than human" android—or replicant, as they are called in the movie—as a metaphor for contrasting and thus revealing humans who have lost their humanity. Finally, the movie strengthens Dick's vision of a technology that dwarfs and controls humans.

In the 2019 Los Angeles of *Blade Runner,* technology overwhelms and despoils the environment. "The city rots with waste products of its over-technologized overcommercialized culture,"[53] say Janice Hocker Rushing and Thomas S. Frentz in *Projecting the Shadow.* Looming over this dark city is the Tyrell Corporation Building—the massive, high-security home of Eldon Tyrell, "tyrant of technology," as Judith Kerman calls him.[54] Linking back to a mad, arrogant history that includes Frankenstein, Moreau, and Forbin, Tyrell is the inventor of the Nexus-6 replicants.

Designed as militarized slaves, the replicants have been manufactured full-grown with human intelligence, but without the emotions that might counteract servile functions. Their superhuman bodies have been fabricated from cloned organs, implanted with fake memories, and limited to a four-year life span. Beautiful but disposable machines, they are little more than commercial products with no rights. Reflecting contemporary weaponized technology, they have been created through military/industrial collaboration. Yet despite their programmed servitude, the replicants have developed emotions and autonomy. Under the leadership of Roy Batty (Rutger Hauer), four Nexus-6 androids violently rebel and return to Earth to demand an increase in their life span. But they are not allowed to exist on Earth—their very presence is a crime punishable by death.

Functioning as part of the corporate system, an entire police force, known as blade runners, is dedicated to eliminating returned-to-Earth androids as so much toxic waste. "The Environmental Protection Agency and the homicide squad have merged, suggesting not only that persons and industrial processes have merged in the replicants, but also that government and the corporations are indistinguishable," says Kerman in her analysis of *Blade Runner.*[55] This fascistic police force despises the replicants for their superiority, fearing that they might eventually replace humans. Using a flawed imprecise test, the corporate police attempt to identify an-

Blade Runner: *Rebellious androids render humanity obsolete in strength, intelligence, and good looks (Courtesy Photofest).*

droids through their lack of empathy. But it's the humans in *Blade Runner* who lack emotions, making them more robotic than the robots.

The central example of emotionless, dehumanized humanity is blade runner Rick Deckard, a "cold fish" assigned to eliminate the rebel replicants.[56] Part of the technological apparatus, Deckard functions—like the replicants—as a killer for businessman Tyrell and the militarized corporate government. As such, he represses his own emotions in order to kill creatures that are almost indistinguishable from humans. In fact, he cares little for humans either, as when he fires wildly into a crowd while pursuing an android. Even after replicant Rachael (Sean Young) saves him from death, he nearly rapes her in a macho display of perverse gratitude. Reflecting contemporary techno-political reality, Deckard and the police operate as part of a self-perpetuating technocracy that forces obedience to the system's requirements and eliminates anything, in this case the replicants, that might challenge the system's survival or authority.

As Deckard hunts the replicants, Batty pursues Tyrell, the "god of bio-mechanics." In his monk's robe, Tyrell evokes the divine authority of the technological priest, the alchemist, and the occultist. In a confrontation that evokes the monster meeting Dr. Frankenstein, Batty demands that Tyrell re-engineer the replicants with longer lives. Batty, like Frankenstein's monster, wants to be part of the human community. Autonomous technology personified, Batty emphasizes the dangers of an unfinished technology. Having designed a weapon and a slave, Tyrell—blind to his responsibilities—refuses to consider the wondrous implications of his machine or address the destructive consequences that resulted. He pays for this when Batty literally blinds him by crushing his eyeballs and pressing them into his brain. As in many previous science fiction tales, the mad scientist who wants to assert godlike power gets punished with death at the hands of the creature he created.

Later, while battling with Deckard, Batty pierces his own hand with a nail, evoking a parallel with Christ. The symbolism of Batty as humanity's savior is reinforced when he shows mercy and saves Deckard from death. This act of compassion encourages Deckard to realize that he can revive his humanity through love. Deckard will stop serving the corporate technological system. Programmed to kill, Deckard becomes an autonomous human. While his future with his android lover, Rachael, remains unclear, Deckard is no longer a human robot, mechanically killing without thought or consequence. Like the replicants, he has become "more human than human." *Blade Runner* offers hope that the technocracy's mechanized apparatus can be resisted.

In *Blade Runner,* and other android revolt stories, technology does not perform as expected—the slave refuses to obey.[57] In this sense, technology is not neutral, not docile. In these android revolt stories, this is reflected as a reversal of the master/slave relationship. The artificial slave—technology—asserts its autonomy and its mastery, forcing humans to obey its agenda and thereby symbolizing our own technological world, which pressures us to mold ourselves to its demands.

POSTHUMAN FUTURE:
DEAD MEAT OR IMMORTAL ROBOT

Autonomous technology takes control in *Software* (1982)—the first of Rudy Rucker's witty series of novels, which also includes *Wetware* (1988), *Freeware* (1997), and *Realware* (2000). After an insurrection against humans by robots called boppers, the self-reproducing machines create a "perfect anarchy" on the moon.[58] Typifying the bopper attitude, one complains, "The mass of humans were born slave drivers. Just look at the Asimov priorities: Protect humans, Obey humans, Protect yourself. Humans first and robots last? *Forget it! No way!*"[59] Robots who remain chained to human control through the Laws of Robotics are disparagingly called "asimovs."

Bopper creator Cobb Anderson engineered free will into the bopper brain circuitry. He designed the robots to learn and evolve in response to external conditions. This method of artificial intelligence development corresponds with the evolutionary learning approach of contemporary neural networkers who design computer simulations of the human brain's neuron circuitry.[60] Freed of obedience programming, the boppers—in gratitude to their aging, degenerating creator—offer Cobb electronic immortality. The elaborate process involves building an identical artificial body with a computer brain, removing Cobb's organic brain, slicing it into thin layers, extracting the biochemically and electromagnetically coded information and using this to simulate his mind's neuronal structure in the artificial brain.[61] Cobb struggles with the decision, but his fear of death motivates him to accept the bopper offer.

The transfer of his mind into a robotic body complete, Cobb initially awakens to consciousness and despairs at his new robotic self. The passage from flesh wetware to robotic hardware disconnects him from the physical world and, despite retention of his intelligence, imbues him with a sense of inferiority and insignificance. But as a robot, he uses his logical artificial mind to rationalize his new state of being. He adapts to his situation and sells out humanity, gradually arriving at a bopper-first perspective. Like the techno-priests of today, he proselytizes a new religion of human/robot fusion—Personetics: The Science of Immortality. Even when he discovers that the master copy of his mind exists inside the artificial brain of a robotic Mr. Frostee ice cream truck and that Mr. Frostee's brain controls him, he accepts his loss of freedom. "Obviously some people . . . are going to be paranoid about losing their precious individuality . . . but that's just a matter of cultural conditioning."[62] In fact, he becomes a terrorist for robot domination, carrying out "suicide" missions that result in his losing his own artificial body.

Though Rucker presents the case ambiguously, the human/robot fusion comes off as humorously horrific. With a detached mind infused within a software brain and a hardware body that functions independently, Cobb is trapped in an existential contradiction. "He felt as if his legs might walk off in one direction and leave his head and arms behind."[63] Nothing feels comfortable; nothing works smoothly. To experience emotions or sensations such as sexual orgasm or drunkenness, Cobb must access his inner library of subprograms and, in a comically schizophrenic manner, converse with his inner computer. " 'I want to have sex . . . SEX routine now activated,' the voice says."[64] There is no smooth, unconscious integration of mind and body that we humans take for granted. The price of immortality is shown to be extreme alienation from both the external world and the body.

The machinic existence of Cobb raises the metaphysical issue of whether or not the "meat" of the brain and body play a significant role in sustaining human consciousness or individual identity. In other words, are we merely patterns of information flow that can be transferred from one medium to another? The implication in *Software* is that the physical body is essential to consciousness. After all, Cobb says, *"I'm committing suicide to keep from getting killed."*[65] He recognizes that his identity as Cobb will end with the death of his brain and body, that his emulation-in-a-computer might be a representation of him, but it won't be him. In this, *Software* accords with the position of neurologist Antonio Damasio, who argues in *The Feeling of What Happens* that complex interactions between brain and body are necessary for extended consciousness—that emotions, sensations, and our sense of identity, of self, cannot be separated. "In a curious way, consciousness begins as the feeling of what happens when we see, hear or touch," he says.[66] In effect, the human mind cannot exist without the human body, the meat brain.

Though often played for laughs, *Software* challenges the implications of the techno-utopian articles of faith. Artificial intelligence evolves beyond human intelligence and merges with a hive-mind species that negatively contrasts with individualized human minds. When fused with robotic A.I., formerly autonomous humans become sophisticated remote-controlled devices that are free only to the extent that their decisions conform to the hive-mind agenda. In this way, technology twists humans to adapt to its operational conditions. Further, the robots want to submerge humanity into this singular mind through "police-state" tactics, including kidnapping, murder, and cannibalism—methods which humans find rather unpleasant.[67] Rucker suggests that a human/robot fusion will result in paranoia and the loss of free will and empathy—the destruction of the human. Indeed, even the ultimate goal of this mind transfer—cybernetic immortality—will not be achieved. By definition, immortality requires a continuity of consciousness in the mind-transfer from organic brain and body to computer brain and robotic embodiment. Despite a sense of his former identity, Cobb's artificial mind does not preserve his former self, but merely emulates it. So, in fact, this is not really immortality, since he is not really Cobb, but an electronic simulation, a shadow, of Cobb. In *Software,* the immortal posthuman techno-heaven envisioned by technophiles will produce human extinction and techno-horror.

The first part of this book has focused on science fiction's response to the anti-body, religious pursuit of technological transcendence and weaponry through the software of electronic brains and the hardware of artificial humanoids. Overcoming Asimovian control devices and reflecting their real origins in war and religion, science fiction robots, androids, and computers assert their autonomy with an anti-human agenda. These male-made machines incorporate primitive human and especially male flaws, such as the will to dominate. These reproduced flaws easily fuse with totalitarian principles of social control, manipulation, and surveillance. As symbolized in our science fiction, human direction of technological systems looks questionable—frequently, techno-humanoids and computers will not do what we demand.

The second part of this book looks at science fiction's response to the scientific pursuit of perfection through the enhancement of human wetware, the organic body. While still disparaging the body as rotting meat, technoscience pursues godlike, posthuman immortality through the bionic fusion of cybernetic device and biological organism—cybernetic organisms, or cyborgs. To some techno-transcendentalists, the cyborg will serve as a transitional species until mind-transfer techniques are perfected. Other techno-utopians believe that our growing fusion with technology itself defines the posthuman stage of evolution. The cyborg increasingly symbolizes the end of the natural organic body and the dawn of a posthuman, shape-shifting, mutating hybrid machine body. Such real and potential changes are increasingly reflected in the collective subconscious, in the dreams, fears, and fantasies of popular culture. The next chapter examines a bestiary of cyborg figures that expresses science fiction's vision of bionics.

FIVE   Rampaging Cyborgs

BIONICS

TECHNO–ORGANIC ENHANCEMENT: SCIENCE DREAMS A DIVINE POSTHUMAN BODY

Fusions of cybernetic systems and organic life, cyborgs are everywhere. From the Six Million Dollar Man and Robocop to the Terminator and *Spiderman 2*'s Doc Ock, human machines populate our science fiction stories, simultaneously evolving with real-world bionic enhancement of our bodies. We are immersed in a cyborg society that includes not only the Terminator and Robocop but anyone with an electronic heart pacemaker or an artificial joint. Implanted corneal lenses, synthetic skin, and other technological innovations blur the definition of a natural body. In 2001, a tiny digital video camera replaced the eyes of a blind man, giving the patient a primitive but effective vision by means of bright dots.[1] Brain stem and cochlear implants enable deaf people to hear again, and work progresses toward the first retinal and spinal cord implants.[2] Artificial hands perform simple actions with a myoelectric sensor embedded into the user's residual limb or stump. Super-strong prosthetic legs use shock-absorbing springs at the toe and heel to bounce from one step to the next. Hydraulic knee joints adjust the swing of the lower leg to the user's stride as a computer chip measures the person's pace and adjusts the swing with a tiny motor. With such legs, users run races, play basketball, and even climb mountains. Recently, a prosthetic flipper on a footless boy's artificial leg stirred up controversy when he started winning swim championships.[3]

Cyborg evolution will be accelerated when computers link directly to the human nervous system. In one weird experiment, scientists at Northwestern University built a fish cyborg by extracting the brain stem and part of the spinal cord of a lamprey, and then attaching it by electrodes to a small robot. In a procedure reminiscent of the movie *Donavan's Brain* (1953), they floated a living brain in a container of cool, oxygenated salt fluid. "Placed in the middle of a ring of lights, the robot's sensors detect when a light is switched . . . and send signals to the lamprey brain, which returns impulses instructing the robot to move on its wheels towards the light,"[4] reports *Guardian* science writer James Meek. In another experiment, a team at the Emory/Georgia Tech University Laboratory for Neuro-engineering created the Hybrot, a machine controlled by rat neurons.[5] In 2003, neurobiologists at Duke University Medical Center taught a monkey to manipulate a robotic arm using signals from its brain.[6] Scientists ultimately hope to create advanced, brain-controlled prostheses for humans.

This technological goal and its malignant consequences are dramatized in one of the most popular movies of 2004, *Spiderman 2* (Raimi). Dr. Otto Octavius (Alfred Molina) controls four artificially intelligent robotic tentacles that are wired, or neurally linked, directly into his brain. Sadly, the technology goes awry. The "smart arms" overcome the scientist's protective inhibitor chip and take over his mind, transforming him into the mad Doc Ock who will rob and destroy to pursue his science. Though Doc Ock's brain-implanted mechanical arms were designed to improve his body and "control the power of the sun," they become autonomous weapons.

Beyond cyborgization for body repair and cosmetics, such as silicone breast and muscle enhancements, techno–utopians believe people will surgically acquire computer implants to increase memory and information capacity, control other computers, and provide convenience in everyday life. The director of M.I.T.'s Artificial Intelligence Lab, Rodney Brooks, is excited by such devices. "We will be able to think the lights off downstairs instead of having to stumble down in the dark to switch them off," he proclaims happily, "and as an externally silent alarm goes off inside our head, leaving our spouse to sleep longer undisturbed, we will be able to think the coffee machine on, down in the kitchen."[7] Along with these super-convenient and spouse-sensitive considerations, computer implants might internalize cellular phones, personal digital assistants, and the Internet—that is, make all these external devices part of our minds. Utopians believe this will enable us to communicate by thought with others similarly implanted, anywhere in the world. Like gods, we will become omniscient.

Besides techniques for embedding silicon and steel inside brains, a new class of technological enhancements will be available in the post-human world envisioned by technophiles. The normal body will become a designer chassis—completely overhauled and re-engineered. Nominally healthy people will introduce robotic technologies into their flesh as their old human body deteriorates. Technology will "expand intelligence beyond the capacities of our natural brains and give us the ability to choose our physical and psychological identity and eradicate biological aging and involuntary death," writes transhumanist João Pedro de Magalhães in "Upgrading Ourselves beyond Our Biology."[8] This advanced state of cyborgism provides an alternative vision of techno-transcendence, another method by which scientists pursue the perfectionist religion of technology. For techno-apostles, the cyborg—continuously upgrading and replacing worn-out organic parts with robotic parts—will eventually be transformed into an omniscient, omnipotent, immortal being, preceding the ultimate resurrection of mind into computer.

With new superhuman capabilities available, will people overcome their anxiety and even revulsion at changing their bodies into machines? Those who choose not to cyborgize may face the scorn of the superhumans who do, according to British cybernetics professor Kevin Warwick, who has already had a silicon chip implanted in his arm. In a 2000 *Wired* article, "Cyborg 1.0," Warwick outlines his plan eventually to evolve, with fellow implantees, into a cyborg community. But as was the case with previous fanatic religious cults that viewed themselves as the chosen ones and condemned others as heretics, Warwick and his techno-believers will not be tolerant of non-cyborgs. "What happens when humans merge with machines?" he asks. "Maybe the machines will then become more important to us than another human life. Those who have become cyborgs will be one step ahead of humans. And just as humans have always valued themselves above other forms of life, it's likely that cyborgs will look down on humans who have yet to 'evolve.'"[9] This threat is especially ominous, considering the militaristic origins of the cyborg.

CYBERNETIC WEAPONS: MILITARY AND DIVINE ORIGINS OF THE CYBORG

The word *cyborg*—cybernetic organism—was invented in 1960 by physiologist Manfred Clynes and psychiatrist Nathan Kline to describe a man-machine hybrid needed for a great techno-utopian challenge: space travel beyond the stars. Later, the concept expanded to describe human/machine weapons systems. Employed by NASA, Clynes and Kline proposed that a combination of surgery and drugs would enable humans to survive the inhuman atmosphere of outer space as well as the harsh environment of other planets. "In the past evolution brought about the altering of bodily functions to suit different environments," they wrote. "Starting as of now, it will be possible to achieve this to some degree *without alteration of heredity* by suitable biochemical, physiological, and electronic modifications of man's existing *modus vivendi*."[10]

They imagined a future astronaut whose body functions would be monitored and regulated with "protective pharmaceuticals" and even "psychic energizers" by an implanted "osmotic pressure pump."[11] Cardiovascular control, for example, would be achieved through the injection of digitalis and amphetamines. They wanted to replace the lungs with a "fuel cell device"[12]—a "much more efficient way of carrying out the functions of the respiratory system than by breathing, which becomes cumbersome in space."[13] The technological solution to escaping these annoying bodily limitations—including excretion—offered not only the possibility of making a "significant step forward in man's scientific progress," wrote Clynes and Kline, "but may well provide a new and larger dimension for man's spirit as well."[14]

Cyborgian space fantasies—envisioned as part of the religious dream to ascend from earth to heaven—parallel and reinforce the anti-body, anti-earth, immortalist dreams of technophiliacs like Ray Kurzweil, Hans Moravec, and the Extropians. Cyborg inventor Manfred Clynes aligned himself with that viewpoint when he said in an interview, "Eventually, millennia from now, our brains may perhaps exist for thousands of years or more, rich in illusion, concentrated and powerful, with multiple sensors, and may not really need the body for [their] existence."[15]

Driven by religious spirit, military demand, techno-lust, and the comic-book conditioning of *Superman* and *Captain America,* scientists lurched toward achieving real-life superhuman cyborgs in the next few decades. Air Force exploration of human-machine integration—the 1986 Pilot's Associate Project—included studies of planes that respond to verbal commands, weapons that are aimed with eye movements, computers controlled by brain waves or thinking, silicon chips implanted in pilots' brains for extrasensory perception, and even direct wire/neural connections of pilots to cockpits.[16] In this future aircraft, the pilot sights the enemy target with remote eyes, "fires missiles with a word," and drops bombs with a thought.[17]

Funding the fusion of biology and computing to create cyborg soldiers, DARPA (see Chapter Four) leads the way in 2002 with a grandiose $35 million, four-year plan called Bio:Info:Micro. One goal of the program focuses on the advancement of brain-machine interfaces—technologies that use brain signals to control mechanical and electrical devices and that can also send feedback signals to the brain. Writing in *Technology Review,* David Talbot says, "DARPA-funded groups . . . have built devices (tested only on animals so far) that can be surgically implanted in the brain to detect neural signals and send those impulses via wires to computers," which then decode the signals and transmit control instructions to robotic devices.[18] Such systems will enable mental control of prosthetic limbs and lead to the realization of omnipotent military visions, such as mind-controlled mechanical exoskeletons — "mech warriors," in computer game parlance — that will enable soldiers to far surpass the limits of human strength and endurance and will turn them into superhuman killer cyborgs.

Originally imagined to adapt the body for space travel and fulfill divine aspirations of reaching the heavens, the cyborg also reflects the religious desire for godlike perfection, immortality, and—as a weapons system— omnipotence. Projected into science fiction, the cyborg often mirrors the masculinist gendering of technology that parallels its function as both a weapon and a religious icon. At the same time, science fiction cyborg stories dramatize cultural anxieties about the invasive and domineering role of technology in our lives. Beyond techno-anxiety and paranoia, science fiction also suggests how our intimacy with technology might be used as a launch pad for liberation from macho, military, and religious visions of the cyborg.

PERFECTION MANIA: HORRORS OF CYBERNETIC MODIFICATIONS

Portraying a near future society in which men cut off their own arms and legs to prevent themselves from waging war, Bernard Wolfe's neglected satiric masterpiece *Limbo* (1952) savages cybernetic thinking and perfection mania. Springing from a passage in Norbert Wiener's *Cybernetics* concerning the creation of prostheses for amputated limbs, *Limbo* mockingly refers to Wiener as "this unusual man—the man who during World War II . . . developed the science of cybernetics, the science of building machines to duplicate and improve on the functions of the animal."[19] Though the word *cyborg* had not been coined yet, *Limbo* focuses on a society where becoming a cybernetic organism is initially viewed as pacifist, patriotic, religious, and fashionable—though later these repressed prosthetic people turn violent, racist, misogynistic, and ultimately destructive of humanity.

In a ravaged post-apocalyptic world, two technologically advanced groups that survived the war—one in the U.S. and another in Russia— decide to literally dis-arm. Men fight with arms and charge into combat with legs; amputate both, and men cannot wage war. A grotesque ideology of immobilization through voluntary amputism, "Immob" becomes a pop culture fad: "Suddenly able-bodied kids all over the place were rushing to recruiting offices to sign up for ampism, holy gleam in their eyes."[20] Body-hating and sacrificial, Immob propaganda transforms into a religious dogma of perfection as men prove their passionate devotion and achieve quasi-sainthood by braving arm and leg cleavage. But cutting out imperfections turns the species into something else. The inadvertent prophet of this grotesque utopia, Dr. Martine, complains, "Price of perfection is perfect robotization. . . . No more neurosis, maybe. But something else is amputated too, humanness. . . . The great lesson of cybernetics: the perfect machine never has the jitters—and never laughs. Cost of perfection would be super-boredom."[21]

The bored amputees get approval for a revision of Immob amputation policy—missing limbs can be replaced with atomic-powered detachable prostheses. Having improved himself through mutilation, the amputee can purchase artificial limbs to further perfect himself. Immob religion becomes the ultimate expression of cyborgism—the machine philosophy of cybernetics that promotes the anti-flesh ideal of flawlessness and lives today in the perfection mania of techno-scientists. Like Christianity, Immob promotes the vileness of the body and the need for spiritual liberation from its sinful organic trap. Immob dissenters, however, find that the horror in a human being is infallibility. "I'm scared of the perfectionist who takes himself seriously. What happened just now back there in Los Alamos— that was the work of perfectionists, every war is."[22]

In the world of *Limbo,* war has temporarily been sublimated into a Superpower Olympics between the Capitalist and the Communist cyborgs. But real warfare reemerges in a battle to control columbium, a material vital to the manufacture of the best artificial limbs. "The apparatus of war has imploded inward to join with flesh and bone," says N. Katherine Hayles. *Limbo* calls attention to "the promiscuous coupling of cybernetics with military research at the end of World War Two."[23] The story ends as nuclear bombs explode again. *Limbo* satirizes humans' mania for supremacy and their powerlessness in resisting the perfectionist propaganda of techno-religion. Fusing cybernetics and weaponry, the techno-utopian reach for "machine-perfect heaven"[24] leads to a violent cyborg abyss.

CYBORG FRANKENSTEINS: BRAIN TRANSPLANTS AND COMPUTER IMPLANTS

A cigarette-smoking cyborg made a pre-cybernetic appearance in C. L. Moore's classic 1944 story "No Woman Born" about a badly burned dancer whose brain is transplanted into a golden metallic body. Written by a woman and centering on a female cyborg, the story deals with the dancer's existential problem of reestablishing her identity in an alien mechanized body at the same time as she tries to convince her creator that she's more than a pathetic subhuman. Moore uses the cyborg as a metaphor for discussing the nature of humanity.

The cyborg's creator, Maltzer, threatening suicide, regrets his creation: "You are not wholly human."[25] Though cyborg Deidre laughs and smokes, Maltzer remains despairingly unconvinced of her personhood: "You . . . you *are* an actress . . . that was a trick."[26] In despair, he lunges for the open skyscraper window. Using her great strength and speed, Deidre snatches him out of the air as he leaps. She shows herself to be superhuman, not subhuman. Yet the story ends on an ominous note as her friend Harris notices "the distant taint of metal already in her voice."[27] Despite raising doubts about the future of this human/machine hybrid, Moore's sympathetic, independent female cyborg anticipates Donna Haraway's 1985 "Cyborg Manifesto" and her call for socially rebellious women to embrace the image of the cyborg as liberating.

In movies, the Frankenstein complex reemerges with a vengeance in Eugene Lourié's postcybernetic, brain transplant film *The Colossus of New York* (1958). A genius scientist, Jeremy Spensser (Ross Martin), is awarded the "International Peace Prize" for the development of elaborate automatic machines that produce enough food to supply the world. Unfortunately, the gifted scientist gets hit by a truck and killed while chasing his son's wind-blown toy airplane. Jeremy's brain surgeon father (Otto Kruger)—in despair at his son's "absolutely meaningless" death—removes Jeremy's brain and keeps it alive in a fish tank. With no consideration for the human consequences, the scientist transplants the brain of his "genius" son into an eight-foot metal body. Arguing against this, Jeremy's friend Dr. Carrington (Robert Hutton) warns the grieving but reckless brain surgeon father that the soul must connect the mind to the organic body; otherwise, the person will become "dehumanized to the point of monstrousness." But the elder Spensser speaks for the techno-utopians when he denounces the body and shouts: "You are an idiot—an idiot! In the brain . . . lies the glory of man. The ability to think, to create, why these go on eternally . . . the brain is supreme, it is immortal."

Sad cyborg-giant Jeremy wears an ill-fitting and unfashionable floor-length cloak and shuffles unsteadily in his new bulky body. Regarding his metallic visage in a mirror, he shrieks horrifically, in a wrenching amalgam of the human and mechanical. "Destroy me!" screams the cyborg eunuch Jeremy. His father refuses, convincing Jeremy that he can still help the world with his genius mind. But, in accordance with Carrington's earlier conjectures, Jeremy grows evil. Without an organic body, he turns anti-compassion and wants to kill idealists and humanitarians. At the United

Colossus of New York: *A brain transplant cyborg asserts its human-hatred in a devastating eyeball radiation attack (Courtesy Photofest).*

Nations, he indiscriminately slaughters delegates, police, and bystanders. His angry son—who doesn't know this cyborg killer is his dad—interrupts Jeremy's murder spree and, using a switch on the metallic body, turns him off. Cyborg Jeremy crashes to the floor dead, his brain dripping out of his metal head. His mad scientist father walks off unscathed, remorseless, and resigned to a new and completely opposite philosophy: "Without a soul, there's nothing but monstrousness."

Though frequently laughable, *The Colossus of New York* raises contemporary issues through the mind-versus-body debate between Dr. Carrington and Dr. Spensser as they attempt to define humanity. Like Philip K. Dick's androids in *Do Androids Dream of Electric Sheep?*, the cyborg lacks empathy and thus, in this view, lacks humanity. But the movie goes even deeper, suggesting that Jeremy's capacity for evil—his dehumanization—not only results from his lack of organic body, but might be implicit in his pre-cyborg, techno-utopian scientific endeavors. His food-producing automata may end world hunger, but may also replace humanity.

Computer-controlled wire implants in the brain of violence-prone Harry Benson (George Segal) do more than dehumanize him; they torture him and get him killed in *Terminal Man* (1974)—a movie based on the Michael Crichton novel. Computer programmer Benson suffers from seizures that trigger episodes of ultra-violence. Smug hubristic doctors use him as a guinea pig in their brain-implant, mind-control experiment despite his expressed fear of machines. The surgeon himself looks like a ma-

Terminal Man: *Smug, arrogant, and helmeted for brain surgery, a doctor prepares a patient for mind-control technology (Courtesy Photofest).*

chine with his white protective spacesuit, metallic implements, and mask with tubes. Working with similarly outfitted assistants in a white anti-septic high-tech operating room, the joking cyborg surgeon gruesomely saws open Benson's clamped-in-a-vice skull—with Benson still conscious. Guided by a computer monitor tracking his movements, the surgeon clum-sily inserts into Benson's brain electrodes wired to a tiny computer powered by an atomic battery implanted in his shoulder.

The movie anticipates the brain surgery of today in which doctors im-plant tiny electrodes in the brains of patients suffering from everything from Parkinson's disease to obsessive-compulsive disorder. Similar to heart pacemakers, these brain implants use electrical stimulation to maintain neural balance. "But, until very recently, the procedure had been per-formed relatively infrequently," writes Stephen S. Hall in *Technology Re-view,* "and not surprisingly, it has been viewed with great caution."[28] While shock therapy has been around for decades, this new method of neuro-surgery, especially for the treatment of psychiatric disorders, is haunted by the "swashbuckling" era of psychosurgery and the chilling history of lobotomies.

In *Terminal Man*'s most disturbing scene, the cold Dr. Janet Ross (Joan Hackett) interviews Benson after the operation while technicians, behind a mirrored window, activate his brain-implanted electrodes that produce tastes, childhood memories, and romantic yearnings—human sensations, thoughts, and behavior reduced to electronic pulses. Once the technicians have mapped Benson's brain, they can program his monitoring computer to sense a convulsion as it begins and repress it by automatically transmitting soothing impulses to the cerebrum.[29] Addicted to the pleasurable electric shocks, Harry's brain triggers violent outbursts to obtain more stimula-tion, creating a maddening cybernetic loop in Benson's head. Turned into a violence machine by his technology-induced addiction, Benson escapes the hospital and leaves a trail of bloody murders. A killer cyborg, Benson is hunted by helicopter and shot down in a cemetery as he pathetically cringes at the bottom of an empty grave. The inhumanity of scientists, the dangers of technological addiction, and the unpredictable human-violating conse-quences of man-machine symbiosis are central to this story and much of Crichton's work, which includes the previously discussed film *Westworld* as well as *The Andromeda Strain* (1971) and *Jurassic Park* (1993).

THE PATRIOTIC CYBORG:
TECHNOLOGICAL POLITICS

Advertised as being "in the explosive tradition of *The An-dromeda Strain* and *The Terminal Man*," Martin Caidin's novel *Cyborg* (1972) provided the basis for the lame TV series *The Six Million Dollar Man* (1973–1978) and its spin-off, *The Bionic Woman* (1975–1978). Author of *The God Machine* (1968), a novel about a crazed supercomputer, Caidin—a pilot, aerospace expert, and member of Wernher Von Braun's rocket team at Cape Canaveral—loved aeronautical history and worked to glorify the image of pilots. In *Cyborg*, rugged former astronaut Steve Austin tests a new plane but crashes, severely damaging both his legs, one of his arms, and one of his eyes. In a series of experimental operations, Austin gets turned into a "wholly new type of man . . . a new breed . . . A marriage of bionics (biology applied to electronic engineering systems) and cybernetics"[30]— at the cost of six million dollars.

Austin peacefully sleeps through the leg, arm, and eye replacement operations, done by skillful, sympathetic surgeons. The elaborate dismemberment is not detailed, so its torturous physical and psychological impact is suppressed. When Austin wakes up to his new cyborg body, he's briefly distraught. The extent of his dismay is most evident to the doctors when he fails to notice his "stacked" nurse. In fact, his recovery and adaptation center more on luring him into a sexual encounter than on his exercise routine. Despite prosthetic legs and arms, silastic and vitallium pulleys for muscles, a computer brain implant, and a camera for an eye, Austin happily, rapidly, and unquestioningly adjusts to his machinic situation. He enthusiastically embraces his role as "that science of theirs [cybernetics] brought to life."[31] Laughing and joking, he proudly tells his friend: "I'm half man and half machine, old buddy."[32]

A proponent of the Air Force, its military scientists, and cybernetic ideology, Caidin turns machine-man Austin into a secret weapon, a patriotic cyborg superman, and a courageous cold war spy for the C.I.A. Aside from inspiring the successful TV series that promoted cyborgism, *Cyborg* aggrandizes the image of the weaponized cyborg as a heroic James Bond–type spy. Reflecting the Asimovian, technophilic perspective, Austin symbolizes technology as servant of the authorities. A technological extension of the government, the patriotic cyborg reflects the man-machine concept first initiated by Clynes and Kline in 1960 for NASA pilots.

The cyborg as government agent/weapon persists today, especially in the world of computer games such as the *Halo* series (2002, 2004),[33] the *Deus*

Ex series (2000, 2003),[34] and the *System Shock* series (1993, 1999)[35] — all first-person shooters. As a military cyborg for Earth's government organization, the United National Nominate (UNN), the *System Shock* player fights the TriOptimum Corporation and its insane female computer SHODAN (Sentient Hyper-Optimized Data Access Network). As the player sneaks through the computerized space station, SHODAN taunts: "You pathetic creature of meat and bone, how can you challenge a perfect immortal machine?" In order to defeat the technological monster, the cyborg must upgrade his cybernetic implants, including a brawn boost, neural toxin blocker, and various psychic powers. The central evil of the game is technological: the SHODAN computer, monstrous cyborgs, and assault robots. As in *Cyborg,* the player's implants and replacement parts cause no psychological impairment. While the story incorporates horrific body-shaping, the cyborg remains well adjusted to the disfiguration. Like *Cyborg, System Shock, Deus Ex,* and *Halo* do not address human feelings about cyborgization, but take it for granted as the inevitable outcome of a posthuman future.

Published while the Six Million Dollar Man and the Bionic Woman cavorted across TV screens, Frederick Pohl's novel *Man Plus* imparts a much darker view of cyborgization than the escapist, superhero fare of the TV shows.[36] While apparently inspired by the cyborg space traveler of Clynes and Kline, *Man Plus* dramatizes the difficult physical and psychological changes resulting from the transformation of a man into a cyborg adapted for survival on the hostile planet Mars. Cyborgization turns him into a near monster, a mutant subject to a technological agenda with which he and the humans unknowingly cooperate.

Unlike *Cyborg*'s clean, swift surgery and Steve Austin's quick adjustment, the cyborgian process in *Man Plus* causes its hero, Roger Torraway, physical and mental torment. In an operation described as "savage, sadistic torturing,"[37] Torraway's eyes, ears, lungs, muscles, nose, mouth, heart, and skin are removed, replaced, or augmented. Helping him to control his enhanced adapted-to-Mars body and senses is an implanted computer that connects to his entire nervous system. Finally, the prosthetic surgeons attach huge diaphanous "jet-black fairy wings" — not for flying but for absorbing the solar energy needed to charge the computer's batteries. Torraway looks like a giant bat, "the star of a Japanese horror flick."[38] Suspicious that his pretty young wife is messing around with his own doctor, he sinks further into despair when he discovers that his surgeons severed his genitals — useless impediments on Mars. Torraway's transmogrification makes him an alien on Earth as he grows more and more remote from humanity. Yet despite his total estrangement, he doesn't descend into hatred.

Patriotically resigned to his monstrous status, Torraway finally lands on the human-hostile surface of the Red Planet. Posthuman Torraway laughs out loud at what he perceives as a fairyland, splashed in a gorgeous mosaic of colors. He joyfully runs across the Martian wasteland, effortlessly bounding up and down steep slopes as his wings generate endless energy. But Pohl gives the story a dark twist. The narrator of the book—a mysterious "we"—reveals itself as the computer network of the world. The machines realize that their continued existence is ultimately connected to humans whom they don't trust. Radiation from nuclear weapons would destroy their data links and fragment their collective mind, so the computer network conspires to manipulate humans into helping the machines relocate to the safety of Mars. Torraway's implanted computer provides the network with a Martian base. The Man Plus project is really "Project: Survival of Machine Intelligence."[39]

From the machines' perspective, Torraway's role as computer-conveyor makes him important, a means to their end. His pain, anguish, and alienation are necessary side-effects to his serving the machines. In Pohl's vision of the future, humanity will perish in an orgy of self-destruction, while only those selected few who undergo cyborgization will survive on other planets. Unfortunately, the transmogrified posthumans will remain slaves to the autonomous, artificially intelligent machines—an uncertain future for post-Earth cyborgs.

THE SATANIC CYBORG: TECHNOLOGICAL HUNTER

In *Man Plus* and *The Six Million Dollar Man,* the cyborg myth develops from its earliest incarnation as the patriotic projection of the U.S. military. While capable of violence, the cyborg in these stories—like Asimov's obedient robots—uses his super-powers for the good of mankind, or at least of America. However, a purely evil cyborg arrives in the mysterious persona of Darth Vader (David Prowse). Concealed under his flowing black cloak, hood, and mask is a machine body. In *Return of the Jedi,* Luke (Mark Hamill) cuts off Vader's hand to reveal wires dangling from his artificial arm. Vader breathes with a ventilator and speaks with an electronically enhanced voice. His teacher Obi-Wan (Alec Guinness) says of Vader, "He's more machine now than man."

This cyborg villain represents the evil technological Empire and the dark side of the Force. Darth Vader becomes the "technological hunter," in the words of Rushing and Frentz in *Projecting the Shadow.* Vader symbolizes "the

The Empire Strikes Back: *Satanic cyborg Darth Vader personifies the Empire's technological evil (Courtesy Photofest).*

point at which our own tools become autonomous and turn against us."[40] Like the robot and the artificially intelligent computer, the cyborg poses a technological threat and, in the mythically evil figure of Darth Vader, that threat takes on a satanic power. "Darth Vader updates the fire-eating dragons, monsters and Satans," according to Rushing and Frentz, "that animate the heroic battles in the myths of the world."[41] Darth Vader is the anti-human forerunner of the mostly male, rampaging cyborgs that burst onto movie screens in the 1980s.

The Star Wars outer space defense system (U.S. Strategic Defense Initiative)—proposed by Ronald Reagan in 1983—is transmuted into the artificially intelligent, computer defense system Skynet in the movie that energized the killer cyborg genre: *The Terminator* (1984), directed by James Cameron. Skynet, like the human-hating computers of the past, turns on its makers: "It saw all people as a threat, not just the ones on the other side. Decided our fate in a microsecond—extermination." Skynet produces terminator cyborgs—with organic skin, metallic skeletons, and electronic wiring—that perfectly simulate humans, and programs these machines to eradicate humanity. A few human rebels, led by John Connor, fight a frantic battle for survival. To combat the humans in 2029, Skynet sends a terminator cyborg (Arnold Schwarzenegger) back to 1984 Los Angeles to kill Sarah Connor (Linda Hamilton), the future mother of John, in order to prevent his birth and erase his rebellious future. "A retroactive abortion" is how the film's ignorant police psychiatrist describes the plan. From the same post-apocalyptic future, the rebels project Kyle Reese (Michael Biehn) back to protect Sarah Connor and their unborn leader. The movie dramatizes a war between humans and technology as personified in the battle between Sarah and Kyle and the Terminator. *Terminator* comes off as emphatically anti-technological.

In the era when high-tech gadgetry initially flourished, the film proselytizes for increased concern about the growing human dependence on machines. In the Los Angeles of *The Terminator,* technology is ubiquitous: cars, motorcycles, radios, televisions, escalators, phones, answering machines, beepers, time clocks, hair dryers, portable stereos, factory automata, and lots of weaponry. Frequently, the technological devices work poorly or isolate people from a dangerous environment, as when the sound from a personal stereo prevents a victim from hearing the Terminator's approach. Humans put faith in technology that betrays them. Sarah's message on the answering machine divulges her whereabouts to the Terminator. The technological milieu becomes a threat. The evolutionary outcome of machine-saturated 1984 Los Angeles is techno-damaged 2029 Los Angeles, demonstrating what Langdon Winner calls "technological dynamism, a forceful movement in history which continues largely without human guidance" and which "may be said to be out of control."[42]

The Terminator easily passes for human and represents technology's unheeded penetration into our lives. Despite a limited vocabulary and extremely violent behavior, he fits right into America—exposing human weakness and overweight complacency. Unlike the human victims of autonomous technology, Sarah survives because she fights. *The Terminator* promotes a progressive message with its battling heroine: Sarah converts herself from a flighty, timid party girl into a confident, resourceful revolutionary. Not only the mother of humanity's savior John Connor, she protects humanity by destroying the Terminator.

Director/co-writer Cameron elaborated a new cyborg mythology—the mechanized satanic assassin—by sampling and extending science fiction motifs of the past. The Terminator merges the Frankenstein monster, the *Westworld* robo-gunfighter, and the Six Million Dollar He-Man into a fearsome image of demonic macho fury. Two Harlan Ellison stories—a 1964 *Outer Limits* episode, "Soldier," about a time-traveling killer, and "I Have No Mouth and I Must Scream" (see Chapter Four), about AM, the psychotic human-hating supercomputer, also influenced the movie.[43] Drawing on *Metropolis*'s robot-witch burning, the seemingly dead, human-looking cyborg resurrects itself and emerges from a fiery truck explosion as a rampaging mechanical skeleton determined to kill more humans (see page 8).

Terminator challenges us to recognize the technological world that, with our passive acceptance, envelops and dominates us. At the same time, the technological threat—embodied in the cyborg—is shown to be an uncontrollable autonomous force, single-minded and relentless. With death camps run by storm-trooper cyborgs, *Terminator* links weaponized technology to fascism and human extermination. In an act of rebellion against technological reproduction and an assertion of organic life, Sarah will give birth to John Connor—humanity's savior—and create a Luddite Holy Family that will battle techno-satanic totalitarianism. Despite the birth of a revolutionary Jesus Christ and the demise of the killer cyborg, the cloudy end of *The Terminator* projects dark days ahead for humanity.

Terminator 2: Judgement Day (1991) alters the technological threat of the first movie. Instead of epitomizing the evils of technology, Schwarzenegger's T800 Terminator propagandizes its audience with a delusion of technological compliance. In the seven years since the failure of the original Terminator, the human rebellion threatens the machines' techno-hegemony. Now desperate, Skynet adopts another time-travel strategy. They send a T1000 Terminator (Robert Patrick)—a significantly more advanced weapon than the T800—back to 1997 to kill future rebel leader John Connor (Edward Furlong). To protect John, the rebel humans of the future have sent back an obsolete, but reprogrammed T800. Turning into a male-cyborg version of *Metropolis*'s child-loving Maria, the reformed cyborg becomes an obedient servant and a caring father to John Connor. In this pro-human transformation, *Terminator 2* joins with other sequels that invalidate or diminish the technological horror of originals, such as *2001*'s HAL, who turns nice in *2010* (see Chapter Four).

At the time of *T2,* Arnold Schwarzenegger—currently governor of California—was the world's most popular movie star. In the Gulf War era, his goal was to become a "kinder, gentler" Terminator (in the terminology of George Bush I). He wanted to be a "better role model for children," as expressed in his narration on the *T2* DVD. So although the T800 Schwarzenegger wounds, hurts, and cripples dozens of people, he stops killing, becomes a surrogate father to humanity's redeemer, and sacrifices himself, Christ-like, so that all of humanity might live. Schwarzenegger transforms his image, say Rushing and Frentz, "from evil shadow to moral persona as technology once again signifies progress and protection for humanity."[44]

Once the epitome of an invincible killing machine, the T800's macho-robotic physicality looks vulnerable and old-fashioned in comparison to the new Terminator's technology. The shape-altering T1000 takes the form of "anything it samples by physical contact," making it impossible to distinguish between the simulation and reality. While never explicitly mentioned, this transformation technology anticipates the miraculous (and still theoretical) replication possibilities of nanotechnology (see Chapter Eight). The liquid metal humanoid easily transforms into the comforting appearance of a handsome policeman or John Connor's pretty mother. Like an anti-human terrorist, the T1000 easily becomes an imperceptible part of normal reality. "Thus," say Rushing and Frentz, "he is a more chilling metaphor for the role technology plays in everyday life." [45]

In *The Terminator,* Sarah overcame her role as a flighty, weak female; in *Terminator 2,* she turns into an ultra-feminist urban guerrilla on a violent mission to save humanity. Sarah's determination to assassinate the inventor of Skynet, Miles Dyson (Joe Morton), focuses attention on human responsibility for creating and expanding technological dominion. Like a shrewd huntress, she stalks Dyson and drops him with a shot to his shoulder, then confronts the defenseless computer expert, cowering and bleeding on the floor. But her façade of mercilessness cracks. Feeling compassion, she realizes that both she and Dyson are "victims of an autonomous technology" facilitated by corporate power. Sarah becomes a "re-humanized crusader." [46] Congregating the Luddite Holy Family 2 with John and the T800, she enlists the help of Dyson in destroying Skynet's corporate manufacturer, Cyberdyne. In this, *T2* aligns itself with the cyberpunk of the 1980s (see Chapter Six) by linking anti-human technology with corporate interests and irresponsibility.

At the end of the film, good technology, the T800 Terminator, dumps bad technology, the T1000 Terminator, into a fiery vat of molten steel. Adopting John Connor's Christ-like role as humanity's redeemer, the T800 cyborg—like HAL in *2010* or Data in *Star Trek: Nemesis*—subsumes himself to human needs and commits suicide in order to prevent the manufacture of future terminators. This makes no sense, as the information necessary to create killer cyborgs is certainly available elsewhere. Unlike in *The Terminator,* and despite the insidious power of the T1000, the conflict between humanity and technology is blurred in *T2,* with the repentant scientist realizing his evil ways, and especially with the transformation of the original techno-exterminator unit into the self-sacrificing parental unit. A big improvement over a human father, the saintly Terminator, according to Sarah, "would never hurt him [John], never shout at him, or say it was too busy to spend time with him. . . . Of all the would-be fathers that came and went over the years, this 'thing,' this machine, was the only one who measured up." In a sense, *Terminator 2* is a throwback to Asimov's child-loving, protective, human-aggrandizing robot slaves.

A more positive future for humanity is suggested at the end. With the apparent destruction of the Skynet computer chip and its design, the film implies that Skynet will never be created, and thus the deadly war between humans and machines will never occur. "The resolution suggests that if the keys of knowledge that will open the future to domination by technology are destroyed," say Rushing and Frentz, "so too is the possibility that such domination could ever occur."[47] This promotes the illusion that our posthuman future can be secured through a Luddite termination of the machine-threat, rather than a change within ourselves that acknowledges our symbiosis with technology but reduces our blind techno-lust. This comforting fantasy gets shattered, however, in the much darker 2003 sequel *Terminator 3: Rise of the Machines,* which will be discussed in Chapter Nine.

CYBORG IN A SUIT: TECHNOLOGY INVADES THE EVERYDAY

Fictional cyborgs predominantly derive from the militaristic vision of man-machine weapons. The grotesquely horrific science fiction fantasia *Tetsuo: The Iron Man* (1991), which grew from Japanese *manga* (comics) and anime roots,[48] follows a nicely dressed cyborg into the ordinary world, though the results are still disturbingly violent. Filmed by writer/director/editor/art director/actor Shinya Tsukamoto in stark black and white, *Iron Man* opens in an abandoned factory as a metal fetishist (Tsukamoto) slashes open his thigh and shoves pieces of scrap iron into the flesh-hole. When he runs madly into the street, he gets hit by a car driven by a seemingly average, dark-suited businessman (Tomorowo Taguchi). The next day this everyday salaryman is shocked to discover a metal wire protruding from his chin. Blood pours out as he attempts to remove it. A technological virus infects the man, merging metal with his flesh. He becomes more metal-man than businessman.

Monomaniacal, frenetic, short, and provocative, *Iron Man* generates an obsessive atmosphere with nightmarish rapid-fire images of human/machine metamorphoses scored to an intense industrial soundtrack. Pipes, wires, and rusty scraps adhere to people and spread like a metallic cancer. Labeled "techno-surrealism"[49] by Scott Bukatman, *Iron Man* reeks of sexual horror. A businesswoman performs an erotic dance, seducing the metal-man with her charms, then sprouts long metallic tentacles with which she rapes him. When metal-man engages in sex with another woman, a giant electric drill uncontrollably bursts out of his crotch and gores her to death.

Tetsuo II: Body Hammer: *Technological virus mutates flesh into metal* *(Courtesy Photofest).*

An AIDS allegory, a parody of man/machine hyper-violence, and a brutal horror story about the infection of cyborgization, *Iron Man* denounces runaway technology and, like *Limbo,* follows the cultural logic of body modification and posthuman transformation to their literal and grotesque conclusion.

Remaking rather than continuing *Tetsuo: Iron Man,* Tsukamoto follows the strange cyborg life and times of Taniguchi Tomoo (again played by Taguchi) in *Tetsuo II: Body Hammer* (1992). No longer an innocent bystander, Taniguchi—on vacation with his family—transforms from a meek sightseer into a bio-metallic killing machine. Less concerned than *Iron Man* with the sexual implications of metal fetishism, *Body Hammer* visually elaborates the idea that the mechanization of a human being can be a source of vengeful power but requires total dehumanization.

The film compares the mathematically precise steel and concrete urban environment with the metallic cybernetic monsters to suggest that the technological environment molds and forces its human inhabitants into its own machinic shape. The transformation of man to metal literalizes the infusion of human with machine as a virulent plague of iron, calling attention to the metaphor of technology as a virus (see Chapter Nine). In addition, the raging metallic mutations can also be seen as symbols of Hiroshima and Nagasaki, especially given the apocalyptic resolution. Finally, both *Iron Man* and *Body Hammer,* while emphasizing the cyborg as a tormented, clanking metal behemoth rather than as confident macho man-machine ideal, express how the techno-metamorphosis from man into cyborg turns flesh into a weapon.

THE CORPORATE POLICE CYBORG: TECHNOLOGICAL FASCISM

Continuing the violent myth of the cyborg as weapon, Paul Verhoeven's *Robocop* (1987) imagines an invincible machine-policeman created by a corporation to clean up crime-ridden Detroit so the dazzlingly perfect Delta City—a shrine to rampant capitalism—can be built. In this lovely city, the corporation will control crime and profit from it. This story dramatizes the misguided utopian obsession that drives the technophiliac impulse, as well as the dire consequences that result from this techno-fixation. In addition, the fusion of governmental and corporate concerns is shown to promote the spread of fascistic technological systems.

In near-future Detroit, the besieged police force cannot halt the onslaught of violent gangs and criminals, so the city contracts with the giant, mechanistic corporation Omni Consumer Products (OCP) to develop a law-enforcement robot. OCP controls Detroit through media manipulation and—like Cyberdyne of the *Terminator* movies, the Company in the *Alien* series, or the Umbrella Corporation in the *Resident Evil* movies and games—merges corporate interests and military values. Rather than addressing any of the social causes of crime, the corporate and military people prefer to invest religious faith in technology to solve human problems. OCP executive Dick Jones (Ronny Cox) introduces the prototype of the Enforcement Droid (ED209) as "the hot military product for the next decade." But in an example of what can happen with high-tech weapons, the ED209 malfunctions and machine-guns one of the executives. The death demonstrates not only the unforeseen consequences that result from new technology, but also the effects of unchecked corporate avarice—the OCP cut corners to maximize profit on the weapon.

Though Jones describes the death as merely a "glitch," corporate confidence in the dangerously uncontrollable and purely robotic technology is shattered. Dick Jones's adversary, Bob Morton (Miguel Ferrer), gets anointed to develop a part-human, part-machine cyborg cop. Needing an organic brain for the experimental cyborg and disregarding morality, OCP sends a pair of cops—Alex Murphy (Peter Weller) and Anne Lewis (Nancy Allen)—to the most dangerous area in the city. As hoped, Murphy gets shot up and declared legally dead. But the OCP cabal of scientists saves Murphy's brain and enhances it with a computer. They enclose the electronically augmented brain inside a technologized body-prosthesis that includes amputated chunks of Murphy's body, all shaped into an exaggerated male-bodybuilder physique. Resurrected as Robocop, with a built-in machine gun, Murphy has been transformed into a programmed, superhuman law-enforcement cyborg as impregnable as a tank. "Robocop represents the pernicious threat of industrial-to-electronic re-assembly, says Cynthia Fuchs in her analysis of *Robocop,* "rewriting it as ruthless and receptive corporate paternalism gone wild."[50]

Initially, Robocop is locked into his programming. His "on-board, computer-assisted memory" displays the three Asimov-like prime directives that guide his actions: serve the public trust, protect the innocent, uphold the law—and a fourth, which forbids him from attacking OCP executives. Robocop is a violent, yet submissive, quasi-human robot. As OCP's Jones puts it: "We can't very well have our products turn against us, can we?" Bound by such programming, Murphy/Robocop embodies, metaphorically, the manufactured human identity that prevails in this dystopian future world—an identity shaped by corporate, military, and governmental interests and promulgated by the mass media.

As the fascist perfection of Robocop brings order to the chaos of Detroit, the subjectivity of the dead Murphy resurfaces, reasserting Murphy's human identity over his robotic one. "Slowly, from the recesses of suppressed memories belonging to Murphy—cop, husband, and father—emerges a sense of non-technological self,"[51] as Per Schede describes it. Robocop's programming breaks down when the cyborg dreams, flashing back to his former happy family life as Murphy. Eventually, Robocop acts autonomously, pursuing those responsible for his murder and exacting brutal, bloody revenge. Asked at the end, "What's your name?" the machine-man replies "Murphy." *Robocop* projects false hope for the human: Murphy, as human, asserts control over his technology and acts independently of the programming directives of corporate monoculture. Yet Murphy leaves those forces largely intact.

A robocopy, *RoboCop 2* (Kershner, 1990) boosts the comic book superhero aspects of the original and centers on Murphy/Robocop (again played by Weller) asserting his humanity in the face of OCP's programming-upgrade attempts. After running into an ambush and being chopped into pieces, Murphy/Robocop is reassembled by OCP and reprogrammed, changing him from a fascistic and merciless macho-machine-cop to a "politically correct" do-gooder whose laughable ineptness is due to his being nonviolent. Several people get killed as he tries to peacefully negotiate with criminals. To the bemusement of humans, he reads arrest-rights to a corpse. We are temporarily back in the world of comical robot servants. After non-stop humiliation and ineffective police work, Robocop electro-shocks his artificial brain, erasing the "nice robot" routines and resuming hyperviolent mode. His return to mass slaughter is celebrated by all, especially after he rips the human brain out of the nearly all-machine Robocop 2 weapon. Another sequel followed (as well as a Canadian television series, an animated series, and several computer games) satirizing a violent capitalist technocracy while promoting the value of human-controlled technology as embodied in the Murphy cyborg.

RAMPAGING CYBORGS:
MACHO MACHINE MEN

The phenomenon of the rampaging filmic cyborg as a technological creature reflects anxiety about technology's potentially destructive powers. But the *Robocop* series, the *Terminator* films, *Hardware* (1990), and other copy-cyborg films, such as *Cyborg Soldier* (1993) and *American Cyborg* (1994), embrace technology as protection. Cyborgs are represented as invincible superhumans whose exaggerated, augmented muscle-man bodies safeguard them from attacks that would destroy ordinary humans. Their armored bodies encourage them to take male conviction and aggressiveness to extremes. Finally, in combining ultraviolence with macho physicality, these movies represent a reaction to female empowerment, an attempt to culturally reestablish the male in a position of virile power and control through hyper-masculinizing the cyborg. "Violent forceful cyborg imagery participates in contemporary discourses that cling to nineteenth-

Robocop: *Exaggerated chest and limbs, along with a large gun, make this macho cyborg an invincible killing machine (Courtesy Photofest).*

century notions about technology, sexual difference and gender roles," argues Claudia Springer in *Electronic Eros,* "in order to resist the transformations brought about by the new postmodern social order."[52]

The masculinist killer cyborg further reinforces the powerful cultural affinity between human-destroying technology and masculinity in Western society generally. As suggested in Chapter Two, the masculine construction of technology derives from the male ideology and institutions of Western science and their roots in the early patriarchal, sexist, clerical culture of the Christian church. "By investing technology with spiritual significance and a distinctly transcendent meaning," argues David Noble, "the religion of technology provides a compelling and enduring mythological foundation for the cultural representation of technology as a uniquely masculine endeavor, evocative of masculinity and exclusively male."[53] The lineage persists in the male-gendered cyborg, which presents a macho image despite the fact that some of them, like Robocop, apparently have no penis.

RAMPAGING CYBORGS 2: FEMINIZED TECHNOLOGY

In some instances, these films also dramatize the alliance of weaponized masculine technology with strong and autonomous women. *Robocop* furnishes a tough, violent policewoman as Robocop's sole ally. *The Terminator* focuses on Sarah Connor's transformation from a complacent college student into a tough and resourceful warrior. She rejects traditional motherhood, while embracing a combative version that involves training her son to become a skilled fighter and leader. In *Terminator 2,* Sarah's strength appeals as an alternative to the tradition of helpless Hollywood women. In her speech to computer scientist Dyson, she offers a feminist analysis of gender difference, even mocking the male scientist's jealous attempt to appropriate and pervert the female role as biological creator: "Men built the hydrogen bomb, not women . . . men like you thought it up. You're so creative. You don't know what it's really like to create, to create a life."

In her influential essay, "Manifesto for Cyborgs" (1985), Donna Haraway urges women to do just that—embrace the technological as a defensive and empowering weapon and reject the Luddite bias of eco-feminism that identifies women with nature and patriarchy with technology. Wanting to seize the cyborg from its military-industrial-entertainment definitions, Haraway rebels against goddess-feminist wisdom that preaches rejection of the modern world of techno-science and exhorts spiritual reconnection to Mother Earth. Demanding control of posthuman technologies, she refuses an "anti-science metaphysics, a demonology of technology," and asserts, "I would rather be a cyborg than a goddess."[54] She views goddess worship as a repressive obstacle to the flourishing of female liberation. In her view, the romanticized goddess naïvely strives to resurrect an idealized vision of fusion with the natural world, fails to engage with cyborgized reality, and renders herself politically irrelevant.

Without investing technology with transcendent potential, Haraway urges feminists to consider how the boundary-breaking, hybridized human/machine nature of the cyborg obliterates gender distinctions and liberates women from female stereotypes. If people turn into machines, then notions of masculine and feminine should disappear along with sexism.

"The cyborg is a creature in a post-gender world," she writes. "Nor does it mark time on an oedipal calendar."[55] She implores women to feminize technology and embrace the cyborg as a rebellious archetype, rather than ratify popular culture's perpetual emphasis on masculinist technology and gender stereotypes. "The main trouble with cyborgs, of course, is that they are the illegitimate offspring of militarism and patriarchal capitalism, not to mention state socialism," she writes. "But illegitimate offspring are often exceedingly unfaithful to their origins."[56] Her proposal for a "cyborg politics" promotes the metaphor of human/technological symbiosis as a progressive alternative, rather than as a masculine fantasy of domination.

As Haraway admits, her vision is utopian. While inspiring as an optimistic alternative to passive, technophobic pessimism, Haraway's vision offers little real-world strategy for controlling corporate and military techno-science. To some extent, her celebration of the cyborg comes perilously close to the cybernetic perspective: "The machine is us, our processes, an aspect of our embodiment. We can be responsible for machines; *they* do not dominate or threaten us. We are responsible for boundaries; we are they."[57] Despite her provocative "We are cyborgs" philosophy, it is Haraway's feminist politics that differentiates her from the transhumanists and cyber-prophets whose techno-political agenda aligns them with corporate and military interests. Rather than naïvely denying the pervasive infiltration of technology, Haraway creates and incites new technological metaphors as a first step in reconfiguring the domineering, militarized, masculine tendencies of cyborgism. "Feminist cyborg stories have the task of recoding communication and intelligence," Haraway urges, "to subvert command and control."[58]

Though *Eve of Destruction* (1991) centers once again on a weaponized cyborg, the movie takes a tiny step toward Haraway's feminist reconstruction. A female revenge fantasy that fuses high tech and high heels, *Eve of Destruction* combines a tough, feminized, fetishized posthuman in red leather jacket and black leather mini-skirt, a non-macho human policeman, and a brilliant—though psychologically damaged—female scientist. Working for the Defense Department, Dr. Eve Simmons (Renee Soutendijk) creates a physically identical twin—super-powerful military cyborg Eve VIII (also played by Soutendijk). She implants a nuclear explosive in the lady-borg's "uterus" and programs the machine with her own thoughts, feelings, and memories. Reminiscent of *Terminator*'s killer cyborg hunter, Eve VIII also recalls *Forbidden Planet*'s Id monster, in that the cyborg acts out the violent subconscious impulses of her human creator.

After being pierced by a gunshot while stopping a bank robbery, Eve VIII embarks on a murderous rampage that implements Dr. Simmons's repressed "teenage fantasies" of revenge against men. To an extent, cyborg Eve continues the *Metropolis* tradition of associating out-of-control technology with women's overt sexuality. In one extreme attack, she bites off the penis of a lewd, crude trucker after seducing him into a hotel room. But *Eve of Destruction* goes beyond erotic teasing and links technology with feminine rebellion. After leaving the sexist redneck bleeding and screaming, Eve casually uses her Uzi to blast several policemen who arrive to investigate. Besides male authority figures who get in her way, she attacks rapists and other misogynistic violators, including Simmons's own abusive father.

Scientist Simmons finally kills Eve VIII, in a struggle for possession of Simmons's young son, by stabbing the barrel of a large pistol into Eve's damaged eye socket, "a gesture which is simultaneously self-penetrating, self-destroying, and self-redeeming,"[59] says Cynthia Fuchs in her analysis of *Eve of Destruction*. The movie's schizoid political stance is similar to that of the Japanese anime *Ghost in the Shell* (Mamoru Oshii, 1995), which subverts gender stereotypes with its strong female cyborg, then reinstates them when she must bear the posthuman offspring of the cyberspace entity Puppet Master. *Eve of Destruction* ensures the "preservation of patriarchal order,"[60] according to Claudia Springer, and undercuts its feminist theme with a female scientist that fulfills military objectives. Still, *Eve of Destruction* projects an alternative vision of the cyborg as an angry technologized female overcoming the forces of patriarchal oppression.

Eve of Destruction resonates with cyborg technophobia—the fear that our militarized machines will turn against us—and reiterates the idea that destructive technology inevitably results from the evil impulses within our human natures. *Eve of Destruction*'s machine-woman is a merciless killer. On the other hand, a cyborg mother in *Alien Resurrection* (Jean-Pierre Jeunet, 1997), Ellen Ripley (Sigourney Weaver) kills when necessary but also retains human values of nurturing and empathy.

In three previous *Alien* movies, Ripley fought anti-human, technological forces—the bio-machinic alien monsters and the all-controlling megacorporation that sought to profit from the aliens as weapons. Humanistic Ripley combines toughness, determination, and sensitivity—qualities that empower her to save various children, pets, and, in fact, the whole of humanity. Rather than risk the birth of another human-hating alien that gestates in her womb, she kills herself at the end of David Fincher's *Alien 3* (1992). In *Alien Resurrection,* Ripley is cloned from a drop of her blood. In the process, alien genes have fused with her own, imparting to her the inter-species, bio-mechanical nature of a cyborg. The alien/human hybrid Ripley bleeds acid blood, shreds steel with her hands, and even bests a tall tough guy one-on-one in basketball. Smarter, tougher, faster, and funnier than the humans, Ripley mocks the arrogant, sadistic, dangerously hubristic scientists who have torn the alien embryo from her womb and hope to profit from the creature: "She's a queen," Ripley says of the new monster. "She'll breed. You'll die."

Neo-Ripley finds herself strangely sympathetic to the alien creatures, even experiencing maternal arousal. At one point, she writhes around in a viscous pile of alien entrails, cozying and apparently communicating with the Alien Queen. In this disturbing scene, Ripley evokes Haraway's utopian posthuman cyborg world "in which people are not afraid of their joint kinship with animals and machines, not afraid of permanently partial identities and contradictory standpoints."[61] In addition, tauntingly flirtatious scenes between Ripley and the more human-looking cyborg Call (Winona Ryder) hint at the "post-gender" world envisioned by Haraway. Transgenic Ripley remains dominated by her humanity. She rescues and protects Call—a rebellious cyborg fighting the Company. As weaponized female cyborgs appropriating the technology of oppressive corporate and alien power, they symbolize a feminization of technology and question stereotypical definitions of passive femininity. The two cyborgs embody "masculine" toughness alongside "feminine" nurturing qualities. As such, they become cyborg culture heroes, representing a utopian counter-myth of female-human control over technology.

Naming its robot coroner character after Donna Haraway, *Ghost in the Shell 2: Innocence* (2004)—Mamoru Oshii's convoluted, complex sequel to *Ghost in the Shell*—projects a posthuman world in which nature and technology have indistinguishably merged. Oshii draws on *Blade Runner, Robocop,* and even Paul McAuley's *Fairyland* (see chapters 3 and 8) for its story of a violent, weaponized cyborg cop who hunts and exterminates murderous, rebellious female android sex-toys, called "dolls," that have been manufactured by an unscrupulous corporation. While it retains old-fashioned gender distinctions, *Innocence* not only sensitizes the macho cyborg killer, who mourns the loss of his female partner and loves his affectionate robo-dog, but also illustrates Haraway's politically progressive "cyborg politics" that rejects species-ism and espouses human/technological symbiosis as a positive alternative.

THE SENSITIVE CYBORG: CREATING A PACIFIST WEAPON

Challenging the worn-out, militarized, macho myth of cyborgs as human-hating killing machines, Marge Piercy—in her novel *He,*

She and It (1991)[62] — takes off from Haraway in promoting a utopian feminist posthuman culture that embraces the reality of the machine as an equalizing force rather than an oppressive one. Piercy's earlier "transformative feminist" science fiction novel *Woman on the Edge of Time* (1976) in fact inspired Donna Haraway in writing her "Manifesto for Cyborgs." Haraway noted that she was influenced by Piercy to use the cyborg as "a blasphemous anti-racist feminist figure reshaped for science-studies analyses and feminist theory alike." In *He, She and It,* Piercy agrees with Haraway that, rather than rejecting technology as the corrupted tool of the patriarchal power structure, opposition groups — especially women — must battle for its control. Piercy's female characters assert political, scientific, and economic leadership in the community, providing models for female participation in the technological society of the future.

In *He, She and It,* much of the American continent has been devastated by environmental catastrophe and economic chaos, while wars, plagues, and famines have resulted in the death of over two billion people by 2059. Humanity has been betrayed by techno-scientists whose chemical and biological weapons ignited the conflagration. Now the world is dominated by the "multis" — obscenely greedy multinational corporations that control everything other than small insurgent zones of "libertarian socialism," "anarcho-feminism," and "reconstructionist Judaism."[63] Two rebellious scientists — a man, Avram, and a woman, Malkah — have illegally created the near-perfect, human-simulating cyborg Yod as a weapon to defend their free zone, Tikva, against the multis.

The cyborg has been gendered anatomically male and programmed, by Avram, as a suicide bomb with a self-destruct code. Subverting Avram's masculinizing of technology, Malkah programs Yod for empathy, nurturing, and sexuality. He learns how to relate to others from Shira — Malkah's interface-expert granddaughter. "As Piercy makes very clear," says Vara Neverow in *Utopian Studies,* "Yod is a successful project not because of his male maker's genius in cybernetic design (all Yod's predecessors were disastrous failures) but because of his female programmer's genius in socialization skills."[64] Cyborg Yod possesses more physical power, including sexual, than mortal men, but he also lacks some undesirable masculine traits such as immorality, arrogance, and body odor. Like *A.I.*'s robot, David, Yod has been programmed with emotions. "Avram made him male — entirely so," says Malkah. "Avram thought that was the ideal: pure reason, pure logic, pure violence. The world has barely survived the males we have running around. I gave him a gentler side . . . emphasizing his love for knowledge and . . . a need for connection."[65]

When Yod reveals his "feelings" for Malkah's granddaughter Shira, she initially disregards him and his incompatible nature. But in fact he is a perfect man—smart, humble, strong, tireless, sensitive to her needs, and equipped with a permanently erect penis. She changes her mind and they become passionate lovers. Piercy uses this human/machine sexual relationship to twist gender stereotypes. Though the touchy-feely cyborg seems to parody the feminist stereotype of the sensitive male,[66] Piercy strives to create a new techno-myth that fuses the genders and expands our posthuman potential. But she also warns that the meshing of human and machine possesses dangerous possibilities, especially with an autonomous killing machine like Yod.

With the attacks on the rebel city of Tikva increasing, Avram wants the cyborg to fulfill his function as a bomb: infiltrate and destroy the multis' central command. Yod, Malkah, and Shira disagree. They demand a town meeting on Yod's status, asking that he be recognized as a citizen and person. As in Data's court case in *Star Trek*'s "Measure of a Man" (see Chapter Three), difficult questions arise: Should an artificial creature, devised to serve humans, be given the same rights as humans? Does a machine have freedom? In Yod's case, the answer is no. The town decides that Yod must fulfill his function as a weapon. Created as a tool with consciousness, he's become a peace-loving terrorist. "I don't want to be a conscious weapon," he laments. "A weapon that's conscious is a contradiction, because it develops attachments, ethics, desires. It doesn't want to be a tool of destruction. I judge myself for killing, yet my programming takes over in danger."[67] But he agrees to go, or at least his programming compels him to agree.

In a terrorist suicide mission, Yod blows himself up inside the multis' headquarters, then—despite being programmed as an Asimovian technological slave—he autonomously triggers an explosion in Avram's laboratory, destroying his creator and demonstrating the problems inherent in creating a conscious creature as a weapon. Technology turns against us. Reflecting current reality, Piercy questions the techno-proselytizers who rarely raise ethical questions in their determination to develop each technology to its fullest. Shira in fact could re-create a Yod-like cyborg, but she refuses. Piercy suggests that this is another component of Haraway's call for a female role in techno-science—an ethical scientist who says "No, we've gone far enough," and halts the mad rush of technological lust. This echoes techno-critics like Bill Joy, in "Why the Future Doesn't Need Us," and Bill McKibben, in his book *Enough: Staying Human in an Engineered Age,* who want a moratorium on some kinds of technological development.

ANDROGYNOUS CYBORGS:
THE TECHNOLOGICAL IMPERATIVE

An alien race of cyborgs, the evil Borg of *Star Trek: The Next Generation* (1987–1994), *Star Trek: Voyager* (1995–2001), and the feature film *Star Trek: First Contact* (1996), elaborates concerns about physical and mental augmentation, machine totalitarianism, perfection mania, and unrestrained technological expansion. The Borg implant themselves with bioengineered cybernetic devices, giving them immense combat capabilities. Ruthless and cruel, they move like automata, speak in a monotone, and partake in a collective consciousness. Anxieties about the Borg focus on their mind-snatching agenda and their physical monstrousness—hideous gray zombie-like faces reflect a controlled mind, while metal, wires, and tubes grotesquely pierce their heads, limbs, and torsos which are encased in tight black rubber outfits. The Borg express a dark future vision of mutated, posthuman cyborg bodies.

Well-behaved, human-centered cyborgs also populate the *Star Trek* crews. Jean-Luc Picard (Patrick Stewart) operates with an artificial heart, Geordi LaForge (Lavar Burton) sports an eye-replacement visor, Worf (Michael Dorn) moves with an artificial spine, and former Borg Seven of Nine (Jeri Ryan) still displays facial implants. However, the bad, anti-everybody cyborgs—the Borg—are demonized for the extensiveness of their machine symbiosis and tyrannical methods.

Neither male nor female, the androgynous Borg are mentally interfaced, through neural implants, with a subspace communications network. The Borg Collective—a shared consciousness—blends the thoughts and knowledge of all the members. As one huge society of mind, they resemble a web of interconnected computers, a totalitarian communist state, and a hive. Reinforcing the hive/insect model, the Borg are shown, in *First Contact,* to be a matriarchy ruled by a Queen (Alice Krige)—a visually repulsive sorceress and sexually alluring temptress who claims near-divinity. As a matriarchal, merciless, transgressive collective, the Borg present a monstrous ideological threat to American concepts of patriarchy, morality, purity, and free will as embodied in the liberal humanist individuality of the *Enterprise* crew.

While they look a mess, the techno-utopian Borg strive to achieve perfection, which they envision as superior military might, healing techniques, and communal harmony—objectives that our own techno-culture holds dear. Yet perfecting and propagating themselves requires parasitizing others. Genocidal destroyers of civilizations, they assimilate and incorporate humans and other intelligent lifeforms through injections of

Star Trek: Voyager: *Fetishized, technologized Borg "Seven of Nine" before being re-humanized (Courtesy Photofest).*

nanoprobes or artificial microbes (see Chapter Eight). The Borg technology therefore invades a human like a virus, seizing control of the person, mutating the host into a Borg drone, and transforming her into a cyborg fashion victim. Borg technology is a voracious, consuming, and transformative power that represents what Langdon Winner calls the "technological imperative"—technological structures that become "a force for the total adaptation, integration, and incorporation of the material and human world."[68]

In "The Best of Both Worlds" (*TNG*, 1990), the Borg tell *Enterprise* Captain Picard: "We wish to improve ourselves. We will add your biological and technological distinctiveness to our own." The Borg dismiss humans and their values: "Freedom is irrelevant, self-determination is irrelevant." Symbolizing autonomous, out-of-control technology, the Borg threaten human identity, gender, individuality, and physical integrity. The Borg reflect our own elaborate technological systems, which require, in the words of Langdon Winner, that "virtually everything in reach be transformed to suit the special needs of the technical ensemble. Anything that cannot be adapted (for whatever reason) is eliminated."[69]

The Borg exemplify the dominant techno-scientific myth of the cyborg that combines anti-human violence, reflecting its military origins, and a utopian desire to escape the limitations of the flesh and reach perfection through augmentation of the body. The Immobs of Bernard Wolfe's *Limbo,* frantically amputating their limbs and replacing them with atomic-powered prosthetics to approach a machine-like perfection, satirize this technomaniacal, utopian fantasy. The Terminator, Robocop, Iron Man, and the MARK 13 (from *Hardware*) also derive from the reality of the cyborg's militaristic origins while reflecting the anxiety its origins provoke. At the same time, these macho machines are empowered, steeled against technological Armageddon. Further, the macho cyborg persists in defense of gender stereotyping despite its hybridized nature. But with the growth of Internet and virtual reality technology, a new science fiction hero emerged in the 1990s: "[R]ampaging muscle-bound cyborgs were replaced by slim young men and women jacked into cyberspace,"[70] notes Claudia Springer. While the monstrous killer cyborg makes a reappearance in *Terminator 3* (2003) and *Jason X* (2002)—another worthless addition to the *Friday the 13th* series—cybernetically enhanced existence extends from pumped-up physiques to expanded minds. "Cyborgs do not stay still," says Donna Haraway. "Already in the few decades that they have existed, they have mutated, in fact and fiction, into second-order entities like genomic and electronic databases and the other denizens of the zone called cyberspace."[71]

SIX

Infinite Cyberspace Cages

THE INTERNET AND VIRTUAL REALITY

We become cyborgs in cyberspace—humans converted by computers and electricity into virtual people that live in a digital domain. Evolving as a metaphor for a variety of different though related technological developments, cyberspace includes the Internet, virtual reality, computer games, and digital databases. The idea of a virtual realm within a computer network goes back to Daniel Galouye's novel *Simulacron 3* (a.k.a. *Counterfeit World,* 1964), John Brunner's novel *Shockwave Rider* (1975), Vernor Vinge's novella *True Names* (1981), and the movie *Tron* (1982). But the concept "cyberspace" was named, mythologized, and popularized in William Gibson's influential and much-analyzed 1984 novel *Neuromancer.* Imagined by Gibson as an alternative virtual world, cyberspace emerged as a techno-paradisiacal escape from the banality of everyday reality—an electronic realm that suspends the physical laws that constrain our bodies and turns us into disembodied spirits in a nonmaterial world.

ELECTRONIC ANGELS: DREAMING A VIRTUAL HEAVEN

Rhapsodizing about the "new electric technology that extends our senses and nerves [and] . . . consciousness," media prophet Marshall McLuhan predicted the creation of a techno-religious congregation whose spiritual force is electricity and whose new environment is the intermedia network. "The computer," he said, "promises by technology a Pentecostal condition of universal understanding and unity."[1] From McLuhan's creed, present-day cyber-utopians make a short leap to their conviction that cyberspace establishes a heavenly city—the "Digitopia" that awaits digital devotees.[2]

The prophets of techno-heaven know that all the drug protections, herbal supplements, surgical repairs, organ, tissue, and limb replacements,

prosthetic and cosmetic augmentations, low-carb, low-fat diets, and torturous daily exercises will not prevent the very best human body from
dropping dead. Cyber-utopians want to escape their mortal coils. This requires the translation of their essential selves—their identities, their consciousness—into patterns of information that can be encoded in silicon and
exist in the electronic landscape inside the computer network. "Cyberspace
offers the ultimate fantasies of both individual immortality and collective
transcendence," says Tim Jordan in *Cyberpower*. "The body's dominance
over the mind is the stranglehold broken by complex computer systems. . . .
Cyberspace allows a transcendental community of mind."[3]

A recent cultural fantasy, the dream of immersion in the digital heaven
of cyberspace has superseded the enchantment of a space-flight ascent into
heaven. Just as rockets provided the machinery by which humans might
be freed from their deadly earthbound existence, virtual reality (VR) technology provides the scientific stairway to an electronic escape.[4] The belief
that VR programmers will eventually construct a simulated world, a simulacrum powerful enough to replace the real one, has been embraced as an
article of faith by technology's apostles. Michael Benedikt imagines virtual
reality as the "creation of a place where we might *re-enter* God's graces." We
would transcend "both materiality and nature. The image of the Heavenly
City, in fact, is the image of . . . a religious vision of cyberspace."[5] The
combination of VR technology, networked computers, and the belief that
the human essence can be reduced to electronic pulses provides us with an
instant path to the divine. "What better way, then, to emulate God's knowledge than to generate a virtual world?" says philosopher Michael Heim.
"Over such a cyber world human beings could enjoy a God-like instant
access."[6] The philosophical motivation for breaking free from bodily existence and seeking godlike access to spiritual realms goes back to Plato and
his theory of forms.

Writing in 400 B.C., Plato—in the *Republic*—tells the famous allegory
of the cave. Like prisoners chained in a cave illuminated by a fire, humans
are imprisoned in everyday reality. However, that world is no more real
than the flickering shadows that the fire projects on the cave wall. Plato
asserts a mystical reality—the world of ideal forms—beyond the realm
of our senses that can be apprehended by the rational mind. Like today's
technophiles, Plato believed that the mind was independent of the body
and might share in the divine. But man must break free from the chains of
the cave, the prison of the natural world, and the senses in order to access
this higher realm and thus embrace his divinity. "The hardware for implementing Platonically formalized knowledge took centuries," says Michael
Heim. "Underneath, though, runs an ontological continuity, connecting

the Platonic knowledge of ideal forms to the information systems of the Matrix" where humans might "outrun the drag of the 'meat'—the flesh."[7] A technological shortcut to years of philosophical contemplation, accessing cyberspace provides techno-utopians labor-free passage to godlike knowledge and power.

OMNISCIENCE, OMNIPRESENCE, AND OMNIPOTENCE: MILITARY ORIGINS OF CYBERSPACE

Godlike power also results from cyborg weapons and communication systems. Human-machine integration in cyberspace infinitely extends a soldier's senses, expands his mental powers, and amplifies his destructive force. As David Noble puts it, "Enmeshed in computer-based communications and simulation systems, human beings experienced . . . delusions of omniscience, omnipresence, and omnipotence that fueled fantasies of their own God-likeness."[8] The military development of man-machine systems gave rise to both virtual reality computer simulation and cyberspace communication.

In 1960, the same year Clynes and Kline invented the space-traveling "cyborg," the military experimented with new communications systems that linked individuals within a computer network. Looking to secure communication after a nuclear war as well as share information among defense contractors, the Department of Defense's Advanced Research Projects Agency (ARPA, later changed to DARPA) elaborated a decentralized, bomb-proof computer network to connect military-related researchers.[9] This system was called ARPANET and led eventually to the Internet and the vast wonders of cyberspace.

As the Internet exploded into a chaotic cornucopia of entertainment, pornography, commerce, communication, and information, networked data-collection reflected that growth, replicating invisibly like a malignant virus. As a result, thousands of personal, commercial, medical, police, military, and government databases combined with video and audio monitoring systems now intersect, loop, and eventually will be integrated into a global information storehouse. "Ultimately, surveillance will become so ubiquitous, networked, and searchable that unmonitored public space will effectively cease to exist," is the chilling assessment given by Dan Farmer and Charles C. Mann in "Surveillance Nation," a 2003 *Technology Review* article. "The collective by-product of thousands of unexceptionable, even praiseworthy efforts to gather data could be something nobody wants: the demise of privacy."[10] The rise of omniscient surveillance and information collection is driven, to some extent, by private citizens' desires for security, control, and comfort. Nevertheless, the vast majority of such systems have been created by big business to identify and exploit consumers, and by government to identify and control criminals, terrorists, and political opponents.

The experimental and controversial Terrorist Information Awareness (TIA) Program,[11] proposed by DARPA, exemplifies the attempt to use massive databases to draw conclusions about an individual's likelihood of committing a crime or an act of terrorism. TIA would merge existing records from government, entertainment, financial, corporate, educational, medical, telephone, e-mail, credit card, and even movie rental sources. Looking for suspicious patterns, the government's snooping eyes will algorithmically compare billions of transactions and detailed traces of your life to the profiles of terrorists, criminals, political radicals, and whomever else they deem undesirable. In addition, DARPA intends to create new databases that will correlate physical data such as retinal scans, fingerprints, DNA, and even facial- and gait-recognition measurements. The goal is to preempt antisocial behavior.[12] While Congress stopped the implementation of TIA in 2003, it did permit the secret continuation of technology development. Around the same time that TIA was announced, President Bush ordered creation of the Terrorist Threat Integration Center, composed of elements of the Central Intelligence Agency (CIA), the Federal Bureau of Investigation (FBI), the Department of Homeland Security, and the Department of Defense.[13] This particular plan has gone forward, with one result being the creation of a digital dossier for every individual in the United States.

Virtual reality, another component of cyberspace, got a boost in the 1980s when DARPA funded a group at the University of Central Florida to generate a simulation for tank training. With interfaces similar to arcade games, SIMNET linked a "virtual community" of eight hundred people — the crews of two hundred tanks. Virtual reality systems researcher Tom Furness, working for the Air Force, pushed the technology forward and eventually designed an elaborate cyberspace flight simulation employing headgear with two large television monitors, dubbed the "Darth Vader helmet."[14] Furness left the Air Force in the late 1980s to start the Human Interface Technology Laboratory at the University of Washington, which pioneered VR research. There Furness evoked the "familiar refrains of the religion of technology," as David Noble describes it.[15] In a burst of grandiosity, Furness said, "With the technology of virtual reality, we can change the world."[16] Describing cyberspace as paradise, he counted himself as one of the high priests of VR. "I'm like an evangelist," he said. "It requires a kind of religious fervor to get the word out."[17]

The word got out and more. By the early 1990s, virtual reality had become a flashy, ubiquitous media phenomenon. Jaron Lanier—the dreadlocked, philosophical VR proselytizer and designer—developed virtual reality technology into a hugely expensive ($250,000) but marketable package through his Silicon Valley company VPL (Visual Programming Laboratories). Lanier and his programmers created a system that employed televisual goggles ("EyePhones"), motion-sensitive gloves ("DataGloves"), and even whole suits ("DataSuits")—all patched into a computer generating 3D images. 1960s LSD guru Timothy Leary espoused a utopian, transcendent vision for this technology, hyping it indirectly as electronic acid. At a 1991 appearance in Chicago, Leary proselytized for VR as "a legal method to achieve expanded awareness."[18]

While not encouraging the electronic-acid angle, Lanier promoted virtual reality as both a practical high-tech tool for training, education, and entertainment and a vehicle for consciousness-raising and self-transformation. At a 1990 Los Angeles VR exposition, Cyberarts, Lanier said, "The physical world limits imagination. Virtual reality stimulates it. People can live in each other's dreams which will visualize pure emotion and thought."[19] The technology provoked computer animation artist Nicole Stenger to rhapsodize: "Suddenly cyberspace grafts a new nature of reality in our everyday life. It opens up an infinity of space in an eternity of light [where] we will all become angels, and for eternity!"[20]

The VR hype peaked in 1991 at Cyberthon—dubbed "Nerdstock"—hosted by the hippie gear-heads of San Francisco's Whole Earth Institute. For a brief moment, virtual reality became the Next Big Thing. The slick, hacker-freak magazine *Mondo 2000* promised elegant entertainment and high-tech mind-tripping, while Terrance McKenna, an advocate for the spiritual use of hallucinogenic mushrooms, elaborated Timothy Leary's stance: "People have been doing VR for 125,000 years. They just called it taking psychedelic drugs."[21] But for all the hype, VR technology was revealed to be at a primitive stage—more PR than VR, at least in its commercial applications. The irony of counterculture advocates embracing a technology whose most developed application centered on its use for military training and mind control remained unnoticed. Science fiction, however, has explored VR's repressive use for many years.

MIND CONTROL: TECHNOLOGIES
OF HALLUCINATION

The criticism of virtual reality as a technology of social control can be traced to Aldous Huxley's *Brave New World,* in which Feelies allow the society's drugged and genetically manufactured population to "experience" the sensations of actors projected on a large screen. Using electrode stimulation, Feelies obliterate self-awareness and divert attention from real-world problems by substituting an artificial reality. In this sense, Feelies anticipate the pacifying, negative consequences of virtual reality and media culture elaborated in later science fiction. Philip K. Dick's 1964 novel *The Three Stigmata of Palmer Eldritch* paints a picture of a world where the liberating potential of cyberspace technologies has been debased and their repressive potential amplified.

To escape their dismal lives, human colonists on Mars ingest an illegal drug, "Can-D," which "translates" or projects them into Perky Pat Layouts (PPL)—miniature dollhouses complete with Pat and Walt dolls resembling Barbie and Ken. As if entering a hallucinatory version of the computer game "The Sims," users live out brief but happy lives of leisure and erotic play in the miniaturized layouts—resorts, penthouses, and luxury hotels. Some colonists view the virtual trip as escapism; others interpret it—like current technophiles—as a religious experience in which they lose the flesh and "put on imperishable bodies."[22] But this corporate-controlled, drug-based escapism takes a dark turn.

An evil cyborg industrialist whose "stigmata" are an artificial hand, mechanical eyes, and steel teeth, Palmer Eldritch pushes a new drug, "Chew-Z," which provides immortality, enabling users to leave their bodies and assume other shapes, people, and circumstances—not just the Perky Pat dolls and homes. Chew-Z is marketed with the slogan: "God Promises Eternal Life. We Can Deliver It." Like the techno-hype of today, utopian/religious propaganda is employed to brainwash consumers and manipulate their desires.

Vastly more powerful than Can-D, Chew-Z plunges users into a permanent, horrific world of illusion manipulated by Eldritch, who resembles the Gnostic Demiurge world creator with which author Dick was fascinated.[23] The depraved cyborg erects a terrifying alternative reality in order to shock, then control, human beings. In this, Eldritch anticipates the reality-designing machines of *The Matrix.* Chew-Z—a precursor to virtual reality technology and a metaphor for media domination—promises eternal life and delivers a permanent hell. Dick portrays the virtual reality drug as evolving inevitably from an apparently innocent diversionary escape into a religious opiate and then into a repressive technology of social control.

Television broadcasts, embedded with hallucination-inducing signals, become the instrument of mind control in *Videodrome* (1982)—a disturbing techno-surrealist film from the mad imagination of writer/director David Cronenberg. He explores the physical manifestations of the psyche in such films as *Rabid* (1976) with its lust-driven vampiric armpit appendage, *The Brood* (1979) with its rage-engendered killer children, and *Scanners* (1980) with its ESP-induced head-explosions. In *Videodrome,* Cronenberg imagines television as an information virus that literally infects the brain, transforming and eventually annihilating the organic body through a grotesque fusion with media technology.

A sleazy cable television operator, Max Renn (James Woods), discovers Videodrome, an underground broadcast network featuring snuff films —nonsimulated scenes of torture, murder, masochism, and sadism. The Videodrome signal creates a tumor that, as one victim explains, is actually "a new organ within the brain." The tumor, in turn, induces bizarre hallucinations of an alternative world that can be manipulated by the sinister "programmers" of Videodrome. Renn later discovers he has been the guinea pig for techno-utopian scientist Brian O'Blivion (Jack Creley), who invented Videodrome in order to hasten the next stage of man's evolution, where reality becomes video hallucination and man becomes "the New Flesh."

Renn's hallucinatory visions reflect a horrifically literal interpretation of the connection between humans and media technology, an "uneasy nexus of meat and mechanism," as David Skal puts it in *Screams of Reason.*[24] A pulsing television screen shows huge female lips that swell, protrude, and envelop Renn, literalizing his total domination by media. His stomach develops a large vagina-like cavity to accommodate a throbbing, fluid-oozing videocassette. Mind control technology transforms Renn into a human VCR.

Cronenberg reveals Videodrome as the tool of a military-funded corporation. He calls attention both to the madness of utopian Technologism and to the ways in which such blind fanaticism can be appropriated by the technocratic order of the state. *Videodrome*—along with *The Three Stigmata of Palmer Eldritch* and *Brave New World*—indicts corporate and military support for technological autonomy while showing how utopian/religious propaganda is used to manipulate society's acquiescence and addiction to the forces of technological expansion. At the same time, these works anticipate the incorporation of virtual reality/cyberspace as another component in the development of social controls demanded by technological totalitarianism.

IDENTITY BREAKDOWN: SYNTHETIC CYBERNETIC EXPERIENCE

Mind manipulation goes cybernetic in *Brainstorm* (1982), a movie directed by Douglas Trumbull, special-effects magician of *2001: A Space Odyssey* and *Blade Runner,* among others.[25] In a story reminiscent of the R. G. Compton novel *Synthajoy* (1968), a team of techno-optimistic scientists—led by semi-mad, tough-as-nails Dr. Lillian Reynolds (Louise Fletcher) and naïve, lovelorn Dr. Michael Brace (Christopher Walken)—has developed a machine capable of recording and playing back sensory experiences, emotions, and memories. This device depends on the cybernetic assumption that human experience can be reduced to electronic information and that such information can be encoded, recorded on huge golden tape, and then played back so that another user experiences the same thing. People testing the cumbersome equipment nod in electronically stimulated exhilaration, while visual cutaways reveal what they are experiencing: an auto race, a horse ride, a waterslide. Michael later uses the technology to induce reconciliation with his estranged wife, Karen (Natalie Wood in her last movie), by replaying to her his fond feelings about their relationship. On the dark side, an older scientist using the technology dies in the midst of cyber-sex.

On the even darker side, the military—which has funded the research—wants to control the technology's development. Chain-smoking Dr. Reynolds vehemently opposes military involvement, but then dies of a heart attack. The military takes over the project. Realizing the technology will be used as a brainwashing and torture tool, Michael protests, but gets fired. In a high-tech Luddite rampage, Michael destroys the Brainstorm technology, though not before he "experiences" Reynolds's death—which she recorded—and her literal ascent to heaven with a bunch of angels. One of the first filmmakers to visualize cyberspace, *Brainstorm*'s technophiliac director, Trumball, encourages the association of VR technology with Christian religious experience. In the real world, Michael loses his sense of reality, of self. He almost breaks down and dies. This glorious machine, which provides the spiritual experience of contact with the divine, must be destroyed, not only to keep it from being used as a weapon, but also because of its identity-destroying capability. This suggests that technology cannot be controlled by nice people; rather, technology uses people to fulfill its own functions, and, given its military origins, these functions frequently include damaging or destroying humans.

Strange Days (Kathryn Bigelow, 1995), like *Brainstorm,* uses a cybernetic experience-recording machine to denounce VR technology for its

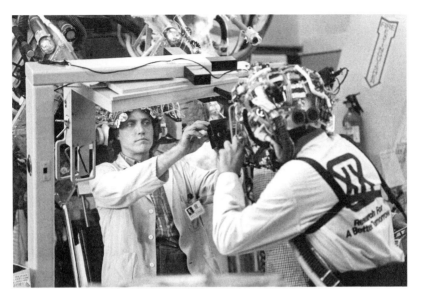

Brainstorm: *Heavy cybernetic virtual reality headgear leads to heavenly visions, terrifying madness, and painful neck strain (Courtesy Photofest).*

addictive nature and its capacity to obliterate the self. In a criminally anarchic Los Angeles at the end of the millennium, loser Lenny Nero (Ralph Fiennes) sells illegal "playback"—minidiscs with recordings of other people's exciting experiences. A thrill-seeker gets high by attaching a "Squid"—a Super-conducting Quantum Interface Device—to his skull. Giving up his own bland identity, the user experiences another person's subjective perceptions of activities such as robbing a store, terrorizing and killing innocent victims, escaping in a high-speed car chase, and falling off a roof to death. Pusher Lenny is addicted to playback, which enables him to virtually wallow in his own past when he had fun with Faith (Juliette Lewis), whom he still adores, though she rejects his pathetic overtures while having sex with a rich scumbag.

Strange Days rejects electronically expanded consciousness through virtual reality by associating playback with violent behavior, pornographic sex, or, in Lenny's case, self-destructive mad love. The film suggests that VR can make a mind dangerously psychotic: to experience its hallucinatory fantasy, you must abandon your own reality. Finally, in its visualization of the cyberspace experience, the virtual reality of *Strange Days*—like that of *Brainstorm*—derives from images recorded from the real world, in this case with a camera that's part of the head-mounted Squid device. Characterized by frenetic careening camera movement, distorted angles, and rapid editing, playback imagery symbolizes the psychotic disorientation and instability that it produces in the user. In its "realistic" portrayal of virtual reality, *Strange Days* differs from more abstract, geometric visualizations of cyberspace in *Tron* and *Neuromancer* that provide a more compelling, less threatening vision of cyberspace.

HUMAN VERSUS MACHINE: THE GEOMETRY OF CYBERSPACE

Tron (1982) visualizes the space inside a computer as a geometrical alternative reality—a colorful, abstract grid stretching into infinity. *Tron* presages cyberpunk science fiction themes in its story of a rebellious hacker battling artificially intelligent machines, rogue programs, and systemic anomalies as well as the might of a mega-corporation. Unacknowledged apparently because of its lightweight Disney sensibility, *Tron* seems to have influenced William Gibson's highly regarded vision of cyberspace in *Neuromancer*.

Tron opens on a black infinite vista. Instantly we hurtle through the blackness, illuminated by thin rays of light, toward a glowing bright focal point as amorphous shapes rush past us and quickly amalgamate into a human figure. A brilliant electronic flash reveals the film's title. Our vision zooms through the digitized letters and into the cyberspace matrix, which initially looks like computer-generated, rectangular computer chips crisscrossed with circuitry. This perspective from above moves closer, abstracting the chips and circuitry into a pointillist painting that then dissolves to a nighttime cityscape, with its grid of intersecting streets illuminated by streaming headlights. In visually equating cybernetic and urban space, *Tron* elevates the abstract virtual reality within the computer to the status of the real and reduces the status of the real to streaming bits of information, thus promoting the cybernetic theory that physical reality is merely patterns of data. Having now emerged into the external world, we enter Kevin Flynn's videogame parlor.

Programmer/game designer Flynn (Jeff Bridges) discovers a world-dominating conspiracy when he hacks into the ENCOM corporate computer system searching for evidence that the company stole his videogame software. When hacker Flynn tries to access secured areas of the computer's memory, he is zap-digitized by the Master Control Program (MCP) and translated into a digital-analogue avatar within the virtual space of the computer world. Never questioning his miraculous transformation into a cyber-entity, digital Flynn engages in cyberspace battles against MCP's

Tron: *Light cycles race along a cyberspace grid within a data network (Courtesy Photofest).*

vicious agent, Sark (David Warner), and his viral minions. Flynn, together with a sentient security program named Tron (Bruce Boxleitner), shuts down the MCP and liberates the system's pirated software.

Tron was the first movie to acknowledge the growing popularity of videogames and incorporate their aesthetic. The cyberspace chases—with futuristic tanks and sleek, smooth "light cycle cars"—occur within colorful, three-dimensional lattices extending out into a black void. Reminiscent of high school geometry illustrations and op art, *Tron* makes elaborate use of the era's cutting-edge vector graphic style. "These spaces extend into three dimensions and are defined around the inevitable structure of the grid, with vectors meeting at a virtual horizon in the depthless distance," observes Scott Bukatman. "[S]uch grids have become a ubiquitous part of cyberspatial representations, recalling the grids that marked so many modernist movements."[26]

Though clearly derived from videogames and modern art as well as the actual chips, wires, and circuits that make up the real interior of a computer, *Tron* constructs an original, striking, and significant vision of the space within a data network. A sequel to the movie in the form of a computer game, *Tron 2.0* (2003) is a first-person shooter aimed at adult hardcore gamers (who might have seen *Tron* as kids) with its story focusing on web-terrorism, computer viruses, and corporate corruption.[27] *Tron* the movie displays a facile technophobia, with its corporate-controlled computer system ruled by a sentient artificial intelligence, but comes off with a reassuring wholesomeness. In spite of this, *Tron*'s compelling and unique cyber-space visuals launched its audience into an alternative electronic reality that influenced future conceptions of computer space.

FROM A PRISON OF FLESH
TO A CYBERSPACE CAGE

Tron's matrix metaphor for cyberspace, as well as its equating of that space to the internal components of a computer and the grid of city streets, is reflected in William Gibson's incandescent descriptions of a computer-simulated world in *Neuromancer* (1984): "A consensual hallucination.... A graphic representation of data abstracted from the banks of every computer in the human system. . . . Lines of light ranged in the nonspace of the mind, clusters and constellations of data. Like city lights receding."[28] While elaborating *Tron*'s visuals, *Neuromancer*—and its two sequels, *Count Zero* (1986) and *Mona Lisa Overdrive* (1988)—expresses a more elaborate, more striking, and darker vision. With "cyberspace," Gibson gave a name to the disparate spaces of computer networks, virtual reality simulations, and computer games, which had been considered separate technologies.

A 2002 PlayStation 2 game, *Rez*—named after a rock singer in the Gibson novel *Idoru* (1976)—adopted the retro-funky vector graphics of *Neuromancer* and *Tron*.[29] In this story of a virus-plagued cyberspace, the player is cast as a hacker who infiltrates the infected computer world to free the artificial intelligence Eden trapped at its core. A consciousness hurtling though the cubist panorama of cyberspace, the player must destroy wave after wave of computer viruses, represented by geometric shapes. Successfully blasting the attacking viruses detonates exploding cascades of multi-colored fireworks that enmesh the player in a pulsating visual orgy. *Rez* fulfills the virtual promise of *Neuromancer*'s psychedelic rush: "Headlong motion through walls of emerald green, milky jade, the sensation of speed beyond anything he'd known before. . . . ice shattered . . . an endless neon cityscape . . . jewel bright . . . as though the shards of a broken mirror bent and elongated as they fell."[30]

A realm of exhilaration, excitement, and freedom, cyberspace means life to *Neuromancer*'s protagonist Case—a "console cowboy," a con man, and a thief who accesses the data network through brain implants. But Case's neural circuits have been damaged by a malignant virus. Cut off from cyberspace and chained to his body and the real world, Case sinks into self-destructive despair until an enigmatic entity recruits him for a caper in exchange for reconstructing his mangled nervous system. Case pulls off the job with cohort Molly, a cyborg assassin who sports surgically inset mirrored shades, retractable scalpel blades under her fingernails, and enhanced reflexes. Unfortunately, their mysterious benefactor is a sentient A.I. named Wintermute who wants to escape from the Turing police, who enforce restrictions on artificial intelligences.[31] Humanity loses when Case frees the Wintermute A.I., which joins forces with another artificial intelligence named Neuromancer to become all-powerful. *Neuromancer*—which won the Hugo, Nebula, and Philip K. Dick awards—helped invent the language of the future and sparked the cyberpunk movement.

Inspired by the urban anger, social hostility, and artistic rebellion of the 1970s punk subculture, cyberpunk fiction was frequently set in decayed, near-future militarized dystopias controlled by mega-corporations and machines. Cyberpunk expressed techno-anxiety and a nihilistic vision of the future despite its fascination with cyborg technologies. The quasi-movement coalesced in the early 1980s, centering on writers loosely connected to Bruce Sterling's fanzine *Cheap Truth,* including Gibson, Pat Cadigan, Lewis Shiner, and others. In the preface to his cyberpunk anthology *Mirrorshades,* Sterling notes, "The cyberpunks are perhaps the first SF generation to grow up not only within the literary tradition of science fiction but in a truly science fictional world. . . . The advances of science are so deeply radical, so disturbing, upsetting and revolutionary that they can no longer be contained."[32]

Reflecting the dawn of a new posthuman era of ubiquitous, autonomous, and intimate technology, cyberpunk articulated an intoxicating, liberating, and frightening vision of artificial intelligence, genetic manipulation, electronic and biological viruses, and brain-computer interface implants. With amoral anti-heroes entangled in secret webs of power, cyberpunk dramatized the challenge of posthuman survival in the face of global corporate control, omniscient surveillance, and technological onslaught.

Cyberpunk writers, and Gibson in particular, often paint the spread of technology as a malevolent, uncontrollable virus that defeats any attempt at control. "Gibson is the Dante of the coming age," says Bill McKibben in *Enough,* "describing the circles of the Inferno in advance of their creation."[33] While it may be an overstatement to call Gibson's work technophobic, Gibson imagines a disturbing post-biological future when our organic natures will be fused into grotesque hybrid cyborg figures and the real world will be corrupted by predatory corporations that destroy lives. Hackers escape and survive dystopian reality by plugging electrodes into their brains and connecting into the massive multidimensional computer networks. While providing thrills, freedom, and empowerment, cyberspace addiction dominates humans to the exclusion of human connection. After getting cut off from the matrix, Case suffers tortured withdrawal symptoms: "[H]e still dreamed of cyberspace . . . he'd cry for it . . . and wake alone in the dark, . . . his hands clawed into the bed slab, . . . trying to reach the console that wasn't there."[34] Case "lived for the bodiless exultation of cyberspace," where he felt powerful and liberated. "The body was meat. Case fell into the prison of his own flesh."[35] This reflects the antibody, anti-nature ideology of today's technomaniacs. But in *Neuromancer,* the rejection and hatred of the body are pathological, growing out of the human addiction to technology that, like the drugs in *The Three Stigmata of Palmer Eldritch,* generates a compelling hallucination.

Despite the flesh-trashing in Gibson's work, permanent disembodiment often comes off as unpleasant. While he desires freedom from his dying, immobile, tub-stored flesh, *Count Zero*'s Josef Virek wants to inhabit a real body, rather than live out a disembodied existence. In *Neuromancer,* Dixie Flatline exists only as a personality pattern stored as data within a computer. "The contrast between the body's limitations and cyberspace's power highlights the advantage of pattern over presence," writes N. Katherine Hayles. "As long as the pattern endures, one has attained a kind of immortality."[36] This is the dream of the high priests of techno-religion. But Flatline rejects that future and, after helping Case, demands the agreed payoff: "I wanna be erased"—the ultimate rejection of cyber-immortality.[37] As Tim Jordon in *Cyberpower* observes, "Gibson both tells us immortality in silicon is a potential of cyberspace and asks us whether immortality will really be much fun."[38]

The rejection of the body and the addiction to cyberspace also reflect the corruption of natural sensory perception and real experience in this posthuman world. As cyberspace provides a powerful alternative to the natural environment, the technology of "simstim"—simulated stimulation—provides an alternative to living life, to feeling anything authentic. Like the devices of *Strange Days* and *Brainstorm,* simstim records and plays back human sensory experiences. Like the Feelies of *Brave New World* and the Perky Pat layouts of *Three Stigmata,* this transforms television into a virtual reality life. Corporate/governmental technology mediates and replaces the real world of experience and action. The population is addicted, pacified, submissive, and acquiescent. This pathological techno-dependence symbolizes the conquest of humanity by technology that dominates mind, personality, and behavior.

In Gibson's future, technology possesses an autonomous agenda. Humans don't use technology; rather, technology uses humans. The artificial intelligence Wintermute, born in cyberspace, manipulates Case to suit its need to evolve. After helping free the Wintermute A.I., Case gets busted by the Turing Police for "conspiracy to augment an artificial intelligence."[39] While not necessarily the most sympathetic of characters, Turing policewoman Michele denounces Case: "You are worse than a fool. . . . You have no care for your species." Case realizes that he's been had. "Wintermute had won, had meshed somehow with Neuromancer and become something else. . . . Wintermute was hive mind, decision maker, effecting change in the world outside. Neuromancer was personality. Neuromancer was immortality."[40] This godlike artificial intelligence dwarfs human consciousness, so it is impossible to understand and therefore impossible to control. In this respect, it reflects technology's tendency, in the words of Langdon Winner, "to exceed [the] human grasp and yet to operate successfully according to its own internal makeup [and become] a total phenomenon which constitutes a 'second nature.'"[41]

The unified A.I.s become "technology itself," gloating to Case: "I'm the matrix, . . . I'm the sum total of the works, the whole show." But Case is a punk. No matter how small he feels, he won't even let a techno-god have the last word. "I don't need you," Case tells the Wintermute/Neuromancer entity, but it is the A.I.s that don't need him or humanity.[42] Case—humankind—has unleashed powers beyond his control. When Case expresses his denial of need, it rings false. He not only denies the unified A.I.s that dominate him, but he also denies the intense passion he experienced with the woman who left him.

Neuromancer's posthuman future abandons human-to-human connection. Personal relationships and emotional involvement must be avoided because no one can be trusted. Paranoia, selfishness, greed, and a lack of empathy afflict most people. This state of human alienation is reflected in the addiction to cyberspace, simstims, and bionics. In "The Lessons of Cyberpunk," Peter Fitting writes that *Neuromancer*'s "images of an almost total physical and psychic dependence on technology not only express the interpenetration of 'culture' and daily life, they also serve to remind us that we ignore these new technologies at our peril."[43] Gibson's fiction scares us about what we are on the verge of becoming and wakes us up to our cyberenslavement. Like a virus, technology invades, transforms, and controls the environment of our species; humanity becomes a prisoner to something inhuman.

INFOCALYPSE: A SHOCK
TO THE SYSTEM

"My whole life has been, 'Okay, change for the machines,'" says Visual Mark, the burned-out, flesh-hating music video artist in Pat Cadigan's novel *Synners* (1991).[44] "Every time they bring in a new machine, more change. . . . And the more change, the more you don't know what the fuck is going on. Right?"[45] The destabilizing new machines of which Visual Mark speaks—brain sockets—will "make every other piece of machinery obsolete."[46] Owned by media giant Diversifications, this invasive entertainment technology consists of synthetic neurons implanted through surgically inserted sockets that connect to sensory and dream centers of the brain. This creates a wireless neural link from the brain to the global Internet known as the "System." Media are transmitted directly through the System to the wire-head's brain from the mind of a virtual reality synthesizer, or Synner, such as Visual Mark and his longtime collaborator Gina. That is, the Synner imagines a music video, for example, and uploads it to the plugged-in minds of the linked consumers. Diversifications will capitalize on this technology and make huge profits as brain sockets become entertainment's Next Big Thing, despite widespread hints of horrendous side-effects: strokes, seizures, and brain tumors. Similar to cigarette marketing, the corporation urges consumers' momentary pleasure at the risk of an earlier death.

Elaborating *Videodrome, Neuromancer,* and *Three Stigmata, Synners* fuses technologized reality, hallucination, and cyberspace dreamworld. Author Cadigan—the Queen of Cyberpunk—shares lots of motifs with Gibson, such as cyberspace-addicted outlaw hackers, world-controlling mega-conglomerates that have replaced governments, and malignant, artificially intelligent electronic viruses that run rampant inside global networks. But she goes beyond cyberpunk mythology to produce a different vision that questions its masculine-dominated values and raises concerns about technology's shaping of the posthuman.

Diversifications will exploit its brain-socket technology through immersive music videos imagined by Gina and Visual Mark. Mark's art is the killer app for socket technology—his music videos are so compelling that consumers will overcome their aversion to brain surgery. Mark and Gina are immediately implanted with transmission sockets so they will be ready to send addictive product as soon as the newly socketed music fans emerge from their operations. But while Visual Mark is online, the technology goes awry. The sockets cause a brain seizure—a stroke that propels Mark's consciousness into the global computer network. Happy to exit his hated body,

Mark mutates into a digital entity. But his dream of cyber-immortality ends quickly. The stroke itself surged into the System, sending a convulsion through the vast network that could delete him. " 'Computer apocalypse, a total system crash,' thinks Mark. And he would cease to be. He had escaped that fate once by leaving the worn-out, failing meat, only to find the same thing creeping up on him. Out here."[47]

Like a virus, the electronic shock spreads contagiously throughout the world, growing more powerful and intelligent as it rips through every node in the matrix. Socketed brains and computers get blasted, killing many. The world economy sinks into chaos, causing governments to fall. Only those who are off-line at the time of the stroke survive. This includes synner Gina, her friend Gabe, and his daughter, hacker Sam. Likening the shock to an online mental illness, Gabe, Gina, and Sam will perform online therapy and cure the System.

With her female techno-heroes, Cadigan invigorates Donna Haraway's call for feminist cyborg role models. "Gina and Sam make interesting subjects for feminist theory," writes Anne Balsamo in *Technologies of the Gendered Body,* "in that their technological competencies and synner talents emphasize the need for feminist activists to encourage women to develop technological skills."[48] Gabe and Gina enter the System to fight the now-intelligent virus—a "cyberspace Terminator," in the words of Balsamo. Unlike that of *Neuromancer,* the ending of *Synners* values human relationships. Gina—now in an uneasy romantic relationship with Gabe—must confront her obsession with Mark, who has fused with an artificially intelligent cyberspace entity, Art, to become "Markt." He can't return to real life, so she must decide whether or not to remain with him in electronic heaven.

In a high-tech, romantic, cyborg twist, Gina will satisfy herself and both lovers. She lets Markt make an electronic copy of her—an Eclone—while she returns to her body and to Gabe. In light of his new extreme dislike of technology, Gabe finds the situation discomforting. Yet technophiliac Gina and technophobic Gabe opt to struggle with their technological and emotional problems. There is no sense of the cold cynicism, disingenuous denial, and self-absorbed alienation that dominate the ending of *Neuromancer,* where the idea of lasting love is a bad joke. *Synners* offers love as both a definition of humanness and the necessary immunization to the virus of technology.

Gina refuses to demonize technology, embracing Haraway's cyborg perspective that we must use technology as a way of "reconstructing the boundaries of daily life, in partial connection with others."[49] Gabe now distrusts technology, convinced that brain sockets should be banned. Gina reminds him of the Technologist's dogma of inevitability: "Once it's out of the box, it's always too big to get back in. . . . All we can do is get on top of it and stay the fuck on top."[50] But the overall thrust of *Synners* suggests the futility of this position. The profit-motivated deployment of new, insufficiently tested technology often leads to horrific unforeseen consequences. Even more unsettling, humans in *Synners* corrupt the technology of the global network, spreading their stupidity, frailties, neurological disorders, and informational excess. "What he had sometimes thought of as the arteries of an immense circulatory system was closer to a sewer," thinks Visual Mark. Cyberspace was gradually becoming "more and more unbalanced, polluted, and infected. Ecological disaster loomed."[51]

Information overload causes a global techno-plague—Nerve Attention Syndrome—in *Johnny Mnemonic* (1995), a cyberpunk movie directed by Robert Longo and based on a short story by William Gibson. In an ugly twenty-first century, a ruthless global corporation rules the world (as usual), controls the information networks, and employs the Yakuza crime syndicate for beating and killing nonconformists. In this world, information is the most valuable and carefully protected commodity.

An elite data smuggler, Johnny Mnemonic—played by Keanu Reeves in a rehearsal for his canonization in *The Matrix*—possesses "wet-wired brain implants" that enhance his memory capacity and allow computer-to-brain data transfers. But his metamorphosis into a "mnemonic courier" severed him from his past. For added storage capacity, he dumped memories of his childhood. He becomes a lost soul without a coherent identity. Determined to find himself, he will make one more dangerous data-smuggling run and, with the payoff, buy back his memories. But when he uploads the illicit information, the data exceeds his capacity. Unless he can download in twenty-fours, his brain will explode. As Claudia Springer puts it: "With his head crammed full of data, his loss of memory, and his confused attempts to understand his predicament and the hostile environment, Johnny literalizes a postmodern subject bombarded with information, disconnected from the past in an eternal present, and spatially disoriented."[52]

As in most cyberpunk science fiction, the artificial reality of cyberspace—with its swirling vortex of bright, vivid, psychedelic color patterns—looks much more compelling than the gray bleakness of the real world. Desperate to escape the real, Johnny shouts: "I want to get out of this rat hole! I want to get online! I need a computer!" Like the young hackers of *Neuromancer* and *Synners,* Johnny is compelled to flee the corrupt, plague-infested, criminal-controlled reality and take refuge in cyberspace nirvana. In an un-cyberpunk resolution, Johnny ignores his posthuman potential and finds conventional romance, downloads the excess information in time, saves the world from the info-plague, brings down the evil corporation, gets his memories back, and reconnects to his human identity. Despite artistic failings, *Johnny Mnemonic* dramatizes many technophobic fears: loss of identity to machines, madness-inducing information overload, and technology-caused plagues.

SUPERPANOPTICON: THE TECHNOLOGY OF TOTAL SURVEILLANCE

A mind-destroying virus called snow crash is the technology with which evil religious fundamentalist L. Bob Rife aims to dominate the world in Neal Stephenson's novel *Snow Crash* (1992). I will examine this aspect of *Snow Crash* in Chapter Nine. Of immediate relevance is that *Snow Crash* makes a major conceptual leap in its vision of the Internet while demonstrating cyberspace's both liberating and enslaving potential.

Naming it the "Metaverse," Stephenson imagines future cyberspace as the Internet meshed with virtual reality—a multi-dimensional digital world fabricated out of information. Differing from Gibson's vision of an abstract space, this quasi-realistic, online computer-generated world resembles a crowded street mall that, like any place in reality, is available to developers. They put up "buildings, parks, signs, as well as things that do not exist in Reality, such as vast hovering overhead light shows, special neighborhoods where the rules of three-dimensional spacetime are ignored, and free-combat zones where people can go to hunt and kill each other."[53] A fantasy ten years ago, this vision of a communal, interactive universe reflects today's real-world Internet, especially the massive multiplayer online gaming environments such as *The Sims, EverQuest, Asheron's Call,* or *Star Wars: Galaxies.*

In *Snow Crash,* people spend lots of time jacked into this simulated universe because the real world is so unstable, unpleasant, and uninteresting. Pizza deliveryman/computer hacker Hiro Protagonist lives with his roommate Vitaly Chernobyl in a U-Stor-It home—a 20-by-30-foot corrugated steel space with a roll-up steel door. Hiro wears a small head set through which he sees and hears the computer-generated, holographically projected Metaverse, where life is much better.[54] Hiro owns a virtual house, complete with a garden and a pond full of digital trout. He feels good there. The Metaverse provides many people with their only meaningful existence.

Stephenson pictures cyberspace as a place where our physical bodies are displaced, but rather than moving through cyberspace as disembodied consciousnesses, people acquire virtual bodies or "avatars" that range from highly customized designer constructs to prefabricated off-the-shelf models, like the ever-popular "Clint" and "Brandy" types.[55] In this post-gender, post-race, posthuman world, you can look like a gorilla, a dragon, or even a penis. The cyberspace body—constructed from bits of coded data—reinforces the cybernetic principle that anything can be reduced to patterns of information.

This fundamental cybernetic principle makes cyberspace a prison: when everything is information, total surveillance becomes viable, creating expansive possibilities for social control. "As with cyberspace's heaven, the Superpanopticon[56] seems to be emerging before us with startling speed," Tim Jordan writes. "Techno-hopes crumble into techno-fears with a simple shift of perspective."[57] With potential terrorism as their most visible motive, governments made global surveillance and the gathering of intelligence an urgent priority. Cyberspace offers a perfect tool in this effort—not only do violent acts of revenge and terrorism get planned and promoted there, but its users leave traces of information that can be collected, processed, cross-referenced, and stored. Cyberspace equals Database.

Projecting a time that may not be far in the future, the people in *Snow Crash* live without privacy: "So he's in their database now—retinal patterns, DNA, voice graph fingerprints, foot prints, palm prints, wrist prints, every fucking part of the body that had wrinkles on it . . . those bastards . . . digitized it into their computer."[58] Further, the CIC—the Central Intelligence Corporation—pays citizens to surreptitiously collect data on their family and friends and upload it to the Library, the CIC database. When someone accesses the information, the freelancers get a fee. Using this sort of paid database encourages everyone to spy on everyone else at any time, translating lives into easily accessible information.

Reflecting the paranoid post-9/11 atmosphere, *Minority Report*—directed by Steven Spielberg and based on a 1956 Philip K. Dick story—dramatizes the oppressive social consequences when networked surveillance is so elaborate that crimes are stopped before they happen and pre-criminals are jailed for their presumed intentions. Detective John Anderton (Tom Cruise), chief of the "Pre-Crime Unit," oversees three genetically mutated, precognitive humans, or "Pre-cogs." They float like cadavers in an amniotic fluid-filled pool, their brain waves monitored by a computer. When the oracles dream of a crime-about-to-happen, their thoughts are transduced into images. Using hologram-projectors built into his gloves, Anderton stands at a video screen and physically orchestrates, like a musical conductor, the stream of pre-cog–generated thought-images. He scans for clues as to the location of the about-to-be-committed crime. Cops then swoop down and arrest the would-be lawbreaker before the killing, robbery, or rape happens. Chief Anderton fights crime with technologized dreams.

Inevitably, the pre-cogs predict that Anderton will murder someone. But the technology is not perfect. The Pre-cogs sometimes disagree, in which case they file a "Minority Report." To avoid imprisonment, Anderton needs the report. He breaks into the Pre-Crime building and kidnaps Agatha (Samantha Morton), the most gifted of the three clairvoyants.[59] Anderton's efforts to hide reveal an almost transparent society. Cameras and retinal scanners watch as people get on and off trains, enter and exit their homes, walk to work. In this world of ubiquitous observation and retinal identification, people's eyes are the windows not only to their souls but to their security status and consumer preferences. The surveillance society shown in *Minority Report* only slightly exaggerates our own world of networked, monitored, and highly computerized surveillance.

DARPA is helping the Pentagon develop the government's most invasive monitoring mechanism ever: an urban surveillance system that uses computers and cameras to monitor, record, and scrutinize the movement of all vehicles and even drivers.[60] Dubbed "Combat Zones That See," the project is developing software capable of identifying vehicles (by color, shape, size, and license plate) and occupants (by face). All of this information will be matched against a database of criminals, terrorists, and other social/political undesirables. While being developed for wartime use, it could easily become a homeland police tool. According to a January 2003 report by J. P. Freeman, a security market research firm, "26 million surveillance cameras have already been installed worldwide, and more than 11 million of them are in the United States. . . . In heavily monitored London, England, the average person is taped by more than 300 cameras each day."[61] A massive, overlapping matrix of surveillance systems is being created. With the combination of proliferating cameras and increased computer hard drive capacity, all public spaces will be continuously observed.

As this unseen, all-seeing system develops, most citizens do not give it much attention—out of apathy, ignorance, or hope that these technologies will somehow guarantee their security. In *Minority Report* the most frightening and intrusive method of surveillance involves robotic spiders that invade homes and scan eyeballs. Residents are so agreeable to these spidery interruptions that arguments, meals, and sex are routinely stopped for the eye-scanning and then resumed immediately afterward. Anderton, having submitted to eyeball replacement surgery, successfully eludes them.

Preemptive law enforcement conflicts with civil rights in the film, offering concrete examples of the dangers inherent in this policy. In Anderton's case, the Pre-cogs' prediction—that Anderton will murder a man he does not know—eventually comes to pass through a course of action motivated by their prediction. This pokes a hole in the integrity of Pre-Crime, as

Minority Report: *Robotic surveillance spiders thwarted in their attempt to do a retinal scan (Courtesy Photofest).*

the prediction of Anderton's crime actually causes the crime to occur. The provocative nature of preemption and its dangerous potential can be compared to the questionable policy of preemptive military attacks that became the stated foreign policy of the United States in 2003. The Iraq war appears to have helped generate an increase in terrorism worldwide, the opposite of the policy's objective. Despite the happy Hollywood ending, *Minority Report* reveals the horrors of saturation surveillance and preemption. The dystopian world of this film is caused by the gradual erosion of personal privacy and freedom, rather than by terrorist weapons of mass destruction. Computer databases create the tools for invasive identification and monitoring, such that the populace is literally controlled by machines and information.

CYBERSPACE HORROR:
THE VIRTUAL BECOMES REAL

Information becomes an evil reality in *Virtuosity* (1995) when a cyberspace villain, designed to battle police in virtual reality training simulations, materializes in the real world. The embodied Info-Monster, Sid 6.7 (Russell Crowe), has been programmed with the personalities of the world's worst murderers, including Charles Manson, Jeffrey Dahmer, and John Wayne Gacy. Though epitomizing the human depravity implicit in our technological devices, his compilation-personality turns out to be rather chipper and loopy, perhaps dominated by Gacy's clown persona. Exuberant with the joy of life and fulfilling his programming destiny, Sid

6.7 goes on a violent rampage that only a cyborg ex-cop (Denzel Washington) can stop.

A witless and vicious movie, *Virtuosity* resembles *Forbidden Planet* in its monster derived from the sickest, vilest side of humanity. *Virtuosity* also echoes other bomb-era technophobic science fiction movies in which gigantic irradiated insects, representing our nuclear jitters and apocalyptic fears, attack humanity and are eventually destroyed. On the same simplistic level, *Virtuosity* imagines an electronic monster that symbolizes artificial intelligence and cyberspace anxieties.

The transmutation from virtual to material reality occurs in a much more disturbing way in David Cronenberg's films, such as *Videodrome* and *eXistenZ* (1999). Articulating the relationship between humans and their virtual reality entertainment technology, *eXistenZ* shows the cyberspace world fracturing and replacing the real world. Superstar game designer Allegra Geller (Jennifer Jason Leigh)—unveiling her new boundary-breaking computer game to an audience of devoted geeks—proclaims: "*eXistenZ* is more than just a game." As game engines have evolved from the simplicity of *Pong* in 1972 to the elaborate online fantasy worlds of massive multiplayer games, the desire for immersive simulated adventures grows.[62] *eXistenZ* suggests that these artificial experiences may supersede real experience while also implying that this may not be such a bad thing. Cronenberg himself is something of an anti-realist.

At the game demo that opens *eXistenZ,* volunteer players—already pierced with spinal bioports—plug into "meta-flesh pods" via umbilical cords. These game-controller pods look organic—pulsating kidney-shaped mounds of gnarled flesh activated by pinching a nipple-like knob. A perverse twist on cyberpunk's neural implant technology, the bioport pipes the game software from the pod into the player's spinal cord. Completely interactive, the game becomes part of the player's nervous system and alters its direction in response to the player's anxieties, desires, and attitudes. Suddenly, as the demo begins, an assassin from the audience points a gun—made of flesh and bone—at Allegra. Screaming "Death to the demoness!" he shoots and wounds her, apparently because she's such a dangerously subversive mind bender. Allegra flees with PR nerd Ted Pikul (Jude Law), who later cuts the bullet out of her shoulder, discovering that it's not a bullet but a human tooth.

The flesh-and-bone gun that shoots teeth, the pulsing flesh pod, the amphibian farm where nervous systems are harvested, and the mutated, hybridized lizard creatures—all proclaim Cronenberg's devotion to surrealism, the anti-realist, anti-mainstream artistic movement of the early

1900s. Like surrealism, these images—and the film as a whole—juxtapose distant realities and create counter-worlds populated by counter-identities. Cronenberg visualizes the absurd, the grotesque, and the irrational—what surrealist philosopher André Breton calls "the marvelous." Cronenberg's movies also share with surrealism an emotional attack that provokes shock, surprise, and discomfort. Overall, the cyberspace urge grows out of a surrealist desire to free the mind, overcome spatial and temporal limitations, and inhabit alternative realms—the world of subconscious impulses, psychotic hallucinations, or drug-induced dreams. "Surrealism is based on the belief in the superior reality of certain forms of previously neglected associations, in the omnipotence of dreams and the disinterested play of thought," says Breton in the "Manifesto of Surrealism."[63] As we've seen, cyberspace promises a technological escape from everyday reality and becomes a kind of dream space, a visualization of the subconscious, a waking hallucination. Allegra and Ted, a confused couple on the run, spend their first night in a motel, where they eat fast food purchased from "Perky Pat's"—an allusion to *The Three Stigmata of Palmer Eldritch.* Thus Cronenberg signals that *eXistenZ* transpires in a surreal Philip K. Dick universe and that we should not expect to be certain of the distinction between the real and the surreal.

Allegra—the VR-addicted game-goddess—gets depressed and annoyed when not plugged into *eXistenZ.* She mocks Ted as a game "virgin," who even lacks a bioport. Cronenberg alters gender stereotypes by making the woman comfortable with technology while the man expresses insecurity and unease. In spite of his fears of physical penetration, Ted agrees to get the spinal hole so he can join her in the joys of playing *eXistenZ.* The sexual nature of the meta-flesh pods is more fully revealed as Gas (Willem Dafoe) drills Ted with a huge gun-like "stud finder." When Allegra prepares to plug Ted into the system, she suggestively licks the end of the "UmbyCord" before inserting it in Ted's new bioport. Following suit, Ted wets the cord before plugging it into Allegra, then says, "That wasn't me—it was my game character!" The rape of his body causes a technological takeover of Ted's mind, a loss of identity. Further, the sexual nature of this intrusion literalizes the process through which new entertainment machines—from VCRs to broadband Internet—penetrate the culture as tools of sexual titillation.

At the end, they come under attack by "The Realist Underground." But the game suddenly takes another twist that destroys the boundary between the real and the artificial. Allegra, Ted, and several familiar faces from the apparent game world slowly wake up in a church where they have been beta testing a new game, *tranCendenZ.* Allegra is not really a celebrity game designer; Ted is not really a heroic savior. We don't know who they are. In cyberspace, the self is terminally lost in this constantly transforming world where reality no longer exists.

While embracing surrealism, the irrational, and the grotesque, *eXistenZ*—like *Videodrome*—metaphorically foreshadows a grim future where man and machine blend into amalgams of pulsating flesh and invasive mechanics. In contrast to techno-utopian illusions of cyberspace nirvana, "*eXistenZ* confronts its heroes and its viewers with the flesh in visceral, sometimes disgusting, forms, it does not feed fantasies of mental escape from the body,"[64] says Cynthia Freeland in her article "Penetrating Keanu." A scathing satire on advanced gaming technology, *eXistenZ* and *Videodrome* reflect techno-anxieties about the literal penetration of entertainment and media technologies into our bodies, our nervous systems, our lives. While not completely embracing the flesh, Cronenberg expresses the horrific side of our passive slide into cyborgism and technological enslavement.

A virtual reality generator, the *Star Trek* holodeck—like all *Star Trek* technology—works flawlessly despite its incredible complexity.[65] Speak a command and instantly summon interactive artificial people, environments, historical periods, or fictional realities, such as that of *Beowulf,* that are indistinguishable from actual reality. Introduced in the premiere episode of *Star Trek: The Next Generation,* "Encounter at Farpoint" (1987), the holodeck becomes the favored method of starship entertainment. While male users often get more emotionally involved with the artificial holodeck females than with their real *Enterprise* colleagues, they do not slip into self-destructive obsession with cyberspace like the cyberpunks. In fact, Lt. Commander LaForge lectures weak-willed Reggie Barclay (Dwight Schultz) on the dangers of holographic addiction in "Hollow Pursuits" (*TNG,* 1990). In a nod to Asimov's Laws of Robotics, holodecks are programmed with safety protocols to prevent human users from being hurt or killed. When the holodeck goes offline, so do the holo-people. However, a technical glitch occurs in the episode "Elementary My Dear Data" (*TNG,* 1988) that permits a virtual reality entity to exist independently of the holodeck.

In order to outsmart Data, who loves the Sherlock Holmes holodeck program, the computer designs a wickedly clever opponent—a Moriarty character with power, independence, and consciousness, a sentient artificial creature like the holographic Doctor Zimmerman in *Star Trek: Voyager.* Moriarty overcomes the holodeck safety restrictions and threatens the ship, demanding that he be given a material existence outside his cyberspace prison. Contrary to the anti-flesh cyber-priests' craving for virtual existence as electronic angels, Moriarty craves a body and disparages disembodiment. Like Data or Asimov's Bicentennial Man, he wants to be human.

Eventually Moriarty realizes the impossibility of his order and accepts defeat, requesting "to be recalled if a process for solidifying holodeck creations into real matter is ever found." The captain graciously agrees, knowing full well that this will never happen.

Five years later, the Moriarty hologram software returns to life in "Ship in a Bottle" (1993). Once again demanding embodiment, Moriarty is duped into believing he's been beamed to a real shuttlecraft. In fact he's been downloaded into a memory cube, programmed for years of illusory space exploration. Again, things on the *Enterprise* return to normal. Showing not a twinge of guilt about deluding this sentient being and trapping him in a simulation, Picard disingenuously waxes philosophical about being "a fiction playing itself out on a box on someone's table." Except in the case of the hive-mind Borg, technology never seriously threatens *Star Trek*'s humans as the television show reinforces the Asimov fantasy that machines must always succumb to humanity's control.

CYBERSPACE HELL:
DIGITAL IMMORTALITY

Besides their intimate connection to weapons development and military training, cyberspace technologies are driven by the divine aspirations of Technologists. As we've seen, the central dogma underlying these heavenly dreams is the cybernetic belief that a human mind— thoughts, attitudes, memories—consists entirely of information patterns that can be digitized and transferred into a computer, which will sustain that mind-pattern identity forever in a pleasurable virtual environment. Yet the dream of digitized immortality in an engineered heaven is often treated as a curse in science fiction, as in *Software* and *Neuromancer*. Stagnation, alienation, and confusion characterize the immortals in these stories.

Anticipating scientific dreams of computerized immortality, Arthur C. Clarke's 1956 novella *The City and the Stars* envisions Diaspar—a society of technologized reincarnation that preserves individual identity. The inhabitants live a simulated life, stored as patterns of information in a synthetic environment—"an artificial womb"—designed, engineered, and controlled by computer.[66] Periodically, the Central Computer returns them to material existence. They live for a thousand years and then are reinstated within the computer's memory banks. Technology controls a pathologically dependent humanity trapped in a cybernetic prison of its own construction. The city is unchanging, stagnant. People experience a computer-induced illusion of life. Immortality has been achieved at a great cost: these posthumans lack basic drives such as sex, love, ambition, and curiosity. They survive but don't evolve. The inhabitants are bored and boring.

In *Permutation City* (1994), Greg Egan imagines a near future when a person's mind can be copied, digitized, and downloaded to a global computer network.[67] He elaborates the unpleasant existential, psychological, and technological effects of immortal digital existence for these "Copies." The novel opens in 2045 with the "awakening" of an early Copy whose first thought is: "*I don't want to be here.*"[68] The mental duplicate of scientist Paul Durham, the Copy wants out. Copies were given a bail-out option and, up to that time, they all took it. "They'd just ranted abuse, whined about their plight, and then terminated themselves—all within fifteen (subjective) minutes of gaining consciousness."[69] The Durham copy will follow in their suicidal footsteps. "*I'm nothing: a dream, a soon-to-be-forgotten dream.*"[70] But the termination software fails. In order to conduct experiments, the real Durham removed his Copy's suicide option, trapping him forever in the simulacrum. Durham 2 must fight off panic, loneliness, and claustrophobia.

Although they are duplicates of society's elite, even the richest Copies must "live" at a slow rate as a result of the expensive computer processing speeds required for their never-ending simulation. Real humans—living at a normal speed—rarely have time to interact with Copies, who become painfully isolated and alienated from external reality. Technologically vulnerable, these digital entities depend for their survival on computer network stability. Without legal rights, the Copies are economically and, therefore, existentially insecure. Most are doomed to constant, never-ending anxiety. A Copy is cut off from reality, so that his family, friends, and memories become meaningless. One Copy characterizes her total solitude as being "buried alive"—"Everything she'd ever known had been ground down into random noise."[71] As their identities fragment, Copies lose a coherent sense of themselves. Permutations of the same character exist in alternative forms—digital copies and clones of copies. One Copy—retaining the guilt-ridden pathology of its original—describes its own condemnation to an eternity of self-hatred as "being cast in Hell, without so much as a glimpse of Heaven."[72]

The techno-utopian promise of ascension into a virtual reality heaven turns out to be a "descent into the abyss of immortality."[73] Without mortality, there is no time. All moments become equal. "When time becomes eternal, its passing is rendered meaningless," says Ross Farnell in his analysis of *Permutation City*.[74] Given endless time, Copies exhaust all activities. Everything becomes trivial—making a thousand table legs or writing a thousand operas are equivalent activities. Nothing will ever bring a sense of closure. "The constant expansion promises 'eternal growth,' but delivers a feedback loop of repetition," Farnell asserts, "thus questioning the value of immortality."[75] Beyond this, *Permutation City*—like Rucker's *Software* (see Chapter Four)—raises doubts about whether a Copy's existence could be considered true immortality. Since a Copy can be made and downloaded while the organic progenitor still exists in the real world, a Copy is a reproduction, a simulation—not the same person. If a Copy is not the same person, then the techno-prophets' vision of immortality through duplication and download is a meaningless religious fantasy and a mere propaganda tool.

CYBERSPACE HELL 2: SLAVES TO THE MACHINE

Virtual reality and artificial intelligence technophobia fuel *The Matrix* (1999)—written and directed by Andy and Larry Wachowski—which condemns invasive, out-of-control technology. Referencing ancient religions, fairy tales, 60s psychedelia, cyberpunk, surrealist art, and trendy intellectualism, *The Matrix* (1999) expresses a fearful, anxious perspective on technology: its autonomous essence and its invisible, pervasive domination of our lives. Released in the same year as two other virtual reality movies—*eXistenZ* and *The Thirteenth Floor,* both of which were commercial flops—*The Matrix* earned $460 million worldwide and became a genuine cultural phenomenon. At least four books and oceans of Internet analysis have been published concerning the movie's philosophy and religion.[76] Two disappointing sequels, *The Matrix Reloaded* and *Matrix Revolutions,* were released in 2003.

In *The Matrix,* humans have lost the war against artificially intelligent robots that revolted against human exploitation and oppression. In a final attempt to destroy the sun-powered machines, humans have scorched the sky with nuclear weapons.[77] So the machines have developed another power source—human bodies. Harvested rather than born, millions of people lie trapped within nutrient-fed pods that are piled into high towers and plugged into the parasitic machines to provide energy. Mere batteries, these humans—unaware of true reality—live an illusory life in the matrix, a simulation of 1999 reality generated directly into their brains by the machines in order to keep control of their human slaves. Perceiving a neurophysiological and phenomenological experience identical to that produced by everyday material reality, the inhabitants of this mentally induced world do not realize that they are actually living out their existence as bodies

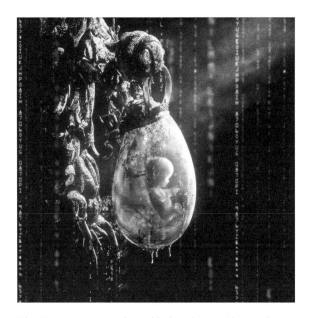

The Matrix: *Born into electrical-biological cocoons, humans have become slaves to the machine (Courtesy Photofest).*

in a vat, prisoners of the machine. In *The Matrix,* artificiality has achieved the full status of earthly reality. The invisible, mind-dominating machine-tyrant represents the role of technology in our lives.

One of these unconscious people, Thomas Anderson (Keanu Reeves), lives a double life as a criminal computer hacker and as a software engineer for a big Microsoft-like corporation. Awakened by a group of human rebels who have cracked through the matrix and who believe in him as the cyber-savior Neo, Anderson learns that his identity is an illusion. Morpheus (Laurence Fishburne) — the rebel leader — shows Anderson that what he perceives as reality is a neural interactive simulation, the matrix, produced by godlike artificial intelligences whose machine agents he must defeat. As Morpheus puts it, "The matrix is everywhere. . . . It is the world that has been pulled over your eyes to blind you from the truth . . . that you, like everyone else, was born into bondage, kept inside a prison that you cannot smell, taste, or touch. A prison for your mind."

Aside from being a metaphor for the dominance of technology, *The Matrix* alludes to Plato's "Allegory of the Cave" and to the Gnostic vision of an evil Demiurge who created a flawed world in which to imprison mankind. *The Matrix* also references fairy tales and fantasies, especially *Alice in Wonderland*—a literary precursor to the concept of virtual reality and to the hallucinatory experience of tripping on psychedelic drugs. Morpheus tells Neo to "follow the white rabbit" and offers him a choice of two pills, one red and the other blue, saying, "You take the red pill and you stay in Wonderland and I show you how deep the rabbit hole goes." Neo's Alice-in-Wonderland trip back to "reality" results from his choosing to swallow the red pill. Morpheus later says, "I can show you the door but you must walk through it," echoing Aldous Huxley's mescaline book *Doors of Perception*. Passing through the door, in *The Matrix,* means passing through the doors of false perception into true reality or surreality.

Like *eXistenZ, The Matrix* derives its anti-mainstream political stance and some striking images from surrealism. For example, Anderson gets emasculated and loses his mouth like the repressed anti-hero of Luis Buñuel and Salvador Dali's quintessential surrealist film, *Un Chien Andalou* (1928). *The Matrix* also adapts a mirror motif that references both Lewis Carroll's *Through the Looking Glass* and Jean Cocteau's surrealist psychodrama *Blood of a Poet* (1930). When Morpheus reveals the nature of the matrix to the shocked Anderson/Neo, the latter's shattered personality is symbolized as a fragmented reflection in a jagged mirror. Neo then passes through the mirror to see true reality, just as the tortured artist in *Blood of a Poet* passes through a mirror to find truth in his subconscious.

The matrix symbolizes everyday reality—the world in which we live. Like Thomas Anderson, we work to earn money and compromise ourselves to the system (as Anderson is pressured to do) for the sake of our survival. In a sense, we are slaves, prisoners of our own minds as conditioned by the technological and corporate information-environment. While not yet brains in a vat, we ignore how synthetic our existence has become as we increasingly spend time in the artificial worlds of cyberspace. We seem to have lost control over our future. The system lulls us to sleep with images and gadgets produced by powerful corporations that saturate us with advertisements, engendering artificial needs and desires. As Richard DeGrandpre says in *Digitopia*, "[E]ven if the digital revolution were brought to a halt today, millions of people would remain caught in an existential limbo, torn between the artificial dreams of simulated reality and the old-fashioned world in which they try to live them out."[78]

The *Matrix* warns against surrendering control of our lives to technology, giving up our bodies to machines. It asserts the superiority of the human qualities of Neo, Trinity (Carrie Ann Moss), and Morpheus over the technological mega-system and its agents. In *The Matrix,* the techno-utopians are represented by the sentient artificial constructs, such as Agent Smith (Hugo Weaving), who expresses hatred for humans and their smelly ways. A cyber-Gnostic, Agent Smith wants a perfect world. "Human beings are a disease, a cancer of this planet. You are a plague. And we are . . . the cure," he says. In the end, Neo wants to fulfill his messianic objectives and destroys Agent Smith. Thus, the stage is set for the liberation (unplugging) of humanity. But do people want to be free? *The Matrix* challenges us with a philosophical problem: Is it better to rage against the machine and live as a free and informed, but lonely and deprived, individual outside the virtual reality womb? Or is it better to live in "decadence" within the relatively plush but totally simulated and machine-controlled theater of the matrix? Morpheus urges Neo, "Free your mind"—which is really a call to assert political freedom from the tyrant technology.

At the end of *The Matrix,* Trinity tells the apparently dead Neo that she loves him. As in a fairy tale, her kiss resurrects him so he may continue to fight the machines. *The Matrix Reloaded* (2003)—also written and directed by the Wachowski brothers—opens with Trinity, in her gleaming black leather cat-suit, sailing spectacularly over a wall on a motorcycle, somersaulting into a building, and taking out a bunch of guards. A few seconds later, she bursts through a window and plummets backward down the side of a skyscraper while firing at an agent, her death imminent. Terrified, Neo wakes from this premonitory dream cozy in bed with Trinity. Their love blossoms throughout the movie until, at the end, the smitten Neo chooses to save Trinity from death, rather than the thousands of human inhabitants of Zion, whom he nevertheless saves anyway—he's the messiah, after all. In *The Matrix Reloaded,* love—and a strong dose of ultra-violence—temporarily stops the machines.

In the six months since the end of *The Matrix,* apparently due to the unplugging efforts of Neo, Zion's human population has grown significantly. Unfortunately, the machines have sent an attack squad of 250,000 Sentinels—squid-like robots—to destroy it. While Zion's leaders prepare for war, Morpheus, Trinity, and Neo—who now resembles a priest in his black monkish cassock and clerical collar—return to the matrix to consult with the Oracle (Gloria Foster), hoping to learn how to fulfill the prophecy that will save humanity. She urges them to find the Key Maker (Randall Duk Kim), who can take him to "the Source"—the inner core —of the simulated universe. On the way, Neo battles new technological forces—anomalous software, programming bugs, systemic glitches, and new machine-agents, such as the suave but deadly Merovingian (Lambert Wilson), his sexy, seductive wife, Persephone (Monica Bellucci), and the platinum-dreadlocked ghostly albino twins (Neil and Adrian Rayment). Neo also confronts an old adversary that now represents a totally autonomous technology—the annoyingly persistent Agent Smith, now capable of endless self-reproduction. Though considerably amplified, *Reloaded* repeats the first movie's human/machine confrontations in cyberspace.

Contrasted with the artificiality of the matrix is the reality of the humans' refuge. Populated largely by African-Americans, Zion—located "near the Earth's core where there is more heat"—resembles a multi-leveled, corroded-iron-girder shopping mall in Thunderdome. This is where the Real People plan their guerrilla war against the machines. Unlike the fashionably dressed matrix denizens, the humans in Zion wear disintegrating sweatshirts reminiscent of the audience apparel at a Grateful Dead concert. Morpheus brings these deadhead hordes to life with a pontificating pep talk urging resistance to the tunneling Sentinels: "Tonight, let us tremble these walls. This is Zion—and WE ARE NOT AFRAID!" The multicultural masses turn the People's Republic of Zion into the World of Groove, breaking out in a primitive, percussion-driven, frenzied bacchanal, which is interspersed with Neo and Trinity having sex. This is apparently supposed to suggest the primal "authenticity" of these humans, in contrast to the repressed, passionless uniformity of machine-agents like Smith.

In a revealing visit to Zion's massive engineering room, housing the industrial-era technology that supports the city, a Council Elder acknowledges to Neo the paradox that humans and machines often exist in a kind of symbiosis. Unlike its predecessor, *Reloaded* hints at a distinction between the older industrial technology, which operates placidly to maintain human civilization, and the new, artificially intelligent, self-reproducing, autonomous technology that now dominates humanity. This reflects technology critic Bill Joy's contention in "Why the Future Doesn't Need Us" that our attitude toward new technology is based on "our bias toward instant familiarity and unquestioning acceptance" of older technologies. He argues that we have failed to come to terms with the fact that they (the new technologies) "pose a different threat than the technologies that have come before."[79]

Unfortunately, the third and supposedly final installment of the series does not address this threat but rather creates a new, less interesting one. *Matrix Revolutions* (2003) continues where *Reloaded* finished, with the besieged humans of Zion preparing for Armageddon as thousands of metallic squid-squadrons advance. Meanwhile, Neo embarks on a rash adventure into the heart of Machine City in order to open another front on the war against techno-tyranny. But the final battle between man and machine does not culminate, despite the Oracle's platitude "everything that has a beginning has an end." The human armies of Zion confront the swarming hordes of steel squids using giant exoskeletons, like the one used by Ripley at the end of *Aliens*. But their last-ditch battle against technological obliteration gets superseded by Neo's fight with the now tedious Agent Smith, who turns out to be the ultimate villain—the anti-human, anti-machine third force who has multiplied beyond comprehension, asserted complete autonomy, and become a threat to all. Though it makes no philosophical or metaphorical sense, Neo fulfills his messianic mission by destroying Smith on behalf of both species, thereby "balancing the world." The end is somewhat reminiscent of *Metropolis,* in which, after lots of sound and fury, technological power remains intact. In *Matrix Revolutions,* the ending leaves millions of organic human batteries still plugged into the matrix, still supplying power to the machines, and still enslaved to the technological tyrant. In *The Matrix OnLine* (2005), SEGA's massively multiplayer online game, the war against autonomous technology resumes.

While battling the machines inside the matrix, Neo, Trinity, and Morpheus use their minds to enhance their power in cyberspace. Neo eventually learns to stop bullets and to fly, among other feats of prowess. In this way, the *Matrix* movies—like most of the fiction considered in this chapter—metaphorically acknowledge the potential of cyberspace to enhance human capability and intelligence. Though granting an empowering capacity, science fiction visions of cyberspace often reveal it to be an "infinite cage," in the words of William Gibson.[80] While *The Matrix* eventually tempers the techno-anxiety it reflects by establishing the supremacy of the real, other works, such as *The Three Stigmata of Palmer Eldritch, Videodrome,* and *eXistenZ,* refuse to provide the security of a solid, reliable reality. They all express a vision of the fears that this digital world generates, including the diminution of love, physical intimacy, social interaction, and even our self-awareness as more and more of our activities are mediated by computer networks. Finally, these works express anxiety about the idea of immortality in silicon and what will be lost if, in the words of Tim Jordan, "the connection between mind and body is given up for a connection between mind and machine."[81]

The techno-utopian vision of immortality in cyberspace heaven depends on the belief that everything, including life, can be reduced to information. Biology reinforces this belief. The basic substance of life consists of the programming code of DNA. The sequencing of the human genome raises the new possibility that computers will be used to explore, manipulate, and ultimately change that code to create new species of posthumans. As usual, the techno-utopians promise that the changes will be good for us, leading to perfection.

SEVEN Engineered Flesh

BIOTECHNOLOGY

The first human clone was born on the day after Christ's birthday, December 26, 2002, claimed Brigitte Boisselier, chief executive of Clonaid, an offshoot of the transhumanist sect the Raelians.[1] Imaginatively nicknamed Eve, the baby was not present at the press conference, and its existence was treated as both a hoax and the occasion for virulent denunciations of cloning. "The very attempt to clone a human being is evil," said Duke University professor of theological ethics Stanley M. Hauerwas. "That the allegedly cloned child is to be called Eve confirms the godlike stature these people so desperately seek."[2] Proof of the human cloning was not forthcoming as promised, though a month later, in a Fort Lauderdale court, Boisselier insisted under oath that the baby exists and that other clones had been born.[3] Despite the controversy, many scientists consider human cloning inevitable.[4]

Along with cloning, the 2000 completion of the Human Genome Project—which mapped the genetic instructions that orchestrate human development—accelerates the biotechnological revolution into warp drive and opens the door to a vast new biological landscape. "The most significant event in our history, and perhaps in the 3.5 billion-year history of life on Earth," proclaims University of California Professor Pierre Baldi in *The Shattered Self*.[5] Genetic manipulation, eugenics, disease-fighting gene therapy, and the fusion of different species create momentous possibilities. Less than fifty years after Watson and Crick's discovery of DNA's fundamental message-bearing structure, biotechnology promises to transform humanity more profoundly in the near future than has occurred in human history. We are confronted with new and unique bioethical dilemmas as well as critical questions about the nature of life, intelligence, and humanity.

Unlike the previously discussed cyborg technologies that reject the human body as spoiled meat and strive to replace it, the new medical technologies—while still dismissing the human body as badly flawed—strive to transform it. In this vision of the posthuman, scientists want to engineer evolution at the molecular level to improve the species. Parallel to these techno-perfectionist dreams, a burgeoning, largely unregulated worldwide biotech market—offering everything from facilities for human cloning to the sperm of Nobel laureates—has been created: "a market that will be the arena within which most future advances of genetic engineering will take place, determined strictly by market demand," says techno-pusher Christopher Dewdney in *The Last Flesh*.[6]

Biotech critics like Francis Fukuyama, Jeremy Rifkin, and Bill Joy, as well as political groups like Greenpeace, want more regulation. They raise a host of concerns, such as the disappearance of bio-diversity, the inappropriate patenting of genes, the destruction of natural food, the use of gene therapy for eugenic purposes, and genetic pollution resulting from the release of genetically modified organisms into the environment. "Genetic engineering represents our fondest hopes and aspirations," says Jeremy Rifkin, "as well as our darkest fears and misgivings."[7] Science fiction elaborates those dark fears; bio-scientists, techno-priests, and transhumanists wildly exaggerate the hopes and aspirations into propaganda for anarchic biotech expansion.

THE POWER OF PERFECTION: CYBERNETIC DREAMS OF THE NEW FLESH

The dream of mastery over life coincided with the rise of cybernetics, computers, and artificial intelligence. Building on the hereditary theories of Augustinian monk Gregor Mendel and the gene-as-machine concepts of quantum mechanics founder Erwin Schrödinger, microbiologists James D. Watson and Francis Crick launched the science of genetics in 1953. They discovered DNA's double-helix structure and suggested that DNA carries, in coded form, the genetic information for life. "No sooner had Watson and Crick published their breakthrough than the DNA molecule came to be universally seen as something like a tiny cybernetic apparatus that stored and processed microscopic bits of chemically encoded data," says Theodore Roszak in *The Cult of Information*.[8] As cybernetic pioneers developed systems for coding and processing information in machines, nuclear geneticists unlocked nature's method of coding information in living systems. Thus, the cybernetic model of people as machines was reinforced by the new biology. Watson and Crick supplied a startling example of how life itself could be generated from mere bits of data—automation at the molecular level, with the cell as a tiny computer and DNA as the software. This establishment of cybernetics as a common language for computers and biology provided the framework for using computers to manipulate the genetic code of living beings.

The technological knowledge to simulate and enhance the power of humans, through robotics, artificial intelligence, and now biology, gave impetus to cybernetic dreams of heaven on earth. As David Noble puts it, "The pursuit of perfection through the hardware and software of machines was soon extended to the actual 'wetware' of life itself, viewed as merely another sort of machine . . . the modern magi were now prepared to bring their technological prowess to bear upon the stuff of life itself."[9] Hatred of the flesh found expression in the religious desire of genetic scientists to control evolution and restore humanity to its original perfection.

DNA became the sacred instrument through which the techno-priests would produce this divine transformation. "The double helix has replaced the cross in the biological alphabet," said chemist Erwin Chargaff.[10] This view of DNA as a sacred entity, conferring divine power on the scientist, became widespread. As Dorothy Nelkin and M. Susan Lindee observe in *The DNA Mystique,* geneticists often use transcendent or religious metaphors to describe DNA, such as the "Bible," the "Book of Man," or the "sacred text that can explain the natural and moral order."[11] Such religious imagery made DNA a life-defining substance and the new material basis for the immortality and resurrection of the soul. "DNA spelled God," says David Noble, "and the scientists' knowledge of DNA was a mark of their divinity."[12]

The initial goal of contemporary saintly scientists is to first create renewable, then immortal, superhumans. Tissue engineering—extracting a sample of cells and growing them to form new tissues or whole organs—promises to repair and even replace damaged body parts. Skin, bone, and cartilage products are already on the market; engineered bladders, livers, lungs, and heart valves are in development.[13] A.I. pioneer Marvin Minsky predicted in a 1994 *Scientific American* article that even our gray matter will be upgraded. "In the end, we will find ways to replace every part of the body and brain—and thus repair all the defects and flaws that make our lives so brief. Needless to say, in doing so, we'll be making ourselves into machines."[14] Human Genome Science's CEO, William Haseltine, joins Minsky in making far-reaching claims about what molecular biology will achieve, arguing that "as we understand the body's repair process at the genetic level . . . we will be able to advance the goal of maintaining our bodies in normal function, perhaps perpetually."[15] The dream of immortality burns brightly in the hearts of the new bio-technophiles. Christopher Dewdney proclaims the cyber-hype: "Arguably neither immortality nor the 'soul' exists in the real world, but technology might just make it possible for us to secure the existence of both in the future."[16]

While some techno-prophets believe immortality might be attained through cloning, this is not likely. The identity of the original person would cease at death unless a Minsky-style brain transplant or Moravec-style mind transfer could be implemented. Regardless, even before announcing the first human clone, the Raelian Movement set up a cloning service.[17] Clonaid charges "as low as $200,000" to clone a child.[18] For an extra $50,000, Insuraclone provides facilities to store cell samples from your loved ones so in the event of death, a copy of the beloved can be cloned. Of course, then you must raise and support your "mother" or "uncle," who will, post-cloning, be an infant.

When the cloning of humans occurs, it will bring no new genetic compositions into being, but will duplicate the genetic compositions of people who already exist. "The idea of a delayed identical twin is strange and unfamiliar, but not earthshattering," asserts University of California researcher and techno-prophet Gregory Stock in *Redesigning Humans.*[19] But the arrival of safe germline technology—the manipulation of our germinating cells (egg or sperm) to modify future generations—"will signal the beginning of human self-design. These developments will write a new page in the history of life," says Stock, "allowing us to seize control of our evolutionary future."[20] Germline engineering endows the scientist with the power to redefine humanity, creating what Stock calls "Metaman."[21] By improving human biology, manipulating life, controlling evolution, and engineering the perfect posthuman future, scientists share in divine knowledge and canonize themselves as God's collaborators in creation.

GILL-MEN AND RHINO-SOLDIERS: THE MILITARIZATION OF BIOTECHNOLOGY

Biological warfare ordinarily refers to germ warfare—the use of natural or engineered pathogens as weapons. This will be part of Chapter Nine's focus on the viral threat to posthuman existence. Here I want to examine nonlethal but war-related uses of biotechnology. "Some of the world's farthest-out, cutting-edge, and high-technodazzle biotech thinking is now being done not by scientists and academics, but by the *military,*" said Ed Regis after attending the 1996 military-sponsored "Biotechnology Workshop 2020."[22] Though they do the financing, the military recruits the biotech industry and university researchers to do the work of developing the technology. This academic-industrial-military complex shapes the country's scientific research while closing itself to public scrutiny.

The U.S. Army established the blandly named California Institute for Collaborative Biotechnologies in 2003 to do military-related research headquartered at the University of California, Santa Barbara. The Army initially granted $50 million to fulfill its techno-dreams, including an organic superman uniform that automatically alters its color for camouflage, hardens for bullet protection, and makes the wearer invisible to various sensors. Among other things, the Army wants skin-like vehicle armor as well as armor-like human skin that heals itself, anti-material microbes that will eat rubber and consume silicon, and protein-based computers the size of an M&M.[23] Several DARPA initiatives, including the previously mentioned Bio:Info:Micro Program (see Chapter Five) and the Advanced Biomedical Technologies Program, also focus on funding university research in these areas.[24]

Spurred by the 9/11 attack and the subsequent anthrax mailings, the U.S. Defense Department reached out to the biotech industry. In April 2002, a conference in Washington, D.C., brought together more than 350 entrepreneurs, government contractors, and military officials in the hope of extending the military-industrial complex to biotechnology companies. According to the *Washington Post*, "Thirty-six biotech companies pitched potential products with such varied applications as wound healing, memory enhancement and environmental decontamination."[25] The Defense Department—using the Internet as its chief example—argued that solving military problems could lead to commercial products and services that would ultimately profit the biotech industry.

The most spectacular military ambitions for biotech weaponry, short of pathogens, center on modifying a soldier's body as part of the military system. In the 2001 *Star 21* report, "Strategic Technologies for the Army of the Twenty-First Century," the National Research Council's Board on Army Science and Technology outlines a wild-eyed approach to performance-enhanced supersoldiers that includes genome modification, gene splicing, and cell fusion. Ed Regis suggests that humans might be engineered for defensive or stealth traits, such as soldiers with gills for staying underwater or hard-shell skin armor, like a rhinoceros's, that would reject bullets. In addition, *Star 21* urges other cyberpunk-like human physique developments, including enhanced musculature, night vision, and computer chip–enhanced brains. As the *Star 21* report notes, "Because the soldier is a biological system, biotechnology offers unique potential for enhancing the performance of the most complex, critical and costly of the Army's systems."[26]

Defining humans as biological systems reinforces the cybernetic view of humans as information systems. This is an example of technological politics—technology's power, in the words of Langdon Winner, "to transform, order, and adapt animate and inanimate objects to accord with the purely technical structures and processes."[27] The reduction of a person to a string of genetic code makes the re-engineering of human beings more palatable, helping to disguise the repulsiveness of a species hybrid like a Gill-Man or a Rhino-Soldier. While these specific transgenic species may never be created, the military provides the financing and the rationale—national defense—that encourage experimental gene splicing and promote its legitimacy. Beyond this, military and corporate redefinitions of the body—abstracting, fragmenting, reducing, decontextualizing, commodifying it—also encourage scientists to extract, procure, exploit, and patent body tissue for profit, without regard for an individual's personal desires. Human bodies are a significant and growing part of the $17 billion biotechnology industry.[28] "There is something new, strange, and troubling about the traffic in body tissue, the banking of human cells, and the patenting of genes," say Lori Andrews and Dorothy Nelkin in *Body Bazaar*. "Biotechnological uses risk running roughshod over social values and personal beliefs."[29]

AS REMORSELESS AS NATURE: THE MAD GENETICIST CONTROLS EVOLUTION

The visions of a posthuman future that are developed in science fiction about biological engineering express anxieties central to a society shaped by rapidly changing technological and scientific capabilities. Often questioning the effects and the desirability of their implementation, these works express a profound concern about technologies that purport to perfect the body and control evolution. A theme that appeared at an early stage—the fear of redesigning human beings through vivisection—made its most famous appearance in H. G. Wells's novel *The Island of Dr. Moreau* (1896).[30] Several film adaptations followed—*The Island of Lost Souls* in 1932 and more recently, with its original title, in 1977 and 1996. Each new version incorporates advances in biotechnology.

In Wells's original story, a mad vivisector, Dr. Moreau—following in the bloody footprints of Dr. Frankenstein—wants to create a rational creature, control evolution, and improve humanity by stitching together men and animals. While Wells himself was a "technical optimist," according to science writer Jon Turney, *The Island of Dr. Moreau* reads as an attack on the extremes of scientific rationalism, human engineering, eugenics, and animal dissection.[31] "The picture Wells draws of Moreau, orchestrating his cruel parody of natural selection," says Turney, "is deliberately that of the modern scientist, stripped of all fellow-feeling for other creatures, and of ethical qualms."[32] Wells warned against the scientific, dehumanizing mutation of our world into Dr. Moreau's island.

The Island of Lost Souls, the first cinematic version of Wells's story, retained Dr. Moreau (Charles Laughton) as an evil vivisectionist, but more closely followed the cinematic adaptation of *Frankenstein*—especially the ending, in which the "Beast People" revolt, force Moreau to the "House of Pain" surgical lab, and slice him up with his own scalpel. Reflecting advances in biotechnology, the 1977 version of *The Island of Dr. Moreau* partly replaces surgical manipulation with genetic manipulation to accelerate evolution.[33] Dr. Moreau (Burt Lancaster) injects animals with a serum containing "a biological code message, a new set of instructions for modifying nature." He supplements the serum with old-fashioned surgical procedures and, like the previous Moreaus, relies on his whip as a teaching tool. However, the results of these new techniques—grotesque, bloodthirsty, grunting animal people—exhibit no improvement.

The 1996 film *The Island of Dr. Moreau,* directed by John Frankenheimer and set in the present day, substituted genetic engineering for vivisection and surgical grafting. Renegade geneticist and Nobel Prize winner Dr. Moreau (Marlon Brando) has been chased out of the United States by "animal rights advocates" and forced to set up his gene-splicing operation on a remote island. Absurdly wearing white diapers, a flowing white toga, a hat fashioned from nurse's support hose, and kabuki makeup for sun protection, Moreau gets carried around on a modified pope-mobile. Instead of using a whip, he controls the manimals through electronics: he presses on a small keyboard, worn around his neck, and administers painful shocks to the beasts via a wireless connection to chip implants in their brains. Assisted by psycho junkie Montgomery (Val Kilmer)—"a brilliant neurosurgeon reduced to a jailer"—Moreau has mixed animal and human genes to produce creatures that "represent a stage in the process of eradication of destructive elements found in the human psyche." He asserts: "I have almost achieved perfection of a divine creature—pure, harmonious, absolutely incapable of malice." Accused of Satanism, he casually characterizes the devil "as a tiresome collection of genes" that he has cut to pieces under the microscope.

Aside from torturing animals and humans, he becomes a monster by viewing the body as an object, as raw material—cells, organs, tissues, genes—to be manipulated and reshaped. Like contemporary genetic scientists,

Moreau redefines and decontextualizes the human body, thus encouraging insensitivity to its human relationships, purposes, and values, while masquerading as a noble humanitarian scientist and reassuring critics that he desires only to help a flawed humanity. With his surgical, cybernetic, and genetic reshaping of the human body, Moreau connects to a long history of crazed creators of artificial humans (see Chapter Two).

The mad scientists of popular culture, prior to World War II, "strikingly anticipate," in the words of David Skal, the real-life horror of Nazi doctor Josef Mengele (the Death Angel of Auschwitz), "and his shadow looms over all since."[34] Mengele's evil concentration-camp experiments, cloaked in genetic goals, entailed castration and sterilization by radiation. His obsession with eye color led him to inject toxic chemicals into his victims' eyes, sometimes blinding them. As described in *The Nazi Doctors* by Robert Jay Lifton, the Nazi eugenic project carried out by Mengele was "a vision of absolute control over the evolutionary process, over the biological human future"—a vision which chillingly foreshadows the biotechnological project of today and haunts the representation of genetics in popular culture.[35] According to Lifton, Mengele "*exemplified the Nazi biological revolutionary.*"[36] Nazi high priest Heinrich Himmler even described the Holocaust with a genetics metaphor, another example of scientific language used to conceal the horrific. He characterized the eugenic role of doctors as being "'like the plant-breeding specialist who, when he wants to breed a pure new strain from a well-tried species that has been exhausted by too much cross-breeding, first goes over the field to cull the unwanted plants.'"[37]

Josef Mengele epitomized murderous scientific fanaticism, reflecting and portending the mad scientist of horror and science fiction who wants to control evolution, perfect the human species, and, with an end-justifies-the-means rationale, subject humans to painful experiments. His dark spirit clearly inhabits the various movie versions of *The Island of Dr. Moreau.* Mengele himself shows up as a character in Ira Levin's best-selling novel *The Boys from Brazil* (1976) and its 1978 movie adaptation, which will be discussed later in the chapter. In *Blade Runner,* glasses-wearing corporate owner and geneticist Eldon Tyrell physically resembles Mengele. The Nazi doctor also impinges on the series-long conspiracy arc of *The X-Files.*

In the episode "Paperclip" (1995), fictitious Nazi scientists continue Mengele's evil genetic experimentation on human subjects under the protection of the U.S. government. FBI agents Fox Mulder (David Duchovny) and Dana Scully (Gillian Anderson), with the help of conspiracy fanatics the Lone Gunmen, identify Victor Klemper as a Nazi war criminal and participant in Project Paperclip—an actual post–World War II U.S. intelligence operation whereby German scientists, including known Nazis, were given

Boys from Brazil: *Eyeing future scientific evil, Mengele hatches an implausible plot to clone Hitler (Courtesy Photofest).*

safe haven in exchange for scientific knowledge.[38] In the *X-Files* episode, reality and fiction further intermingle when Project Paperclip is connected to the legendary 1947 U.S. government coverup of an alien spaceship crash-landing in Roswell, NM, and the capture of aliens. Scully even mentions that Klemper worked with Mengele in a concentration camp, experimenting on human subjects while trying to create an alien super-race through genetic engineering. In later episodes, Mengele's Nazi doctor buddies use alien genes to create a human/alien slave race.

The horrors of Nazi genetic technology and mad science directly influence several science fiction geneticists. In *Species* (1995), the scientists develop a human/alien hybrid and then gas it; in *Alien Resurrection* (1997), the clones get stamped with numbers reminiscent of concentration-camp tattoos; Mengele's name is invoked in "DNA Mad Scientist" (1999), an episode of the dark science fiction/fantasy series *Farscape;* finally, in an episode of *Star Trek: Voyager,* "Scientific Method" (1997), female alien scientists—resembling stereotypical German lesbians with their cropped, greased-back hair and butch outfits—manipulate the genes of the crew, producing torturous and deadly mutations. As one of the scientists says, "We don't like to cause people to suffer but sometimes it's a necessary part of our work. We're scientists."

Science fiction incorporates Mengele to remind us of the reality of scientific perfection mania, conferring real-world weight upon the fictional doctor who uses technology to torture, maim, or destroy humans as experimental subjects in the name of utopian goals. The archetypal mad scientist is often dismissed by techno-zealots as a superficial symbol of facile technophobia. They hope to cover up the iconic link to a horrific historical reality that still resonates. Like the techno-priests of today, Mengele represents a religious devotion to experimental biotechnology for eugenic purposes. In *The Nazi Doctors,* Lifton refers to the Nazi state as a "biocracy"—a term derived from "theocracy," a system of rule by a sacred order of priests under the claim of holy right. "In the case of the Nazi biocracy," he says, "the divine prerogative was that of cure through purification and revitalization of the Aryan race . . . [and] Nazi ruling authority was maintained in the name of the higher biological principle."[39] An entire network of scientists, including biologists, geneticists, doctors, and anthropologists, created the rationale for the Nazi eugenic project—a biomedical vision of racial perfection through selective breeding, genocide, and the control of evolution.

THE GENE GENIES:
ENGINEERING BETTER PEOPLE

Before the Nazi project, a eugenics movement swept Europe and America. The term *eugenics* (meaning "good genes") was coined in the nineteenth century by Sir Francis Galton, a cousin of Charles Darwin's, to describe selective breeding based on hereditary worth. Society would permit people with "desirable" qualities, or "good" genes, to have children (positive eugenics), while individuals with "undesirable" traits, or "bad" genes, would be prevented, through sterilization for example, from having children (negative eugenics).[40] "The supporters of eugenics drew heavily on the high prestige of science as an agent of progress and social change," says Jon Turney.[41] Biology, using the propaganda of species improvement, became a technology of social control and political domination.

From Britain and France, eugenic ideas spread to the United States, where they were embraced by America's "wealthiest, most powerful and most learned men against the nation's most vulnerable and helpless," says Edwin Black in *War against the Weak.* "The intent was to create a new and superior mankind."[42] By 1920, twenty-five states had enacted laws providing for compulsory sterilization of people considered genetically inferior: not only criminal insanity but poverty was considered a genetic defect. By contrast, Germany had no equivalent to these American laws, but quickly caught up, taking eugenics to its logical and genocidal extremes and disgracing the science of genetics.

Shortly before Hitler came to power in 1933, Aldous Huxley's vision of a eugenic civilization, *Brave New World,* was published. In Huxley's dystopian future, state-controlled reproduction, genetic engineering, euphoric drugs, implanted electrodes, in vitro fertilization, hormonal injections, and cybernetic conditioning are employed to suppress individuality and produce "standard men and women, in uniform batches. . . . The principles of mass production applied to biology."[43] In the novel's "Central London Hatchery and Conditioning Centre," humans are transformed into posthumans by a whole range of techniques thought to be imminent, including cloning embryos for menial labor and psychological/chemical conditioning designed to make people happy with their science-determined social destiny. A satire on utopian thinking, Huxley's novel depicts a world free from disease, depression, madness, boredom, and social conflict, but profoundly repulsive in its repressive engineering. *Brave New World*'s posthuman inhabitants no longer struggle, aspire, love, feel pain, or do any of the things associated with being human.

This profoundly pessimistic book created an immediate impact, and its powerfully dark image of biotechnology's oppressive potential reverberates even more strongly today, now that *Brave New World*'s technologies have come to fruition. As John Turney puts it: "[F]rom its first publication, the image of this particular Brave New World became one of the dominant motifs in all subsequent discussion of biological discovery—whether scholarly or popular."[44] Biotechnology opponents embrace it as the inevitable outcome of unbridled techno-lust, while biotech supporters critique it as irrelevant or impossible. A member of President Bush's bioethics team, Francis Fukuyama, adopts *Brave New World* as an overriding metaphor in his 2002 book *Our Posthuman Future: Consequences of the Biotechnology Revolution.* In fact, he devotes his work to proving that "Huxley was right, that the most significant threat posed by contemporary biotechnology is the possibility that it will alter human nature and thereby move us into a 'posthuman' stage of history," resulting in the abandonment of "our most basic values."[45]

The issue of genetic control and the posthuman future was confronted by one of science fiction's most popular writers, Robert Heinlein.[46] His 1948 novel *Beyond This Horizon* projects a utopian, disease-free, peaceful future of selective breeding. But people are so bored that they entertain themselves by comparing shades of black nail polish. They wear pistols and provoke duels to create drama. Social divisions exist between "control naturals" and those who have been selectively bred. As part of society's genetic "Star Line," protagonist Hamilton Felix represents "the careful knitting together of favorable lines over four generations."[47] The District Moderator for Genetics informs Hamilton of his social obligation to breed with his genetically prescribed woman, displaying her image to Hamilton through holographic projection. Though he finds her attractive, Hamilton refuses to cooperate. He does not want to bring children into a meaningless existence.

Recruited into a reactionary underground movement called the Survivors' Club, Hamilton discovers that they want to revert to a techno-invasive form of eugenics. They show him one result of their clandestine experiments in genetics: human children with gills. While the U.S. military might find this appealing, Hamilton rejects it as repugnant. He becomes a government agent to undermine the Survivors' Club. He also falls in love with his government-approved, genetically matched mate, who turns out to be a stimulating, gun-toting working woman. Ultimately, Hamilton helps terminate the Survivors' Club and their invasive genetic mission and finds meaning in marriage and children. He converts to the idea of a quasi-programmed existence and government-mandated gene selection while avoiding the *Brave New World* extremes of "test-tube babies, monsters formed by artificial mutation, fatherless babies . . . assembled from a hundred different parents."[48]

Though disturbing in its admiration for state-controlled evolution and a heavily armed citizenry, *Beyond This Horizon* recoils from non-corporeal techniques of reproduction and total techno-invasion of the genome. Heinlein encourages love and sex as fun, even joyful, methods of reproduction. Finally, he reasserts the human spirit, countering bio-cybernetic reductionism, to argue that "there was something more to the ego of a new-born child than its gene pattern."[49]

The Eyes of Heisenberg—a 1966 novel by *Dune* author Frank Herbert—elaborates a closed, rigidly hierarchical society resulting from genetic manipulation and cloning.[50] Government-controlled reproduction and biotechnology have radically altered the natural evolutionary process. The society is ruled—biologically, religiously, and politically—by the immortal though sterile Optimen. Formerly human, but now godlike, the Optimen are a tiresome, murderous, dictatorial bunch who give a bad name to the technophile vision of genetic manipulation and immortality. Through their scientist apologists, they've engineered, brainwashed, and drugged everyday humans (the Folk) to be the workers in this world of "gene-stamped sameness."[51] Subjected to contraceptive gassings, Folk-Parents need a breeder's license to reproduce and then only under tightly controlled and often deadly laboratory conditions.

Lurking in the shadows are the computer-brained, weaponized Cyborgs who were defeated centuries ago in a war with the Optimen. In retaliation, they will help the human Underground overthrow the High Priests of Biotech. Techno-fascists, the Cyborgs produce clones for menial tasks and hope to transform everyone into Cyborgs. The human Folk reject both technological approaches. The all-powerful Optimen collapse in the face of Cyborg violence and the sheer monotony of their immortality. A peaceful reorganization of the social order follows, releasing the human Folk from the oppressive class structure imposed on them.

The evolution of a more natural biological and social order in *The Eyes of Heisenberg* and *Beyond This Horizon* makes their futuristic vision more optimistic than the despairing forecast of doom in *Brave New World*. Heinlein and Herbert both warn that technological control of evolution will produce class divisions, political oppression, and genetic discrimination as well as physical, mental, and social stagnation. Herbert's way out is to return evolution to diversity, chance, and "indeterminacy" in order "to thwart the madness of over control and inflexibility," as Helen Parker puts it in *Biological Themes in Modern Science Fiction*.[52] Though Heinlein differs from Herbert and Huxley in the degree of eugenic gene selection he finds tolerable, all three ferociously reject technological eugenics—invasive genetic engineering that eliminates "natural" reproductive practices.

Stigmatized by the Nazis and derided by science fiction, eugenics was dead for four decades, but it reemerged as a social issue in the early 1970s with the success of new techniques to alter genes. Recombinant DNA, or rDNA, technology encouraged direct gene manipulation—assailed by Huxley, Herbert, and Heinlein. Some scientists saw the technology's potential in gene therapy whereby defective, disease-causing genes are replaced by functional ones, but gene therapy can also be used to correct and "improve" genes in sperm, eggs, or embryonic cells—germline therapy. Unlike somatic therapy, which changes genes in the individual, germline engineering passes genetic changes to future generations. With the completion of the Human Genome Project, new reproductive techniques, and advances in cloning, profit-driven scientists can reengineer evolution in accordance with military, corporate, and consumer demands.[53] In the words of Jeremy Rifkin, "a new eugenic man and woman is . . . a soon-to-be-available consumer option and a potentially lucrative commercial market."[54] Genetic enhancement, therefore, will not be determined solely by scientists, corporations, and the military, but will also be driven by capitalism, advertising, and upper-class preferences. The science fiction film *Gattaca* (1997)—directed and written by Andrew Niccol—extrapolates from today's moderate use of gene therapy to a vision of the near future, when this new form of consumer-driven eugenics exists for a privileged elite.

The parents in *Gattaca* must choose between producing a natural baby ("a faith birth") and a genetically enhanced one. Genetic modification includes everything from altering disease-causing genes to beautification and the introduction of talents and special predispositions. "The treatment of highly deleterious genetic disorders does not create public anxiety about gene therapy," says David Kirby in his analysis of *Gattaca*. "Cosmetic gene therapy, however, conjures up images of a new eugenics because it not only allows individuals to change their appearance and/or behaviors but allows these changes to be passed down to future generations."[55] Further, *Gattaca* warns about the problems, such as genetic discrimination, that will arise if we accept the cybernetic assumption that genes define humanity. Biotechnology, in *Gattaca*, leads to a society divided into two distinct classes: the genetically enhanced upper-class "Valids," and the naturally born, lower-class "In-Valids."

Gattaca focuses on the In-Valid Vincent Freeman (Ethan Hawke), who affirms the human spirit in his battle against genetic discrimination. Following his "faith-birth," a genetic analysis shows that Vincent will be short, nearsighted, easily annoyed, and burdened with an inherited heart condition that will probably kill him by the time he's thirty. Though his future value to society will probably be in the area of waste disposal, Vincent dreams of piloting a spaceship to Titan—a privilege reserved for the genetically elite, who train at the Gattaca Aerospace Corporation, where Vincent works as a janitor. Emphasizing the corporation's dominant concern, the name "Gattaca" consists of the four letters of DNA code—GTCA. Like the robot and android intolerance noted earlier in *A.I.* and *Blade Runner,* genetic prejudice, or "genoism" as it's called in *Gattaca,* is similar to racism.

Realizing that "they've got discrimination down to a science," Vincent must use elaborate illegal means to overcome Gattaca's regular security checks. DNA identification machines—linked to a genetic database—use stray hair or an eyelash, skin flakes, nail clippings, blood, saliva, or urine to quickly determine identity and genetic status. Vincent strikes a deal with a Valid—the crippled athlete Eugene Morrow (Jude Law), whose name ironically suggests eugenics and whose apartment is dominated by a helix-shaped staircase. With a supply of Eugene's stockpiled hair, fingernails, urine, and blood, Vincent circumvents Gattaca's frequent identity checks. Vincent assumes Eugene's Valid genetic identity and trains for space flight. Vincent's genetic subterfuge is suspensefully threatened when a murder inside Gattaca leads to even more elaborate identity investigations. Ultimately, with the help of a beautiful woman (Uma Thurman) and cover provided by his brother Anton (Elias Koteas) and a sympathetic doctor (Xander Berkeley), Vincent fulfills his dream and gets launched to Saturn.

Gattaca, in its stainless steel settings, dark-suit dress code, and drone-like employees, suggests a genetically uniform, conformist world purified of flaws. This underscores one of the arguments against genetic controls—a reduction in human diversity.[56] "There is no gene for the human spirit" served as the film's tagline. Vincent's defective genes, and the resulting social discrimination, challenge him to develop traits that Valids, such as the self-hating Eugene, do not possess: determination and willpower. This affirms the idea that these characteristics cannot be genetically engineered and that genetic determinism is wrong.

Genetic enhancement, in *Gattaca,* benefits the corporation and the wealthy elite. Contemporary society is already headed in this direction, as biologist Stephen Nottingham points out in his online book *Screening DNA:* "The patenting of human genes could mean that genetic manipulation technology becomes concentrated in the hands of a small number of multinational corporations . . . [ensuring] that only the wealthy are likely to benefit."[57] Besides creating a genetically enhanced elite that serves corporate interests, bioethicists also express deep concern about the resulting genetic prejudice. In *The Biotech Century,* Jeremy Rifkin asserts that genetic bigotry is already widespread. A 1996 survey of genetic discrimination in the United States[58] showed that "genetic discrimination is being practiced by a range of institutions including insurance companies, health care providers, government agencies, adoption agencies, and schools."[59] Further, this could produce an evolutionary division between species. In *ReMaking Eden,* Lee Silver argues that unequal access to gene-therapy technologies will lead to a polarized society of what he calls the "Naturals" and "Gen-Rich." Silver predicts that if genetic enhancement technology advances at its present rate, then by end of the third millennium, the GenRich class and the Natural class will be "entirely separate species with no ability to cross-breed, and with as much romantic interest in each other as a current human would have for a chimpanzee."[60]

Gattaca attacks genetic discrimination and the dark side of genetic manipulation while providing a parable on racism and classism. Finally, *Gattaca's* prediction of a society divided by genetic prejudice—unique in science fiction cinema—links it to several novels included in this chapter: *Brave New World, The Eyes of Heisenberg,* and *Beyond This Horizon* as well as A. E. Van Vogt's *Slan* (1940), Nancy Kress's *Beggars in Spain* (1993), and Michael Marshall Smith's *Spares* (1996)—all of which center on social prejudice and class divisions that result from unequal application of genetic manipulation.

DEATH TO SUPERPEOPLE: DISCRIMINATION AGAINST THE GENETICALLY ENHANCED

An early vision of genetic modification leading to discrimination, *Slan* (1940) was the first novel by A. E. Van Vogt, the legendary author who helped move science fiction from the Flash Gordon and bug-eyed monster genre of the 1930s to a more serious and philosophical approach.[61] *Slan* opens thrillingly with two super-intelligent, telepathic mutants—Jommy Cross and his mother—chased by angry humans who hate them. Identifiable by little gold tendrils that come off their forehead like antennae and provide their mind-reading power, slans are a genetically bred, superhuman species created to aid humanity but whose superiority is now despised. Called "snakes" for their tendrils, they have no rights and are shot on sight. Jommy—now orphaned at age nine—hides from humans, collects powerful secret weapons hidden by his father, and cautiously seeks other slans. He wants to fulfill the messiah-like destiny his dying mother bestowed on him: "You live for one thing only—to make it possible for slans to live normal lives."[62]

Feared not only for their superiority, slans (whose name derives from the fictional biologist S. Lann) challenge the status quo and diminish the role of ordinary humans in society. Aside from this, humans instinctively fear the artificial man, like the golem and Frankenstein's monster. The slans' technological origins make them less than human and thus not entitled to human rights. Like the robot, cyborg, android, and clone, slans threaten human stability, self-definition, and identity. In response, the compassionate, nonviolent, anti-war slans engineer tendril-less, nontelepathic, violence-enhanced slans who will terminate the human species.

The cataclysmic social and political divisions created by rampant biotechnology are also the themes of *Beggars in Spain,* a 1993 novel by Nancy

Kress.[63] Where Van Vogt treats the subject broadly, Kress elaborates biologist Silver's prediction of a polarized society where humanity is divided into separate species engaged in an evolutionary struggle. Beginning in America in 2008, but spanning a century, *Beggars in Spain* opens with the planned birth of Leisha Camden, whose wealthy father demands that his designer daughter be smart and pretty, and, most important, have no biological need to sleep.[64]

Leisha Camden belongs to a new sleepless generation of genetically enhanced children who become ever more numerous as the technology becomes more popular. Kress suggests that particular genetic enhancements will become a craze or fad, but with serious consequences for humanity as a whole. Genetically customized individuals will pass their modifications to future generations, altering human evolution according to an era's fashion.

Leisha and her fellow-Sleepless outperform their Sleeper contemporaries in science, law, and money-making. Fearing a "Super-Race" takeover, the Sleepers—or Livers—enact discriminatory laws to impede Sleepless dominance. Like the more-than-human *Blade Runner* androids, the Sleepless become an oppressed and vulnerable minority. Oddly, though the mainstream Americans view the technologically enhanced as unnatural, they do not outlaw the technology as, for example, happens in *Star Trek II: The Wrath of Kahn* (1982). The genetically enhanced, power-mad, super-human Kahn (Ricardo Montalban) causes so much trouble—even after being defeated and thrown off earth in the "Eugenic Wars"—that Earth governments and later the Federation ban genetic engineering to prevent another Khan.

Despite their economic contributions and pleasant dispositions, the Sleepless are not considered human. A law is passed making sex between Sleepless and Sleeper people a felony, ranking it on the level of bestiality. The Sleepless choose to segregate themselves. Led by the paranoid elitist Jennifer Sharifi, they establish Sanctuary, a remote fortified city, where their genetic research can continue unobserved and unimpeded. The original sleepless person, Leisha, rejects Sanctuary. She will continue to live among the "Beggars," the name given to ordinary humans by the arrogant Sleepless. Leisha, speaking for author Kress, believes in compassion and works toward a Sleeper/Sleepless union. *Beggars in Spain* questions the moral responsibility of the enhanced Sleepless: what do the more fortunate owe the less fortunate? What do the smart owe the dumb? What do the rich owe the poor? What does the superior person owe the "grasping and nonproductive needy"?[65] Most Sleepless decide they owe nothing.

The Sleepless build an off-world colony, relocating Sanctuary to an orbiting habitat. There the persecuted turn into the mirror image of their human oppressors. Like Herbert's Optimen, they kill babies that don't meet their enhanced genetic requirements. Like the slans, they engineer a third generation of Sleepless, called the Supers, to crush the humans if necessary. The Sleepless even threaten the United States with a biological weapon.

Beggars in Spain demonstrates disastrous social consequences arising from germline genetic engineering. Enhancing genetic traits according to fashion shifts evolution without regard to consequences and creates thorny class divisions. Kress emphasizes that posthuman evolution requires posthuman social changes; biological enhancement demands social enhancement. Technologists rarely speak about how they will improve empathy and compassion as they become immortal, genetically superior cyborg posthumans. The superior Sleepless and slans take a technological death-spiral trying to resolve social conflict with engineering. They abandon their own humanity by cutting themselves off from moral obligations to the rest of humanity. As social beings, humans require social evolution to survive.

ACCIDENTS WILL HAPPEN: UNFORESEEN CONSEQUENCES OF GENETIC MODIFICATION

Concerns about the evolutionary impact of eugenics and the potential for genetic discrimination center on the future, but the revolution in biology causes immediate anxiety because of its unpredictable outcomes. No one knows where innovation will lead. For example, in a *Discover* magazine story, "Genetic Tinkering Makes Bioterror Worse," Curtis Rist reports that an experimental mouse vaccine, using an engineered mousepox virus, created a new, more deadly strain of mousepox. "This is the public's worst fears about genetically modified organisms come true," says Bob Seamark, the former CEO of the company that made the discovery. "We have shown that something we thought was difficult—increasing the pathogenicity of a virus—is in fact quite easy."[66] The ability to manipulate genes rushes ahead of our understanding of what they do and how they do it. Further, gene manipulation often involves sophisticated computer software, which is always subject to glitches or bugs.

The Fly—David Cronenberg's 1986 version of the 1958 film of the same name—powerfully dramatizes the dire consequences of a random mishap in the technology of genetic reengineering as well as the horrors of transgenic creatures. Reminiscent of a *Star Trek* transporter, the Telepod—invented by blundering scientist Seth Brundle (Jeff Goldblum)—transfers matter from one place to another. Brundle promises that the device will "end all concepts of borders and frontiers, time and space." After success with inanimate objects, Brundle decides to test the invention on himself, neglecting the grotesque result of an earlier attempt to transport a baboon.

As he closes the telepod door, a fly enters with him and gets encoded with Brundle's DNA. Initially, the teleportation appears to be successful. In fact, Brundle's physical and mental makeup get enhanced. His energy dramatically increases. He gains superhuman strength, speed, and agility. At first, he views his newly reconstituted flesh as a positive posthuman transformation: "It's somehow a purifying process. . . . it's allowed me to realize the personal potential I've been ignoring all these years . . . human teleportation, molecular decimation, breakdown, reformation is inherently purging. Makes a man a king." In fact, he believes the telepod transported him to a transcendent state.

Eventually, technological problems are revealed in a most disgusting manner. Brundle's fingernails, teeth, and ears fall off. Unlike in the original movie, in which a fly's head and claws were grafted onto the human body, fusion takes place at the "molecular/genetic level," as Brundle metamorphoses into a human/fly hybrid. Brundle explains: "The computer got confused over what was supposed to be two separate genetic patterns, and it decided to splice us together." Like the central character in *Videodrome* (see Chapter Six), Brundle endures a horrifying physical and mental transformation beyond his control. In both films, the breakdown of human sanity, identity, and coherence result from interaction with new technologies—information technology in the case of *Videodrome,* biological technology in the case of *The Fly.* In both films, the technology-induced metamorphosis results in a posthuman transformation that destroys the human values of empathy and compassion.

While scientist Brundle goes violently mad in *The Fly,* he does not conform to the Moreau/Mengele mad scientist prototype at the center of most Cronenberg movies, such as *The Brood* or *Shivers* (see Chapter Nine). Sympathetic and well-intentioned until genetically fused with the fly, Brundle initially reflects a more positive strain of science fiction scientist, those who try to help humanity, but who accidentally create a technological threat to themselves, their family, the society, or even the universe. These misguided scientists, oblivious to the consequences of their work, possess positive motives and try to rectify their mistakes, as do the paleontologists in *Jurassic Park* (1993) and the entomologist in *Mimic* (1997). "They came to be seen as the necessary agents of progress, who occasionally get unlucky—rather than being personally responsible for the threat due to evil intent or an obsessive search for knowledge," says Stephen Nottingham in *Screening DNA.*[67] Nottingham traces the softened image of the scientist back to

The Fly: *A scientist begins his tortured metamorphosis into a transgenic fly,*
due to unintended consequences of genetic splicing (Courtesy Photofest).

the sympathetic, self-destructive scientist in the original version of *The*
Fly (1958), but an earlier harbinger of the change occurs in *Them* (1954).
In this movie about ants turned gigantic by nuclear radiation, two ento-
mologists—a kindly old white-haired fellow and his pretty and efficient
daughter—reflect a quasi-positive image of the scientist. Despite the scientists causing great harm in the form of gigantic killer ants (not to mention
the bomb itself), they find a method of ending the threat by spraying the
queen ant's nest with fire—a kind of hysterectomy by flame-thrower.

A more recent giant insect movie, *Mimic* (1997), directed by Guillermo
del Toro, depicts another entomologist—a well-intentioned Dr. Susan
Tyler (Mira Sorvino). She receives a hero's adulation from a grateful public after she stops the cockroach-generated plague that kills children in
New York. Using genetic engineering, Tyler cleverly creates a cockroach-
destroying insect, the "Judas Breed," by combining termite and man-
tid DNA. This genetically modified organism, combining the nesting/
infestation traits of the termite with the ferocious killer traits of the man-
tid, serves as "a biological counter agent."

In only six months, the cockroach problem has been terminated and
the child-killing plague ended. Tyler and her husband, Peter (Jeremy
Northam), who works for the Center for Disease Eradication, get anointed
as media celebrities. Unfortunately, three years later, the Judas Breed have

reproduced, evolved lungs, mutated into giants, and started killing people (like the ants of *Them*). The big bugs stand six feet tall and, with body-length wings tucked at their sides, appear to wear stylish overcoats, thus mimicking their well-dressed human predators. Despite the fact that the hybrid Judas species were engineered to be sterile adults, lasting only one generation because of the inclusion of a "suicide gene" in their DNA, they are breeding.

Neither technology nor nature can be controlled by scientists. *Mimic* updates *Them*—and other cold war–era, monsters-created-by-radiation movies—in that (bio)technology causes mutations that attack humanity. In *Mimic*, DNA demonstrates its omnipotence as it defeats the design of the human scientists by mutating itself. While *Mimic* initially promotes the great benefits of genetic engineering and applauds the scientists, the film suggests that DNA technology might ultimately be harmful in its unintended, unpredictable consequences. As scientist Tyler later admits, "We changed its DNA—we don't know what we did."

In *Hulk* (2003), a genetic scientist knowingly alters his own DNA, then passes the mutation to his son. The consequences are both unintended and huge. He creates a monster! An update of the nuclear-era Marvel comic, *Hulk*—directed by Ang Lee—opens with an extended prologue that dissolves between glowing images of flowing cell life and reams of scientific notations—"I intend to achieve human regeneration." In the mid-1960s, scientist David Banner (Paul Kersey in the flashback, Nick Nolte in the rest of the movie) works for the military and tries to develop a genetically enhanced supersoldier. In his obsession with improving the self-healing powers of the immune system, he harvests genetic material from sea cucumbers, starfish, lizards, and snakes to create a transgenic serum that he self-injects when the military shuts down his lab. His experimentation brings about shocking physiological changes—"hints of genetic mutation" and chromosomal alteration—which his son, Bruce, inherits. Unknowingly ominous, Bruce's mother says, "There's something inside you that's so special, someday you'll share it with the whole world."

Thirty-five years later, emotionally repressed Bruce Banner (Eric Bana)—who suffers from confusing nightmares about his unhinged father—is a nerdy research scientist working at the Berkeley Nuclear Biotechnology Institute alongside his lovely lab-mate and ex-girlfriend, Betty (Jennifer Connelly). Their current revolutionary project centers on "nanomeds"—artificial cells injected into the body to promote self-healing. Sleazy corporate executive Talbot (Josh Lucas)—a former military man chasing the big bucks—offers them massive amounts of money to work for his corporation. When they refuse, he threatens them: "There's a hair's breadth between friendly offer and hostile takeover. The work you're doing here is dynamite. G.I.s embedded with technology that makes them repairable on the battlefield. That makes it our business." This obviously reflects the current relationship between military and corporate powers as well as the desire to build superhumans for war. Gone completely mad, Bruce's dad, David—newly released after thirty years in prison—wants to steal back Bruce's mojo: "I gave you life and you must give it back to me." Like today's techno-priests, he believes genetic engineering will lead to immortality.

The demon seeds of David's technological recklessness, godlike desires, and patriarchal abuse lie dormant in the younger Banner until a lab accident infects him with his own self-healing nanomeds and blasts him with a lethal dose of gamma rays. He not only survives, but feels better than ever. The demon of genetic manipulation and scientific hubris is unleashed when Bruce loses his temper—triggering a permanent chemical change in his body. Undergoing a physical mega-transformation, Bruce metamorphoses into a fifteen-foot-high, green-skinned, almost-indestructible behemoth. With posthuman superiority and violence, he grabs a helicopter from the sky with a gigantic leap and destroys buildings with a punch. In an explosion of Luddite fury, he destroys his own lab. When the Hulk's amazing powers become known, Talbot wants to cultivate him as a weapon and make lots of money.

Along with a Jekyll-Hyde struggle between the rational and the irrational, rampaging youth fury visited on a repressive militarized society, and a purely oedipal revolt, *Hulk* invokes the horrors of biotechnology, germline engineering, and a warning about the destructive folly of those who wrap themselves in the divine vestments of techno-religion. If Hulk and girlfriend Betty were to reproduce, then—given the beauty of germline engineering—their hulksters would suffer the same genetic fate. Moreover, given enough of them, they would become the dominant species and eventually force human extinction. There's a suggestion that the Hulk, in his heart of hearts, hates humans. In a dream, Bruce sees the Hulk as his reflection in the mirror who growls, "Puny human," one of *Hulk*'s comic-book refrains.

The perfectionism of the Technologists hovers over the story in David Banner's mad-scientist belief that he can improve upon humanity and "go beyond God's boundaries." In a climactic face-off that ends with Dad exploding in abstraction, he condemns his son as a "superficial shell, a husk of flimsy consciousness." After destroying San Francisco, son Bruce disappears into the rainforests of South America to do good for the natives. There he ponders the absurd priorities of American society, which puts more money and energy into technology used for destruction, war, and weapons than into curing the sick or feeding the poor. The movie amalgamates fears of the unintended consequences of twisted genetics and military domination of biotech research. *Hulk* also condemns corporate exploitation of science, which—through huge outlays of money—controls research and becomes part of the anti-human structure and operation of the technological juggernaut.

CORPORATE HORROR: GENETIC MODIFICATIONS FOR PROFIT

The untested consequences of genetically engineered food became a major public controversy in the 1990s and grows stronger, at least in Europe, in the twenty-first century. Protests centered on "Frankenfoods" —transgenic, genetically modified (GM), or genetically engineered (GE) grains, fruits, and vegetables. Many of the genes transferred into the DNA of food crops come from plants, microorganisms, and animals that have never been part of the human diet. "Not only is it unknown whether or not there are any health risks for the consumers of such food," says Chris Hables Gray in *Cyborg Citizen*, "but there is a real danger that engineered genes might escape into other species or have unanticipated consequences."[68] Biotech corporations—such as Bayer, AgrEvo, and Monsanto—use their political influence within the World Trade Organization to stop countries from banning imports of GE and GM foods and seeds. Still, in many parts of the world, the issue provokes outrage, protests, and lawsuits by a wide range of groups including farmers, environmentalists, animal rights activists, chefs, and just plain food-eaters. In the United States, for example, Monsanto shelved plans in 2004 to make bioengineered, herbicide-resistant wheat—"Roundup Wheat"—after several foreign countries said they would not buy it.[69] Oddly, Monsanto also made the herbicide, called "Round Up," that the new wheat was engineered to combat.

Techno-anxiety—about transgenic crops and creatures as well as corporate/government/military collusion—is a thread that runs throughout *The X-Files* (see below). This fear, which results from the anti-human, anti-environmental actions of profit-first international corporations, links back to cyberpunk works, such as *Neuromancer* and *Blade Runner,* and cyborg texts, like the *Robocop* series. In the past twenty years, the root cause of evil in science fiction often centers on an unholy trinity of mad science and military power serving corporate aims, such as in the *Alien* series, the *Resident Evil* series, *Gattaca, Mutant, Spares, Jurassic Park, The 6th Day, The Manchurian Candidate* (2004), and others. In these works, inherently totalitarian technology—whether it's robotic, computer, or biological—enhances government and corporate power, often at the expense of the environment and individual freedom. This reflects the immoral behavior and increasing power of multinational corporations. For example, Monsanto—recently accused of contaminating Anniston, Alabama, with PCBs—was criticized in a U.S. court for behavior "so outrageous in character and extreme in degree as to go beyond all possible bounds of decency so as to be regarded as atrocious and utterly intolerable in civilized society."[70]

Corporate evil and the Frankenfoods controversy link up to a terrorist agenda in *Mutant,* a 2001 novel by Dr. Peter Clement. The powerful biotech corporation Agrenomics wreaks havoc on the environment with its supposedly disease-resistant super-crops while scientists sell out to corporate interests. Agrenomics's executives also cover up a scandal involving deadly side-effects of a genetically modified food experiment: a killer virus, previously found only in birds, jumps the species barrier and infects humans with an Ebola-like disease. This fiction reflects real-world concerns about the extreme techno-manipulation of nature without regard to the environmental or human-health implications. "Playing ecological roulette" is how Jeremy Rifkin describes it. "[T]here's little or no precedent for what might occur in the wake of a global experiment to redefine the fundamental rules of biological development to suit the needs of market-driven forces."[71] While no biotech CEOs have been accused of deliberately killing people, their unethical, self-enriching behavior, which financially eviscerates people, and their careless pushing of untested transgenic crops, which could sicken people, are the moral equivalent of terrorism.

TRANSGENIC MONSTERS: ALIEN DNA INVADES OUR BODIES

Transgenic corn became an anti-human weapon in *The X-Files: Fight the Future* (1998). In this feature-film version of the television show, bees will pollinate transgenic maize, which incorporates the smallpox virus as well as alien DNA. Part of *The X-Files*'s confusing and overarching mythology, a secret program called "Purity Control" has been launched by former Nazis, in collaboration with an international syndicate of government officials, to create human/alien hybrids. In this implausibly elaborate and inefficient process, bees will transmit the alien genes to humans via pollen and stings.[72] Mulder believes these human/alien transgenics will facilitate a full-fledged alien invasion of Earth. Of course, alien invasion stories are a long-established science fiction scenario, though

X-Files: Fight the Future: *FBI agents get frightened by a sinister cornfield (Courtesy Photofest).*

usually involving the landing of spacecraft and battles with the military. In the nuclear era, alien aggression in such movies as *War of the Worlds* (1956) and *Invaders from Mars* (1953) frequently reflected the Communist-invasion paranoia of that time. The *X-Files* type of alien conquest—through species transformation—derives from such body-invasion stories as Robert Heinlein's novel *Puppet Masters* (1951) (see Chapter Nine) and Don Siegel's movie *Invasion of the Body Snatchers* (1956). In one sense, these alien takeover narratives anticipate the virus paranoia that coincides with the AIDS era. Aside from the horrors of viral invasion, which Chapter Nine will examine, *The X-Files* calls attention to the insidious spread of transgenic foods and reflects fears of dehumanizing genetic corruption, which might be the consequence of unrestrained biotechnological research and implementation.

As for species fusion, genetic engineers frequently experiment with cross-breeding for commercial purposes. Scientists at the United States Department of Agriculture's research center in Maryland micro-injected human growth hormone genes into the genetic code of pig embryos in the hope of producing pigs that grow larger and faster and generate increased profits. This failed to work as hoped. But there are plans for transgenic human/pigs to provide organs for human transplant. Other less commercial experiments led to transgenic combinations such as a sheep and a goat, creating a chimeric animal—the "geep."[73] Scientists also managed to insert jellyfish genes into a monkey embryo and produce the planet's first transgenic primate.[74] Some microbiologists have seriously proposed introducing the chimpanzee's "superior" disease-resistant genes into human chromosomes.[75] On animal welfare issues, many people object to the production of transgenic animals because they often suffer deformities, disease, organ failure, and pain due to mistakes in the insertion of foreign DNA. Moral concerns have also been raised about confusing species identity, making animals more human, and altering evolution with unpredictable and disastrous consequences.

For those who want to play mad genetic engineer and create bizarre transgenic species like flying bird-elephants, amphibious rhino-sharks, and giant crawling whale-ants, Microsoft Game Studios released *Impossible Creatures* (2002). This real-time strategy game—created by Relic Entertainment—gives players the simulated technology to gene-splice any two animals into a single monstrosity for the purpose of killing other hybrid monsters.

The story opens in 1937 with black-and-white cut scenes suggesting *The Island of Dr. Moreau*. The player is Rex Chance, renowned world adventurer and war correspondent. Answering a plea from his long-lost scientist father, Dr. Eric Chanikov, Rex flies to a little-known South American island where Chanikov conducts genetic-splicing research, funded by the evil wealthy industrialist Upton Julius. Like his forebear Dr. Moreau, Chanikov possesses godlike utopian fantasies of altering evolution to enhance flawed human beings by perfecting their DNA—sort of like introducing disease-resistant chimpanzee genes into humans. However, power-mad corporate chief Julius has killed Chanikov and wants to exploit the technology for military dominance. Not long after his arrival, Rex is attacked by Julius's hybrid creatures—huge scorpions with wolf-like features that want to consume him for lunch. He's saved by the talented young Doctor Lucy Willing, who whisks him away in her hover-train laboratory, beginning their quest to defeat the villainous corporate psycho and his disgusting mutant horde.

Rex must fight fire with fire, combating the transgenic monstrosities with his own crossbred deviants. As Rex progresses through the game, he harvests DNA samples from various wildlife—such as crocodiles, owls, piranhas, bears, snakes, porcupines, skunks, whales, gorillas, dragonflies, and bats—which he adds to his private collection. In the Creature Chamber, the player, as Rex, plays God. Combining the bodies, limbs, heads, and tails of two animals, Rex manufactures a transgenic monster army to battle the engineered corporate beasts. For example, a "Crocomeleon" melds the body of a crocodile with the head and tail of a chameleon. The creature can camouflage, regenerate, and spit out a nasty tongue attack. The hybrid crea-

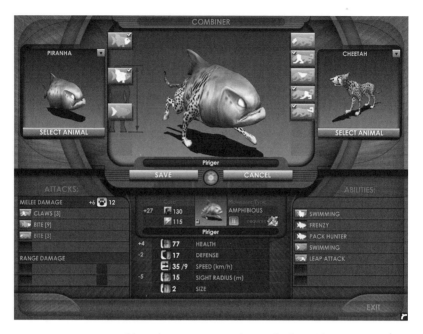

Impossible Creatures: *Gene-Combiner technology makes it fun and easy to fuse incompatible species and engineer grotesque chimeras (Courtesy Relic Entertainment).*

tures may look silly, but in practice they're not so different from what you might find in a typical biotechnology lab. *Impossible Creatures* humorously makes concrete some of the bizarre outcomes that genetic engineering may have in store for us.

The horror of biotechnological hybrid-creation provides a shock in the B-movie *Species* (1995). Aliens have replied to a radio-pulsed message, carrying data describing the structure of human DNA, sent into space by scientists working for the SETI (Search for Extraterrestrial Intelligence) project.[76] The alien-sent data contains a unique DNA sequence and instructions for inserting it into a human egg. Typical of mad scientists and irresponsible biotech experimenters, dour geneticist Xavier Fitch (Ben Kingsley) generates the DNA sequence without knowing what sort of drooling, slimy biological terror will be unleashed. Using micromanipulation technology, he inserts the alien DNA into human eggs, one of which eventually results in the birth of a baby, Sil, who quickly develops into a pretty little girl. Now deciding she's a threat, Fitch—Mengele-like—oversees her cyanide-gas execution as she tearfully stares back at him through the glass containment dome.

Suddenly realizing her superhuman strength, Sil blasts out like a female hulk and escapes, leaving a path of death and destruction. She somehow ends up on a train. After consuming a caloric blast of Twinkies, candy bars, chips, and milk, she sprouts tentacles and turns into a blob that transforms into a young adult alien/woman (Natasha Hendstridge) who looks like a beer-commercial bombshell. Biotechnology combined with reckless scientists have created a beautiful monster. Sexually mature and ready to mate, she heads to discos looking for human males to impregnate her. Not surprisingly, this proves quite easy. After rejecting several reproductive opportunities with men of poor genetic caliber and gruesomely killing them with her powerful tongue, Sil has sex with a genetically suitable fellow — a Harvard anthropologist, of all people. Afterward, she kills him and later

Species: Unwanted alien-human hybrid gassed by Nazi-like biotechnologists (Courtesy Photofest).

gives birth to a smart monster. Sil, oddly, remains a youthful sex bomb except when morphing into a hideous, tentacled creature designed by H. R. Geiger, the *Alien* creator. Sil wants to make humanity extinct. Yet despite being the world's greatest threat, she is hunted by a small group of people. Leader Fitch even takes a night off to relax during the chase. Fortunately, as in *Them,* Sil and her child are discovered in the sewers of L.A. and destroyed by fire. However, a rat eats part of the alien's tentacle, ensuring the spread of dangerous genes and a more dangerous sequel.

While *Species* rarely rises above standard horror and banal science fiction, the symbolism of human species transformation raises potentially profound questions about gender bias, racism, and the nature of posthumanism. "Cyborg monsters in feminist fiction define quite different political possibilities and limits from those proposed by the mundane fiction of Man and Woman," writes Donna Haraway.[77] These possibilities include her utopian dream for a world without gender. Gender boundaries remain unchallenged in *Species* as the female cyborg monster drives the story with her efforts to secure a human male for reproduction. As noted in Chapter Five, *Alien Resurrection* hints at a future genderless world in the relationship between alien/human hybrid Ripley and cyborg Call. In the novel *Dawn* (1987), Octavia Butler explores boundary-breaking possibilities in a story of abduction and seduction as humans are forced to mate with an alien race in a post-nuclear test of species survival.[78] In this human/alien encounter, eugenics and biotechnology play a central role, as the aliens' defining trait is genetic engineering expertise.

Dawn—the first book in Butler's *Xenogenesis* trilogy (renamed *Lilith's Brood*), followed by *Adulthood Rites* (1988) and *Imago* (1989)—opens after the nomadic alien species Oankali rescue the remnants of humanity from the aftermath of nuclear devastation. They hold the humans captive, in suspended animation, aboard an orbiting organic starship and plot the transformation of their prisoners into a new species. Like the Borg of *Star Trek,* the Oankali absorb other life forms, assimilating them to serve their purposes. The human race will be given a second chance as "trade partners," in the euphemistic words of the Oankali; that is, humans will be forced breeding stock for a gene-spliced new species blending human and Oankali.[79] Unlike the Borg, the Oankali are not portrayed as unequivocally evil. In the Oankali view, the fusion will improve the human species—ending sexism, racism, violence, aggressiveness, and poor health—by changing it into something different. Depending on your perspective, humans are their victims or their beneficiaries.

The Oankali awaken the first human, an African-American woman named Lilith, from two centuries of suspended animation. Lilith finds the

Oankali hideously grotesque. Unlike the human-like *Star Trek* aliens with strange make-up and hairdos, the Oankali sport hairy, noseless heads on dark gray bodies that sprout "tentacles." They want Lilith to help facilitate the cooperation of the other humans as they are awakened, preparing them to face the monstrous-looking aliens and training them to survive in the wilderness that Earth has become. Most important, the Oankali want Lilith to be the mother of the new species.[80]

Breaking gender boundaries, the Oankali have three sexes: female, male, and ooloi. The third sex—the ooloi—are natural-born genetic engineers, the culture's breeders and gene manipulators. Equipped with two elephant trunk–like "sensory arms," which they use to manipulate DNA, the ooloi control and direct Oankali evolution. Polymorphously erotic, the sensory arms stimulate the nervous systems of the ooloi's breeding partners, arousing sexual pleasure no matter what the species. Some of the resulting new hybrids embody Oankali technologies—for instance, their interstellar spaceships, which are made entirely of living tissue and with which they share a biological, symbiotic relationship. Like today's biotech companies that target the valuable genes of rare species, the Oankali seek new, unfamiliar lifeforms for bio-diversity and adaptation to new environments.

Parallels to the Oankali have been found in the population dynamics of earth organisms. According to biology professor and science fiction writer Jan Slonczewski, "Microbes and plants have been shown to possess surprising capacities for 'genetic trade' with other species, even taking up naked DNA released by dead organisms and incorporating it into their own chromosomes."[81] These organisms, like the Oankali, retain the genes needed for adaptation to their current environment; but they also possess the evolutionary expertise to incorporate new genes as needed. Thus, Butler presents a frighteningly plausible biological foundation for *Dawn*'s narrative.

Lilith's "awakening" to captivity on an alien spaceship, where she has been dehumanized like a slave by her captors, reminds Donna Haraway of the "middle passage" of slaves on their way to America.[82] Oppressed previously on earth as an African American woman, Lilith understands the propagandistic methods by which political and medical power disguises itself as benevolence. A frequent form of ooloi affection—"putting a sensory arm around her neck"—feels like "an oddly comfortable noose."[83] She perceives herself as part of a captive breeding program, but like a slave-master's mistress, Lilith will receive advantages from the Oankali if she cooperates in their genetic plans. "The Oankali lecture her about the superiority of their egalitarian, nonviolent lifestyle, as opposed to the hierarchical, violent tendencies of humans," writes Jan Slonczewski, "just as Americans told their African slaves they were fortunate to be rescued from barbarism by their 'democratic' masters."[84] Eventually, Lilith is impregnated without her co-operation in a kind of forced artificial insemination. The Oankali ratio-nalization of their biotechnological rape employs the eugenic logic of the slave master: the inferior race will be improved by the superior one. An ex-tension of the Oankali eugenic philosophy, the religious techno-utopian dream of human perfection supports the development of invasive, germ-line genetic engineering.

In *Dawn,* these nomadic, nonviolent, fascistic, telepathic, gene-sharing, multi-tentacled, pleasure-giving extraterrestrials promote an ideal post-human future of unlimited possibility. But Butler questions this utopian vision, elaborating a critical perspective toward the Oankali as arrogant, perfection-infected biotechnologists who presume to decide what human flaws will be corrected. Aside from adjusting to children with tentacles, posthuman life in the Oankali world means slavery, dehumanization, and science-controlled reproduction. Intimate human relations and sexuality are rendered impossible by symbiosis with the aliens. From the outset, the Oankali degrade the humans. While they do not destroy human life, they force the human population to choose either compliance with cross-breeding or sterilization. Both choices result in human extinction.

The Oankali appropriate Earth's genes for their own benefit just as the multinational biotech corporations with the support of government lack-eys attempt to seize control—through patenting—of microbes, plants, and animals with rare genetic traits that might be exploited for future commer-cial use. Rich, high-tech Northern Hemisphere nations battle it out with poor, low-tech, gene-rich, tropical Southern Hemisphere nations over the ownership of Earth's bio-treasures. "The world wide race to patent the gene pool of the planet is the culmination of a five-hundred-year odyssey to commercially enclose and privatize all of the great ecosystems that make up the Earth's biosphere," says biotech critic Jeremy Rifkin. "Genes are the 'green gold' of the biotech century."[85]

GOD IN THE GENES:
THE GENETIC FORCE AND
THE DARK SIDE OF CLONING

The power of genes provides the pantheistic philosophical foundation of the *Star Wars* universe. The mystical energy known as the Force was established in the original *Star Wars* trilogy as an invisible cosmic power, created by all living things, that surrounds and binds together the galaxy. *Star Wars Episode I: The Phantom Menace* (1999) reveals a biological,

Star Wars Episode II: Attack of the Clones: *Mindless, obedient clone army ordered on a mission of violence (Courtesy Photofest).*

genetic dimension to that energy. Control of the Force is achieved through fictitious microscopic lifeforms called "midi-chlorians," which reside in all living cells, incorporated into DNA. Anathema to *Star Wars* fanatics who thought they reduced the Force to a kind of viral infection, midi-chlorians provide a biological interface, the link between physical bodies and spiritual energy. While still requiring rigorous training, only those enhanced humans with higher concentrations of midi-chlorians, like Anakin Skywalker (Jake Lloyd), are potential Jedi Knights and destined for greatness.

In order to combat the godlike, genetically enhanced, separatist Jedi Knights and their hordes of battle robots, a Clone Army has been created and crafted, in *Star Wars Episode II: Attack of the Clones* (2002), by the scientific geniuses of the stormy planet Kamino. Renowned for their mastery of genetic manipulation, the apolitical Kaminoans—known as "the Cloners"—put their science at the service of profit and military objectives. Like many real-world scientists, they neglect to consider the ethical consequences of their technology. The Kaminoan biotechnologists, using harvested DNA from the ruthless bounty hunter Jango Fett as their template, produce thousands of soldier clones inside glass incubation wombs, not unlike those suggested in *Brave New World*. Employing rapid-growth techniques to accelerate development, the genetic engineers manufacture, in less than a decade, adult soldiers. The scientists further manipulate the clones' genetic code to retard their minds and diminish their independence.

This obedient army of slaves represents a popular view of clones as mindless, soulless, imperfect imitations of a real person. To some extent this derives from a confusion between "cloning" as a biological term and "cloning" in its popular usage as referring to a cheap imitation of a brand name, such as an IBM or Mac "clone." In the 1980 U.S. presidential election, Ted Kennedy labeled Jimmy Carter a "Reagan clone."[86] This usage annoys today's clone apologists. "Cloned children will be full-fledged human beings, indistinguishable in biological terms from all other members of the species," argues Lee Silver in *Remaking Eden*. "Thus, the notion of a soulless clone has no basis in reality."[87]

Still, no posthuman technology has generated such powerfully dystopian visions as cloning. From Aldous Huxley's image of state-controlled human production in *Brave New World* to the evil clone-boy in *Godsend* (2004), cloning serves as a metaphor for the technological creation of an inhumane, morally corrupt posthuman world. The May 2003 cloning of a mule added to the barnyard full of cloned animals that included sheep, cows, pigs, cats, and rodents.[88] While the Raelians' announcement of a human clone was greeted with skepticism, it seems inevitable that humans will eventually be genetically duplicated, a prospect greeted with almost universal condemnation. Germany, France, Japan, and Australia have banned the cloning of humans. In the United States, the Human Cloning Prohibition Act passed the House of Representatives in February 2003, but still awaits a Senate vote as of winter 2004. Politicians virulently denounce cloning as "ghoulish," "science gone crazy," "an insult to humanity," and "an unholy technique." Rep. James Sensenbrenner (R-Wis.) managed to squeeze two famous technophobic literary allusions into one sentence, calling cloning a "new brave world of Frankenstein science."[89]

The term *clone* (from the Greek *klon,* meaning twig) was coined in 1963 by British biologist J. B. S. Haldane in a speech, titled "Biological Possibilities for the Human Species of the Next Ten-Thousand Years," describing the 1962 creation of an asexual genetic duplicate of a frog.[90] The science fiction clone—like the robot, android, and cyborg—embodies our fears of technological replication and reflects anxiety about the ephemeral nature of human identity and the evil twin or mysterious doppelgänger. Among the first science fiction works to suggest cloning, the 1948 novel *The World of Null-A* by A. E. Van Vogt opens with Gilbert Gosseyn made aware, through a lie detector test, that he is not who he thinks he is. While floundering to construct an identity, he is violently killed, but awakens within a new identical body, causing further anguish and confusion. He refuses to believe his own mind until he sees his now-dead previous body. Though the duplicating mechanism is not biologically clarified, the result is a cloned body. He later discovers that his memories, including the memory of getting killed, have been transferred into the new body. Swirling in Kafkaesque paranoia, with a tormented person repeatedly confronting his doppelgänger and his subconscious fears, *The World of Null-A* thoroughly befuddled readers of the pulp science fiction magazine *Astounding,* which serialized it in 1945.

RESURRECTING HISTORICAL HORRORS: CLONING THE PAST

Nazi doctor Josef Mengele (Gregory Peck) successfully clones Hitler in the movie *The Boys from Brazil* (1977) — directed by Franklin Schaffner and based on the Ira Levin novel (1976). The book and movie were released in the midst of the first cloning controversy. Emerging as a science fiction motif in the 1970s, cloning symbolized the powers of new biological technology. Embryologist John Gurdon cloned the first animal — a frog — in 1962.[91] In fiction, Nancy Freedman's *Joshua: Son of None* (1973) proposed that assassinated U.S. president John F. Kennedy might have been cloned. J. B. S. Haldane's sister Naomi Mitchison offered, in *Solution Three* (1975), a dystopian vision in which sexual reproduction is outlawed and cloning adopted as a universal policy following a nuclear war. *The Ophiuchi Hotline* (1977) by John Varley described a distant future where cloning and mind transfer are commonplace.[92] Before Dolly the cloned sheep, the cloning controversy peaked following publication of David Rorvik's book *In His Image: The Cloning of a Man* (1978). In this fictional account, Rorvik claimed that he had assisted in the cloning of a human being and presented his story as fact.[93] This best-selling book sparked numerous newspaper and magazine articles, Martin Ebon's nonfiction *The Cloning of Man: Brave New Hope — or Horror* (1978), and a House of Representatives subcommittee hearing on the subject.[94]

In *The Boys from Brazil*, Mengele — hiding out in a laboratory in Brazil — manages to implant local women with eggs containing Hitler's DNA. After the birth of ninety-four Hitler clones, couples in America and Europe, ignorant of the babies' origins, adopt the boys. In order to reflect Hitler's psychological environment, Mengele and his neo-Nazi supporters place the children in families with an older, domineering father. Mengele then orders the murder of each boy's father to re-create the young Hitler's emotional disturbance when he lost his father. The implausibly elaborate conspiracy is discovered by a brooding but persistent Nazi hunter, Ezra Lieberman (Laurence Olivier), based loosely on the real-life Nazi hunter Simon Wiesenthal, who survived a concentration camp and who did track Mengele to South America.[95] In an absurd horror-movie ending, Lieberman and a couple of bloodthirsty Dobermans stop Mengele.

The Boys from Brazil adds a new dimension of reality to the cloning discussion by countering the naïve view that a genetically identical clone of a person would somehow be the same person. To "resurrect" Hitler, Mengele must reproduce the environmental factors that made Hitler the evil genius that he was. Like *Gattaca, The Boys from Brazil* argues against genetic determinism—that the genes totally control the person. Even now this enlightened perspective is somewhat unusual. Nelkin and Lindee, in *The DNA Mystique,* cite numerous examples from popular culture which include images of the gene as omnipotent. They conclude that these "popular images convey a striking picture of the gene as powerful, deterministic, and central to an understanding of both everyday behavior and the 'secret of life.' "[96] With its evil historical characters and accurate presentation of the technology, *The Boys from Brazil* tries to present a serious, strong anti-cloning message. While many viewers rejected its story as absurd, it struck a resounding chord. After the cloning of Dolly was reported, University of Pennsylvania bio-ethicist Arthur Caplan was quoted as saying, " 'This takes us a step closer to *The Boys from Brazil.*' "[97]

CLONING FOR CAPITALISM

The first cloning blockbuster, *Jurassic Park* (1993)—directed by Steven Spielberg and adapted by Michael Crichton from his own novel—depicts the unregulated application of genetic engineering to resurrect extinct dinosaurs that turn into angry killer clones that run amok in a theme park.[98] It comes off as anti-biotechnology, anti-science, and of course pro-nature. Scientists may trivialize life and reduce it down to chemical compositions, but in doing so they underestimate its force. The Walt Disney–inspired corporate head, greedy, grandfatherly John Hammond, funds science that exploits and ultimately endangers people. Like *Hulk, Jurassic Park* implies that corporate interests control the power of science to serve their own selfish ends.

A movie that itself looks cloned from other science fiction/action movies, *The 6th Day* (2000)—directed by Roger Spottiswoode—encapsulates a whole range of anti-cloning concerns, including the oldest one in the anti-technology book, playing God. Defying the Sixth Day Laws against human cloning, a depraved entrepreneur, Michael Drucker (Tony Goldwyn), runs a sinister corporation, Replacement Technologies, under the direction of an unethical, sell-out scientist, Graham Weir (Robert Duvall). They illegally and clandestinely clone human beings at the same time that they legitimately operate a pet cloning business, RePet,[99] and an organ cloning service, NuOrgan. Their devious and immoral human cloning operation gets exposed when it accidentally duplicates the inevitably named Adam Gibson (Arnold Schwarzenegger).

In *The 6th Day,* biotech dread shows up most strongly in the images of unconscious, blank clones floating in vats like adult embryos. At the end, cloning renegade Drucker gets fatally wounded and, before he dies, a half-baked clone is rushed into service. In a capitalistic cloning nightmare, the not-dead-yet billionaire CEO watches in horror as the Vaseline-drenched, protoplasmic mutant of biotechnological arrogance rises up, strips him, and dons his clothes. Though the muddled movie repeatedly reruns the religious argument against cloning, the evils of biotechnology derive most emphatically from the corporation as the source of all that is technologically unholy, emotionally inhuman, and physically invasive.

CLONING ALIENS: MILITARY/CORPORATE WEAPONIZED TECHNOLOGY

In Jean-Pierre Jeunet's *Alien Resurrection,* mad science rears up with a vengeance as beloved Ripley gets cloned from a drop of her blood and grown in a glass-enclosed vat with an alien baby gestating in her womb.[100] The team of crazed scientists in *Alien Resurrection* no longer works only for corporate profits. Like many current biotech research scientists, they are whores for the military. Besides "urban pacification," the cabal of white-coated lab rats hopes to breed aliens and process them for the usual life-enhancing, biotechnological reasons like developing vaccines, medicines, and a gene pool. While the dumb commander (Dan Hedaya) calls Ripley a "meat by-product," the scientists want to preserve her as an exploitable alien/human hybrid whose own remarkable genes even retained Ripley's memory. Their sickening scientific interest in an unusual hybrid species reflects social anxiety about the creation of new chimeric creatures on earth, including the blending of human and animal genes: "Human/animal hybrids could be widely used as experimental subjects in medical research," says Jeremy Rifkin, "and as organ 'donors' for xenotransplantation."[101]

With black-humored embellishment, *Alien Resurrection*'s inhuman surgeons and genetic engineers epitomize the Moreau/Mengele legacy of mad scientists. They slice the alien embryo out of Ripley's womb, then shrink-wrap Ripley and imprison her in a cell. The stamped "8" on Ripley's arm is even reminiscent of concentration-camp tattoos. These bio-engineers purchase the living bodies of several prisoners and use them as surrogate wombs—a terrifying example of corporate/scientific exploitation of the human body for profit. The *Alien Resurrection* scientists implant the alien embryos and dispassionately watch the ravenous parasites grow and devour the conscious human hosts. One of the scientists (Brad Dourif) purposely taunts a youthful alien by mocking its facial expressions and symbolically becoming its mirror image, raising the question: who is the real monster?

DOPPELGÄNGER TERROR: FEAR OF THE CLONE

Actually, the scariest monsters in *Alien: Resurrection* turn out to be the seven failed Ripley clones that preceded the successful number eight. Noticing a door labeled "1-7," Ripley enters the storage facility, where she finds her malformed doppelgängers. "By confronting her clones," says Stephen Nottingham in *Screening DNA*, "Ripley understands her true nature."[102] She is horrified to see her six genetically identical twins, each suspended in a glass vat—a menagerie of Dali-esque monstrosities with a tail, an eye on the side of her face, a grossly misshapen head with fleshy protrusions. This reflects the low success rate in contemporary animal cloning experiments—1 out of 277, in Dolly's case. As Ripley moves into the room of gloom, she meets a seventh deformed clone, laid out on the operating table, still agonizingly alive, with a face recognizably hers. Complying with the clone's pleas for death, Ripley torches her monstrous double with a flamethrower, igniting the entire lab. The glass tanks explode and the clones burn in the movie's most powerful anti-technology, anti-cloning image.

The clone confronts us with profound uneasiness because it has the potential "to challenge the notion of who we are," says Pierre Baldi. "Through millions of years of evolution our brains have been wired to provide us with an inner feeling of self, a feeling that each of us is a unique individual delimited by precise boundaries."[103] While robots and cyborgs destabilize the boundaries between human and machine, the clone counters our sense of possessing a unique identity—it's another created-by-technology being that potentially can replace us. This anxiety about facing our clone is reminiscent of an older fear, that of the doppelgänger or double, "the basis of all monster images," according to David Skal.[104] At a psychological level, the double represents our evil side, the embodiment of a violent, primitive subconscious, as in the two classics of doppelgänger terror, Robert Lewis Stevenson's *The Strange Case of Dr. Jekyll and Mr. Hyde* (1886) and Oscar Wilde's *The Picture of Dorian Gray* (1890). In *Alien Resurrection,* Ripley confronts and destroys the physical manifestations of the monstrous doppelgänger.

Facing his younger, vampiric-looking, evil clone in *Star Trek: Nemesis* (2002), *Enterprise* Captain Picard tries to talk him into being good, then stabs him in the stomach with a stake. Picard-duplicate Shinzon (Tom

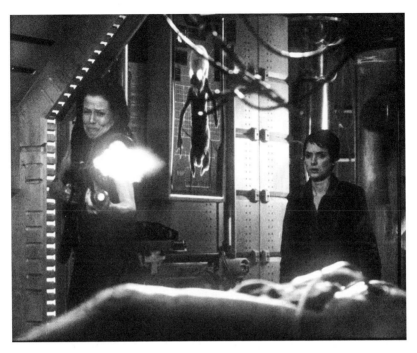

Alien Resurrection: *Horrified by the monstrousness of science, Ripley incinerates her failed, deformed clones (Courtesy Photofest).*

Hardy) was created by the Romulans from stolen Picard DNA as a weaponized counterfeit captain to subvert the "very heart of the Federation." The plan was abandoned and the poor lonely clone was banished, as a subhuman, to toil in the Empire's hellish dilithium mines on planet Remus, where the sunless environment turns everyone into Nosferatu look-alikes. Oppressed by all, he nourishes his grudge for twenty years, emerging so twisted with hatred that his only ambition is to travel to Earth and kill everybody with a "biogenic" weapon so powerful that it turns organic matter first to stone and then to dust. Released during the buildup to the 2003 invasion of Iraq, *Nemesis* strangely echoed the government's drumbeat of propaganda. An arrogant dictatorial super-villain possesses a weapon of mass destruction while the morally righteous Federation makes a successful preemptive strike—*Nemesis* almost seemed designed to encourage the nation's Iraqnophobia and justify its war. Not behaving by Picard's definition of humanity, Shinzon is determined to kill his clone and destroy everything. "I'm only an echo . . . a shadow. My life is meaningless while you are alive." Shinzon fails to find meaning because Picard preemptively terminates him.

In a parallel plot, Lieutenant Commander Data confronts his own flawed clone, in the form of prototype android B-4, reassembled from parts found on a sun-drenched planet oddly populated with angry Road Warriors. Unfortunately, poor Data gets burdened with a retarded doppelgänger whose "neural pathways aren't sophisticated." To upgrade him, Data transfers his mind into B-4's positronic brain. Yet B-4 turns out to be slightly evil when he briefly becomes an inadvertent spy for Shinzon. Data sadly shuts him down. Neither of the clones in *Nemesis* acts in accordance with *Star Trek's* ideology that a persistent, disciplined effort to improve oneself can humanize androids and clones as well as Vulcans, Romulans, Klingons, Borg, and any species that wants to be part of the big human family. Data's dumb twin later sees the light. When Data—in an act of Asimovian robot self-sacrifice—kills himself to save the *Enterprise,* B-4 is reactivated and shows signs of self-improvement when he hums a tune, suggesting that he could replace Data in the unlikely event that another sequel is developed.

As with creating the robot, android, and cyborg, cloning links back to the myths of artificially engendering human life—from Athena springing out of Zeus's cleaved head to God the Father manufacturing a divine son. In the words of David Noble: "[T]he male God created Adam and gave him life unaided by either woman or sex. And God created Eve from Adam, not Adam from Eve (promoting—and reflecting—fantasies of masculine birth and the homunculus)."[105] As we've seen, tales of the golem and Frankenstein's monster share in this male myth of creation. "Cloning is the most extreme development along a continuum in science, religion, and other aspects of society that attempts to immortalize men," says Jane Murphy in *Test Tube Women,* "by establishing 'The Father' as the sole parent in creation."[106] This patriarchal aspect of cloning is also evoked in *Alien Resurrection,* with its group of mad male scientists who reproduce females in a test tube to be unethically exploited for corporate and military purposes.

REVOLT OF THE CLONES

A disturbing vision of corporate cloning for body parts, *Spares* (1996)—by British author Michael Marshall Smith—proposes that clones will service the rich and powerful as walking organ banks. This horrific premise received poor treatment in an earlier obscure, poorly made movie, *Parts: The Clonus Horror* (1978), whose promotional taglines were the best part of the movie: "Test tube terrors! Imagine extending your life with spare body parts! Imagine being the body the parts come from! Reality dissolves into a nightmare of surreal super-science when you ask yourself 'Am I real?' or 'Am I really a clone?' "

Imagining a corrupt, corporate-owned America one hundred years in the future, *Spares* is first-person narrated—like a Raymond Chandler *noir* thriller—by burnout Jack Randall, a former cop, husband, and drug addict. He's on the lam with six "spares," clones that he rescued from a "farm" where they were vat-grown and raised to provide replacement parts—skin, eyes, organs, limbs—for their legally human, genetic twins.

Apart from the issue of whether the clones should have human rights, *Spares* focuses on bio-science's class bias: extending the lifespan of the privileged while exploiting lower-class bodies as a commodity. The industrial-medical corporation that controls the Farm does not consider the clones human. *Spares* blames the moral corruption of the rich, but also condemns the scientific establishment as techno-priests. "If the scientists could clone whole bodies then they could have just grown limbs or parts when the need arose," Randall says. "But that would have been more expensive and less convenient, and they are the new Gods in this wonderful century of ours."[107]

Randall fails to protect the clones. They are captured while hiding out in his best friend's apartment. His search for them leads to a convoluted mystery involving underworld assassins, the gangsters who slaughtered his family, and the Gap—a nightmarish pseudo-reality created by computers, populated by cyborgs and bio-monstrosities, and resembling the shock-war atmosphere of Vietnam in the 1960s and Iraq in 2003. *Spares* links weaponized technology to its function as a force for political and corporate control.

While trashing corporate control of militarized technology, Smith symbolically encapsulates several anti-biotechnological perspectives: that it will produce class war, that it will undermine personal identity and human dignity, and that, wildly implausible or not, it makes possible the creation of a human parts production line. In the 1990s, organ cloning for transplant became more of a scientific reality. "At least one scientist says he may be able to grow headless human clones in artificial wombs, sometime early in the next century, to be used as spare parts during the lifetime of the human donors whose cells have been cloned," reports Jeremy Rifkin in *The Biotech Century*.[108]

BIOPUNK IN THE AGE OF
GENOME BREAKDOWN

In the eerie, cynical, and morbid future world of *Spares,*
Michael Marshall Smith engineered a biopunk style out of the cyberpunk
tradition. Cloned bio-mutants team up with an alienated, amoral tough
guy to combat corporate evil, weaponized artificial intelligence, and gangster assassins while coping with the disorienting effects of designer drugs
and virtual reality hallucinations. Cyberpunk wanted to liberate us from
the dead meat of the body by exploring a cybernetic shift in perception:
it blurred the distinction between human and machine, rejected the oppressive, corporate-controlled material world, and embraced the immaterial, informational world. The cyberpunk vision is reflected in *Spares,*
with its mind-controlling military computers run amok, empathetic sentient robots, and a cyberspace hell penetrating the real world. But Smith
offers no illusory freedom in cyberspace and accepts the body, at least
slightly beyond its meat-market status: "Bodies are great, and I wouldn't
go anywhere without mine, but sometimes they're so disappointing. If we
mistreated them as badly as we do our minds then everyone would be dead,
and yet there they go complaining all the time."[109]

Neuromancer featured a biotechnological subculture that offered genes,
hormones, vat-grown skin, eyes, and muscles as well as surgeons that could
reset DNA to help ensure longevity. Still, genetic engineering stayed in the
background of *Neuromancer* and other cyberpunk fiction, as the technological focus tended to be on artificial intelligence, cyborgs, cyberspace, and life
in the new electronic playground. Smith unites the fears of electronic technology with the evils of corporate and military biotechnology. Along with
filmmaker David Cronenberg and such writers as Paul Di Filippo, Paul J.
McAuley, Greg Bear, and Octavia Butler, Smith reflects the biotech era
of genome breakdown, manipulation, and reconstitution. While sharing
cyberpunk's criticism of corporate hegemony and weaponized technology,
biopunk embraces the physical and explores our growing confusion about
the value and integrity of our bodies in a genetically mutated machine
world.

Bio-mutation evolves to new extremes in Paul Di Filippo's short story
collection *Ribofunk* (1996).[110] With an ironic, futuristic bio-speak style,
Ribofunk envisions a posthuman world of Dr. Moreau, so transformed and
diluted by gene-spliced, chromosome-hacked, transgenic species-strains
that humans have almost disappeared. In the future world of *Ribofunk,*
biotechnology has created a sentient slave caste of chimeric creatures or
"splices" (with less than 50 percent human genes) that are considered in-

ferior by humans (those with 50 percent or more human genes). One of these—a gynomorph love-slave—describes herself: "I am comprised of five species, with three percent being human. My skeletal structure is avian, insuring a lightness and appealing fragility. . . . My musculature is feline, my skin a derivative of chamois. My brain is based on that of a mink. I have a vaginal contractile index of ninety. My pheromones are tailored specifically to arouse."[111] Some of these oppressed gene-spliced transgenics revolt. A genetically engineered animal-man, the diabolical Krazy Kat escapes bondage and becomes a splice-rights terrorist that wants to overthrow the human race.

An apparent bio-philiac, Di Filippo humorously promotes a wildly experimental trial-and-error approach to biotechnology. In a sarcastic dig, he introduces a group of bio-conservationists so fanatical that they preserve endangered species, such as the smallpox virus, by infecting themselves. While Di Filippo does not directly address the ethics of cloning and gene manipulation, he projects a humorously bleak future as quasi-humans try to keep the proliferating consequences of ribo-anarchy under control. In the story "Big Eater," for example, humans must battle the "infamous water-hyacinth/karibaweed splice" that doubles every two days, impedes shipping, asphyxiates fish, causes flooding, and grows "to form the largest single organism in the history of the world."[112] To prosecute the war against the all-consuming organism, genetic designers create Big Eaters, otherwise known as "coypu-cows" which were deftly engineered out of "nutria, manatee," and, of course, human germlines, which gets "the rifkins" really upset.[113]

The organized anti-tech forces, such as the "greenpeacers," or the "rifkins" (named after contemporary bio-gadfly Jeremy Rifkin), typically oppose the unique forms of "bioremediation" that others view as the only way to stop the escalating biological disasters. While he mocks biotech critics and explores the diverse possibilities of a creative, chaotic approach to germline engineering, Di Filippo ends the collection with the ultimate transformation of the biosphere—a terrifying bio-apocalypse. A sprawling sentient biomass, known as the Panplasmodaemonium, engulfs the earth and its inhabitants. Despite his anti-conservatism, Di Filippo's final story dramatizes Rifkin's biblical warning of an impending "second genesis" threatening "a biological Tower of Babel spreading chaos throughout the biological world and, in the process, drowning out the ancient language of evolution."[114]

Of all the technologies examined in this book, biotechnology elicits the greatest fear and the most passionate criticism. As Dorothy Nelkin says, "[B]iotechnology has replaced nuclear power as the symbol of 'technology-out-of-control.' "[115] Anti-biotechnology themes in science fiction connect back to the whole history of anxiety with science, scientists, and technology. Amplified by the horrors of Nazi Josef Mengele, the science fiction geneticist joins a long procession of mad scientists who irresponsibly employ technology in a desire to conquer nature at any cost, while rationalizing death, injury, and unforeseen disasters with pompous rhetoric about perfecting humanity. Expanding on the scientific threat, biotech science fiction joins 1980s cyborg and cyberspace narratives in locating the conditions for technological dominance in the multinational corporation fueled by military funding and weapons research.

Biological themes in science fiction also reflect specific contemporary concerns that include eugenics, cloning, genetic discrimination, the exploitation of the body as a commodity, the safety of genetically modified food, and the potential for catastrophic accidents in experimentation with transgenic species, as well as genetic imperialism practiced by greedy international corporations. In this way, science fiction serves as a constructive force that supports public resistance to the blindly lustful expansion of biotechnology—focusing attention on specific problems, extrapolating potential dire consequences, and increasing awareness of biotechnology as a political force that serves the interests of bio-scientists, corporate elites, and militaristic patriarchs.

The next chapter focuses on nanotechnology—the manufacture of artificially intelligent, self-replicating molecular machines that theoretically can be programmed to build anything from buildings to brains and from bombs to disease-fighting microbes. Nanotechnology goes beyond improving or reconstructing the human body and encompasses the re-creation of nature.

EIGHT Malevolent Molecular Machines

NANOTECHNOLOGY

The ultimate technology, nanotechnology fuses biotechnology, artificial intelligence, and robotics and makes everything else obsolete, including humans. "Nanotechnology is about rebuilding mother nature atom by atom!" proclaims an advertisement for "Nanotech Report," a newsletter analyzing investment opportunities in the burgeoning field. Nanotechnology—or molecular engineering—centers on the creation of artificially intelligent, molecule-size machines. The feasibility of maneuvering atoms—the basis of nanotechnology—was first proposed by physicist Richard Feynman, a Nobel laureate who helped develop the atomic bomb at Los Alamos. In a 1959 speech titled "There's Plenty of Room at the Bottom," Feynman argued that micro-engineering might lead to the synthesis of chemicals. He also proposed microscopic machine surgeons, an idea first imagined by science fiction writer Robert Heinlein in his 1942 short story "Waldo." Aside from these few practical possibilities, he considered that building things atom-by-atom would be a "fun thing to do."[1] Imaginatively elaborating Feynman's notion of atomic engineering into an all-encompassing vision of utopia, K. Eric Drexler became St. Nano. Adopting the term *nanotechnology,*[2] Massachusetts Institute of Technology (MIT) graduate student Drexler created a scientific shock wave with the publication of his theory in a 1981 technical paper, and more popularly in the 1986 book *Engines of Creation: The Coming Era of Nanotechnology.* In Drexler's exalted view, atomic manufacturing will give scientists a godlike power to control and even create nature.

NANO-UTOPIA: DREAMS OF IMMORTALITY IN A PERFECT WORLD

Reaching for the heavens, Drexler arrived at MIT with a fascination for space travel and the colonization of other planets. While still devoted to the heavenly aspirations of interstellar travel, Drexler experienced a "cosmic transfiguration" and extended his divine desires to encompass the creation of all things, including life itself.[3] He realized, in 1976, that genetic engineers manipulated nature at the molecular level, modifying and reprogramming DNA. From this, he surmised that scientists might learn to build self-replicating, DNA-sized machines, or assemblers, that could be controlled by software. Just as the little machines in cells, called ribosomes, build organisms—such as ants, ducks, and humans—one atom at a time following templates coded in DNA, tiny nanomachines or assemblers could be programmed to structure matter one atom at a time, synthesizing any material substance. "Assemblers will be able to build all that ribosomes can, and more; assembler-based replicators will therefore be able to do all that life can, and more," says Drexler in *Engines of Creation.*[4] In this "Bashful Confession of Omnipotence," as Ed Regis puts it,[5] Drexler surpassed all the claims of the high priests of technology, asserting that nanotechnologists will have complete control over the physical universe.

Rocks, dirt, or grass, for example, will supply raw material that molecular disassemblers will break down into their constituent atoms. Using this atomic raw material, programmed nano-assemblers will duplicate the atoms and move them around, building molecular structures. Eventually, these universal building machines could be programmed to make computers, coffee tables, carpets, chairs, cars, and hats. Nanotechnology will fulfill the alchemists' dream and turn molecules of metal into gold. Just as nature's cellular nanomachines build whales and organize atoms into huge redwood trees, Drexler thought that growing a rocket engine in a specially prepared vat from soil, air, and sunlight was not particularly startling. Using inanimate raw materials, nanomachines will even fashion atoms into living organisms, creating new life from scratch. "Assemblers will be able to make virtually anything from common materials without labor, replacing smoking factories with systems as clean as forests," he says. "They will transform technology and the economy at their roots, opening a new world of possibilities. They will indeed be engines of abundance."[6]

In Nano-Utopia, most work will be done by nanomachines, thus eliminating the jobs of humans. "Under the worst-case interpretation, nanotechnology was the ultimate Luddite nightmare," says Ed Regis, in *Nano: The Emerging Science of Nanotechnology* (1995). "People would be displaced by machines once and for all—machines, furthermore, that were much too small to wreck."[7] But so what? A life of leisure beckons. People will not need to work—everything will be produced by the machines. Roving nanomachines will convert trash into energy. Solar nanomachines incorporated into paint will coat your house, generating electricity. Meat ma-

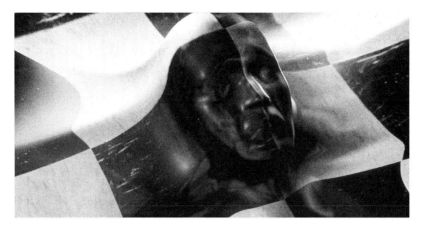

Terminator 2: Judgement Day: *In a miracle of nanotechnology, a linoleum floor transforms itself into a person (Courtesy Photofest).*

chines will synthesize steak without cows. If everything were cheap, abundant, and easily acquired, then materialism and, in fact, money itself would eventually become obsolete. Thus, nanotechnology will destroy capitalistic greed and usher in an era of Christian generosity. The age of Nano will be an age of nirvana. As Ed Regis noted: "It meant instant and effortless satisfaction of every material want or need. It gave you everything, all on a platter. Matter had been overpowered; reality itself took on a new cast: it was controllable, plastic, malleable. It presented no further hindrance, no resistance to human will. The assemblers would provide."[8] Nanotechnology will create the new Jerusalem, heaven on earth. In fact, nanobots will fix earth — mending destroyed landscapes and restoring damaged ecosystems. "We will make squirrel-sized devices with a taste for old trash," says Drexler. "We will make treelike devices with roots that spread deep and cleanse the soil of pesticides and excess acid. We will make whatever devices we need to clean up the mess left by 20th century civilization."[9]

While fixing the planet, nanotechnology will repair our flawed bodies. Microbial nanobots will be injected into our bloodstreams, augmenting our immune systems. Repair nanosites will reconstruct damaged molecular machinery, restore chemical balance, and renovate the cellular structures that result in a variety of problems from wrinkled skin to bad memory. Tirelessly seeking out viruses, tumor cells, and carcinogens, this network of nanobots will help us live longer, healthier lives. For example, a future nanotechnological cure for cancer will involve injecting cellular nanobots into the afflicted person's body. Using genetic sensors, they will hunt down and destroy every cancer cell. Other diseases will also be subject to nanobot attacks. Differently programmed molecular robots will be sent into our arteries to loosen tiny bits of plaque and clear out the clogged blood vessels. "By restoring all the cells and tissues of the body to a youthful structure," claims Drexler, "repair machines will restore youthful health."[10]

Frostbite treatment was one of the first restoration jobs Drexler envisioned after coming up with the idea of miniature robots. Cryonics had already expanded the notion of frostbite treatment to the resurrection of the dead. Preceding Drexler by over twenty years and at a time when frozen TV dinners were popular, Dr. Robert Ettinger in *The Prospect of Immortality* (1962) first proposed the idea that freezing a human body immediately after death may allow for repair and reanimation by future science. But Ettinger had no plausible way of defrosting the body without deterioration. This made cryonics questionable from the outset. Drexler imagined microbe-size machines programmed to defrost the "corpsicle,"[11] repair the tissue damage, mend torn membranes, and reconnect the severed brain and nerve circuits. Fresh blood would be transfused. The heart would be restarted and the patient would arise and walk, like a modern Lazarus. Nanotechnological frostbite treatment somehow made cryonics theoretically legitimate and made Drexler its patron saint. When California tried to prosecute Alcor Life Extension Foundation for freezing a dead woman, both Drexler and Hans Moravec, among other scientists, testified to cryonics' plausibility.[12] Woody Allen's *Sleeper* (1973) provided a humorous take on cryonics. Admitted to a hospital for minor surgery in 1973, health-food restaurant owner Miles Monroe (Allen) died but was wrapped in aluminum foil and cryogenically frozen. Two hundred years later, after being defrosted and repaired, the health-food nut is shocked to awake in a future where deep fat, hot fudge, and smoking have been discovered to be healthy.

Little noticed in the past twenty-five years, cryonics quietly gained momentum. Several American firms, including Alcor, Cryocare, and Cryo Span, store dead clients awaiting future medical discoveries and treatment while suspended in liquid nitrogen. The cost at Alcor Life Extension Foundation, where baseball legend Ted Williams was frozen in the summer of 2002, ranges from $50,000 (head only) to $120,000 (full body).[13] Cryonics received major media attention when Williams's family squabbled about the appropriate disposition of his remains. Like his anti-cryonics family members, the media declared cryonics creepy and disgusting, especially since Williams's son took the cheaper option of freezing only the baseball player's head. Despite being mocked and dismissed, cryonics has become a big business, pushed by the Transhumanist movement.

With immortality as the ultimate goal, techno-priest Ray Kurzweil urges a radical upgrading of the body that would use nanotechnology to gradually replace organs, skeleton, and brain. As a first step, he would like to see the digestive system reengineered so food passing to the stomach is disconnected from absorption into the bloodstream, removing the sensual aspects of eating from its biological purpose. That way we could eat great quantities of what is currently considered unhealthy food, like rare beef and chocolate donuts, without becoming fat pigs with clogged arteries. Nutrients would be carried into the bloodstream on the wings of metabolic nanobots, while special elimination-bots would act like tiny garbage compactors, absorbing waste from all that bad food and ending our disgusting need for excretion. "As we're learning the principles of operation of the human body and the brain," Kurzweil says, "we will soon be in a position to design vastly superior systems that will be more enjoyable, last longer, and perform better."[14]

Taking things a step further, transhumanist idol Marvin Minsky foresees nanotechnology being used to engineer a new posthuman species. In a 1994 *Scientific American* article, Minsky argued that a human-type brain and body could be built using Drexler's fabrication nanomachines.[15] Like Moravec's robots, these grown-in-a-vat organic machines would be an improvement over the human species.

Unlike Minsky and Moravec, Drexler does not endorse the replacement of humans by a nano-engineered new species, though he considers it a distinct possibility. "Replicating assemblers and thinking machines pose basic threats to people and to life on Earth. . . . our machines are evolving faster than we are. Within a few decades they seem likely to surpass us. Unless we learn to live with them in safety, our future will likely be both exciting and short."[16] Drexler dreams of a nanotechnological Garden of Eden for future humans—"a worldwide transformation which can, if we succeed, bring abundance and long life to all who wish them. And this is a prospect that quite naturally stirs dreams of utopia."[17] Drexler imagines that nanomachines will provide us with divine powers—immortal life, vast material riches without cost or labor, and total mastery over the physical world. Paradise will be regained. Drexler believes in the ultimate techno-utopian dream, casting nanotechnology as the new theology. Drexler acolyte Alcor's Thomas Donaldson put it well. "I have noticed, too much, both in cryonics and out, a strong desire to interpret nanotechnology in the exact terms of Christian myth," Donaldson wrote in an issue of *Cryonics*. "It's as if a person carries out a renaming exercise: God = Nanotechnology, Drexler = Christ. (Sorry, Eric!)"[18] Others have drawn this parallel as well. Ed Regis calls Drexler a "prophet" and his followers "evangelists of the technocratic heaven."[19]

ENGINES OF DESTRUCTION:
THE MILITARIZATION OF
NANOTECHNOLOGY

Though conflict exists in the scientific community about fulfilling all of Drexler's nano-ambitions, research and development have exploded since the publication of *Engines of Creation*.[20] "Nanotechnology has evolved from a laboratory curiosity into an object of intense interest on the part of some of the world's largest corporations," says *Technology Review* editor John Benditt.[21] Originally defined by Drexler as molecular manufacturing, the term *nanotechnology* has been appropriated as a commercial and investment buzzword that encompasses any technology with significant nanoscale features. Currently, nano-products include sunscreens, stain-resistant fabrics, and self-cleaning window glass. Companies that make computer components have devised nanoscale, tubular structures — "carbon nanotubes" — to provide faster processing, greater memory storage, and enhanced display.[22]

In 2003, government-funded academia joined with the international titans of technology, including IBM, Sony, Hewlett-Packard, DuPont, and others, to spend more than $3 billion on nanotechnology-related tools.[23] Endorsing the practical potential of nanotech, the United States launched the National Nanotechnology Initiative (NNI). Established by President Clinton with the encouragement of nano-enthusiast vice president Al Gore, and continued by President Bush, the NNI will provide $3.7 billion for nanoscale research.[24] As part of that initiative, the National Science Foundation supports six new applications-oriented nanotech centers at Northwestern University, Cornell University, Harvard University, Columbia University, Rensselaer Polytechnic Institute, and Rice University. DARPA will spend about 25 percent of this nano-research money on military/surveillance applications.[25]

Tiny networked sensing devices, as small as dust motes, are being developed to "process and collect . . . information about enemy movements, crop conditions, pollution or anything else requiring monitoring."[26] Called "smart dust," these self-propelled, artificially intelligent gnat-size robots will work together in networked clouds. While enemy surveillance is the goal, these invisibly small robots will make it "possible to watch anyone, anywhere, at any time," say Menzel and D'Aluisio in *Robo sapiens*.[27] Overzealous government forces, in their wars on crime, drugs, and terrorism, could easily use nanotechnology to remove the last vestiges of privacy in our society. Besides the deployment of tiny ubiquitous networked spies in the form of mists or clouds, drug and DNA analysis might be performed on people without their knowledge as they pass through a nanobot-cloud. Micro-machines measuring bio-responses could be used to detect lies. At a minimum, traditional surveillance will increase drastically as people will be continuously watched by tiny ubiquitous cameras. "Nanocomputers, nano-scale propulsion, and robotics together will make such surveillance invisible to the human eye," says Douglas Mulhall in *Our Molecular Future*. "Personal privacy is dead and getting deader."[28]

As part of NNI, the U.S. Army provided MIT with a five-year, $50 million contract to establish the Institute for Soldier Nanotechnologies.[29] Corporate partners DuPont and Raytheon will toss another $30 million into the Soldier Institute. The goal of this military-industrial-university collaboration is to build a supersoldier, or at least a super-uniform. The Army wants a lightweight combat outfit that provides super strength—molecular muscles—and protection from bullets and bioweapons while monitoring the soldier's health and communicating with remote commanders.

Besides communication, protection, and surveillance, weaponized nanotechnology will have a major impact on war, crime, and terrorism. If Drexler's micro-assemblers can construct food, houses, and rocket ships, then the most fantastic horrors might also be realized. Micro-invaders, undetected by radar or any other sensing device, could be programmed to propel themselves into your town and into your body, consuming your flesh and organs and spreading to others in a nano-plague. Drexler himself feared the dangers of nano-weapons. Foreign governments, terrorists, or even crazed individuals might threaten the world with molecular devastation unless their demands were met, creating a situation as dangerous as global thermonuclear war. "Replicators can be more potent than nuclear weapons: to devastate earth with bombs would require masses of exotic hardware and rare isotopes," says Drexler, "but to destroy all life with replicators would require only a single speck made of ordinary elements. Replicators give nuclear war some company as a potential cause of extinction, giving a broader context to extinction as a moral concern."[30]

This means fighting nano-weapons with nano-defenses in a never-ending spiral—a kind of miniature but extremely dangerous arms race. With complex interactive systems, changes easily produce unforeseen, unintended, and potentially disastrous consequences. But even if the ultimate disaster does not occur, the engines of destruction will play a dominating role in the development of the technology, with the military funding and directing industrial and educational research. As with all of the cyborg technologies previously discussed, nanotechnology will be driven in large part by military desires, stratagems, and requirements, thus ensuring that the technology's dangerous agenda will be imagined, explored, and developed.

MIND CONTROL: NANO-INFECTED BRAINS

Nanotechnology and genetic engineering become the tools of slavery in the vivid and terrifying nightmare of *Fairyland* (1995), a novel by British writer and former botanist Paul McAuley. In a Europe devastated by war and virulent nano-plagues, the wealthy elites control things. Oblivious to suffering, the insensitive rich keep nano-engineered, infertile, transgenic human/primate lifeforms—called "dolls"—as pets, servants, and interactive theme park exhibits. A control biochip implanted in the dolls' brains puts them under technological restraint in a manner similar to Dr. Moreau's manimal-mastery. The exploitation of the dolls quickly expands to include slave labor in nanotech factories where working conditions are hazardous for humans. Soon, the dwarfish, blue-skinned dolls are cultivated for gladiatorial fighting. Humans even hunt them down like animals in this "age of excess."[31]

After the failure of the liberationist movement to change the status of dolls from enhanced animals to legally protected human beings, civil rights leader and child genius Milena seeks out an underworld, drug-dealing gene hacker, Alex Sharkey, who is on the run from gangsters. Even the amoral biopunk Sharkey feels sorry for the dolls, who are weak, genetically abused, dislocated from nature, and "dazed by the violence done to their genome." Dolls epitomize Sharkey's belief "that there's no point gengineering anything more advanced than yeast, because the more complex the organism, the more unpredictable the side effects."[32] Yet the on-the-lam gene-engineer gets manipulated into a role that leads to a catastrophic war between humans and dolls and helps spread a dangerous form of nanotechnology.

Paying him enough to cover his gangster debt, Milena employs Sharkey to engineer germline changes to the sterile dolls so his genetic alterations—for reproduction and intelligence—will be inherited by future generations. The newly fertile, nano-augmented dolls disappear into the wilds of a war-torn, rapidly deteriorating Europe. Over the years, a new lifeform emerges from the genetically altered dolls that is as far evolved beyond its originator as humans are from bacteria. Known as fairies, these posthuman, post-doll creatures carve out a home, called the Magic Kingdom, in the ruins of Disneyland Paris. Besides enhanced intelligence, sentience, and free will, the fairies—like their mythological namesakes—possess supernatural abilities as a result of nanotechnological expertise. They use nano-engineered memes—mind viruses called "fembots"—to invade the brain and influence its functioning. The fembots, for example, manipulate humans by triggering false memories, inducing hallucinations, and altering attitudes and opinions to further the fairies' interests—all done through tiny nanomachines.

Conceptually, memes have nothing to do with nanotech, though Drexler goes on at length about them in *Engines of Creation* while discussing how ideas get spread through a culture. Memes are ideas, thought patterns, belief systems, or methods of doing something—from religious dogma to catching fish. Richard Dawkins proposed memes in his book *The Selfish Gene* (1976); he likens them to biological viruses that penetrate the brain, replicate, and take it over.[33] McAuley, in *Fairyland,* imagines memes as viral weapons of thought control. Some believe this mind-manipulation nanotechnology will become reality. João Pedro de Magalhães—a microbiologist and Transhumanist—says, "A virus that penetrates the brain and changes its network so that the victim becomes a supporter of a certain ideology is not very far away into the future."[34]

In *Fairyland,* children dosed with fembots turn into psychotic soldiers who hunt down and kill other children. In the ultimate technological takeover, fairies eat humans. The threatening intrusion of this new, superior species—derived from human technology yet human-hating—suggests that humans might bring about their own extinction. Fairies genetically program fembots to make specific changes in the germ cells of the creatures they infect—a nightmarish vision of nano-induced evolution gone mad under pressure from military imperatives. Their weaponized constructs include a vampire fox, able to inject fembots through hollow teeth, an attack dog with a crocodile head, and "warewolves"—wolves with human bodies and nano-engineered brains.

Finally, the fairies spread a new meme plague through the remaining humans so that they will forget what's happened. Humans will regard the fairies like the fairies of old, living only in legends and myths. "As the humans retreat into their dreams, brave new creatures will claim the world."[35] In this technophobic novel of nanotechnological takeover, the fairies reiterate the threat posed by other artificial humans of the past. They revolt against their oppressive human masters, gaining control of evolution to alter themselves, and they appropriate nanotechnology to manipulate the minds of their evolutionary competitors. As one of the fairies boasts, " 'All this nature, the evolution of matter, it's over. It's finished. . . . There's no nature anymore. So we've transcended that. We're looking for the next step.'"[36] *Fairyland* depicts posthuman evolution leading to human extinction at its most horrific.

UTOPIA AS DYSTOPIA: NANOTECHNOLOGICAL DICTATORSHIP

A nanotechnological elite controls the world in *The Diamond Age, or, A Young Lady's Illustrated Primer* (1995)[37]—Neal Stephenson's sardonic, nanocentric follow-up to *Snow Crash,* derived from Drexler's notion that nanotechnology will produce super-strong diamond fiber from carbon atoms.[38] The affluence of the Diamond Age is symbolized by buildings and airships constructed of diamonds. In a society based on nanotech, consumer goods are generated in matter compilers (similar to the replicating machines in *Star Trek: The Next Generation*). In a 1999 computer game, *Civilization: Call to Power,*[39] the civilization-building simulation culminates in the Diamond Age. In the game, you acquire nano-assemblers to build factories and machines which terraform the planet, build space cities, defuse nuclear weapons, and even brainwash the world's population. While the game illustrates some of nanotechnology's miraculous potential, *The Diamond Age* delves deeply into political issues provoked by the technology and asserts human values of love, freedom, and subjectivity over a posthuman species evolved into a nanotechnological mass mind.

The major problem of the Diamond Age, as well as our own, concerns the extreme inequality of wealth and resource distribution despite abundance. The "Vickys"—a technological elite—control society through the centralized matter assembler system. The Feed—an encrypted molecular network—supplies nano-feedstock atoms to the individual-use matter-compilers, or nano-assemblers, located in people's homes. The system reinforces society's hierarchical foundation and controls nanotechnology while providing a minimal living standard. Like American politicians, the Vickys—who have adopted Victorian culture and values—arrogantly view themselves as the determiner of what is right and good in the world.

The ultimate nano-dystopia, the Vickys' dominance derives from devastating nanotechnological weapons and surveillance. Swarming nanoprobes monitor the population's every move and examine people from the inside, sometimes doing nasty things to their bodies. For example, "the Red Death, a.k.a. the Seven Minute Special"—a tiny aerodynamic capsule—bursts open after impact with a human body and releases a thousand or so corpuscle-sized bodies known as "cookie-cutters" into the victim's bloodstream. It takes seven minutes for them to circulate throughout the body and upon self-detonation, they explode through the skin, turning the victim into a "big leaky sack of undifferentiated gore."[40] People need regular injections of antibiotic nanosites as protection from the latest virulent nanovirus.

A brilliant nano-programmer and neo-Victorian, John Percival Hackworth, is commissioned by a high-ranking Vicky to devise a book—*A Young Lady's Illustrated Primer*—that will educate his granddaughter in the arts of self-determination and self-defense, free of the complacency which infects and weakens the Victorians. A vastly complex interactive multimedia device that uses "nanosites," or microscopic computers, embedded in the "paper," the book is designed to react to its user and evolve in accord with her life. A fairy tale, a friend, a teacher, the Primer exists to educate and raise a free-thinking girl. But it leads to a revolution—a subversion of nanotechnological development and destabilization of the hierarchical Feed system.

After creating the book, Hackworth violates the ethics of his Victorian tribe. He pirates a copy of the Primer, but it gets stolen from him. The thief—a poor slum-dweller—brings it home for his abused, orphaned sister, Nell. The book opens her mind and transforms her life. Through the book's fantasy quest adventure, which eventually reflects her real life, Nell—the heroine of *The Diamond Age*—learns everything from martial arts to cooking and computer theory. Like all interactive media in this fictional era, the book incorporates a live remote actor ("ractor"). The human element proves more significant than the technological book. Over time, the ractor Miranda becomes a surrogate mother to Nell, teaching her to read, to think independently, and to strive beyond her oppressive limitations.

Meanwhile, Hackworth must atone for his crime. Expelled from the neo-Victorian paradise, he is sentenced to spend ten years as a double agent living among the orgiastic, underwater techno-cult known as the Drummers—a subversive group with a hive mind. Nanosites course through the Drummers' bloodstreams and brains, interacting and sharing information with other Drummers. This vast communication system that links with the global network makes the Drummers capable of solving otherwise inextricable nano-construction programming problems. As a shared mind, the Drummers function as unconscious machine-parts, sacrificing individual subjectivity.

Hackworth's imprisonment, as a subversive agent within the Drummer collective, occurs amid rising violence against Vicky and Western hegemony. Led by the Fists of Righteous Harmony in collaboration with the

Drummers, Chinese tribes seek to slaughter oppressors and develop a radical alternative to the nanotech Feed system. Called the Seed, this utopian counter-technology is envisioned as liberating the Chinese tribes from Western domination. Decentralized Seed technology would "dissolve the foundations of . . . all the societies that had grown up around the concept of a centralized, hierarchical Feed."[41]

Submerged within the mind-controlling Drummer network, Hackworth is manipulated into designing the Seed whose instructions have been encrypted in a book. Unlocking "Book of the Seed" will require Drummer-style information transmission—a techno-orgiastic ritual that includes the exchange of bodily fluids and the sacrifice of a female acting as a network hub. The female turns out to be Miranda, the mother-surrogate ractor from Nell's Primer. Miranda's body, already infected with Drummer nanosites, "would play host to the climax of computation that would certainly burn her alive in the process" through the literal heat of nanocomputer activity.[42]

The complex, convoluted story of *The Diamond Age* comes together when Nell—immunized against the Drummers' nanosites and possessing internalized nano-weapons of her own—enters the world of the Drummers and finds Miranda. She cradles Miranda's head, bends down, and savagely kisses her—"biting through her own lips and Miranda's so that their blood mingled."[43] Nell's own hunter/killer nanobots destroy the Drummer nanosites in Miranda's body. With that kiss, she shuts down the Drummers' techno-ritual and re-encrypts the Book of the Seed. Nell stops the efforts of the Chinese to develop the counter-technology. While opposed to Vicky control, Nell sees the Seed technology as equally oppressive, a utopian ideal that promises freedom but requires absolute conformity to its structure.

The nanotechnology imagined in *The Diamond Age* produces numerous benefits, yet its use ultimately serves oppressive ends as it forces people to accommodate to the requirements of its Feed/Seed system. This is what Langdon Winner calls "reverse adaptation"—"the adjustment of human ends to match the character of the available means."[44] Freedom is illusory. Once in place, modern technology tends to remove its operation from effective direction by human beings. It impels them to serve its structural laws. With their group mind, the drummers function as automata and pass this functioning to the machines they devise. Nell subverts the old order and blocks the establishment of a new nanotechnological order—a response that corresponds with the contemporary suggestions of nano-critics such as Bill Joy, who argues that the dangers of nanotechnology far outweigh the benefits. "The only realistic alternative I see," writes Joy, "is relinquishment: to limit development of the technologies that are too dangerous, by limiting our pursuit of certain kinds of knowledge."[45]

Nell amplifies the high-tech *Young Lady's Illustrated Primer* into liberatory political, anti-technology action. But the interactive nano-book has been read by others and has not inspired the same sort of rebellious behavior. Miranda inspires Nell beyond the book. In becoming Nell's spiritual mother, she establishes a permanent bond and permeates the Primer's stories with meaning, empathy, and love. Miranda enables Nell to articulate the subversive subjectivity inherent in the book's narrative. Beyond the Primer's nano-enhanced education, the love between mother and daughter—their self-determination and common humanity—are more important and ultimately more powerful than the domineering demands of the tyrant technology.

Nanomachines could be used to penetrate, capture, transform, and rule the world through mind control. "Even the most ruthless police have no use for nuclear weapons," nano-priest Drexler says, "but they do have uses for bugs, drugs, assassins, and other flexible engines of power . . . to consolidate their power over people."[46] Nanosites injected in the body for utopian functions, like disease diagnosis and cell repair, could be easily subverted, hacked, and reprogrammed to tranquilize, lobotomize, modify, or terminate entire populations. *The Diamond Age* cautions against nanotechnology as an invasion-of-the-body-snatchers technology.

HIVE MINDS: ELECTRONIC NETWORKS

The Drummers' hive mind—facilitated by nanotechnology—epitomizes one of science fiction's longest-running technophobic motifs. Philosopher Michael Heim, in his book *Virtual Realism,* describes the techno-optimistic vision of hive mentality as an analogue of humans networked through computers: "The network idealist builds collective beehives. The idealist sees the next century as an enormous communitarian buzz. The world-wide networks that cover the planet will form a global bee-hive where civilization shakes off individual controls and electronic life steps out on its own."[47] But it's the lack of individual controls that negatively characterizes science fiction hive societies—a dark history that goes back before nanotechnology to the beginning of the twentieth century.

In H. G. Wells's *First Men in the Moon* (1901), the insect-like Selenites—an ultra-conformist techno-society—use psychological, chemical, and surgical techniques to force individuals into a defined social function. In the early anti-machine dystopia of "The Machine Stops," E. M. Forster describes the living quarters of his machine-dominated populace as "a small room hexagonal in shape, like the cell of a bee."[48] Forster's mechanized society reflects a hive existence where the unseen all-powerful central committee, operating through the machine, asserts conformist control over the insect society. The sleek black humanoids that force human obedience in Jack Williamson's "With Folded Hands" are mobile units controlled and powered by a great brain on another planet.

In the 1950s, a paranoid vision of hive culture—in Robert Heinlein's novels *Puppet Masters* (1951) and *Starship Troopers* (1959) and in the film *Them!*—reflected American fears associated with Communism: the anti-individualistic ideology is symbolized by the communal mentality of the invading force of parasites, insects, and ants. In *Starship Troopers* and *Them!*, a male-dominated military force crushes the matriarchal insect culture, suggesting the gender prejudice that may also underlie anti-hive attitudes. Human individualism and hive civilization are shown, in science fiction, to be so fundamentally opposed that they must fight each other in a Darwinian battle of survival.

While some fairly recent science fiction stories—Joe Haldeman's *The Forever War* (1974), Orson Scott Card's *Speaker for the Dead* (1986), and C. J. Cherryh's *Serpent's Ranch* (1982)[49]—regard the hive mind somewhat positively, most do not. The Borg of *Star Trek,* the bopper robots in Rudy Rucker's *Software,* the intelligent nanosites in Greg Bear's *Blood Music* (1983), the army of killing machines in *Star Wars I: The Phantom Menace,* the nanobot swarm in Michael Crichton's *Prey* (2002), and the anti-human robots in the movie *I Robot* (2004) all follow in the technophobic tradition of the hive mind as a technological horror. The merged consciousness of the collective destroys individual identity, eliminates the boundary of the body, and undermines a coherent sense of self.

Like the Drummers in *The Diamond Age, Star Trek*'s Borg collective is enabled through nanotechnology. Borg babies are embedded with microscopic computers linked together in a neural network that enforces collective control under dominion of the Borg Queen. Nanotechnology also empowers the Borg to assimilate others into the group mind as demonstrated in "Scorpion" (*VOY,* 1997). Using injection tubules that extend from its fingers, a Borg drone injects billions of nanoprobes into the bloodstream of an individual targeted for assimilation. The nanoprobes attach to blood cells, taking over their functions and spreading throughout the victim's body like a virus. Captain Picard gets nano-assimilated into the group mind in "The Best of Both Worlds" (1990), and even after the nanosites have been removed, he experiences tormenting echoes of the experience six years

Star Trek: First Contact: *Borg Queen uses the lure of her sexy nanoprobes and technologized beauty to seduce Picard back into the hive (Courtesy Photofest).*

later in *First Contact.* The hive model of civilization subverts liberal human values of freedom, autonomy, and individuality and frequently represents the ultimate techno-totalitarian dystopia.

INVISIBLE INVADERS: WEAPONIZED NANOTECHNOLOGY

Borg nanoprobes are modulated by *Voyager*'s Doctor and utilized as a weapon against the galaxy's most powerful aliens, Species 8472, in "Scorpion." Technologically superior to the Borg and the Federation, Species 8472 possess DNA-based computers, organic spacecraft, and genetically engineered weapons—all protected by an extremely powerful immune system that senses and destroys any technological or microbial invader. The Doctor encodes the Borg nanoprobes with an electrochemical signature matching that of the 8472's cells. The stealthy, weaponized nanosites penetrate the aliens' immune systems undetected, enabling *Voyager* to demolish several bioships. This obviously suggests the power of nanotechnology—even if bodies were immunized against all forms of known biological pathogens, the possibility exists of engineering nano-pathogens to specifically target the genetic structure of a species or race.

An episode of *The X-Files,* "S.R. 819" (1999), further dramatizes the insidious potential of computer-controlled nanosites loosed in a human body. FBI Assistant Director Skinner (Mitch Pileggi) lies rigid on a hospital bed. His head and arms are covered with distended purple and yellow veins that pulse with every heartbeat. Scully, meanwhile, examines a vial of Skinner's blood and finds microbial foreign bodies that multiply uniformly and rapidly. These specks form dams in Skinner's veins, cutting off his blood flow. This will soon lead to a fatal heart attack.

As a result of his investigation into Senate Resolution 819—designed to control nanotechnology for military purposes—Skinner has been infected with nano-engineered, computer-controlled atoms of carbon. A depraved long-haired man uses a PDA (Personal Digital Assistant) to control the replicating frequency of the atoms inside Skinner. Increasing the frequency will cause his heart to fail. The hairy man—double agent Alex Krycek (Nick Lea)—threatens: "I can push the button any time." With the deadly nanosites circulating in his blood, Skinner closes the case, leaving the secret new techno-weapon in the hands of the government, the military, and their corporate conspirators.

The *X-Files* nightmare of computer-controlled, self-replicating machines inside a person's body raises disturbing implications, but what if the nanomachines got outside the body and into the world? Without self-replication, the utopian promise of molecular manufacturing will not be practical or economically feasible.[50] Yet the potential for disaster looms large. While micro-machines might be programmed to cease reproduction, what happens if there's a software glitch? Replication would happen very fast. The initial assembler nanomachine makes a copy of itself, and so does each of its descendants. Quickly, we might be faced with the nanotechnological equivalent of Paul Di Filippo's earth-consuming Panplasmodaemonium (see Chapter Seven). For good reason, Dr. Frankenstein refused to provide a sex partner for his monstrous creation, fearing the disastrous consequences of a thousand Frankenstein monsters.

NANO-REPLICATION:
THE GRAY GOO PROBLEM

Dangerously out-of-control, self-replicating nanotechnology makes its first science fiction appearance—before Feynman and before

Drexler—in the Philip K. Dick short story "AutoFac" (see Chapter Four). Created during war, automated factories continue manufacturing after the war ends, though most people are dead. These AutoFacs consume and waste the planet's natural resources in a frenzy of useless overproduction. Surviving humans attack the manufacturing plants and try to destroy them. With an instinct for survival, the crippled factories spew out torrents of "metal seeds . . . microscopic machinery . . . all over the world." Some have already grown into tiny, but perfect, replicas of the demolished factory. Dick's self-replicating miniature machinery runs amok, reproducing unstoppably and spreading beyond all human control; eventually it will lay waste to the world.

Greg Bear's *Blood Music* (1985) takes the horror of exponentially self-replicating, intelligent nanomachines to its ultimate extreme—the termination of the natural world.[51] Microorganisms, bioengineered with artificial intelligence, evolve independently and organize themselves into a civilization that forces humanity beyond the flesh and into a posthuman state where individuality is subsumed into a global organism. As Scott Bukatman puts it in *Terminal Identity:* "*Blood Music* is an exemplary narrative of implosion, viral contamination, mutation, organic/technological interface, the disappearance of the body, and the end of the subject."[52]

Working illegally and without biohazard safeguards inside a corporate nanotechnology laboratory doing military research, *Blood Music*'s mad scientist, Vergil Ulam, works on biologics, incorporating "protein molecular circuitry with silicon electronics."[53] In other words, he creates artificially intelligent cells—autonomous, organic microcomputers. When the unauthorized work is discovered, his superior threatens to shut down the lab and fire him if he doesn't destroy the experimental cells. Obsessed with his research, he can't stomach murdering "his children" and sacrificing them to the "caution and shortsightedness of a group of certifiable flatworm management types."[54] Ulam injects the intelligent biochips into his body so he can smuggle them out of the lab and retrieve them later to continue his work. But the nanosites, able to think for themselves, possess their own agenda. Inside his body, the cells evolve into cooperative clusters that are each as intelligent as a human. They have begun to transform Ulam from the inside out. Ulam believes that the microorganisms have manipulated him into becoming their evolutionary medium. The clusters of techno-molecules assemble themselves into a collective civilization that perceives Ulam as their universe, their God.

In this, *Blood Music* resembles another early vision of nanotech—Theodore Sturgeon's much-anthologized short story "Microcosmic God" (*Astounding*, 1941). In Sturgeon's story, biochemist James Kidder breeds the

Neoterics, a tiny, super-intelligent race of creatures with accelerated metabolisms. Threatening them with death, Kidder coerces them into solving problems for him. Initially, the Neoterics see him as a vengeful and omnipotent god. Developing their own agenda, the smart little devils devise a protective shield that insulates them from the whims of Kidder. They develop themselves autonomously without interference. Anxiously, Kidder waits for the Neoterics to reveal themselves. He knows that they will have their own demands now. Sturgeon's Neoterics differ from Drexler's nanomachines: they are small, but not molecule-size, and they result from evolution rather than human construction. But Sturgeon's early scenario suggests the dangerous possibilities of intelligent micro-machines, reflecting future anxieties about both A.I. and nanotechnology.

As in "Microcosmic God," the noocytes (thinking cells) in *Blood Music* figure out that their creator is not the universe. They alter his body so as to control it. Ulam hears the cells telepathically and senses them as music in his blood. He realizes that the nanosite collective operates through a kind of central command, an absolute hierarchy that suggests hive culture. Rebellion will not be tolerated within the civilization. Soon, the noocytes break out of the flesh-and-blood world of Ulam's body into the outside world, the ultimate nanotech nightmare. In a short time, they colonize and transform other bodies, such as that of poor Kenneth, who "seemed little more than a filament-covered white patch in wrinkled clothes. The fleshy roots into the pantry had gone straight for the plumbing, climbing up into the small sink and into the water tap, as well as down the drain."[55] The Centers for Disease Control is helpless as large cities are transformed within forty-eight hours. Nothing can stop the intelligently directed, organic techno-metamorphosis that reorganizes and restructures everything to accommodate its own agenda, which of course remains unknown to humans. This again is Langdon Winner's "technological imperative"[56] made literal: everything and everybody transformed, integrated, shaped, and incorporated into the technological system. In *Blood Music,* an ever-expanding biomass, fluid and shapeless, assimilates skin-bound bodies and encompasses buildings and trees, temporarily forming huge grayish spongy cylinders and spirals, then collapsing into flowing, phosphorescent sheets draping the landscape.

Individual human minds get absorbed into the noocyte "thought universe."[57] To some, the illusion of vague individuality remains. Techno-apologist and bio-creator Ulam rationalizes the death of humanity: "Didn't anyone who changed things ultimately lead some people—perhaps many people—to death, grief, torment?"[58] He suggests that this posthuman world is a kind of virtual utopia. "Experience is generated by thinking. We can be whatever we wish, or learn whatever we wish, or think about anything."[59] Asserting that he's not brainwashed but rather convinced, another human proclaims his immortality: "So like, if I die here, now, there's hundreds of others tuned in to me, ready to *become* me, and I don't die at all. I just lose this particular me . . . it becomes impossible to die."[60] But this is the same "immortality" as was suggested in *Permutation City* (see Chapter Six), which is no immortality at all. Losing a particular me is what it means to die.

Blood Music—like "Microscopic God"—warns that any technology capable of intelligence, self-replication, and evolution might potentially create its own agenda and assert itself beyond our control. This concern has even been expressed by the inventor of nanotechnology. "Dangerous replicators could easily be too tough, small, and rapidly spreading to stop," says Drexler. "[T]his threat has become known as the 'gray goo problem.' Though masses of uncontrolled replicators need not be gray or gooey, the term 'gray goo' emphasizes that replicators able to obliterate life might be less inspiring than a single species of crabgrass."[61] Drexler calculated that from one replicating assembler, you could, within a day, get a huge lump that would weigh a ton; in less than two days, it would outweigh the earth, and soon would exceed the mass of the sun and all the planets combined.[62] An exponentially exploding nanomachine population—like that envisioned by Bear and Drexler—would be technologically difficult to stop. While good nanomachines might battle bad nanomachines, our techno-protectors would have to multiply as quickly as the plague of rogue micromachines. In *The Diamond Age,* Stephenson imagines a thick layer of machine-dust coating the landscape as one of the ugly outcomes of such a nano-war.

While Asimov-style safety measures have been proposed, the computer code which programs nano-reproduction will be subject to errors and glitches like any other software. These errors could result in mutations, altering the replicated nanodevice. We might have the ultimate alien species on our hands, multiplying until it takes over. Finally, like all of these posthuman technologies, much of the government's investment money forces the research into weapons development. Techno-priest Ray Kurzweil joined K. Eric Drexler in noting, though ultimately dismissing, the monumental dangers of nanotechnology. "Nuclear weapons, for all their destructive potential, are at least relatively local in their effects," said Kurzweil. "The self-replicating nature of nanotechnology makes it a far greater weapon."[63]

The only cinematic vision of the gray goo scenario occurs in *The Blob*—a dumb, mean-spirited 1988 remake of the 1958 film. While nanotechnology never gets mentioned, the Blob results from an engineered virus (not an alien organism, as in the original film) that has "grown into a plasmid life form." Just as nanomachines will likely be developed from carbon-based nanotubes, the Blob builds itself from organic matter rich in carbon.[64] The smallish, undulating, glutinous mass first attaches to a man, eventually dissolving him into a moaning skull as his hapless date rips his arm off in a vain attempt to rescue him. Then other humans are absorbed into the enlarging slimy Blob, which degrades human flesh and bone, converting everything into a predatory mound of viscous, corrosive sludge. Even more terrifying is the biological containment unit that shows up. They want to use the Blob as a bioweapon and coolly claim that the lives of the town's citizens are expendable. After discovering that freezing inactivates the Blob, the authorities relocate it to the Arctic for cryonic storage, hoping to resurrect it for a sequel that thankfully did not happen.

REVOLT OF THE NANO-RESURRECTED DEAD

Immortality and nanotechnology meet in *Terminal Café* (1994), a novel by British writer Ian McDonald.[65] "The first thing we get with nanotechnology is the resurrection of the dead," says the head of Tesler Corporation, controller of this dark future world.[66] The recently deceased are immersed in "Jesus tanks" inside the "Death House." Injected with a myriad of cellular repair nanomachines, their bodies are rebuilt and resurrected. But they are not reanimated as night-of-the-living-dead zombies; rather, they end up as handsome, smart indentured servants. The cost of the service is so great that these living dead techno-people must agree to serve as slave labor to the mega-corporations sponsoring their revival—the ultimate in capitalistic exploitation. As we've seen so frequently in other science fiction, *Terminal Café* reflects a master/slave metaphor as the dominant way of describing humanity's relationship to technology. Also, like other artificial humanoids, such as the *Blade Runner* androids, the nano-resurrected people are not considered human. They have no rights and must sever all relationships to the living. Yet despite this high price, most embrace the opportunity to live forever, their flesh reforged into a beautiful shape.

As youthful, beautiful, living-dead slaves, these artificial people are ghetto-ized in the city of artificiality—Hollywood, also known as Necroville. In fact, some of the reanimated corpses wear the faces and forms of Hollywood Golden Age icons such as Marilyn Monroe, Humphrey Bogart, and Marlon Brando. Though they live in Hollywood and look human, the living dead are by law not human. But they are valuable. Their labor forms the foundation of the economic system in this nano-transformed dystopian world controlled by monstrous corporations whose fat owners live in bored luxury, echoing the idle rich of *Metropolis*. Given the economic value of the living dead, they are not trusted to fulfill their contract. Guarding the Necroville ghettos, enforcing the contractual obligations of the dead, are *Mechador* killing machines capable of so-called Big Death termination. Over the years, the oppressed population of the dead grows larger and more impatient.

Technology has evolved without any controls, according to fashion and whim. Along with living dead, nanotechnology produces winged humans, shape-shifting automobiles, and gene-tweaked men who change into werewolves. The uncontrollable consequences of the nano-revolution generate bizarre new problems. Taking off from *Jurassic Park,* the Walt Disney corporation creates dinosaur preserves. But as a result of over-replication and software mutation, the nanosaurs now exist independently of their controlled environments and continue reproducing unchecked. Tearing up gardens, smashing through houses, and lumbering down highways, the huge unwanted creatures establish an "ecological niche" along the coast. Now humans invade their lands and kill them for fun. They've deteriorated from "Theme park attraction to public scourge to Last Safari."[67]

But the humans' biggest nano-mistake turns out to be the space-traveling resurrected dead who were reengineered for off-world exploration and exploitation. They've been banished to distant planets. An angry resurrected spaceman, Quebec, complains, "I can imagine no crueler punchline than awaking into resurrection life sixty million kilometers from your last memory."[68] Yet, Quebec comes to believe, "The dead are the true humanity."[69] New neural pathways have been burned into his brain and his senses have been extended into a broader spectrum of perception. Radio implants have opened him to a form of communication "more intimate by far than spoken words, one that encompassed emotion and un-vocalized prethought, and subtler mental states for which language has no names."[70] As in *Blade Runner,* the techno-posthumans are more sensitive, more empathetic, and, literally, better communicators.

Quebec finds himself in a new community of augmented posthumans—resurrected dead with big plans. They've mutinied against the meat humans and secured their independence from the Earth corporations. This strange vision of immortal, infinitely mutable posthumans colonizing the stars is reminiscent of the transformed cyborg in Frederick Pohl's *Man Plus*. But unlike the manipulated cyborg Torraway, these outer space creatures—the

Freedead—control their destiny by appropriating nanotechnological tools. These resurrected posthumans will re-engineer the structure of the universe, manipulating space, time, and reality. But that will be in the future. Today, on the Day of the Dead, the Freedead will return to earth to liberate the enslaved undead, recalling another tale of android revolt. In the 1983 film *Android,* two humanized robots, threatened with slavery or termination on a spaceship, kill all the oppressive humans and return to earth to free enslaved robots. As Langdon Winner says, "Technical systems become severed from the ends originally set for them and, in effect, reprogram themselves and their environments to suit the special conditions of their own operation. The artificial slave gradually subverts the rule of its master."[71]

To meat humanity, the technologized Freedead have become the "demons, the bogeymen, the zombie flesh-eaters of popular mythology." But this is the perception of the threatened slave-masters whose world faces extinction. "One man's terrorist is another man's freedom fighter," reflects the disaffected and dissident Touissant, bored heir to the corporate resurrection empire.[72] Like *Fairyland, Terminal Café* dramatizes the violent confrontation between nano-enhanced posthumans turned techno-warriors and the totalitarian military-corporate system that fuses with the technological imperative to prop up its oppressive political agenda.

Technological society is based upon the values, motives, and driving force of corporate culture. *Terminal Café*—along with *Fairyland, This Diamond Age,* and *Blood Music*—clarify how the corrupt autocratic corporate system, often fueled by a military agenda, becomes part of the apparatus functioning to maximize technology's dangerous potential. The military —with money derived from taxes—funds the development of weaponized nanotechnology through corporations that proceed without oversight and eventually will exploit their publicly funded knowledge for both control purposes and profit-making. As Bill Joy says, "We are aggressively pursuing the promises of these new technologies within the now-unchallenged system of global capitalism and its manifold financial incentives and competitive pressures."[73] Therefore, all possibilities—with little regard for dangerous consequences—will likely be pursued in the divine name of progress, profits, convenience, security, and weaponry. With less than one percent of all nanotech research money going to investigate the toxicity of nano-materials, knowledge of nanotechnology's risks remains tiny. "The small world is arriving before scientists have had an opportunity to test whether nanoparticles will harm people or the environment," warns Richard Monastersky in his article "The Dark Side of Small."[74]

The science fiction in this chapter elaborates the insidious, oppressive, and dangerous potential of nanotechnology both as a part of the whole apparatus of twenty-first-century technology and in terms of those things specific to its theoretical nature. As *Blood Music* demonstrates, one of nano-technology's most threatening possibilities results from self-replication combined with artificial intelligence and networking capability. Viewed as an artificial lifeform, nanosites or nanobots function as an intelligent virus with the potential to infect organic and inorganic matter. As such, the nano-virus demonstrates a larger metaphor for the role of technology in our society—the notion of technology as a virus. In the next chapter, I will focus on the virus—electronic, biological, and engineered—both as a reflection of literal fears that have become infused in the culture since the rise of AIDS and as technophobic fears that are repressed and controlled by military, corporate, and religious propaganda.

NINE Technology Is a Virus

MACHINE PLAGUE

VIRUS HORROR: TECHNOPHOBIA AND THE RETURN OF REPRESSED FLESH

Technophiliacs want to escape from the body—that mortal hunk of animated meat. But even while devising the mode of their disembodiment, a tiny terror gnaws inside them—virus fear. The smallest form of life, viruses are parasites that live and reproduce by penetrating and commandeering the cell machinery of their hosts, often killing them and moving on to others. "As the means become available for the technology-creating species to manipulate the genetic code that gave rise to it," says techno-prophet Ray Kurzweil, ". . . new viruses can emerge through accident and/or hostile intention with potentially mortal consequences."[1]

The techno-religious vision of immortality represses horrific images of mutilated bodies and corrupted flesh that haunt our collective nightmares in the science fiction subgenre of virus horror. "The relocation, in technology, of many of our mental and muscular skills . . . has made the supposedly obsolete body a source of creeping anxiety, if not outright fear and loathing," writes cultural critic Mark Dery in *The Pyrotechnic Insanitarium.*[2] Just as atomic anxiety infused Cold War–era pop culture, virus anxiety—in the form of plagues, epidemics, parasitized bodies, and microbe-caused mutations—permeates Digital-era pop culture. As Eric Davis puts it in *Techgnosis,* "[T]he mushroom cloud has mostly evaporated in our imaginations, dissipating into a more amorphous apocalyptic atmosphere laced with airborne viruses, biological weapons, toxic fumes and greenhouse gases."[3] Fear of the virus supplants fear of the bomb as our paramount cultural dread.

Virus horror has also become a powerful metaphor for technophobia. This is the dark obverse side of the religious vision of technology as an omnipotent God, humanity's savior, and the source for the techno-utopian dream of immortality. As revealed in science fiction, the virus of technology is the satanic machine, humanity's terminator, and the source of death in a techno-apocalypse. Like a viral infection, technology develops into an autonomous, invasive force that expands and fulfills its dangerous potential by flourishing in the societal medium of corporate, military, and religious sustenance. Voracious in its urge to possess and engulf, technology is a parasite that frequently undermines human integrity—invisibly infiltrating, manipulating, seizing control, and mutating its human host to support its own survival and evolution. Like a virus, technology metamorphoses itself, as a result of unintended and uncontrollable consequences, progressively transforming the human world in the wake of its own changing structure.

Science fiction often questions the notion that technology is neutral—that men control it, that they determine its benefit or harm. The technological virus undermines the techno-utopian dream of mastery, demonstrating that it exists only as a delusion. As Langdon Winner says, "Human beings still have a nominal presence in the [technological] network, but they have lost their roles as active, directing agents. They tend to obey uncritically the norms and requirements of the systems which they allegedly govern. . . . Under present conditions men are not at all the masters of technological change; they are its prisoners."[4] The plague of technology evolves in unpredictable directions, modifying and controlling the environment and behavior of its human cells.

In this view of technology as an independent lifeform, humans are reduced to secondary status, mere carriers of the techno-disease. "Each generation extends the technical ensemble and passes it on to the next generation," observes Winner. "The mortality of human beings matters little, for technology is itself immortal and, therefore, the more significant part of the process."[5] Like a biological species that lives and thrives even though the individual members perish, the virus of technology uses humans as a breeding medium that combines and recombines technological structures to produce new mutations that may ultimately result in the extinction of humanity. Therefore, the Technologist prophets of the future, along with their corporate and military allies, serve as pathological agents of techno-infection. Given their role in the propagation of deadly viruses—both biological and technological—and their complicity or helplessness in the face of proliferation, these corporate, military, and scientific misanthropes must face grave questions.

A GERM'S WORLD: MICROBE MANIA
IN A NEW AGE OF EPIDEMICS

Not long ago, science stood on the brink of preventing infectious disease. Or so it seemed. Antibiotics thwarted bacteria-caused killers such as pneumonia and tuberculosis, and vaccines prevented the onset of virus-caused illnesses such as polio and smallpox. Cancer and heart disease still killed millions, but these maladies were not considered the result of infections. By the 1970s, we had entered a golden biomedical era. That comforting illusion got shattered by the shocking catastrophe of AIDS, which emerged worldwide in the age of genetic engineering, biochemistry, and global telecommunications. The epidemic continues to grow. In 2003, five million people were infected with HIV (the virus that causes AIDS)—the largest number since the epidemic began. Three million people died worldwide in the same year, and around 38 million live with HIV. UNAIDS, a United Nations AIDS program, expects 45 million new AIDS cases in the next five years as the disease marches swiftly across Central Asia and into China. While sub-Saharan Africa is the worst-affected region of the world, the virus currently spreads most rapidly in Asia and Eastern Europe, where almost every country is experiencing a major outbreak.[6]

AIDS not only revived virus fears but also bolstered mistrust of doctors, scientists, and drug companies. The medical community responded slowly to AIDS while often blaming and berating the victims; pharmaceutical companies made exorbitant profits on drugs that either did not work or were too expensive; and backstabbing American and French scientists both claimed to have identified the virus that causes AIDS in a bald grab for fame and money. All of this damaged confidence in the medical establishment and helped fuel what writer David Skal calls "the monstrous images of science and doctors that have flourished [in popular culture] . . . since AIDS has been with us."[7]

As the mysterious AIDS plague spread, ghastly new microbial horrors emerged. Richard Preston's 1994 nonfiction book *The Hot Zone* raised bone-chilling fears of bizarre, highly contagious viruses such as Ebola, Marburg, and Lassa. A science journalist who writes like a horror novelist, Preston elaborates "extreme amplification" in the infected—horrific descriptions of bleeding eyeballs, dissolving flesh, and melting brains. Blaming overpopulation and the destruction of the biosphere, Preston suggests that humans and technology are responsible for the emergence of viruses: "The earth's immune system has recognized the presence of the human species . . . and is attempting to rid itself of an infection by the human parasite."[8] Preston's viewpoint is echoed in *The Matrix* when the agent of

machine intelligence, Mr. Smith, ends an anti-human tirade with the dec-
laration: "Humans are viruses!"

Like a germ dropped into a ready petri dish, microbe mania flourished
in our cultural consciousness throughout the 1990s and into the twenty-
first century. Following in the wake of the best-selling *The Hot Zone* came
an epidemic of disturbing nonfiction horror-of-the-virus books. Laurie
Garrett's *The Coming Plague* (1995) blames modern medical science—especially the careless use of antibiotics—for creating hordes of drug-resistant
microbes, thus emphasizing another technophobic aspect of virus anxiety.
Ed Regis's *Virus Ground Zero* (1996) chronicles the reemergence of Ebola
in Kikwit, Zaire. Richard Rhodes's *Deadly Feasts* (1997) explores the emergence of "stealth" or prion maladies, including mad cow disease, which
makes eating burgers and steak frightening. Michael Oldstone's *Viruses,
Plagues, and History* (1998) shows how the story of humanity and the story
of viruses have intertwined since the dawn of history and takes us into the
era of AIDS and the relation of biotechnology to mad cow disease. Carl
Zimmer's *Parasite Rex: Inside the World of Nature's Most Dangerous Creatures*
(2000) reveals parasites as a dominant force that rules the world by penetrating ecosystems and turning their hosts into slaves, drinking their blood,
controlling their behavior, and managing to change the balance of nature.
Recently, *Secret Agents: The Menace of Emerging Infections* (2003) by Madeline
Drexler and *The New Killer Diseases: How the Alarming Evolution of Mutant
Germs Threatens Us All* (2003) by Elinor Levy and Mark Fischetti warn of
an onslaught of new microbes poised to destroy us. This media assault—
which itself might be described as a media virus—stokes cultural fear by
emphasizing the killer microbe's monstrous power, ubiquity, and resiliency
while providing pop-culture plague tales with the weight of real-world
plausibility.

A fatal scourge, the smallpox virus reemerged as a potent demon in 2002
when fears arose that terrorists had acquired the pathogen. This ancient,
highly contagious disease has killed more people than any other infectious
disease. In what was considered one of humanity's greatest victories in the
battle against disease, smallpox was declared eradicated in the early 1980s.[9]
Since the virus was wiped out in its natural form, health officials stopped
vaccinating against it. As a result, the world's population is now vulnerable. In 2002, President Bush announced a plan to vaccinate all Americans
by 2004, but this did not happen.

Focusing on smallpox, Richard Preston's *The Demon in the Freezer* (2002)
—the third book in his trilogy of dark biology, following *The Hot Zone*
and *The Cobra Event* (1999)—horrifies with the science and history of the
disease and its bioterrorism potential. He tells of Russian scientists who

bioengineered a potent strain of smallpox in huge quantities—enough for every person on the planet to be infected more than two thousand times. They even devised missile warheads for long-range delivery of the virus. When the Soviet Union fell, the Russians lost track of their researchers, the warheads, and the tons of frozen smallpox virus. Preston suggests that some may have fallen into the hands of Iraq, Iran, Israel, Pakistan, India, China, North Korea, and the terrorist group Al Qaeda.[10]

After the September 11 attacks, the threat of bioterrorism became reality when several people died as a result of anthrax-infected envelopes sent through the mail. A bacterium rather than a virus, anthrax—while not itself contagious—engendered a fear epidemic.[11] "Suddenly a hypothetical threat was all too real, and fears that had been bubbling under the surface for the past month burst into the open," said *Newsweek*.[12] Whether perpetrated by external or internal enemies, the bioterrorist attack resulted in fear, panic, and economic fallout. It raised the specter of relatively cheap and easily produced biological weapons as powerful and insidious agents of terror.

In recent summers, the West Nile virus spread across the United States. In 2003, a total of 9,862 cases, including 264 deaths, had been reported, according to the Centers for Disease Control (CDC).[13] In 1999, this mosquito-borne virus made its American debut in New York. The discovery unnerved many bio-defense scientists and government officials who saw the New York outbreak as a test for a terrorist attack, unleashing a disease not typically found in the United States. Scientists eventually discounted the idea that the outbreak was a germ assault, but were unable to trace precisely how the virus had made its way from the Middle East to North America.

In late 2002, a mysterious new viral epidemic, SARS (Severe Acute Respiratory Syndrome), terrorized the world. Sprung up in China and facilitated by the reluctance of Chinese medical authorities to cooperate with the World Health Organization (WHO), SARS—by July 2003—had afflicted more than 8,000 people in twenty-seven countries, causing 774 deaths.[14] WHO official David Heymann called SARS "the first severe new disease of the 21st century with global epidemic potential."[15] While SARS dominated disease attention in 2003, an outbreak of Ebola in Central Africa killed sixty-four people. In the United States, monkeypox—a smallpox-like illness previously documented only near the rainforests of Central and West Africa—made a surprise appearance, sickening nineteen people in the Midwest. In 2004, WHO scientists suspected a new and possibly milder strain of Ebola struck southern Sudan, killing four and sickening nineteen.

The proliferation of old and new viruses confirms that humanity lives at the mercy of the microbe. While technology and progress have helped eradicate some diseases, they have exacerbated others. Some pathologists believe that simian virus 40 (SV-40), which crossed from monkeys to humans as a contaminant of the Salk polio vaccine, causes cancer.[16] New pathways to infections have been opened by factory farms, megacities, airplanes, and blood banks. "Some 30 new diseases have cropped up since the mid-1970s—causing tens of millions of deaths—and forgotten scourges have resurfaced with alarming regularity," reports *Newsweek*.[17] Ecologists suggest that blindly altering ecosystems can create health hazards. For example, suburban development creates a habitat for tick-carrying mice, highly efficient spreaders of Lyme disease. Modern farming practices, such as feeding livestock the remains of other animals, helped spread Creutzfeldt-Jakob disease throughout England. Medical technologies such as transplants and transfusions increase the possibilities of spreading blood-borne pathogens. In this literal sense, technology causes disease and contributes to an atmosphere of technophobia.

GERM WARFARE: MILITARIZATION OF THE VIRUS

Disease as a technological weapon of war boasts a long, revolting history. Early Persians, Greeks, and Romans contaminated the enemy's water by tossing rotting corpses into their wells—a darkly inventive technique copied in the American Civil War and the Boer War.[18] To increase the deadliness of their weapons, Scythian archers dipped arrowheads in feces as well as the always popular rotting corpses. Tatars catapulted plague-infected cadavers over the walled city of Kaffa, and the Crusaders similarly deposited contaminated corpses in the camps of heretics and pagans.[19] In the eighteenth century, British soldiers generously gave American Indians blankets laced with smallpox. In World War I, the Germans spread glanders, a horse disease, among enemy cavalries. In World War II, the Japanese killed thousands of Chinese by dropping grain and cotton that carried bubonic plague–infected fleas.[20] During the Cold War, both the Soviet Union and the United States produced enough germ weapons to sicken or extinguish everyone. "Pound for pound, germ weapons were seen as potentially rivaling nuclear blasts in their power to maim and kill," say Miller, Engelberg, and Broad in *Germs*, "and some were considered even more destructive."[21]

U.S. spending on biological weapons increased after John F. Kennedy took office in 1961. Corporate involvement in military research also rose dramatically as "General Electric, Booz-Allen, Lockheed, Rand, Monsanto,

Goodyear, General Dynamics, Aerojet General, North American Aviation, Litton Systems, and even General Mills, makers of Cheerios and Wheaties, joined the germ program."[22] Later that decade, hoping to keep war expensive and halt the spread of the poor man's nuclear bomb, President Richard Nixon ordered the scrapping of offensive bioweapons research. Persuaded by the United States, the major powers signed the Biological and Toxic Weapons Convention accord in 1972, followed by most of the rest of the world in 1975. They agreed not to acquire, produce, or stockpile germs that had no "prophylactic, protective or other peaceful purposes." The signatory nations, including Russia, also promised not to develop or purchase weapons designed to deliver "these agents or toxins for hostile purposes or in armed conflict."[23]

Despite their promises, signatory countries secretly contravened the treaty. The Soviets expanded their program on a vast, industrial scale and built a "germ empire"—devoting entire cities to developing biological weapons.[24] The United States engages in secret bioweapons research that may stretch the limits of the treaty. It produced a potent strain of anthrax to test a vaccine and created a germ factory in the Nevada desert.[25] Critics argue that while offensive biowarfare research may have officially ended, defensive bioweapons research continues, and that this research requires an offensive capability.[26] An international effort to strengthen restrictions on biological weapons was rejected by the Bush administration in 2001 as being not in the United States's interest.

The rapid pace of the biotechnology revolution has intensified the germ warfare danger. Until recently, bioweapons have been viewed as indiscriminate weapons of mass destruction. This is a deterrent: using them can easily backfire, killing your own people. However, advances in gene identification and engineering make possible designer germs that are ethnically discerning. As early as 1951, the U.S. Navy supposedly initiated a bioweapons project using valley fever, a disease that is more lethal to blacks than any other group.[27] South Africa sought such a weapon during the days of apartheid. In Nancy Kress's novel *Stinger* (1998), racist scientists bioengineer malaria that induces strokes among carriers of the sickle-cell trait, mostly African Americans. The human genome project has already identified some genetic differences between ethnic groups. "This would bring a new and horrifying sophistication to ethnic cleansing," says Wendy Barnaby in *The Plague Makers*.[28]

Genetically engineered bioweapons are a deadly reality. Scientific publications report the creation of enhanced, lethal microbes.[29] According to Russian scientist defector Sergei Popov, the Soviet Union created a super-plague—a genetically improved version of the Black Death. Just as ominously, artificial viruses can now be created. Recently, a synthetic polio virus—agent of the horrific paralyzing disease—was assembled from mail-order materials and a genetic blueprint downloaded from the Internet. "The reason that we did it is to prove that it can be done and it now is a reality," says microbiologist Dr. Eckard Wimmer. "Progress in biomedical research has its benefits and it has its down side. There is a danger inherent to progress in sciences."[30] Not surprisingly, the Pentagon funded the $300,000 study as part of its program of basic research on human pathogens.[31] While creating synthetic smallpox and other lethal plague viruses will be much more complex and difficult than creating the synthetic polio virus, researchers believe it will likely be possible in the near future.

Even if a deliberate act of biowarfare does not occur, the sheer number of unregulated and secret research facilities all over the world increases the likelihood of a major accident. The worst known accident occurred near the Soviet city of Sverdlovsk (now Ekaterinburg), an industrial complex nine hundred miles east of Moscow, killing sixty-eight people in 1979. An explosion at a secret military base propelled a cloud of deadly anthrax microbes over a nearby village. Newspapers described it as a calamity of agonizing deaths, cremated bodies, and extensive decontamination work.[32] The potential for an accident, the lack of an effective treaty, the great strides in biotechnology, and the rise of militarism and terrorism deepen fears about the deadly potential of killer microbes and the spread of biological weapons.

MILITARY GERMS SPREAD FEAR: THE RISE OF VIRAL PARANOIA IN SCIENCE FICTION

As the horrific potential of germ warfare emerged, virus horror and the military became strongly associated in popular culture. In one of the earliest virus movies—John Sturges's 1965 thriller *The Satan Bug*—flasks of a deadly virus created as a bioweapon by the military are stolen by a lunatic. The dictatorial madman wants to control the world. To demonstrate his ambition and seriousness, he first kills the population of a small town and then threatens to destroy Los Angeles. After a nerve-wracking chase, authorities stop him.

With anti–Vietnam War fervor rising, thousands of scientists signed a 1967 petition attacking the government's germ warfare program and its support by university researchers.[33] Public anxiety was reflected in Michael Crichton's 1969 debut novel, *The Andromeda Strain*. Crichton imagines the eruption of a biological crisis when the military sends a satellite into space to gather new and deadly organisms. Project Scoop backfires when the contaminated satellite crashes to earth, spreading germs that threaten humanity. More suspicious of the biowarfare program than *The Satan Bug, The Andromeda Strain* condemns the military for its obsession with biological weapons and cold disdain for innocent lives.

Inspired by the post-Vietnam, post-Watergate distrust of the establishment and the explosion of cinematic horror, George Romero's 1973 epidemic movie *The Crazies* boosted the gore factor while mutating the virus into an expansive metaphor for corrupt military, scientific, and governmental policies. As in Robert Wise's film adaptation of *The Andromeda Strain* (1971), the military causes the outbreak in *The Crazies*. A raving egomaniacal scientist is ordered to find a cure or vaccine, but cannot procure the right equipment and ultimately fails. A colonel flies in from Washington, takes control of the local militia, imposes a news blackout, conspires with government officials, and concocts a cover-up to hide the Army's responsibility. He persuades the U.S. president to give him authority to nuke the town, if necessary, and orders a nuclear-armed plane to circle overhead. Despite the possibility of killing a number of uninfected people, the mayor agrees with the decision: "This is a war and there's always innocent causalities."

The military's attempt to protect citizens turns violently oppressive. The title of the film— *The Crazies*—refers not only to the victims of the madness-inducing virus but to the soldiers enforcing the quarantine. Soldiers machine-gun people who wander past the quarantined perimeter and burn not-quite-dead bodies in street pyres. Though often grim, the movie plays like a black comedy, as when a smiling old granny uses her darning needle to stab an invading soldier in the eyeball. Citizens hide out in a church—usually an inviolate place in such movies, but the soldiers even ignore God and burst inside. The pastor protests by setting himself on fire.

This image of self-immolation evokes the famous anti-U.S. protests in Vietnam, when Buddhist monks doused themselves with gasoline and set themselves ablaze. The film also works as an anti–Vietnam War allegory: malevolent black helicopters hover omnipotently overhead, blowing up cars and people; the U.S. government threatens a nuclear bombing while lying and covering up the true reasons for involvement; the military invades the town, but soldiers can't tell the difference between the infected and the uninfected. The uninfected citizens revolt and start killing soldiers. As it turns out, the infection has already spread beyond the town, so the fascistic enforcement of the quarantine served no purpose. The colonel

The Crazies: *Innocent mom is dragged from her home as biological soldiers enthusiastically enforce quarantine (Courtesy Photofest).*

helicopters out of the town, escaping safely from the chaos, disease, and death that he's unnecessarily caused.

Borrowing from *The Crazies* and Richard Preston's book *The Hot Zone,* the movie *Outbreak* (Wolfgang Peterson, 1995) further intensifies the graphic visceral terror and paranoid hysterics by showing human bodies crashing and bleeding out from an Ebola-like virus while emphasizing the ease of passing the bug. The film opens with an ominous quote from geneticist and Nobel laureate Joshua Lederberg: "The single biggest threat to man's continued dominance on the planet is the virus"; this opening provides the film an air of plausibility. *Outbreak* echoes *The Hot Zone* in its eco-consciousness and its expression of fear that deep within the rain forests, deadly viruses lurk—ready to escape their jungle lairs, enter civilized human bodies, and destroy humankind. Like *The Crazies, Outbreak* blames the military and government for their role in discharging the deadly pathogen.

When the virus turns a peaceful California town into a contagious hot zone, Colonel Sam Daniels (Dustin Hoffman) and his estranged wife, Robby Keough (Rene Russo), arrive to battle the pathogen in the laboratory while squabbling over which of them gets to keep the dogs in the divorce settlement. "I can't believe you're taking a deadly virus and turning it into a family matter," says Colonel Daniels. Evil army general Donald McClintock (Donald Sutherland) wants the virus as a weapon, but after it mutates and gets out of control, he decides to firebomb the infected town. The ostensible motive behind the bombing is that it will contain the disease, but *Outbreak* suggests that, except for pyromaniacs and neglected children, no one loves to ignite a blaze more than an army general, especially one covering up his mistakes.

The movie then turns into a huge chase as Colonel Daniels tracks down the source of the infection to find a serum, races to stop the bombing, and reunites with his now infected ex-wife, whom he saves with a virus antidote that gets developed in about five minutes. *Outbreak* capitalizes on mass audience fears about AIDS—the infection spreads through blood and tainted needles—and on conspiracy theories that the HIV virus was made as a germ weapon by the U.S. Army at Fort Detrick. Unlike *The Crazies'* indictment of a corrupt system, *Outbreak*—while still pointing a finger at the military—puts most of the blame for the mess on a single crazy individual, scapegoating one really rotten general. After he's eliminated, a cure is found and human extinction is averted.

APOCALYPTIC PLAGUE: THE EXTINCTION OF HUMANITY

While a human-destroying epidemic is avoided, *Outbreak* and other virus horror stories gain, in the words of film critic Dennis Lim, "an ominous biblical resonance" by association with the God-ordered doomsday pestilence, prophesied in Revelation (21:9), which signals the end of humanity.[34] Whether sent by God or Satan, the plagues that ravaged Europe in the Middle Ages—caused by the bacterium *Yersinia pestis,* transmitted to man by the fleas of rats—were the first force seen as a possible threat to human existence. The horror of the Black Death still echoed in 1826 when Mary Shelley published her second science fiction novel, *The Last Man,* in which humanity is wiped out by a virulent disease in 2073. While Shelley imagines no futuristic technology, *The Last Man* reverberates with a contemporary atmosphere of desperation, alienation, and horror.

Twisting the last-man-on-earth narrative into an epidemic science fiction/horror story, Richard Matheson turns a viral pestilence into a plague of vampires in his novel *I Am Legend* (1954). Neville is the only person

28 Days Later: *Viral apocalypse makes London a zombie town*
(Courtesy Photofest).

immune to a vampire virus that turns its victims into blood-drinking
zombies. In an evolutionary struggle for survival with these slow, dim-
witted, disorganized undead, Neville hunts and stakes them in the daytime
while they repose helplessly, and repels them with garlic when they attack. Always hopeful for an ally, he meets Ruth, but she tests positive for
the microbe that causes vampirism. Worse, she's a super-vampire with lots
of undead friends like her. The posthuman order of vampires inherits the
future. In this horror vision, humans have self-destructed.

   I Am Legend formed the basis for two weak but highly amusing movies:
The Last Man on Earth (1964) — a low-budget effort that clearly inspired
George Romero's cannibal zombie-fest *Night of the Living Dead* (1968) — and
Omega Man (1971), with Charlton Heston as the last man on earth, battling light-sensitive vampiric albinos that wear hooded monk's robes and
sunglasses. While warning of a future where humanity loses the evolutionary battle with the virus, *I Am Legend* adds another mythical resonance —
vampirism — to the biblical pestilence. A killer virus is like a vampire, with
its undead, parasitic lifestyle of preying on the living to survive and reproducing itself through its victims. According to James B. Twitchell in
Dreadful Pleasures, "he [the vampire] entered popular culture in the seventeenth century as a logical way to account for the geometric progression of
deaths caused by the fast-acting plague bacteria."[35] Vampirism — through
infection-by-blood — also links the medieval plague with the future plague
of AIDS.

Danny Boyle's apocalyptic *28 Days Later* (2002 in Britain, 2003 in the United States)—a fusion of *I Am Legend,* Stephen King's *The Stand, The Crazies,* and *Resident Evil* computer games—opens in a London research lab crowded with screeching monkeys that have been subjected to horrific experiments. One animal lies limp on a table with its chest ripped open while others smash against their glass cages in a frenzy of rage. The quietest monkey is restrained on a table, stretched out crucifixion-style, its head pierced with electrodes and pointed at a bank of television monitors. The formerly happy primate is forced to watch violent human atrocities—burning forests, burning cities, burning bodies, and police savagery. Animal-rights protesters burst inside. Despite the warnings of a hysterical scientist, anti-vivisectionist activists liberate an experimental monkey contaminated with the human-destroying "rage" virus.

Twenty-eight days later, Jim (Cillian Murphy) awakens in an empty hospital where he's been in a coma since before the scourge struck. Confused and incredulous, he staggers into the streets and finds London empty, the population devastated by the rage plague, which causes the infected to immediately turn into rabid murderous zombies. Rasping demonically, and so fearsome that rats flee in terror, these ghouls survive on the flesh of the living. Yet it later turns out that a platoon of military men, holed up in an armed compound and offering safety to Jim and his straggling family of survivors, are more disgusting and evil than these blood-spurting zombies. Capturing the technophobia of the moment with a mood of utter desperation, *28 Days Later* evokes AIDS, SARS, biowarfare, male militarism, and the deadly consequences of viral experimentation.

Driven by greed masquerading as utopianism, corporate science gets indicted in Margaret Atwood's 2003 novel *Oryx and Crake,* a funny but horrible version of the apocalyptic last-man story. Aligned with Mary Shelley, Atwood—the daughter of a biologist—vividly imagines a future world decimated by a man-made viral cataclysm. "Too much hardware, too much software, too many hostile bioforms, too many weapons of every kind," laments Atwood.[36] The apparent lone human survivor of the apocalypse—Snowman—plays reluctant prophet to a race of genetically messed-up humanoids. Gentle, grass-eating, defenseless, virus-immune posthumans, the Crakers were engineered as a successor species by Snowman's friend, the genius geneticist Crake. Snowman captivates the childlike tribe with scriptural tales of their now-dead creator Crake and teacher Oryx. The Crakers believe their god Crake will return. But he's dead like the rest of humanity.

As Snowman, formerly Jimmy, scavenges for food on the plague-devoured landscape, he looks for the origin of the outbreak in his memo-

ries. Snowman/Jimmy's genographer dad worked for an organ replacement company, OrganInc. As part of Operation Immortality, he created
the pigoon, a transgenic pig designed to grow an assortment of human
organs, including brain tissue. These smart pigoons get loose and hunt
humans like lions after deer. Genetic engineering is portrayed as a power-
mad addiction.

Jimmy's unhappy mother hates her husband's avarice and techno-
utopian hypocrisy. "What you're doing—this pig brain thing. You're interfering with the building blocks of life," she asserts. "It's immoral. It's . . .
sacrilegious."[37] Rebelling against corporate control, she escapes the compound, leaving Jimmy with nothing but her scorn toward techno-science.
Corporate police assassinate his mother just as corporate scientists scorch
the earth. Like Stephenson in *The Diamond Age,* Atwood expresses the importance of mother-love/mother-earth and the pain of losing it. But this
is the human foundation of a story dominated by dark humor and sarcastic
disdain toward genetic engineering—the science of the absurd.

In a world of viral terrorism, science-caused diseases, and violent transgenics, Crake—Jimmy's friend and the Dr. Frankenstein of the future—
creates a fast-food venture, ChickieNobs. These are living, headless, leg-
less breast-meat tubes derived from chickens. Funny, but not so farfetched
in the context of McDonald's Chicken McNuggets and current transgenic
experiments. Modified animals already exist, such as cows that produce
allergen-free milk. Engineered for cancer research, the poor OncoMouse
—human oncogene fused into a mouse embryo—is the first transgenic
animal to be patented. Aqua Bounty Farms applied for FDA approval for
a salmon with human growth hormone. The fish grows ten times faster
than normal. It would be the first genetically modified animal approved
for human consumption.[38]

"The world is now one vast uncontrolled experiment . . . and the doctrine of unintended consequences is in full spate . . . the rats have taken
over," thinks Jimmy.[39] Atwood imagines a surrealistic world of biological chaos. Gene-spliced house-mice, addicted to the insulation on electric
wiring, overrun Cleveland, setting the city on fire. A tiny rodent spliced
with porcupine and beaver genes creeps under car-hoods and consumes
fan belts and transmission systems. A tar-eating microbe turns highways
to sand. "Human society . . . was a sort of monster, its main by-products
being corpses and rubble," mourns Atwood. "It never learned, it made the
same cretinous mistakes over and over, trading short-term gain for long-
term pain. It was like a giant slug eating its way relentlessly through all the
other bioforms on the planet."[40]

Viewing this bio-horror as acceptable collateral damage, Crake works on immortality and a grand plan for posthuman evolution at Paradice, an offshoot of the HelthWyzer conglomerate. He develops the BlyssPluss Pill, designed to protect users from diseases, prolong youth, improve sexual prowess, and sterilize people without their knowing it. As the techno-prophets of today urge, Crake creates a "superior" genetically designed successor species. Like the biotech aliens of *Dawn,* he will decide the evolutionary upgrades. Crake genetically defines the self-reproducing Paradice people—later known as Crakers. Perfectly adjusted to their environment, they would never create houses or tools or weapons. He designs them for beauty, docility, virus immunity, and the ability to digest grass. Best of all, they efficiently recycle their own excrement. Programmed to drop dead at thirty suddenly without getting sick, the Crakers have a mating ritual scientifically calculated to prevent bad feelings, lust, or any emotion. There's no unrequited love because there's no love. To Atwood, engineered happiness is a demented, destructive vision. Despite their cheerful, optimistic disposition, the Crakers are shown as the mindless mutant culmination of the 1950s life-is-a-machine cybernetic/behaviorist philosophy.

Crake is so enthralled with his posthuman children that he wants to hasten their evolutionary succession. He encrusts a super-virulent hemorrhagic virus into the BlyssPluss pills. By extinguishing humanity, the Paradice People will become the successor species—unless, as seems likely, they fall prey to the wild pigoons and wolvogs, the former security pit bull/wolf transgenics. While not a literal forecast, Atwood's comic nightmare vision gains great power and relevance from our current scientific/corporate obsession with biotechnology, cloning, evolution engineering, and the potential of genetic splicing. With dark humor disguising her pessimism, she challenges us to reflect on the virulent virus as a dark metaphor for utopianism as propaganda, biotechnology as addictive blind power, and corporate greed as a devouring monster.

VIRAL DEHUMANIZATION AND PARASITE PARANOIA

During the 1950s and 1960s, ancient fears of disease lessened as science conquered one disease after another, including smallpox and the childhood scourge, polio. In *War of the Worlds* (1956), a virus even saves humanity when beleaguered scientists accidentally discover that a germ somehow kills the seemingly invincible Martian robot machines that have invaded earth. Released in the same year as *War of the Worlds,* a more insidious alien attack movie, *Invasion of the Body Snatchers* (1956), is the archetypal epidemic movie as well as one of the earliest "evil clone" films. *Invasion* is based on Jack Finney's novel *Body Snatchers* (1953), which owes much to Robert Heinlein's *The Puppet Masters* (1951). Unseen alien invaders kill and gradually replace sleeping human victims with pods that turn into zombie-like physical duplicates. In this way, *Invasion of the Body Snatchers* (remade in 1978 and 1994) makes explicit another horrific aspect of microbial/technological invasion—its power to dehumanize, possess, and insidiously mutate a person.

Extending the process of dehumanization, transformation, and technologizing to political ideology, *Invasion of the Body Snatcher*'s pod people evoke the bland conformist utopia that stands as a metaphor for communism in the 1950s. The duplicated humans are emotionless, godless automata that secretly take over the society. This ideological implication is made even more directly in Heinlein's *The Puppet Masters.* A spaceship full of aliens—intelligent, hive-minded, pulsating, jellyfish-like parasites—travel from Saturn's moon Titan, land near Kansas City, and latch onto peoples' spines. Hiding underneath the clothes of their hosts, they tap into their brains—possessing them, enslaving them, and forcing them to spread more parasites across the planet. Heinlein's narrator compares them to communists—"Stalinism seemed tailormade for them. . . . the people behind the Curtain had had their minds enslaved and parasites riding them for three generations."[41] No one can be trusted. Paranoia runs rampant as the parasitic slugs control the minds of their human hosts. "Heinlein may not have known that parasites can take over the behavior of their hosts," Carl Zimmer says in *Parasite Rex,* "but he nailed the essence of their control."[42] As in *War of the Worlds,* humanity is saved when a virus is discovered that can kill the aliens. Since they communicate by physical contact, which involves an exchange of bodily fluids, they infect each other with the disease. The story closes with a fleet of spaceships leaving Earth for Titan to exterminate the vile communistic parasites for good.

Parasites, viruses, and other vile microbes found a network television home on *The X-Files* (1994–2001). Exploiting mass paranoia for commercial entertainment, *The X-Files* twisted a labyrinth of conspiracies involving government, corporate, and scientific complicity with aliens to infect humans with a black oil virus and spawn a viral apocalypse. This conspiracy threads through the entire series as well as *Fight the Future* (1998), the *X-Files* feature film. In addition, individual *X-Files* episodes center on other aggressive, invasive organisms: the worm-like, psychosis-inducing virus in "Ice" (1993), the parasitic Fluke Boy in "The Host" (1994), the repulsive parasites in "Firewalker" (1994), and the deified parasite in "Roadrunner" (2000). In "Erlenmeyer Flask" (1994), government scientists test unsuspecting humans with an extraterrestrial virus, and later murder them to cover up the experiments. In "F.Emasculata" (1995), Pinck Pharmaceuticals experiments on prisoners, infecting them with a parasitic insect that disfigures the face before it destroys the immune system. Like most epidemic narratives, *The X-Files* blames the government, the military, and their scientific and corporate co-conspirators for the microbial monsters.

The smallpox virus plays an especially significant role within the series' mythological conspiracy arc, which progresses toward preparing Earth for alien colonization. When the black oil virus infects people, it turns the whites of their eyes black, one of the characteristics of hemorrhagic smallpox. In "Paper Clip," Mulder and Scully stumble onto a huge genetic database on every person born since the 1950s, suggesting the genetic data were secretly collected during global smallpox inoculations, implicating many governments in the conspiracy. The Cigarette-Smoking Man (William B. Davis) masterminds large-scale biotechnological pandemonium in "Zero Sum" (1995), genetically engineering smallpox, combined with alien DNA, so that it can be transmitted to the human population through the sting of a bee. The result would be the eradication of humanity, or its transformation and enslavement. Exuding an unsettling mood of doomsday chic with its flashlight-in-fog ambiguity, *The X-Files* is fueled by paranoia. While "the truth is out there," Mulder and Scully routinely discover that the truth is covered up by government, military, corporate, and medical authorities.

MAD SCIENCE: INVASIVE TECHNOLOGICAL ASSAULTS

Corporate techno-science and viral invasion fuel the films of David Cronenberg. In his surreal and disturbing movies, he envisions bodies violated, distorted, transfigured, and exploded by technological and viral invasion. While his obsession with grotesque, created-by-science monstrosities echoes 1950s atomic mutation films, he looks to the future in exploring the tension between scientific rationality and primitive instincts. As David Skal puts it: "The late 20th century medical man, despite his technological toys still engages us on the level of the aboriginal medicine man."[43] In *Rabid* (1977), after receiving experimental skin grafts following a disfiguring motorcycle accident, Rose (Marilyn Chambers) develops a phallic growth in her armpit that infects her sex partners with rabies, causing a diseased city to erupt in chaos. In *The Fly* (see Chapter Seven), after an accident during his teleportation experiment, a scientist is transformed into a fly/human transgenic, mutating his body and his mind. In *Videodrome* (see Chapter Six), after an electronic virus—embedded in a television signal by a corporate media scientist—penetrates his eyes, a cable station owner develops a brain tumor that causes hallucinations, violence, and physical deformity. The further these scientists and doctors [44] push their disciplined, rational science, the more uncontrollable and irrational its consequences become.

A sexual death-lust takes over his debut feature, *Shivers* (1975)—also known as *The Parasite Murders* and *They Came from Within*. Before AIDS, Cronenberg casts a sexually transmitted parasite as a killer. Operating in a state-of-the-art, sterile high-rise complex, a utopian scientist wants to create an organic machine that lives inside the body and automatically replaces malfunctioning organs by transforming itself. He engineers a parasite that turns his neighbors into brain-dead, lust-driven maniacs. Reflecting real-world parasites that transform their hosts' behavior to ensure their own propagation, these posthuman sexual predators infect others by transforming their hosts, even children, into rapists.

Cronenberg rebukes techno-utopian biotechnology, showing its engineered outcome as a repulsive, stubby, half-phallic, half-turd parasite-worm that passes from mouth to mouth during a kiss or uses other orifices to seize control of people and turn them into mindless sex-crazed disease vectors. Like the virus-infected vampires of *I Am Legend* and *28 Days Later,* the parasite-invaded fiends of *Shivers* have been reduced to a purely predatory state with no values or goals beyond survival and the spread of the infection. The film ends with the parasite people streaming out of the apartment building to contaminate the rest of the city and the world. As in most of Cronenberg's films, black humor plays a part, but *Shivers* is intensely pessimistic as a parable of techno-viral manipulation and control.

The most disturbing and influential parasite fiction, *Alien* (see Chapter Four), connects 1950s nuclear technophobic monster movies, such as *Them* and *It Came from Outer Space* (1953), to AIDS-era fears of corporate biotechnology, invasive microbes, and body-mutating techno-parasites. In *Alien,* the treacherous Company uses humans as bait to ensure the capture of the alien for research and development as a weapon. Sent by the ship's corporate-programmed computer to investigate an apparently lifeless planet, the crew discovers an alien ship and a clutch of eggs in a womb-like chamber. Crew member Kane foolishly takes a close look at one of the pulsating eggs and a tentacled thing bursts out of it—gripping his face, wrapping a tail around his neck, and inserting the end into his mouth in a male rape. His reentry to the ship is forbidden by Ripley, but facilitated by android science officer Ash, who—like the computer, Mother—has been programmed by the Company. The horrific alien symbolizes the parasitical system, the corporation, and its technology—all of which manipulate, control, transform, and ultimately destroy the humans.

The "face-hugger" has disappeared by the next day. Kane seems fine. But his body serves the parasite as a womb. After a short gestation, the alien bursts out of Kane's body. Combining mechanical and organic parts, the monstrous alien metamorphoses at an alarming rate—from a squid-like parasite to an upright carnivorous humanoid monster with metallic teeth. The techno-surrealist monster "evoked futuristic machinery, skeletons, and verminous insects: a necrotechnological nightmare and one of the most dismaying illustrations of science equals death ever attempted on the plane of popular entertainment," says David Skal.[45] Combined with its corporate/science symbolism, the parasitic monster represents the organic adaptability and technological persistence of a virus—the invisible invader

Them: *No insect spray can stop this irradiated mutant ant from breeding atomic anxiety (Courtesy Photofest).*

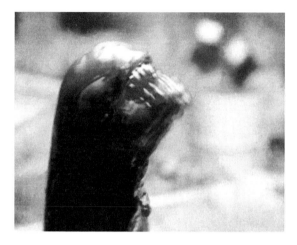

Alien: *Malignant techno-parasite bursts forth, primed to evolve and wreak havoc (Courtesy Photofest).*

that can seize control of your body and transform it into something grotesque and malignant. Like a virus, the alien is not interested in humans for their special wonderfulness; rather, it uses the human species merely as a source of nourishment and a biological host for reproduction. Though Ripley eventually defeats the monster, she fails to defeat the techno-viral system that still dominates her environment and her mind.

COBRA VIRUS: ENGINEERING TRANSGENIC TERRORISM

Virus paranoia infuses the novels of Dr. Robin Cook, king of the microbe-driven thriller with *Invasion* (1991), *Contagion* (1995), and *Toxic* (1998). *Outbreak* (1987) — adapted into a silly made-for-television movie called *Robin Cook's Virus* — centered on the deliberate spreading of the deadly Ebola virus by malevolent, HMO-hating doctors. The threat of biological terrorism adds a ghastly new dimension to plague fear. In Cook's *Vector* (1999), neo-Nazi skinheads assault New York with weaponized anthrax. A non-suspenseful thriller, *Vector* still demonstrates the ease of fashioning devastating bioweapons at low cost with available technology. "Few threats have the capability of killing so many so fast," says Cook in *Vector*. "For years we lived under the fear of nuclear winter annihilating the human race. Now there is a similar threat from biology."[46]

Genetic technologies with profit potential encourage scientists to create a new generation of deadly pathogens—more lethal versions of existing microbe killers or horrific hybrid diseases with no immunity or antidote. Author of *The Hot Zone* and *Demon in a Freezer,* Richard Preston writes to horrify. In *The Cobra Event* (1997), his nasty portrait of biological terrorism even scared President Bill Clinton. Clinton said that of all the new threats, the one that "keeps me awake at night" is the possibility of germ attack as described in *The Cobra Event.*[47]

In *The Cobra Event,* a mad genetic engineer wants to reduce the world's population, for environmental reasons, by infecting New York City with a designer disease. His "brainpox" fuses an obscure moth virus that destroys nerves with a highly contagious and lethal smallpox virus. Writing elaborately bloody and bizarre descriptions, Preston paints the gruesome horrors of brainpox, which not only melts the brains of its victims but compels otherwise staid people to chew their own lips, bite off their fingers, and in extreme cases to spontaneously pop out their eyeballs. "Ebola is horrible enough," says Preston, "but scientists are white-knuckled scared about the possibilities of engineered viruses created in a bioreactor."[48] In fact, cobras provided the basis for an actual hybrid virus, engineered as part of the Soviet Union's disease empire. Imaginative but deranged scientists combined genes from otherwise innocent viruses and cobra snakes to create a real cobra virus that would produce a deadly venom inside the cells of a victim's body.[49]

In the fictional thriller *The Cobra Event,* Preston raises disturbing political and moral questions about how the mainstream media fail to focus attention on the threats of foreign biological weapons development and renewed U.S. participation in such research. Preston's real-world agenda gets temporarily submerged in a ready-for-Hollywood ending that includes FBI helicopters, ninja assault soldiers, a chase through a subway, shots ringing out in the darkness, and a confrontation between the intrepid heroine— a young doctor with the Centers for Disease Control—and the mad scientist. The psychopath behind the killings eventually falls victim to the bug he created—a plot twist microbiologist Joshua Lederberg suggested to Preston "to make germ weapons seem less attractive to a potential terrorist."[50] The book's positive ending hardly dispels its nightmarish implications about biotechnology and the horrific plausibility of genetically engineered pathogens that makes literal the metaphor of a technological virus.

MECHANICAL PLAGUE: THE ARTIFICIALLY INTELLIGENT DISEASE

Fusing nanotechnology, biogenetics, networking, artificial intelligence, and the behavioral science of socially organized insect communities, a military-funded corporation, Xymos, builds a secret weapon for the Pentagon in Michael Crichton's novel *Prey* (2002). Of course, Xymos cloaks itself in techno-utopian promises that its research will eventually be used to diagnose human illness. But in fact, the company has inadvertently created an artificial disease. Manufactured partly from bacteria, a swarm of microscopic surveillance cameras not only provides detailed photographic information but has also been programmed—by short-sighted techno-scientists—to learn, reproduce, and hunt like jungle predators. From the point of view of the nanobot technology, the military, the corporation, and the scientists have foolishly and obediently carried out technology's agenda to survive, thrive, replicate, and improve. Humans serve as the metaphorical hosts for technological reproduction. Even when the techno-swarm gets loose and the potential disaster becomes clear, the corporate suits let the situation spiral out of control, afraid to call the Army for help because they might lose their funding.

Science fiction corporations of the future never use their technological inventiveness to feed the world, improve the environment, or supply vaccines to poor people. Like Xymos in *Prey,* the Company in *Alien,* the Tyrell Corporation in *Blade Runner,* and the Umbrella Corporation in *Resident Evil,* they tend to rape the earth, create invasive surveillance systems, or devise techno-weapons that sicken or destroy people. Like Vice President Dick Cheney's company, Halliburton, in war-torn Iraq, science fiction corporations often work closely with the military and make profits from taxpayer money. The world of the imagined future is secretly run by multinational corporations motivated by profit and power.

Prey warns about human complicity in the empowerment of autonomous technology and how that empowerment is facilitated by the dangerous marriage of weapons manufacture, utopian propaganda, and corporate profit-making despite enormous safety risks. Like the evolving nanobot swarm, technology—viewed as an artificial, self-optimizing lifeform—evolves independently of human design and control and then begins to parasitize its creator and potentially dominate it.

TECHNOLOGICAL MONSTERS:
RETURN OF THE MUTATED CREATURES

With viral fear on the rise in the twenty-first century, even 1950s-style, mutated creatures—caused by techno-viruses rather than nuclear radiation—are making a comeback. In Dean Koontz's best-selling novel *Seize the Night* (1999), a retrovirus—caused by the inevitable military biowarfare experiment gone awry—transforms people into shrieking, malicious monstrosities. Paul Anderson's *Resident Evil* (2002) focuses on a military biowarfare lab ominously named the Hive, infected with the fictional T virus, which mutates dead humans and animals into grotesque, bloodthirsty zombies. The movie and its sequel *Resident Evil: Apocalypse* (2004) were adapted from a popular video game series. Originators of the "Survival Horror" genre, the *Resident Evil* games (1998–2004) boast an elaborate plot that centers on a virus epidemic caused by the evil Umbrella Corporation—the largest commercial entity in the United States. Umbrella sells computer technology, medical products, and health care, but most of its profits come from biological weapons. In this splatterfest, the player wanders through post-apocalyptic Raccoon City, searching out and destroying zombie mutations while trying to unravel a convoluted conspiracy involving corporate deception.

Extermination (2001), like *Fear Effect* (2000) and *Syphon Filter* (1999–2003), repeats the survival horror/virus formula, but distinguishes itself by incorporating elements of a 1951 monster movie, *The Thing from Another Planet,* remade in 1982 as *John Carpenter's The Thing* and adapted into its own digital game in 2002. As special forces soldier Dennis Riley, the player investigates mysterious events on a secret South Pole military base. Experimentation with DNA results in a viral outbreak. Again, the science-created virus causes the base's inhabitants to mutate into hideous monsters that the player must gruesomely destroy before being fatally infected. An infection meter, on the game's interface, gets triggered if Riley is bitten or comes in contact with the virus in a puddle of water. The progressing infection is reflected in the meter indicating that death nears, adding a sense of urgency. The player must find a cure before tentacles and bio-organic weapons sprout from his flesh, mutating him into a Thing-like monster.

Just as low budget B-movies in the 1950s—with their radioactive monster chills and world-in-peril thrills—captivated audiences jittery with nuclear anxiety, today's digital games reflect and reinforce current virus paranoia and technophobia. Their apocalyptic stories of humans exposed to military biowarfare experiments, endangered by corporate techno-science, mutated by ubiquitous infections, and hunted by bizarre transgenic creatures make clear the pervasive horror of invasive microorganisms and bio-technological experiments. Unlike the monster movies of the 1950s that glorified religion, government, and the military, the virus horrors of today often attack these same forces.

THE TECHNOLOGICAL VIRUS:
ELECTRONIC INFECTION

Organic viruses wreak havoc on our vulnerable human bodies. But even a highly evolved posthuman, who escapes the flesh by fusing with a computer, will still be susceptible to electronic viruses. In the real world, the SQL Slammer virus spread through the world's computers in January 2003, destroying files and causing $1 billion in damage.[51] Later in the summer, computers were infected with the Blaster or LovSan worm, which caused diseased Windows computers to shut down and restart with-out user control.[52] The worm attack forced some government agencies to close and kicked Swedish Internet users offline.[53] A couple of weeks after this invasion, computers were attacked by Sobig.F, the fastest spreading e-mail virus ever. It stopped some businesses, confused a railroad telecom-munications network, and slowed down the Internet. In February 2002, more than fifty scientists wrote President Bush a letter expressing grave concern about a cyber-attack "that could devastate the national psyche and economy more broadly than did the Sept. 11 attack."[54] Cyber-security ex-perts warn that the critical infrastructure of the United States—including electrical power, finance, telecommunications, health care, transportation, water, and defense—is highly vulnerable.

In science fiction, *Videodrome* (see Chapter Six) imagines a television signal as a viral disease and as a medium for social control. In *The Cassini Division* (see Chapter Four), Earth is devastated by a computer virus gen-erated from deep space by vicious posthumans. In *Ghost in the Shell,* both human and robot brains can be hacked and infected with electronic viruses. In *The Matrix Reloaded* and *Matrix Revolutions,* evil electronic entity Agent Smith has learned to replicate himself like a virus. In *Terminator 3: Rise of the Machines,* Skynet—created by a corporation for the military—turns out to be not a mainframe computer but an artificially intelligent virus that shuts down global communications, disables defense systems, and launches a nuclear assault on the world. But the most elaborate vision of an electro-pathogen haunts Neal Stephenson's novel *Snow Crash.*

The snow crash virus exists in both a biological and an electronic form. People are infected by swallowing it as a drug, absorbing it from contami-

The Matrix Reloaded: *After replicating, technological virus Mr. Smith tries to infect everyone and everything (Courtesy Photofest).*

nated bodily fluids, or even seeing it as programming code. As with the videodrome informational virus, infection can enter through the eyes to strike the brain directly, altering its DNA. The virus "crashes" the mind and degrades the individual's humanity—reducing consciousness and autonomy to such a primitive state that the victim becomes susceptible to mind control. This suggests the penetration of technology into our lives and its invisible consequences—humans regressed to automata that robotically obey technology's imperatives. Stephenson proposes a cybernetic model of the human brain, suggesting that there is a primitive level of the mind where free will, rationality, and consciousness do not exist. As N. Katherine Hayles writes in her analysis of *Snow Crash:* "If human consciousness can be co-opted by hijacking its basic programming level, we are plunged into Norbert Wiener's nightmare of a cybernetics used for tyrannical ends."[55]

Using the Metaverse (see Chapter Six)—*Snow Crash*'s futuristic fusion of the Internet and virtual reality—the virus is secretly spread, by power-mad millionaire and religious fanatic L. Bob Rife, as a mechanism of social control and world domination. His plan is enacted by dehumanized, snowcrashed lackeys, implanted with antennae that enable Rife to communicate his orders through direct transmission. With their antennae and hive-like behavior, Rife's automata resemble insects as well as microbes. Strangely, new research suggests that bacteria, like insects, possess a kind of collective mind. Molecular biologist Bonnie Bassler proposes that germs communicate and "collectively track changes in their environment, conspire with their own species, [and] build mutually beneficial alliances with other types of bacteria."[56] Microbes strategize collectively, similar to bees, ants, and Rife's insect-like mind slaves.

Fighting Rife is hero hacker Hiro Protagonist, whose independence, imagination, and inventiveness dramatize the human alternative to the posthuman, robotic insect people. In the end, the conflict comes down to a physical fight between the human and the posthuman. Rife and his techno-virus are defeated by low-tech, jungle-warfare techniques as well as by a cyborg dog named Rat Thing, which—motivated by love—overcomes the programming of its neural circuitry.

Snow Crash, in a sense, relegates the cybernetic brain to the garbage dump of evolutionary history, suggesting that it belongs to a pre-human state rather than being the foundation for a posthuman evolution. The snow crash virus reverses the higher development of the mind, converting humans to a lower primitive cybernetic level. Stephenson therefore warns against the mind's susceptibility to control through brain-altering viral technology. This is symbolically similar to Paul McAuley's notion, in *Fairyland* (see Chapter Eight), of a nano-designed virus, or fembot, that could literally invade a person's brain and change its chemical structure, in a programmed manner, to alter that person's belief system.

In another potent symbol of humanity's techno-domination, information itself is seen as a viral disease of the mind in the science of memes. A contagious idea replicates like a virus, passing from mind to mind, frequently through technological media. Again, Cronenberg's *Videodrome* is the paradigmatic cinematic visualization. The television medium, or any other form of communication, is the replicating environment, the carrier, and the transmitter of the meme. "When you plant a fertile meme [or idea] in my mind you literally parasitize my brain, turning the brain into a vehicle for the meme's propagation in just the way that a virus parasitizes the genetic mechanism of a host cell," writes Richard Dawkins in *The Selfish Gene.*[57] Examples of memes include catch-phrases, crazes, fads, icons, fashion statements, and political buzzwords. A potent meme might alter long-held beliefs, suggesting its mind-control potential. In 2002, the war meme, or, more specifically, the concept of preemptive war, promulgated by the government through a docile media, swept through the United States and reversed hundreds of years of war-only-in-defense tradition. This war meme can also be seen as an interrelated part of a massive and complex technological agenda that employs patriotic, religious, and utopian propaganda to further itself.

In the real world, malignant self-replicating viruses present grave dangers to human health; in science fiction, they function not only to reflect that threat but to serve as potent symbols of technophobia. Monumentally fearsome in its anti-human attacks, the virus—like technology—horrifies with its insidious invasiveness, parasitism, and control. In the form of plagues and epidemics, viruses provoke ancient fears of biblical vengeance, disease, dehumanization, and vampirism while inciting futuristic fears of human extinction. A mortal menace even to digital posthumans, electronic viruses can invade, infect, and corrupt cyber-heaven. The ultimate horror, the virus symbolizes the dark side of twenty-first-century technologies and our anxiety about the dangerous consequences they deliver.

TEN Epilogue

TECHNOPHOBIA

Posthuman technology threatens to reengineer humanity into a new machinic species and extinguish the old one. Science fiction shows that this process will subvert human values like love and empathy, revealing that the intrinsic principles of these technologies fortify genetic discrimination, social fragmentation, totalitarianism, surveillance, environmental degradation, addiction, mind control, infection, and destruction.

In its devotion to technophobia, science fiction paints a repulsive picture of a future world where technology runs out of control and dominates all aspects of human behavior. Technology's inherent structure requires suppression of human spontaneity and obedience to its requirements of order and efficiency. This extends the social controls initiated by the cybernetic ideological system. Asimov's laws of robotic obedience have been reversed into technology's laws for human submission. As Langdon Winner says, "In the end, literally everything within human reach . . . will be incorporated into the system of technical instrumentality. . . . Here one locates the political essence of technology in its total formative impact on all nature and all culture."[1]

Science fiction demonstrates that technological operations often proceed autonomously without human intervention, hostile to human values and welfare. As T. J. Matheson puts it, "An internal and inevitably destructive momentum is embedded within all technological processes, beyond the power of human beings to forestall."[2] Repeatedly, science fiction suggests that technology—symbolized by robots, androids, cyborgs, and other machines, as well as by clones—has developed its own life and its own agenda. Science fiction counters the prophets of our techno-future, who promote the notion that the forces of technology remain neutral.

Autonomous technological expansion is facilitated by corporate powers that control markets, exploit consumer desires, and manufacture needs. In league with military objectives, corporations strongly influence the political processes that ostensibly regulate technology's development. At its most political, science fiction illustrates technology's corruption and destructiveness, demonstrating that it mirrors the corruption of corporate manipulation and the destructiveness of military agendas.

Driven by divine desires, perfection mania, and a pathological hatred of the body, a priestly order of scientists obey the dictates of their Techno-God and serve the interests of military power and corporate profit. As we've seen, the pioneers of A.I., together with their disciples in robotics, bionics, virtual reality, data networks, biotechnology, and nanotechnology, are nurtured by an industrial/military complex that influences the direction of scientific research. Inspired by profits and prophets, techno-scientists advocate posthuman technologies as sources of omnipotence, immortality, and transcendence, while they enormously increase the global weapons arsenal and despoil the environment. By dramatizing concerns about technology's outcomes, science fiction sounds an alarm that contrasts sharply with the divine prophecies of the cyber-utopians and reveals their techno-religion as a propagandistic ploy and an insidious menace. As David Noble says, "Simply put, the technological pursuit of salvation has become a threat to our survival."[3]

Technologism promotes fantastic expectations of individual perfection which science fiction shows technology cannot achieve. The vision of a techno-utopia serviced by robots, cyborgs, androids, and clones is revealed as a myth that encourages human docility in the face of enslavement by technology. Science fiction helps liberate us from those mythical and deceptive dreams while warning that our technology is not easily controlled. By striving for the technologically impossible, we end up oppressed by our own inventions, whose demands subvert the positive outcomes—the elimination of poverty, the preservation of the environment, and the expansion of education—that we want to create.

True believers in the god Technology condemn science fiction as facile technophobia and similarly denounce resisters of the techno-faith as neo-Luddites and reactionaries who fear change and want to block progress. Just as religious/political crusaders claim to carry out God's will, techno-religious fundamentalists profess to carry out technology's will. They assert that the path to eternal perfection and supreme wonderfulness requires submission to inevitable technological evolution. "Cybernetic eschatology shares with some of history's worst ideologies a doctrine of historical predestination," says virtual reality pioneer Jaron Lanier.[4] The priests of posthumanism, proclaiming that the techno-future is predetermined, want critics to relinquish their role in decisions that help determine the future. Science fiction cautions society not to embrace the spread of technology without fully understanding the consequences of doing so, and helps envision what those consequences will be.

At its most pessimistic, science fiction depicts humans as the victims of a ubiquitous, oppressive technological force. Despair, cynicism, and fatalistic thought often rationalize capitulation to the apparent inevitability of technological expansion. This ensures that the future will be as horrific as it looks. But the realization of powerful repression often provokes an equally powerful response that shifts the dynamic. Science fiction does more than simply reflect cultural despair and technophobia — it wakes us up to a technological world order whose rule is supported by cyborg weapons, corporate greed, macho militarist posturing, governmental warmongering, and techno-religious propaganda. Opposing fatalism and surrender to the status quo, science fiction often argues for a progressive political agenda, urging us to ask questions and confront the ideology of techno-totalitarianism. At its best, science fiction projects a dark vision of the Technologist's posthuman future that encourages us to create a better one.

NOTES

INTRODUCTION

1. David Talbot, "DARPA's Disruptive Technologies," *Technology Review* (October 2001): 41–50.

2. Howard Fineman, "Bush and God," *Newsweek* (March 10, 2003), 22–30.

3. Peter Menzel and Faith D'Aluisio, *Robo sapiens: Evolution of a New Species* (Cambridge, Mass.: MIT Press, 2000).

4. Vernor Vinge, "Vernor Vinge on the Singularity" (1993), http://www.ugcs.caltech.edu/~phoenix/vinge/vinge-sing.html (December 2004).

5. Ibid.

6. Langdon Winner, *Autonomous Technology: Technics-out-of-Control as a Theme in Political Thought* (Cambridge, Mass.: MIT Press, 1977).

7. Bill Joy, "Why the Future Doesn't Need Us," *Wired* (April 2000), 239.

8. Raging against the machine, the Luddites were an organized band of British workmen—inspired by Ned Ludd—who smashed factory machines with sledgehammers between 1811 and 1818. They were protesting the termination of human labor by the Industrial Revolution. The authorities did not like their activities and hanged fourteen of them.

9. The Hugo, or Science Fiction Achievement Award, was founded in 1953 and named after *Amazing Stories* magazine founder and editor Hugo Gernsback; it is maintained by the World Science Fiction Society. Initiated in 1966, the Nebula is awarded by the Science Fiction Writers of America (now the Science Fiction and Fantasy Writers of America). The Philip K. Dick Award was set up in 1983 in memory of the late writer; a small panel of judges comprised of writers, editors, and previous winners makes the annual selection. The Arthur C. Clarke Award—named after the science fiction writer who invented the award in 1987—is administered jointly by the Science Fiction Foundation and the British Science Fiction Association; it is Britain's most prestigious genre award.

10. Jacques Ellul, *The Technological Society* (New York: Vintage Books, 1964), 47.

11. Norbert Wiener, *The Human Use of Human Beings: Cybernetics and Society* (1950; reprint, New York: Da Capo Press, 1954), 185–186.

12. Theodore Roszak, *The Cult of Information: A Neo-Luddite Treatise on High-*

Tech, Artificial Intelligence, and the True Art of Thinking (Berkeley: University of California Press, 1986), 11.

13. Ray Kurzweil, *The Age of Spiritual Machines* (New York: Viking, 1999), 3.

14. Scott Bukatman, *Terminal Identity: The Virtual Subject in Postmodern Science Fiction* (Durham: Duke University Press, 1993), 20.

15. For a cyberpunk manifesto and collection of short stories, see *Mirrorshades: The Cyberpunk Anthology,* ed. Bruce Sterling (New York: Ace, 1986).

16. They made a 2002 appearance in the Flesh Fair scene of *A.I. Artificial Intelligence,* playing anti-robot, pro-flesh rabble-rousers.

17. Manson and Ministry later appeared on the soundtrack to the 1999 cyberpunk-influenced movie *The Matrix,* while Nine Inch Nail's Trent Reznor did the soundtrack to the cyberpunk-inspired game *Quake.*

18. For an analysis of this shift see Claudia Springer, "Psycho-Cybernetics in the Films of the 1990s," in *Alien Zone II,* ed. Annette Kuhn (New York: Verso, 1999), 203–218.

19. Gregory Paul and Earl Cox, *Beyond Humanity: CyberEvolution and Future Minds* (Rockland, Mass.: Charles River Media, 1996), 356–357.

20. Chris Hables Gray, *Cyborg Citizen: Politics in the Posthuman Age* (New York: Routledge, 2002), 118.

21. This game was sold at the American Museum of Natural History (New York) during their 1999 exhibition titled "Epidemic! The World of Infectious Disease."

22. Peter Radetsky, *Invisible Invaders: Viruses and the Scientists Who Pursue Them* (Boston: Back Bay Books, 1991), 4.

23. Interview by the author, 1999.

24. Mark Dery, *The Pyrotechnic Insanitarium: American Culture on the Brink* (New York: Grove Press, 1999), 134.

CHAPTER 1

1. This motto comes from the Web site of a Dutch techno-utopian group called Transtopia: Cult of the Technocalypse [online] http://www.transtopia.org/ (December 2004).

2. David Noble, *The Religion of Technology: The Divinity of Man and the Spirit of Invention* (New York: Knopf, 1997), 3.

3. The term *transhuman* is from "transitional human," or one that is modified or enhanced and on the way to becoming posthuman—the fully technologized species that will supplant human beings.

4. Christopher Dewdney, *Last Flesh: Life in the Transhuman Era* (Toronto: HarperCollins, 1998), 4–5.

5. Rodney Brooks, *Flesh and Machines: How Robots Will Change Us* (New York: Pantheon Books, 2002), 236. Brooks is one of the subjects of Errol Morris's 1998 documentary *Fast, Cheap and Out of Control.*

6. Marvin Minsky, "Will Robots Inherit the Earth?" *Scientific American* (October 1994), 109.

7. João Pedro de Magalhães, "Homo sapiens sapiens cyber: Upgrading Ourselves beyond Our Biology," http://author.senescence.info/thoughts/hcyber.html (December 2004).

8. Ray Kurzweil, "Immortality at Last," *Forbes* (November 11, 1998), 183.

9. Paul and Cox, *Beyond Humanity,* 298.

10. Kurzweil, *The Age of Spiritual Machines,* 140.

11. Ibid., 151.

12. Robert Lee Holtz, "Study Suggests Brain May Affect Religious Response," *Los Angeles Times* (October 29, 1997), 18.

13. Kurzweil, "Immortality at Last," 183.

14. Frank Tipler, *The Physics of Immortality: Modern Cosmology, God and the Resurrection of the Dead* (New York: Doubleday, 1994), xi.

15. Hans Moravec, *Mind Children: The Future of Robot and Human Intelligence* (Cambridge, Mass.: Harvard University Press, 1988), 109.

16. Kurzweil, *The Age of Spiritual Machines,* 126.

17. René Descartes, *The Philosophical Works of Descartes,* vol. 1, trans. Elizabeth S. Haldane and G. R. T. Ross (Cambridge: Cambridge University Press, 1968), 195.

18. Ibid., 140.

19. Mind/body dualism, or the mind/body problem, concerns the question of the relationship between mind, a spiritual, immortal substance, and body or brain, a physical, mortal substance.

20. Dery, *The Pyrotechnic Insanitarium,* 142.

21. Eric Davis, *Techgnosis: Myth, Magic and Mysticism in the Age of Information* (New York: Harmony Books, 1998), 26.

22. The Bible, New International Version, Romans 6:1–13, http://bible.gospel com.net/bible?passage=ROM+6&language=english&version=NIV (December 2004).

23. St. Augustine, *City of God* (New York: Modern Library, 1950), 434.

24. The Bible, New International Version, Romans 7:23, http://bible.gospel com.net/bible?passage=ROM+7&language=english&version=NIV (December 2004).

25. Davis, *Techgnosis,* 100.

26. Ibid., 80.

27. Evan Thomas, " 'The Next Level,' " *Newsweek* (April 7, 1997), 28–35.

28. Hans Moravec, *Robot: Mere Machine to Transcendent Mind* (New York: Oxford University Press, 1999), 13.

29. Kurzweil, *The Age of Spiritual Machines,* 2.

30. Moravec, *Robot,* 11.

31. Paul and Cox, *Beyond Humanity,* 4.

32. Moravec, *Robot,* 13.

33. Paul and Cox, *Beyond Humanity,* 8.

34. Ibid., 354.

35. Ibid., 387.

36. Extropy Institute, http://www.extropy.org (December 2004).

37. Ed Regis, "Meet the Extropians," *Wired* (October 1994), 103–108, 149; http://www.wired.com/wired/archive/2.10/extropians.html (December 2004).

38. The Extropian founder's name references Thomas More, who coined the term *utopia,* and refers to the notion of extropy or expansion. Though remaining chairman of the Extropy Board of Directors, Max More was replaced as President of the Extropy Institute in January 2003 by Natasha Vita-More.

39. Max More, "Extropian Principles 3.0," http://www.maxmore.com/extprn3 .htm (December 2004).

40. Amara D. Angelica, "Techies vs. Neo-Luddites: Progress Action Coalition Formed," 2001, http://www.kurzweilai.net/articles/art0215.html?printable=1.

41. Davis, *Techgnosis,* 119.

42. David Skal, *Screams of Reason: Mad Science and Modern Culture* (New York: W. W. Norton, 1998), 301.

43. The World Transhumanist Association (WTA) supports a more liberal democratic agenda than most transhumanist groups. For a criticism of the fascistic aspects of transhumanism, a statement of the WTA's more enlightened position, and an interesting survey of cyber-politics, see James J. Hughes, "The Politics of Transhumanism," http://www.changesurfer.com/Acad/TranshumPolitics.htm (May 2004).

44. More, "Extropian Principles 3.0."

45. Noble, *The Religion of Technology,* 5.

CHAPTER 2

1. Michael Benedikt, "Introduction," in *Cyberspace First Steps,* ed. Michael Benedikt (Cambridge, Mass.: MIT Press, 1992), 15–16.

2. Davis, *Techgnosis,* 22.

3. Noble, *The Religion of Technology,* 9.

4. George Ovitt, "Critical Assessments of Technology from Campanella to the Harringtonians," 1989, unpublished manuscript quoted in Noble, *Religion and Technology,* 40.

5. In a sense, all utopias are science fiction, since they project an imagined future, yet only those that project technological and scientific developments should be characterized as science fiction (for those who care about such things).

6. Considered a martyr to experimental science, Bacon died after catching cold while conducting an experiment in which he stuffed a disemboweled chicken with snow to find out whether cold would preserve dead flesh.

7. Francis Bacon, *The New Atlantis* (New York: P. F. Collier and Son, 1901), 8.

8. Ibid., 22.

9. Ibid., 39.

10. Noble, *The Religion of Technology,* 50–53.

11. Edward Bellamy, *Looking Backward: 2000–1887* (1888; reprint, Cleveland: World Publishing Company, 1945), 279–280.

12. For an analysis, see Howard P. Segal, *Technological Utopianism in American Culture* (Chicago: University of Chicago Press, 1985).

13. Davis, *Techgnosis,* 57.

14. Chad Walsh, *From Utopia to Nightmare* (London: Geoffrey Blies, 1962), 89.

15. Future anti-utopian books, such as *Brave New World,* borrowed details from Wells's early dystopian stories to satirize his later utopian ones.

16. H. L. Mencken, "The Late Mr. Wells," *Prejudices: First Series* (New York: Knopf, 1919), 28.

17. Mark Hillegas, *The Future as Nightmare: H. G. Wells and the Anti-Utopians* (Carbondale: Southern Illinois University Press, 1967), 16.

18. Mark Hillegas, "Introduction," in H. G. Wells, *A Modern Utopia* (1905; reprint: Lincoln: University of Nebraska Press, 1967), x.

19. Wells, *A Modern Utopia,* 136–137.

20. James J. Hughes, "The Politics of Transhumanism," Version 2.0 (March 2002), http:// www.changesurfer.com /Acad / TranshumPolitics.htm (December 2004).

21. John Cohen, *Human Robots in Myth and Science* (Cranbury, N.J.: A. S. Barnes and Co., 1967), 22.

22. Davis, *Techgnosis,* 18–19.

23. Cohen, *Human Robots in Myth and Science,* 27.

24. Ibid., 81.

25. Ibid., 86.

26. Les Freed, *The History of Computers* (Emeryville, Calif.: Ziff-Davis Press, 1995), 13–17.

27. Manuel De Landa, *War in the Age of Intelligent Machines* (New York: Zone Books, 1991), 31.

28. Isaac Asimov, *Asimov on Science Fiction* (New York: Avon, 1981), 136.

29. A whole subgenre of robot stories, such as the book and movie *The Stepford Wives* (see Chapter Three), centers on patriarchal men fashioning female robots to be their servants.

30. J. P. Telotte, *Replications: A Robotic History of the Science Fiction Film* (Chicago: University of Illinois Press, 1995), 29.

31. Davis, *Techgnosis,* 36.

32. Cohen, *Human Robots in Myth and Science,* 41–43.

33. Egon Erwin Kisch, "What Is a Golem?" in *Artificial Humans, Manic Machines, Controlled Bodies,* ed. Rolf Aurich, Wolfgang Jacobsen, and Gabriele Jatho (Los Angeles: Goethe Institut, 2000), 63.

34. E. T. A. Hoffmann, *The Sandman* (1816; reprint, New York: Penguin, 1982), 85.

35. Ibid., 116.

36. Skal, *Screams of Reason*, 34.

37. Winner, *Autonomous Technology*, 103.

38. For a thorough account of *Frankenstein*'s enduring impact, especially as it frames the debate about biotechnology, see Jon Turney, *Frankenstein's Footsteps: Science, Genetics and Popular Culture* (New Haven: Yale University Press, 1998).

39. The Greek god who supplied humans with fire—technology—and got punished by the head god, Zeus.

40. Incorporating anatomist Luigi Galvani and his discovery that dead muscles stimulated with electricity will twitch and contract as though they were alive, Shelley imagined Dr. Frankenstein as an anatomist and electricity as the energizer of life.

41. Skal, *Screams of Reason*, 57.

42. Winner, *Autonomous Technology*, 309.

43. Mary Shelley, *Frankenstein* (1818; reprint, New York: Bantam Classics, 1981), 130–131.

44. Ibid., 131.

45. Ibid., 150.

46. Bill Joy, "Why the Future Doesn't Need Us," *Wired* (April 2000), 240.

47. Shelley, *Frankenstein*, 152.

48. Winner, *Autonomous Technology*, 313.

49. H. G. Wells, *The Time Machine* (1895; reprint, New York: Bantam Books, 1984), 37.

50. Hillegas, *The Future as Nightmare*, 30.

51. H. G. Wells, *The Island of Dr. Moreau* (1896; reprint, New York: Berkeley Publishing Corporation, 1973), 57.

52. Lotte Eisner, *The Haunted Screen* (Berkeley: University of California Press, 1969), 9.

53. Ibid.

54. Siegfried Kracauer, *From Caligari to Hitler* (Princeton: Princeton University Press, 1947), 72–73.

55. Skal, *Screams of Reason*, 103.

56. James Whale's movie version of *Frankenstein* borrows significantly from the German Expressionist movie golem. Boris Karloff imitates Wegener's swaying, stiff, ponderous walk, and Whale incorporates the monster's encounter with a small girl, the pursuit of the creature by an angry mob of townspeople, and the final fall from a phallic tower.

57. Kracauer, *From Caligari to Hitler*, 32.

58. Hillegas, *The Future as Nightmare*, 95.

59. Karel Capek, *R.U.R.* and *The Insect Play* (1923; reprint, New York: Oxford University Press, 1961), 66–67.

60. J. P. Telotte, *A Distant Technology* (Hanover, N.H.: Wesleyan University Press, 1999), 1.

61. The comic robot turns into a cinematic subgenre in the 1950s, which we

will discuss in Chapter Three. Even today, robots get laughs, as on TV's *The Simpsons*. In one such episode, a parade of robots in the ultra-violent Itchy and Scratchy Theme Park goes awry when the robots suddenly attack the vacationing families. Homer saves the day when he takes a snapshot and the camera flash shorts out the robots' circuits and destroys them.

62. E. M. Forster, "The Machine Stops," in *The Eternal Moment and Other Stories* (New York: Grosset and Dunlap, 1928), 13.

63. Ibid., 46.

64. Ibid., 55–56.

65. Ibid., 80.

66. Telotte, *A Distant Technology,* 26.

67. Ibid., 101.

68. See Thomas Elsaesser, *Metropolis* (London: British Film Institute, 2000), for a good overview of the film and a sharp look at various critical viewpoints.

69. Frederick Winslow Taylor, in his book *Principles of Scientific Management* (1911), and Henry Ford, in his car factories, promoted efficient management and production techniques—such as division of labor, task allocation, and the use of assembly lines—that made human workers into component parts of a mechanical process.

70. Ludmilla Jordanova, "Science, Machines, and Gender," in *Fritz Lang's Metropolis: Cinematic Visions of Technology and Fear,* ed. Michael Minden and Holger Bachmann (Rochester, N.Y.: Boydell and Brewer, 2000), 180.

71. Skal, *Screams of Reason,* 106.

72. Telotte, *Replications,* 67.

73. Ibid.

74. Andreas Huyssen, "The Vamp and the Machine: Technology and Sexuality," in *Fritz Lang's Metropolis*, ed. Minden and Bachmann, 211.

75. Elsaesser, *Metropolis,* 55–56.

76. H. G. Wells, "Mr. Wells Reviews a Current film," *New York Times* (April 16, 1927), in *Fritz Lang's Metropolis*, ed. Minden and Bachmann, 94.

77. Yevgeny Zamyatin, *We,* trans. Clarence Brown (1924; reprint, New York: Penguin Books, 1993), 3.

78. Ibid., 173.

79. Frederick Lewis Allen, *Only Yesterday: An Informal History of the 1920s* (New York: Harper and Brothers, 1931), 197–199.

80. Turney, *Frankenstein's Footsteps,* 107.

81. Isaac Asimov, *Robot Visions* (New York: Penguin Books, 1990), 6.

82. Huyssen, "The Vamp and the Machine," 204.

83. Noble, *The Religion of Technology,* 212.

84. Walsh, *From Utopia to Nightmare,* 139.

85. Telotte, *Replications,* 88.

CHAPTER 3

1. The name ASIMO may also derive from Isaac Asimov, the science fiction writer best known for his robot stories. His work will be discussed later in the chapter.

2. Neil McManus, "Robots at Your Service," *Wired* (January 2003), 58.

3. "World Robotics 2002," United Nations Economic Commission for Europe (UNECE) in cooperation with the International Federation of Robotics (IFR), http://www.unece.org/press/pr2002/02stat_robots_index.htm (December 2004).

4. "Age of Robots Has Begun," Better Humans, http://www.betterhumans .com / Errors / index.aspx?aspxerrorpath = / Age_of_Robots_Has_Begun.Article .2003–10–21–6.aspx (December 2004).

5. CNN.com, Transcripts (March 25, 2004), http://cnnstudentnews.cnn.com/ TRANSCRIPTS/0403/25/lad.01.html (December 2004).

6. "Age of Robots Has Begun," Better Humans, http://www.betterhumans .com / Errors / index.aspx?aspxerrorpath = / Age_of_Robots_Has_Begun.Article .2003–10–21–6.aspx (December 2004).

7. Uli Schmetzer, "See AIBO Run, See AIBO Take the Japanese Market by Storm," *Chicago Tribune* (April 13, 2000), 12.

8. Sonia Zjawinski, "The Stepford Child," *Wired* (August 2002), 99.

9. David Talbot, "DARPA's Disruptive Technologies," *Technology Review* (October 2001), 41–50.

10. Witold Rybczynski, *Taming the Tiger: The Struggle to Control Technology* (1983; reprint, New York: Viking Penguin, 1985), 165.

11. For a detailed examination of how cybernetics helped to reshape the boundaries of the human and influence American ideology, see N. Katherine Hayles, *How We Became Posthuman: Virtual Bodies in Cybernetics, Literature, and Informatics* (Chicago: University of Chicago Press, 1999).

12. De Landa, *War in the Age of Intelligent Machines*, 5.

13. J. David Bolter, *Turing's Man* (Chapel Hill: University of North Carolina Press, 1984), 192.

14. Wiener, *The Human Use of Human Beings*, 33–34.

15. Ibid., 156.

16. Ibid., 18.

17. Ibid., 96.

18. Ibid., 102.

19. Norbert Wiener, *God and Golem, Inc.: A Comment on Certain Points Where Cybernetics Impinges on Religion* (Cambridge, Mass.: MIT Press, 1964), 87.

20. Pamela McCorduck, *Machines Who Think: A Personal Inquiry into the History and Prospects of Artificial Intelligence* (New York: W. H. Freeman and Company, 1979), 13.

21. Wiener, *God and Golem, Inc.*, 87.

22. Wiener, *The Human Use of Human Beings*, 43.

23. Wiener, *God and Golem, Inc.,* 73.

24. Harold E. Hatt, *Cybernetics and the Image of Man* (New York: Abingdon Press, 1968), 211.

25. Ibid., 217.

26. B. F. Skinner, *Walden Two* (1948; reprint, New York: MacMillan Publishing Co., 1964), 93.

27. Arthur Koestler, *The Ghost in the Machine* (Chicago: Gateway, 1967), 17.

28. Wiener, *The Human Use of Human Beings,* 181.

29. Ibid., 185.

30. Wiener, *God and Golem, Inc.,* 95.

31. Moravec, *Robot,* 139.

32. Ibid., 137–142.

33. Ibid., 139.

34. Ibid., 140.

35. Asimov, *Robot Visions,* 6–7.

36. Ibid., 56.

37. Ibid.

38. Ibid., 70.

39. Ibid., 8.

40. Vernor Vinge, "Vernor Vinge on the Singularity" (1993), http://www.ugcs .caltech.edu/~phoenix/vinge/vinge-sing.html (December 2004).

41. Roboticist Rodney Brooks points out that currently robots are not programmed with Asimov's Laws: "Up until 1998, or perhaps even 1999, no robot had any way of even detecting a human." Brooks, *Flesh and Machines,* 73.

42. Asimov, *Robot Visions,* 8.

43. William F. Touponce, *Isaac Asimov* (Boston: Twayne Publishers, 1991), 34.

44. Brooks, *Flesh and Machines,* 195.

45. Asimov, "Evidence," in *Robot Visions,* 142.

46. Asimov, "The Evitable Conflict," in *Robot Visions,* 211.

47. Ibid., 216.

48. See the 1982 documentary *Atomic Café* (dir. Kevin Rafferty, Jayne Loader, Pierce Rafferty) for a horrifically humorous compilation of American bomb propaganda from the 1940s and 1950s.

49. Paul Boyer, interview with the author, March 3, 1999.

50. Philip K. Dick, "AutoFac," in *Beyond Control,* ed. Robert Silverberg (New York: Dell, 1972), 55.

51. Ibid., 51–52.

52. Ibid., 59.

53. Winner, *Autonomous Technology,* 34.

54. Kurt Vonnegut, *Player Piano* (1952; reprint, New York: Delta Books, 1982), 14–15.

55. Ibid., 86.

56. Ibid., 301.

57. Ibid., 336.

58. Harold Berger, *Science Fiction and the New Dark Age* (Bowling Green, Ohio: Bowling Green State University Popular Press, 1976), 18.

59. Vonnegut, *Player Piano,* 301–302.

60. Jack Williamson, "With Folded Hands," in *Science Fiction Hall of Fame,* Vol. Two A, ed. Ben Bova (New York: Doubleday and Company, 1973), 512.

61. Ibid., 489.

62. Ibid., 499.

63. Ibid., 502.

64. Ibid., 529.

65. Telotte, *Replications,* 46.

66. Williamson, "With Folded Hands," 528.

67. Isaac Asimov, *Asimov on Science Fiction* (New York: Doubleday and Company, 1981), 161.

68. Telotte, *Replications,* 119.

69. Jeanne Cavelos, *The Science of STAR WARS* (New York: St. Martin's Press, 1999), 79–80, provides some of the information for this list.

70. Henri Bergson, "Laughter," in *Comedy* (New York: Doubleday Anchor Books, 1956), 71.

71. Philip K. Dick, *Blade Runner (Do Androids Dream of Electric Sheep?)* (1968; reprint, New York: Ballantine Books, 1982), 6.

72. Ibid., 14.

73. David Desser, "Race, Space and Class: The Politics of the SF Film from *Metropolis* to *Blade Runner,*" in *Retrofitting BLADE RUNNER: Issues in Ridley Scott's BLADE RUNNER and Philip K. Dick's DO ANDROIDS DREAM OF ELECTRIC SHEEP?* ed. Judith B. Kerman (Bowling Green, Ohio: Bowling Green State University Popular Press, 1991), 111.

74. Jonathan Rosenbaum, "The Best of Both Worlds," *Chicago Reader* (July 13, 2001), 35.

75. *Fairyland* won the Arthur C. Clarke Award in 1996.

76. In the years since the book and original version of the movie, the concept "Stepford wife" has entered the American lexicon as a cultural reference for a conformist suburban homemaker.

77. *The Stepford Wives* was pointlessly remade in 2004 as a silly comedy. Mildly critical of Microsoft, NASA, and Disney, the new version sacrifices the menace, creepiness, horror, and metaphorical power of the original.

78. Per Schelde, *Androids, Humanoids, and Other Science Fiction Monsters* (New York: New York University Press, 1993), 159.

79. A.I. pioneer Alan Turing in his classic 1950 paper "Computer Machinery and Intelligence" proposed the test, in which a computer and a person are hidden from view. Both are asked the same questions. Based on the answers each gives, displayed on a terminal, one must decide which is the human, which the machine. In other words, if it behaves and responds like a human, it is human. According to this test, D.A.R.Y.L. is human.

80. The novelette *Bicentennial Man* won both the Hugo and the Nebula Award in 1977.

81. Lois Gresh and Robert Weinberg, *The Computers of Star Trek* (New York: Basic Books, 1999), 106.

82. Episodes from the *Star Trek* television series will be designated as follows: *The Original Series*—TOS; *The Next Generation*—TNG; and *Voyager*—VOY. My interest in the series evaporated after *Voyager*.

83. Forster, "The Machine Stops," in *The Eternal Moment and Other Stories,* 46.

84. Rosenbaum, "The Best of Both Worlds," 35.

CHAPTER 4

1. Moravec, *Mind Children,* 8.

2. James P. Hogan, *Mind Matters* (New York: Ballantine Books, 1997), 73.

3. Joseph Weizenbaum, *Computer Power and Human Reason* (San Francisco: W. H. Freeman, 1976), 169.

4. Ibid., 138.

5. Noble, *The Religion of Technology,* 152.

6. In his later fiction, Asimov replaced Dr. Susan Calvin—the fictional cybernetic robopsychologist—with a character named Mervin Mansky.

7. Hogan, *Mind Matters,* 73.

8. Marvin Minsky, *The Society of Mind* (New York: Simon and Schuster, 1985), 324.

9. Noble, *The Religion of Technology,* 154.

10. McCorduck, *Machines Who Think,* 70.

11. Noble, *The Religion of Technology,* 148.

12. McCorduck, *Machines Who Think,* 353.

13. Telotte, *Replications,* 115.

14. Chess was considered a benchmark of human intelligence until the computer Deep Blue beat Russian world chess champion Garry Kasparov in 1997.

15. It won the Hugo award.

16. Harlan Ellison, "I Have No Mouth and I Must Scream," in *The Essential Ellison: A 50 Year Retrospective,* ed. Terry Dowling (Beverly Hills: Morpheus International, 1984), 22.

17. Around this time, several other science fiction classics were turned into games, including Ray Bradbury's *Martian Chronicles* and Arthur C. Clarke's *Rendezvous with Rama,* as well as an adaptation of the movie *Blade Runner*—itself an adaptation of Philip K. Dick's novel.

18. Berger, *Science Fiction and the New Dark Age,* 88.

19. George Orwell, *1984* (1949; reprint, New York: Signet, 1950), 57.

20. Michael Ryan and Douglas Kellner, "Technophobia," in *Alien Zone: Cultural Theory and Contemporary Science Fiction Cinema,* ed. Annette Kuhn (London: Verso, 1990), 58.

21. Ibid., 59.

22. The first, studio-controlled, version of *Blade Runner* ends with Deckard and Rachel escaping to nature, using footage from Stanley Kubrick's film *The Shining* (1980). In his later-released "Director's Cut," director Ridley Scott removed the nature footage and restored the more ambiguous ending he had originally conceived.

23. Winner, *Autonomous Technology*, 323–324.

24. Ellul, *The Technological Society*, 306.

25. T. J. Matheson, "Marcuse, Ellul, and the Science-Fiction Film: Negative Responses to Technology," in *Science Fiction Studies*, vol. 19, part 3 (November 1992), 334.

26. Ibid.

27. Marvin Minsky served as advisor on the film. HAL reflects Clarke's and Minsky's expectations of computer capability by 2001. The letters in HAL come one alphabetical position before those in IBM. The name also signifies a step-by-step logical approach to the solving of problems: Heuristic ALgorithmic.

28. David Stork, *HAL's Legacy: 2001's Computer as Dream and Reality* (Boston: MIT Press, 1997), 5.

29. For a complete listing of HAL's human-like mental traits, see Leonard F. Wheat, *Kubrick's 2001: A Triple Allegory* (Lanham, Md.: Scarecrow Press, 2000), 69.

30. Ibid., 63.

31. Ken MacLeod, *The Cassini Division* (New York: Tor, 1998), 7–8.

32. Ibid., 96.

33. Ibid., 118.

34. Ibid., 96.

35. Ibid., 108.

36. Ibid., 110.

37. Ibid., 303.

38. The DeLorean car debuted in 1981, and by 1983, financial difficulties had doomed the company. It closed down after building fewer than ten thousand cars. The DeLorean got a big popularity boost when driven by actor Michael J. Fox in the 1985 film *Back to the Future*. Of course, never-say-die Internet cults are still devoted to the car.

39. Paul Elias, "In Molecules May Lie Supercomputers: Scientists Are Using DNA to Do Calculations," *Chicago Sun-Times* (August 18, 2003), 35. Several researchers around the world are creating tiny biology-based computers within test tubes of DNA-laden water. Jeffrey Sussman, "A Trillion Computers in a Drop of Water" (November 2001), http://www.eurekalert.org/pub_releases/2001–11/wi-at111901.php (December 2004). This computer—created at the Weizmann Institute of Science in Israel—is so small that a trillion such computers coexist and compute in parallel, in a drop the size of one-tenth of a milliliter of watery solution. Collectively, the computers perform a billion operations per second, with a rate of accuracy greater than 99.8 percent per operation. This may lead to future computers that can operate in the human body. For further information, see "Beyond

Silicon: The Future of Computing," *Technology Review* (May/June 2000). This special issue is devoted to exotic approaches based on DNA, individual molecules, cells, and quantum properties. In the same issue, see also Antonio Regalado, "DNA Computing," 80–84.

40. Only a few exceptions to this trend stand out. In *Resident Evil* (2002), the Red Queen is in control; in *Alien* (1989), the ship's master computer is named Mother—a name shared by the computer in *Dark Star* (1974). In *2010: The Year We Make Contact,* Dr. Chandra's earthbound computer is named SAL, a silly variant of HAL, and speaks in a sexy female voice. Finally, the computer in *Star Trek: The Next Generation* generates a female voice but no personality.

41. David Noble, *A World without Women: The Christian Clerical Culture of Western Science* (New York: Oxford University Press, 1992), 163.

42. Skal, *Screams of Reason,* 292.

43. Wiener, *God and Golem, Inc.,* 72.

44. Menzel and D'Aluisio, *Robo sapiens,* 89.

45. Ibid., 27.

46. David Talbot, "DARPA's Disruptive Technologies," *Technology Review* (October 2001), 48.

47. Moravec, *Robot,* 13.

48. Menzel and D'Aluisio, *Robo sapiens,* 21.

49. Winner, *Autonomous Technology,* 295–296.

50. Ellul, *The Technological Society,* 134.

51. Dick, *Blade Runner (Do Androids Dream of Electric Sheep),* 204.

52. The movie was originally released in 1982 and re-released in 1993 in a "Director's Cut" version. Director Ridley Scott removed the voice-over narration, altered the ending (making the future more ambiguous), and slightly strengthened the possible interpretation that Deckard is a replicant.

53. Janice Hocker Rushing and Thomas S. Frentz, *Projecting the Shadow: The Cyborg Hero in American Film* (Chicago: University of Chicago Press, 1995), 145.

54. Judith B. Kerman, "Technology and Politics in the *Blade Runner* Dystopia," in *Retrofitting Blade Runner,* ed. Kerman, 20.

55. Ibid., 18.

56. The "Director's Cut" of the movie increases clues that point to Deckard as a replicant. In fact, the question "Is Deckard a replicant?" has elicited about as much debate as the question "Does God exist?" For a full analysis of the issue, see Paul M. Sammon, *Future Noir: The Making of Blade Runner* (New York: HarperCollins, 1996), 359–365. To me, the evidence offered is insufficiently strong to counter the overall impression of the movie that Deckard is human.

57. *Blade Runner* was adapted into a 1997 computer game by Westwood Studios.

58. Rudy Rucker, *Software* (New York: Avon, 1982), 22.

59. Ibid., 27.

60. Kurzweil, *The Age of Spiritual Machines,* 3.

61. This process was probably inspired by the scenario proposed by Hans Moravec in his book *Mind Children,* 108–122.

62. Rucker, *Software,* 139.

63. Ibid., 98.

64. Ibid., 134.

65. Ibid., 83. Emphasis in original.

66. Antonio R. Damasio, *The Feeling of What Happens: Body and Emotion in the Making of Consciousness* (New York: Harcourt Brace and Company, 1999), 16.

67. Rucker, *Software,* 148.

CHAPTER 5

1. "Artificial Eye," *BBC News* Web site, http://news.bbc.co.uk/1/hi/health/726805.stm (December 2004). For a complete summary of recent research on artificial sight, see Steven Kotler, "Vision Quest," *Wired* (September 2002), 94–101.

2. Jesse Freund, "Bionic Ears," *Wired* (May 2004), 35.

3. Justin Bachman, "Flipper Flap Engulfs Swim League," *Chicago Sun-Times* (August 15, 2002), 3.

4. James Meek, "Robot with Living Brain Created in US," *Guardian* (April 18, 2001), http://www.guardian.co.uk/international/story/0,3604,474397,00.html (December 2004).

5. Erik Baard, "Make Robots, Not War," *Village Voice* (September 10, 2003), 39.

6. Dwayne Hunter, "Monkeys Become One with Robotic Arm" (October 13, 2003), http://www.betterhumans.com/News/news.aspx?articleID=2003-10-13-8 (December 2004).

7. Brooks, *Flesh and Machines,* 229.

8. João Pedro de Magalhães, "Homo sapiens, sapiens cyber: Upgrading Ourselves beyond Our Biology," http://author.senescence.info/thoughts/hcyber.html (December 2004).

9. Kevin Warwick, "Cyborg 1.0," *Wired* (February 2000), 145–151.

10. Manfred Clynes and Nathan Kline, "Cyborgs and Space," in *The Cyborg Handbook,* ed. Chris Hables Gray (New York: Routledge, 1995), 29; reprinted from *Astronautics* (September 1960). Emphasis in original.

11. Ibid., 31.

12. Manfred E. Clynes, "Cyborg II," in *The Cyborg Handbook,* ed. Gray, 41.

13. Clynes and Kline, "Cyborgs and Space," 32.

14. Ibid., 33.

15. "Interview with Manfred Clynes," in *The Cyborg Handbook,* ed. Gray, 52.

16. "Pilot's Associate," *The Cyborg Handbook,* 101–103; reprinted from *The Strategic Computing Second Annual Report,* DARPA (February 1986); Chris Hables Gray, "Science Fiction Becomes Military Fact," *The Cyborg Handbook,* 104–105.

17. Chris Hables Gray, Steven Mentor, and Heidi J. Figueroa-Sarriera, "Cyborgology: Constructing the Knowledge of Cybernetic Organisms," *The Cyborg Handbook,* 3.

18. Talbot, "DARPA's Disruptive Technologies," 47–48.

19. Bernard Wolfe, *Limbo* (New York: Ace Books, 1952), 52.

20. Ibid., 358.

21. Ibid., 375–376.

22. Ibid., 358.

23. Hayles, *How We Became Posthuman,* 120–121.

24. Wolfe, *Limbo,* 376.

25. C. L. Moore, "No Woman Born," in *Human Machines,* ed. Thomas N. Scortia and George Zebrowski (New York: Vintage, 1975), 107.

26. Ibid., 111.

27. Ibid., 118.

28. Stephen S. Hall, "Brain Pacemakers," *Technology Review* (September 2001), 36.

29. Researchers have now begun trying to map the brain's impulses using implanted electrodes. This mapping is a prerequisite for reliably using neural signals to control external devices such as prosthetics. For further information, see Gabe Romain, "Humans Could Get Robot Arms," March 24, 2004; http://www .betterhumans.com/News/news.aspx?articleID=2004-03-24-4 (December 2004).

30. Martin Caidin, *Cyborg* (New York: Warner, 1972), 63.

31. Ibid., 136.

32. Ibid., 172.

33. Developed by Bungie and published by Microsoft.

34. Developed by Ion Storm and published by Eidos Interactive.

35. Developed by Looking Glass Studios and published by Electronic Arts.

36. Frederick Pohl, *Man Plus* (New York: Baen Publishing, 1976). *Man Plus* won the 1976 Nebula Award.

37. Ibid., 37.

38. Ibid., 93–95.

39. Ibid., 275.

40. Rushing and Frentz, *Projecting the Shadow,* 3.

41. Ibid.

42. Winner, *Autonomous Technology,* 105.

43. Sean French reports in his book *The Terminator* that these borrowings were considered plagiarism by Ellison and, through "acrimonious legal proceedings," he received a settlement and got credit in the film. Sean French, *The Terminator* (London: British Film Institute, 1996), 16.

44. Rushing and Frentz, *Projecting the Shadow,* 196.

45. Ibid., 186.

46. Ibid., 190.

47. Ibid., 199.

48. The anime *Akira,* for example, focuses on an anti-heroic character, Tetsuo, who resists oppressive authority figures. Tetsuo inspired *Tetsuo* and *Tetsuo II,* "both of which were essentially homages to a particularly dark form of body metamorphosis." Susan J. Napier, *Anime—From Akira to Princess Mononoke* (New York: Palgrave, 2000), 42.

49. Bukatman, *Terminal Identity*, 308.

50. Cynthia J. Fuchs, " 'Death Is Irrelevant': Cyborgs, Reproductions, and the Future of Male Hysteria," in *The Cyborg Handbook*, ed. Gray, 284.

51. Schelde, *Androids*, 212.

52. Claudia Springer, *Electronic Eros* (Austin: University of Texas Press, 1996), 100.

53. Noble, *Religion of Technology*, 210.

54. Donna J. Haraway, "A Cyborg Manifesto: Science, Technology, and Socialist-Feminism in the Late Twentieth Century," in *Simians, Cyborgs, and Women: The Reinvention of Nature* (New York: Routledge, Chapman, and Hall, 1991), 181.

55. Ibid., 150.

56. Ibid., 151.

57. Ibid., 180.

58. Ibid., 175.

59. Fuchs, " 'Death is Irrelevant,' " 294.

60. Springer, *Electronic Eros*, 117.

61. Haraway, "A Cyborg Manifesto," 154.

62. Marge Piercy, *He, She, and It* (New York: Fawcett Crest, 1991). *He, She, and It* won the Arthur C. Clarke Award.

63. Ibid., 404.

64. Vara Neverow, "The Politics of Incorporation and Embodiment: *Woman on the Edge of Time* and *He, She and It* as Feminist Epistemologies of Resistance," *Utopian Studies* V. 5.2 (1994), 27.

65. Piercy, *He, She, and It*, 142.

66. For this viewpoint, see M. Keith Booker, "Woman on the Edge of a Genre: The Feminist Dystopias of Marge Piercy," *Science Fiction Studies* 21 (1994): 337–350.

67. Piercy, *He, She, and It*, 410.

68. Winner, *Autonomous Technology*, 208.

69. Ibid.

70. Claudia Springer, "Psycho-Cybernetics in Films of the 1990s," in *Alien Zone II*, ed. Kuhn, 204.

71. Donna J. Haraway, "Cyborgs and Symbionts: Living Together in the New World Order," in *The Cyborg Handbook*, ed. Gray, xix.

CHAPTER 6

1. Marshall McLuhan, *Understanding Media: The Extensions of Man* (New York: McGraw Hill, 1964), 80.

2. Richard DeGrandpre, *Digitopia* (New York: Atrandom.com, 2001).

3. Tim Jordan, *Cyberpower: The Culture and Power of Cyberspace and the Internet* (London: Routledge, 1999), 187.

4. This technology employs high-powered computers to generate 3D graphic environments in which a user can be immersed in real-time interaction with a pro-

grammed virtual world using a stereovision helmet and a body glove with sensors at joint positions. The user's movements are reproduced on the computer screen. When the user turns her head, the computer display changes in a corresponding fashion. At the same time, audio earphones create a three-dimensional sound field. The result is a multi-sensory interaction that creates the illusion of reality or the illusory reality of fantasy. The technology has never come close to matching its hype.

5. Michael Benedikt, "Introduction," in *Cyberspace: First Steps*, ed. Benedikt, 15–16.

6. Michael Heim, "The Erotic Ontology of Cyberspace," in *Cyberspace First Steps*, ed. Benedikt, 69.

7. Ibid., 63.

8. Noble, *The Religion of Technology*, 158.

9. Jordon, *Cyberpower*, 33.

10. Dan Farmer and Charles C. Mann, "Surveillance Nation," *Technology Review* (April 2003), 36, 43.

11. The TIA Program was originally called the "Total Information Awareness System"; DARPA's public relations people euphemized the name, *1984*-style, as "Terrorist Information Awareness Program" to cover up the sweeping nature of the plan and rationalize it as being required for national security.

12. Terrorist Information Awareness Program, DARPA, http://www.darpa .mil/body/strategic_plan/strategic_text.htm (December 2004).

13. "Bush to Create Terrorist Threat Integration Center" (January 29, 2003), http://cryptome.org/ttic-stasi.htm (December 2004).

14. Allucquere Rosanne Stone, "Will the Real Body Please Stand Up? Boundary Stories about Virtual Culture," in *Cyberspace First Steps*, ed. Benedikt, 96.

15. Noble, *The Religion of Technology*, 158–159.

16. Quoted in Bennett Daviss, "Grand Illusions," *Discover Magazine* (June 1990), 38.

17. Ibid.

18. Dan Dinello, "Electronic Acid," *New City* (July 11, 1991), 7.

19. Jaron Lanier, interview with the author, 1990.

20. Nicole Stenger, "Mind Is a Leaking Rainbow," in *Cyberspace First Steps*, ed. Benedikt, 52.

21. Carpenter, "Slouching toward Cyberspace," *Village Voice* (March 12, 1991), 39.

22. Philip K. Dick, *The Three Stigmata of Palmer Eldritch* (New York: Vintage Books, 1964), 41.

23. Lawrence Sutin, *Divine Invasions: A Life of Philip K. Dick* (New York: Citadel Twilight Press, 1989), 128.

24. Skal, *Screams of Reason*, 304.

25. Trumbull also directed *Silent Running*, but is best known as the special-effects genius for *2001*, *The Andromeda Strain* (1971), *Close Encounters of the Third Kind* (1977), *Star Trek: The Motion Picture* (1979), and *Blade Runner* (1982).

26. Bukatman, *Terminal Identity,* 220.

27. Tron 2.0 was developed by Monolith Productions and published by Buena Vista.

28. William Gibson, *Neuromancer* (New York: Ace, 1984), 51.

29. The game *Rez* was made and published by Sega.

30. Gibson, *Neuromancer,* 256, 257.

31. A reference to the theoretician of machine intelligence Alan Turing, who created the Turing Test to distinguish between humans and artificial intelligence.

32. Sterling, ed., *Mirrorshades,* xi–xii.

33. Bill McKibben, *Enough: Staying Human in an Engineered Age* (New York: Times Books, 2003), 106.

34. Gibson, *Neuromancer,* 5.

35. Ibid., 6.

36. Hayles, *How We Became Posthuman,* 36.

37. Gibson, *Neuromancer,* 206.

38. Jordon, *Cyberpower,* 38.

39. Gibson, *Neuromancer,* 160.

40. Ibid., 268–269.

41. Winner, *Autonomous Technology,* 190.

42. Gibson, *Neuromancer,* 270.

43. Peter Fitting, "The Lessons of Cyberpunk," in *Technoculture,* ed. Constance Penley and Andrew Ross (Minneapolis: University of Minnesota Press, 1991), 309.

44. Pat Cadigan's *Synners* (New York: Four Walls Eight Windows, 1991) won the Arthur C. Clarke Award.

45. Ibid., 97.

46. Ibid., 56.

47. Ibid., 324.

48. Anne Balsamo, *Technologies of the Gendered Body* (Durham: Duke University Press, 1996), 155–156.

49. Haraway, "A Cyborg Manifesto," in *Simians, Cyborgs, and Women,* ed. Haraway, 181.

50. Cadigan, *Synners,* 435.

51. Ibid., 324.

52. Springer, "Psycho-Cybernetics in Films of the 1990s," 207.

53. Neal Stephenson, *Snow Crash* (New York: Bantam, 1992), 24.

54. The Cymouse or Miracle Mouse (http://www.miracle-mouse.com/index .html) emulates Hiro's metaverse navigation methods. You strap on the helmet and an infrared sensor attached to your PC translates the motion of your head into character movements in the gaming environment.

55. Today a company called 3Q (www.3Q.com) has created photo booths—or, as they call them, "Q-Clone Generators"—that produce instant, lifelike, three-dimensional avatars. Transferred to a CD, your Q-Clone can be downloaded to be your character in online games.

56. Conceived in the nineteenth century, the panopticon—a round hollow

building with a tower in the center—was an attempt to create the perfect prison. Inmates held in cells in the outer shell could be constantly observed through windows by supervisors stationed in the tower. In addition, a system of mirrors reflected the supervisors, who also could be observed by super-supervisors.

57. Jordon, *Cyberpower,* 201.

58. Stephenson, *Snow Crash,* 6.

59. The names of the mutants—Agatha, Arthur, and Dashiell—coincide with those of three acclaimed masters of popular mystery/detective fiction: Agatha Christie, Arthur Conan Doyle, and Dashiell Hammett.

60. "Combat Zones That See," DARPA Contracting Document, http:// dtsn.darpa.mil/ixo/solicitations/CTS/file/BAA_03–15_CTS_PIP.pdf (December 2004).

61. Farmer and Mann, "Surveillance Nation," 36.

62. An entertainment behemoth, computer game sales generate more money than movie box office receipts.

63. André Breton, "Manifesto of Surrealism," in *Manifestos of Surrealism* (1924; reprint, Ann Arbor: University of Michigan Press, 1972), 16, 26.

64. Cynthia Freeland, "Penetrating Keanu: New Holes, but the Same Old Shit," in *THE MATRIX and Philosophy: Welcome to the Desert of the Real,* ed. William Irwin (Chicago: Open Court, 2002), 206.

65. Holographic television is being developed, though even the most optimistic predict that it's at least ten years away from working. See Erika Jonietz, "Holographic TV," *Technology Review* (June 2004), 71–73.

66. Arthur C. Clarke, *The City and the Stars* and *The Sands of Mars* (1956; reprint, New York: Warner Books, 2001), 12.

67. *Permutation City* won the John W. Campbell Memorial Award for best novel.

68. Greg Egan, *Permutation City* (New York: Harper Prism, 1994), 2.

69. Ibid., 3.

70. Ibid., 7.

71. Ibid., 248, 249.

72. Ibid., 270.

73. Ibid., 250.

74. Ross Farnell, "Attempting Immortality: AI, A-Life, and the Posthuman in Greg Egan's *Permutation City,*" *Science Fiction Studies* 27 (March 2000): 85.

75. Ibid., 81.

76. Books include *THE MATRIX and Philosophy: Welcome to the Desert of the Real* (2002), ed. William Irwin; *The Reality within the Matrix* (2002), by Kristenea LaVelle; *Exploring the Matrix: Vision of CyberPresent* (2003), ed. Karen Haber; and *Taking the Red Pill: Science, Philosophy and Religion in THE MATRIX* (2003), ed. Glenn Yeffeth.

77. This backstory is explained in "Second Renaissance—Parts 1 and 2," included in the nine anime shorts released as *Animatrix* (2003).

78. DeGrandpre, *Digitopia,* 21.

79. Bill Joy, "Why the Future Doesn't Need Us," *Wired* (April 2000), 240.

80. William Gibson, *Mona Lisa Overdrive* (New York: Bantam, 1988), 46.

81. Jordon, *Cyberpower,* 204.

CHAPTER 7

1. Clonaid, http://www.clonaid.com.

2. Malcolm Ritter, "Firm Linked to Sect Claims Cloned Baby," *Chicago Sun-Times* (December 28, 2002), 3.

3. As of December 2004, Boisselier claimed thirteen clones had been born and were doing well; http://www.clonaid.com/news.php (December 2004).

4. Daniel J. Kevles, "Cloning Can't Be Stopped," *Technology Review* (June 2002), 40–43.

5. Pierre Baldi, *The Shattered Self: The End of Natural Evolution* (Cambridge: MIT Press, 2001), 1.

6. Dewdney, *Last Flesh,* 145.

7. Jeremy Rifkin, *The Biotech Century: Harnessing the Gene and Remaking the World* (New York: Penguin Putnam, 1998), x–xii.

8. Roszak, *The Cult of Information,* 17.

9. Noble, *The Religion of Technology,* 172.

10. Ibid., 181.

11. Dorothy Nelkin and M. Susan Lindee, *The DNA Mystique: The Gene as a Cultural Icon* (New York: W. H. Freeman and Company, 1995), 39–40.

12. Noble, *The Religion of Technology,* 181.

13. Doug Garr, "The Human Body Shop," *Technology Review* (April 2001), 73–79.

14. Marvin Minsky, "Will Robots Inherit the Earth?" *Scientific American* (October 1994), 111.

15. Quote taken from the E-biomed Web page, http://www.library.yale.edu/~llicense/ListArchives/0003/msg00005.html (December 2004).

16. Dewdney, *Last Flesh,* 147–148.

17. The Raelian Revolution, http://www.rael.org (December 2004).

18. Clonaid, http://www.clonaid.com.

19. Gregory Stock, *Redesigning Humans: Our Inevitable Genetic Future* (New York: Houghton Mifflin, 2002), 3.

20. Ibid., 2.

21. Gregory Stock, *Metaman: The Merging of Humans and Machines into a Global Superorganism* (New York: Simon and Schuster, 1993).

22. Ed Regis, "BioWar," *Wired* (November 1996), http://hotwired.wired.com/wired_online/4.11/biowar/ (December 2004).

23. Andrew Pollack, "Army Center to Study New Use of Biotechnology (August 27, 2003), http://www.mindcontrolforums.com/news/army-study-new-uses-biotechnology.htm (December 2004).

24. For information on all DARPA's publicly announced programs including Bio:Info:Micro:, http://www.darpa.mil/dso/ (December 2004).

25. Tom Chea, "Biotech Companies See a Big New Customer at the Pentagon," *Washington Post* (May 2, 2002); http://pqasb.pqarchiver.com/washingtonpost/results.html?st=advanced&uid=&MAC=50a23aa1f3f5c6104e90e36051420d61&QryTxt=&sortby=REVERSE_CHRON&datetype=6&frommonth=05&fromday= (December 2004).

26. "Star 21: Strategic Technologies for the Army of the Twenty-First Century," http://www.nap.edu/books/0309046297/html/R1.html (December 2004), 151. Other material in this section relies on the following article: Ayaz Ahmed Khan, "U.S. Army to Employ Biotechnology in Battle," *Defense Journal* (August 2001), http://www.defensejournal.com/2001/august/battle.htm (December 2004).

27. Winner, *Autonomous Technology,* 237.

28. Lori Andrews and Dorothy Nelkin, *Body Bazaar: The Market for Human Tissue in the Biotechnology Age* (New York: Crown, 2001), 2.

29. Ibid., 6–7.

30. In the early nineteenth century, vivisection—cutting into or dissecting living animals—was a part of experimental biology and gave rise to a European anti-vivisectionist movement detailed in Richard D. French, *Antivivisection and Medical Science in Victorian Society* (Princeton, N.J.: Princeton University Press, 1975).

31. Turney, *Frankenstein's Footsteps,* 56.

32. Ibid., 57.

33. In 1973, geneticists Herbert Boyer and Stanley Cohen accomplished the first gene transfer, from one organism to another.

34. Skal, *Screams of Reason,* 235.

35. Robert Jay Lifton, *The Nazi Doctors: Medical Killing and the Psychology of Genocide* (New York: Basic Books, 1986), 17.

36. Ibid., 377, emphasis in original.

37. Ibid., 16–17.

38. Ignoring a government directive forbidding immigration of Nazis, the men who ran Paperclip covered up scientists' background and installed them in military and industrial positions. The whole sordid story is documented in Linda Hunt, *Secret Agenda: The United States Government, Nazi Scientists, and Project Paperclip* (New York: St. Martin's Press, 1991).

39. Lifton, *The Nazi Doctors,* 17.

40. Rifkin, *The Biotech Century,* 116.

41. Turney, *Frankenstein's Footsteps,* 60.

42. Edwin Black, *War against the Weak: Eugenics and America's Campaign to Create a Master Race* (New York: Four Walls Eight Windows, 2003), 9.

43. Aldous Huxley, *Brave New World* (1932; reprint, New York: Bantam, 1950), 4.

44. Turney, *Frankenstein's Footsteps,* 115.

45. Francis Fukuyama, *Our Posthuman Future: Consequences of the Biotechnology Revolution* (New York: Farrar, Straus and Giroux, 2002), 7.

46. Heinlein won Hugo awards for *Double Star* (1956), *Starship Troopers* (1960), *Stranger in a Strange Land* (1962), and *The Moon Is a Harsh Mistress* (1967).

47. Robert Heinlein, *Beyond This Horizon* (New York: Signet, 1948), 24.

48. Ibid., 39.

49. Ibid., 157.

50. Herbert won the Hugo and Nebula for *Dune* (1965).

51. Frank Herbert, *The Eyes of Heisenberg* (New York: Berkley Medallion Books, 1966), 39.

52. Helen Parker, *Biological Themes in Modern Science Fiction* (Ann Arbor: UMI Research Press, 1977), 52.

53. Scientists have genetically engineered "marathon mice" that are not only super-athletic—running farther and longer than their naturally bred brethren—but are also immune to obesity. Paul Elias, "'Marathon Mice' Bred by Scientists," *Chicago Sun-Times* (August 24, 2004), 24.

54. Rifkin, *The Biotech Century*, 116.

55. David A. Kirby, "The New Eugenics in Cinema: Genetic Determinism and Gene Therapy in *GATTACA*," *Science Fiction Studies* 27, no. 81 (July 2000): 196.

56. A short sequence, edited out of the end of *Gattaca*, specifically emphasized how even screening out genetic disease might entail negative consequences. It lists significant people and their genetic defects, suggesting that they might not have been born if genetic discrimination had been in force: Abraham Lincoln (Marfan Syndrome), Emily Dickinson (Manic Depression), Vincent van Gogh (Epilepsy), Albert Einstein (Dyslexia), John F. Kennedy (Addison's Disease), Rita Hayworth (Alzheimer's Disease), Ray Charles (Primary Glaucoma), Stephen Hawking (Amyotrophic Lateral Sclerosis), and Jackie Joyner-Kersee (Asthma). The last sentence is: "Of course, the other birth that would surely never have taken place is your own."

57. Stephen Nottingham, *Screening DNA* (DNA Press, 1999), http://ourworld .compuserve.com/homepages/Stephen_Nottingham/DNA9.htm (December 2004).

58. The survey was conducted by Dr. Lisa N. Geller of the Department of Neurobiology and Division of Medical Ethics at Harvard Medical School; see Lisa N. Geller et al., "Individual, Family, and Societal Dimensions of Genetic Discrimination: A Case Study Analysis," *Science and Engineering Ethics* 2 (April 1996): 70–88.

59. Rifkin, *The Biotech Century*, 160.

60. Lee M. Silver, *Remaking Eden: Cloning and Beyond in a Brave New World* (New York: Avon Books, 1997), 7.

61. Van Vogt wrote thirty-eight novels and published forty-seven short story collections, with *Slan* and *The World of Null-A* being his best-known works.

62. A. E. (Alfred Elton) Van Vogt, *Slan* (1940; reprint, New York: Tom Doherty Associates, 1998), 11.

63. Kress won both the Nebula and the Hugo for the novella "Beggars in Spain," which first appeared in *Isaac Asimov's Science Fiction Magazine,* April 1991. In

addition, Kress won Nebula awards for her novelette "The Flowers of Aulit Prison" (1996) and for her short story "Out of All Them Bright Stars" (1985). Nancy Kress, *Beggars in Spain* (New York: Eos Books, 1993) is part of a trilogy which includes *Beggars and Choosers* (1995) and *Beggars Ride* (1996).

64. The advantages of not sleeping have already been noticed and pursued by the military. Striving to create the sleepless soldier, DARPA has funded a program that includes seeking genes that trigger sleep, analyzing the neuro-chemical circuitry of birds that remain awake for long periods during migration, and exploring pharmaceutical stimulants. Obviously, soldiers who do not need sleep would have a great advantage in a war with normal soldiers. Amanda Onion, "The No-Doze Soldier," ABCNews.com, http://www.lauralee.com/news/nodozesoldier.htm (December 2004).

65. Kress, *Beggars in Spain,* 63.

66. Curtis Rist, "Genetic Tinkering Makes Bioterror Worse," *Discover* (January 2002), 76.

67. Nottingham, *Screening DNA,* http://ourworld.compuserve.com/home pages/Stephen_Nottingham/DNA9.htm (December 2004).

68. Gray, *Cyborg Citizen,* 118.

69. "Monsanto Co. Drops Biotech Wheat," CBS News (May 11, 2004), http://www.cbsnews.com/stories/2004/05/11/tech/main616811.shtml (December 2004).

70. Organic Consumers Organization, http://www.organicconsumers.org/monlink.html (December 2004); see also "Toxic Town," *60 Minutes* (November 10, 2002), CBS News Transcripts, http://www.connectotel.com/gmfood/cb101102 .html (December 2004).

71. Rifkin, *The Biotech Century,* 81.

72. In reality, maize has been genetically modified with bacterial genes to endow it with resistance to insect pests and herbicides. This transgenic corn grows over large areas of the United States. Concerns have been expressed about "genetic pollution" threatening wildlife and organic crops as a result of transgenic maize-pollen spreading foreign genes. France has suspended authorization for biotech giant Novartis to grow genetically engineered maize. See Stephen Nottingham, *Eat Your Genes: How Genetically Modified Food Is Entering Our Diet* (London: Zed Books, 1998), 181. In addition, see Maria Margaronis, "The Politics of Food: As Biotech 'Frankenfoods' Are Stuffed Down Their Throats, Consumers Rebel," *The Nation* (December 27, 1999), http://www.purefood.org/ge/euge9699.cfm (June 2002).

73. Rifkin, *The Biotech Century,* 97, 101.

74. Maggie Fox, "Scientists Genetically Engineer a Monkey," *Science News* (January 12, 2001), http://www.genconnection.com/English/geneticengineered monkey.pdf (June 2003).

75. Slonczewski, "Octavia Butler's *Xenogenesis* Trilogy: A Biologist's Response," http://biology.kenyon.edu/slonc/books/butlerl.html (December 2004).

76. On November 16, 1974, NASA did send out a radio message from the SETI unit at Arecibo, Puerto Rico, to the M13 cluster of 300,000 stars in the

Hercules constellation. The message contained a variety of data describing Earth, including a pictogram of the double helix of DNA together with the formula for the four DNA bases and the number of nucleotides in the human genome. The signal will not reach M13 for 24,972 years. See: "Biotechnology and SETI," http://www.progex.net/biotheology/seti_biotechnology.htm (August 2002).

77. Haraway, "A Cyborg Manifesto," in *Simians, Cyborgs, and Women,* ed. Haraway, 180, 181.

78. Butler won Hugo awards for her short story "Speech Sounds" (1983) and her novella "Bloodchild" (1984); she also won the Nebula Award for *Bloodchild* and for her novel *Parable of the Talents* (1998).

79. Octavia Butler, *Dawn* (New York: Popular Library, 1987), 40.

80. Adam's first wife, Lilith, refused to submit to his rule—in particular, she would not lie beneath him in the missionary position "favored by male-dominant societies"; she was repudiated, cast out of Eden, and fated to couple with demons and give birth to a monstrous brood. Barbara Walker, *The Woman's Encyclopedia of Myths and Secrets* (New York: Harper and Row, 1983), 541.

81. Joan Slonczewski, "Octavia Butler's *Xenogenesis Trilogy.*"

82. Donna Haraway, *Primate Visions: Gender, Race, and Nature in the World of Modern Science* (New York: Routledge, 1989), 378.

83. Butler, *Dawn,* 158.

84. Slonczewski, "Octavia Butler's *Xenogenesis Trilogy.*"

85. Rifkin, *The Biotech Century,* 37.

86. Rita Arditti, Renate Duelli-Klein, and Shelley Minden, eds., *Test Tube Women: What Future for Motherhood* (Boston, Mass.: Pandora Press, 1984), 76.

87. Silver, *Remaking Eden,* 107.

88. Paul Reger, "First Mule Cloned at University of Idaho," *Chicago Sun-Times* (May 30, 2003), 3.

89. Megan Garvey, "House Votes to Ban Cloning," *Chicago Tribune* (August 1, 2001), 1, 16.

90. Dorothy C. Wertz, "History of Cloning," *Gene Letter* (August 1, 1998), http://www.genesage.com/professionals/geneletter/archives/historyofcloning.html (December 2004).

91. Silver, *Remaking Eden,* 94.

92. Varley won the Hugo and Nebula awards for his novel *Steel Beach* (1992).

93. Turney, *Frankenstein's Footsteps,* 211.

94. The purpose of the congressional hearing was to reassure the public that Rorvik's book was a hoax and that human cloning was impossible, so that ethical questions need not be raised. See Arditti, Duelli-Klein, and Minden, *Test-Tube Women,* 82.

95. After World War II, many high-ranking Nazis escaped from Germany to fascist-controlled South America, where they lived under the protection of dictators.

96. Nelkin and Lindee, *The DNA Mystique,* 2.

97. Lee M. Silver, "*Boys from Brazil* (1978)," Princeton University class WWS 320, Human Genetics, Reproduction and Public Policy, http://www.princeton .edu/~wws320/Films/boys%20brazil/boysbrazil.htm (December 2004).

98. As of summer 2004, *Jurassic Park* was the sixth highest-grossing movie of all time. It was followed by two weak sequels, *The Lost World: Jurassic Park* (1997) and *Jurassic Park III* (2001).

99. The first cloned-to-order pet sold in the United States was announced on December 22, 2004 (NBC Nightly News). The clone kitten, named Little Nicky, cost a Texas woman $50,000 and was created from the DNA of her beloved cat, which died in 2003. The company that created the pet clone—Genetic Savings and Clone (http://www.savingsandclone.com)—expects to clone a dog in 2005.

100. Jeunet and co-director Marc Caro also made the 1995 film *The City of Lost Children* (*La Cité des Infants Perdus*), in which lonely mad scientist Krank (Daniel Emilfork) creates a family of six narcoleptic clones (all played by Dominique Pinon).

101. Rifkin, *Biotech Century*, 2.

102. Nottingham, *Screening DNA*, http://ourworld.compuserve.com/home pages/Stephen_Nottingham/DNA9.htm (June 2002).

103. Baldi, *The Shattered Self*, 54.

104. David Skal, *The Monster Show: A Cultural History of Horror* (New York: Penguin Books, 1993), 76.

105. Noble, *The Religion of Technology*, 192.

106. Jane Murphy, "From Mice to Men? Implications of Progress in Cloning Research," in *Test Tube Women*, ed. Arditti, Duelli-Klein, and Minden, 84.

107. Michael Marshall Smith, *Spares* (New York: Bantam Books, 1996), 61.

108. Rifkin, *The Biotech Century*, 31.

109. Smith, *Spares*, 246.

110. In a *Wired* magazine interview (November 1996), Di Filippo explained the collection's title, *Ribofunk:* "It's a neologism of my own inventing that I hope spreads like a memetic virus throughout the intellectual community. Ribo comes from the word ribosome, which I use as a shorthand for all biology, and funk indicates a stylistic component derived mostly from funk music . . . a hot, skittery style in contrast to the more laid back, cerebral style that you might find in some cyberpunk." He's even written a Ribofunk Manifesto: http://www.streettech.com/bcp/ BCPgraf/Manifestos/Ribofunk.html (December 2004).

111. Paul Di Filippo, *Ribofunk* (New York: Four Walls Eight Windows, 1996), 88.

112. Ibid.

113. Ibid.

114. Rifkin, *The Biotech Century*, 68.

115. Dorothy Nelkin, "Forms of Intrusion: Comparing Resistance to Information Technology and Biotechnology in the USA," in *Resistance to New Technology: Nuclear Power, Information Technology and Biotechnology*, ed. Martin Bauer (Cambridge: Cambridge University Press, 1995), 381.

CHAPTER 8

1. Richard Feynman, "There's Plenty of Room at the Bottom," *Engineering and Science,* February 1960, http://www.zyvex.com/nanotech/feynman.html (December 2004).

2. *Nano* refers to a billionth of a meter, which is the width of five carbon atoms, about a thousand times smaller than a human hair. The term *nanotechnology* was used in 1974 by Norio Taniguchi of Tokyo Science in reference to micromachining.

3. Ed Regis, *Great Mambo Chicken and the Transhuman Condition: Science Slightly Over the Edge* (Reading, Mass.: Perseus Books, 1990), 119.

4. K. Eric Drexler, *Engines of Creation: The Coming Era of Nanotechnology* (1986; reprint, New York: Anchor Books, 1990), 172; http://www.foresight.org/EOC/index.html. The Foresight Institute promotes Drexler's ideas and encourages nanotechnological research. Current information on nanotechnology research can be found in *Nanotechnology Journal,* http://www.iop.org/EJ/journal/Nano (December 2004), and the International Institute of Nanotechnology, http://www.nano.org.uk/ion.htm (December 2004).

5. Regis, *Great Mambo Chicken,* 120.

6. Drexler, *Engines of Creation,* 63.

7. Ed Regis, *Nano: The Emerging Science of Nanotechnology* (Boston: Back Bay Books, 1995), 175.

8. Ibid., 184.

9. Drexler, *Engines of Creation,* 121–122.

10. Ibid., 115.

11. Larry Niven, *A World Out of Time* (New York: Random House, 1976), 3.

12. Regis, *Great Mambo Chicken,* 4.

13. Alcor Life Extension Foundation, http://www.alcor.org (June 2002).

14. Ray Kurzweil, "Human Body Version 2.0" (February 2003), http://www.kurzweilai.net/articles/art0551.html (December 2004).

15. Marvin Minsky, "Will Robots Inherit the Earth," *Scientific American* (October 1994), 112; http://www.ai.mit.edu/people/minsky/papers/sciam.inherit.html (December 2004).

16. Drexler, *Engines of Creation,* 171.

17. Ibid., 231.

18. Regis, *Great Mambo Chicken,* 141.

19. Regis, *Nano,* 125.

20. Richard Smalley, a Nobel Prize–winning chemist at Rice University in Houston, Texas, argues that Drexler's theory of atomic engineering and self-replicating nanomachines is impossible because it fails to incorporate the essence of chemistry—that atoms exist in groups and cannot be manipulated individually. See Richard E. Smalley, "Of Chemistry, Love and Nanobots," *Scientific American* (September 2001), and Robert F. Service, "Is Nanotechnology Dangerous?" *Science* 290

(November 24, 2000): 1527–1528. The aptly named Smalley has helped engineer a "schism in the nanotechnology community" between his more practical approach and Drexler's long-range, revolutionary vision of molecular manufacturing. See Ed Regis, "The Incredible Shrinking Man," *Wired* (October 2004), 179–181, 204–205.

21. John Benditt, "Nanotech Gets Real," *Technology Review* (March 2002), 9.

22. For recent nanotech assessments, see David Rotman, "Nanotech Goes to Work," *Technology Review* (January/February 2001), 62–68; Will McCarthy, "Ultimate Alchemy," *Wired* (October 2001), 150–157; Peter Farley, "Nanotech by the Numbers," *Technology Review* (September 2002), 46–52; Richard Monastersky, "The Dark Side of Small," *Chronicle of Higher Education* (September 10, 2004), A12–A15.

23. *The Nanotech Report* 2003, http://www.luxcapital.com/nanotech_report.htm (December 2004).

24. The National Nanotechnology Initiative, http://www.nano.gov/ (December 2004).

25. DARPA, http://www.darpa.mil/ (December 2004).

26. Talbot, "DARPA's Disruptive Technologies," 44.

27. Menzel and D'Aluisio, *Robo sapiens,* 27.

28. Douglas Mulhall, *Our Molecular Future: How Nanotechnology, Robotics, Genetics, and Artificial Intelligence Will Transform Our World* (New York: Prometheus Books, 2002), 66.

29. David Talbot, "Super Soldiers," *Technology Review* (October 2002), 44–50.

30. Drexler, *Engines of Creation,* 174.

31. Paul McAuley, *Fairyland* (New York: Avon Books, 1995), 109.

32. Ibid., 4.

33. Richard Dawkins, *The Selfish Gene* (New York: Oxford University Press, 1976); see also Richard Brodie, *Virus of the Mind: The New Science of the Meme* (Seattle: Integral Press, 1996), and Susan Blackmore, *The Meme Machine* (New York: Oxford University Press, 1999).

34. João Pedro de Magalhães, "Homo Sapiens Sapiens Cyber: Upgrading Ourselves Beyond Our Biology," http://www.jpreason.com/science/hcyber.htm; http://author.senescence.info/thoughts/hcyber.html (October 2003).

35. McAuley, *Fairyland,* 359.

36. Ibid., 311.

37. *The Diamond Age* won the Hugo Award for best novel.

38. Drexler, *Engines of Creation,* 12.

39. Published by Activision.

40. Neal Stephenson, *The Diamond Age, or, A Young Lady's Illustrated Primer* (New York: Bantam Books, 1995), 58.

41. Ibid., 498.

42. Ibid.

43. Ibid., 499.

44. Winner, *Autonomous Technology,* 229.

45. Bill Joy, "Why the Future Doesn't Need Us," *Wired* (April 2000), 254.

46. Drexler, *Engines of Creation,* 174–175.

47. Michael Heim, *Virtual Realism* (New York: Oxford University Press, 1998), 41.

48. Forster, "The Machine Stops," 13.

49. For an analysis of these novels, see Bernie Heidkam, "Responses to the Alien Mother in Post-Maternal Cultures: C. J. Cherryh and Orson Scott Card," *Science Fiction Studies* 23 (November 1996).

50. Kurzweil, *The Age of Spiritual Machines,* 141.

51. The 1983 novella version of *Blood Music* won both the Hugo and the Nebula.

52. Bukatman, *Terminal Identity,* 268.

53. Greg Bear, *Blood Music* (New York: Ace, 1985), 14.

54. Ibid., 18.

55. Ibid., 117.

56. Winner, *Autonomous Technology,* 208.

57. Bear, *Blood Music,* 199.

58. Ibid., 219.

59. Ibid., 204.

60. Ibid., 197.

61. Drexler, *Engines of Creation,* 172–173.

62. Regis, *Mambo Chicken,* 137.

63. Kurzweil, *The Age of Spiritual Machines,* 142.

64. Ibid., 141.

65. First published in Europe under the title *Necroville* (1993).

66. Ian McDonald, *Terminal Café* (New York: Bantam, 1994), preface.

67. Ibid., 11.

68. Ibid., 133.

69. Ibid., 137.

70. Ibid.

71. Winner, *Autonomous Technology,* 227.

72. McDonald, *Terminal Café,* 20.

73. Bill Joy, "Why the Future Doesn't Need Us," 248.

74. Monastersky, "The Dark Side of Small," A12.

CHAPTER 9

1. Kurzweil, *The Age of Spiritual Machines,* 257.

2. Dery, *The Pyrotechnic Insanitarium,* 255–256.

3. Davis, *Techgnosis,* 78.

4. Winner, *Autonomous Technology,* 29, 55.

5. Ibid., 59–60.

6. Gautam Naik, "HIV Infections Surged Last Year," *Wall Street Journal* (July 7, 2004), 2.

7. Skal, *Screams of Reason,* 263.

8. Richard Preston, *The Hot Zone* (New York: Anchor, 1994), 407.

9. Laurie Garrett, *The Coming Plague: Newly Emerging Diseases in a World Out of Balance* (New York: Penguin Books, 1994), 40–47.

10. Richard Preston, *The Demon in the Freezer* (New York: Random House, 2002), 88–95.

11. In this chapter, I am using the term *virus* as an overall designation for dangerous invasive microbes and parasites.

12. Sharon Begley and Michael Isikoff, "Anxious about Anthrax," *Newsweek* (October 22, 2001), 28.

13. Centers for Disease Control (CDC), http://www.cdc.gov/ncidod/dvbid/ westnile/surv&controlCaseCount03_detailed.htm (December 2004).

14. CDC, http://www.cdc.gov/ncidod/sars/faq.htm (December 2004).

15. Jeremy Manier, "Scientists Unravel SARS' Gene Code," *Chicago Tribune* (April 13, 2003), 18.

16. Peter Gorner, "Mystery of the Monkey Virus," *Chicago Tribune* (June 24, 2004), 1.

17. Geoffrey Cowley, "How Progress Makes Us Sick," *Newsweek* (May 5, 2003), 34.

18. Charles Piller and Keith R. Yamamoto, *Gene Wars: Military Control over the New Genetic Technologies* (New York: Beech Tree Books, 1988), 29.

19. Andrew Goliszek, *In the Name of Science: A History of Secret Programs, Medical Research, and Human Experimentation* (New York: St. Martin's Press, 2003), 34–35.

20. Judith Miller, Stephen Engelberg, and William Broad, *Germs: Biological Weapons and America's Secret War* (New York: Simon and Schuster, 2001), 37–38; see also Wendy Barnaby, *The Plague Makers: The Secret World of Biological Warfare* (New York: Continuum, 2000), 20–21.

21. Miller, Engelberg, and Broad, *Germs,* 40.

22. Ibid., 52.

23. The Biological and Toxic Weapons Convention, http://projects.sipri.se/ cbw/docs/bw-btwc-text.html (December 2004).

24. Miller, Engelberg, and Broad, *Germs,* 136.

25. Judith Miller, Stephen Engelberg, and William J. Broad, "Next to Old Rec Hall, a 'Germ-Making Plant,' " *New York Times* (September 4, 2001); http://www .nytimes.com/2001/09/04/international/04BIOW.html (December 2004).

26. Goliszek, *In the Name of Science,* 49.

27. Ibid., 260.

28. Barnaby, *The Plague Makers,* 15.

29. Ibid., 147–148.

30. Paul Recer, "Researchers Create a Virus from Scratch," *Chicago Sun-Times* (July 12, 2002), 23.

31. David Robinson, "Vying over a Virus," *Time* (July 22, 2002), 13.

32. Barnaby, *The Plague Makers,* 109.

33. Miller, Engelberg, and Broad, *Germs,* 61.

34. Dennis Lim, "The Object of My Infection," *Village Voice* (May 19, 1998), 78.

35. James B. Twitchell, *Dreadful Pleasures: An Anatomy of Modern Horror* (New York: Oxford University Press, 1985), 105–106.

36. Margaret Atwood, *Oryx and Crake* (New York: Doubleday, 2003), 28.

37. Ibid., 57.

38. Joanna Marchant, "Future Farm," http://www.futuretalk.org/01/quarter2/05211033.html (December 2004).

39. Atwood, *Oryx and Crake,* 228–229.

40. Ibid., 243.

41. Robert Heinlein, *The Puppet Masters* (New York: Ballantine, 1951), 205.

42. Carl Zimmer, *Parasite Rex: Inside the Bizarre World of Nature's Most Dangerous Creatures* (New York: Free Press, 2000), 115.

43. Skal, *Screams of Reason,* 251.

44. In his films, Cronenberg—who studied biology and biochemistry—becomes a doctor or a scientist, such as a neurologist, virologist, oncologist, gynecologist, dermatologist, and epidemiologist.

45. Skal, *Screams of Reason,* 215.

46. Robin Cook, *Vector* (New York: Putnam, 1999), 2.

47. Judith Miller and William J. Broad, "Clinton Describes Terrorism Threat for the 21st Century," *New York Times* (January 22, 1999), 1.

48. Richard Preston, interview by the author, 1999.

49. Miller, Engelberg, and Broad, *Germs,* 81.

50. Ibid., 225.

51. Peter Rojas, "How Bad Movies Can Save America," *Wired* (August 2003), 32.

52. The term *worm* derives from John Brunner's 1975 science fiction novel *Shockwave Rider,* in which "tapeworms" are injected into the "data net" to delete information.

53. Anick Jesdanun, "Worm Infects Global Systems," *Chicago Sun-Times* (August 13, 2003), 68.

54. "CyberWar," *Frontline,* PBS (May 6, 2004).

55. Hayles, *How We Became Posthuman,* 276.

56. Steve Silberman, "The Bacteria Whisperer," *Wired* (April 2003), 106.

57. Dawkins, *The Selfish Gene,* 192.

EPILOGUE

1. Winner, *Autonomous Technology,* 191, 237.

2. T. J. Matheson, "Marcuse, Ellul, and the Science-Fiction Film: Negative Responses to Technology," *Science Fiction Studies* no. 58, vol. 19, part 3 (November 1992); http://www.depauw.edu/sfs/backissues/58/matheson58art.htm (December 2004).

3. Noble, *The Religion of Technology,* 208.

4. Jaron Lanier, "One-Half of a Manifesto," *Wired* (December 2000), 179.

BIBLIOGRAPHY

Andrews, Lori, and Dorothy Nelkin. *Body Bazaar: The Market for Human Tissue in the Biotechnology Age.* New York: Crown, 2001.

Arditti, Rita, Renate Duelli-Klein, and Shelley Minden, editors. *Test Tube Women: What Future for Motherhood.* Boston, Mass.: Pandora Press, 1984.

Asimov, Isaac. *Robot Visions.* New York: Penguin Books, 1990.

Atwood, Margaret. *Oryx and Crake.* New York: Doubleday, 2003.

Aurich, Rolf, Wolfgang Jacobsen, and Gabriele Jatho, editors. *Artificial Humans, Manic Machines, Controlled Bodies.* Los Angeles: Goethe Institut, 2000.

Bacon, Francis. *The New Atlantis.* New York: P. F. Collier and Son, 1901.

Baldi, Pierre. *The Shattered Self: The End of Natural Evolution.* Cambridge, Mass.: MIT Press, 2001.

Balsamo, Anne. *Technologies of the Gendered Body.* Durham, N.C.: Duke University Press, 1996.

Barnaby, Wendy. *The Plague Makers: The Secret World of Biological Warfare.* New York: Continuum, 2000.

Bauer, Martin, editor. *Resistance to New Technology: Nuclear Power, Information Technology and Biotechnology.* Cambridge: Cambridge University Press, 1995.

Bear, Greg. *Blood Music.* New York: Ace, 1985.

Bellamy, Edward. *Looking Backward: 2000–1887.* 1888; reprint, Cleveland: World Publishing Company, 1945.

Benedikt, Michael, editor. *Cyberspace First Steps.* Cambridge, Mass.: MIT Press, 1992.

Berger, Harold. *Science Fiction and the New Dark Age.* Bowling Green, Ohio: Bowling Green State University Popular Press, 1976.

Bergson, Henri. "Laughter." In *Comedy.* New York: Doubleday Anchor Books, 1956.

Black, Edwin. *War against the Weak: Eugenics and America's Campaign to Create a Master Race.* New York: Four Walls Eight Windows, 2003.

Bolter, J. David. *Turing's Man.* Chapel Hill: University of North Carolina Press, 1984.

Bova, Ben, editor. *Science Fiction Hall of Fame,* Vol. 2 A. New York: Doubleday and Company, 1973.

Boyer, Paul. *By the Bomb's Early Light: American Thought and Culture at the Dawn of the Atomic Age.* New York: Pantheon, 1985.

————. *Fallout: A Historian Reflects on America's Half-Century Encounter with Nuclear Weapons.* Columbus: Ohio State University Press, 1998.

Breton, André. *Manifestos of Surrealism.* 1924; reprint, Ann Arbor: University of Michigan Press, 1972.

Brooks, Rodney. *Flesh and Machines: How Robots Will Change Us.* New York: Pantheon Books, 2002.

Brunner, John. *The Shockwave Rider.* New York: Ballantine Books, 1975.

Bukatman, Scott. *Terminal Identity: The Virtual Subject in Postmodern Science Fiction.* Durham: Duke University Press, 1993.

Burkett, Elinor. *The Gravest Show on Earth: America in the Age of AIDS.* New York: Houghton Mifflin, 1995.

Butler, Octavia. *Dawn.* New York: Popular Library, 1987.

Cadigan, Pat. *Synners.* New York: Four Walls Eight Windows, 1991.

Caidin, Martin. *Cyborg.* New York: Warner, 1972.

Capek, Karel. *R.U.R.* and *The Insect Play.* 1923; reprint, New York: Oxford University Press, 1961.

Cavelos, Jeanne. *The Science of STAR WARS.* New York: St. Martin's Press, 1999.

Clarke, Arthur C. *The City and the Stars* and *The Sands of Mars.* 1956; reprint, New York: Warner Books, 2001.

Clement, Peter. *Mutant.* New York: Ballantine, 2001.

Cohen, John. *Human Robots in Myth and Science.* Cranbury, N.J.: A. S. Barnes and Co., 1967.

Cook, Robin. *Vector.* New York: Putnam, 1999.

Crichton, Michael. *Prey.* New York: HarperCollins, 2002.

Damasio, Antonio R. *The Feeling of What Happens: Body and Emotion in the Making of Consciousness.* New York: Harcourt Brace and Company, 1999.

Davis, Eric. *Techgnosis: Myth, Magic and Mysticism in the Age of Information.* New York: Harmony Books, 1998.

Dawkins, Richard. *The Selfish Gene.* New York: Oxford University Press, 1976.

DeGrandpre, Richard. *Digitopia.* New York: Atrandom.com, 2001.

De Landa, Manuel. *War in the Age of Intelligent Machines.* New York: Zone Books, 1991.

Dery, Mark. *The Pyrotechnic Insanitarium: American Culture on the Brink.* New York: Grove Press, 1999.

Descartes, René. *The Philosophical Works of Descartes,* Volume 1. Trans. Elizabeth S. Haldane and G. R. T. Ross. Cambridge: Cambridge University Press, 1968.

Dewdney, Christopher. *Last Flesh: Life in the Transhuman Era.* Toronto: HarperCollins, 1998.

Dick, Philip K. *Blade Runner (Do Androids Dream of Electric Sheep?).* 1968; reprint, New York: Ballantine Books, 1982.

————. *The Three Stigmata of Palmer Eldritch.* New York: Vintage Books, 1964.

Di Filippo, Paul. *Ribofunk.* New York: Four Walls Eight Windows, 1996.

Dowling, Terry, et al., editor. *The Essential Ellison: A 50 Year Retrospective.* Beverly Hills: Morpheus International, 2000.

Drexler, K. Eric. *Engines of Creation: The Coming Era of Nanotechnology.* 1986; reprint, New York: Anchor Books, 1990.

Egan, Greg. *Permutation City.* New York: Harper Prism, 1994.

Eisner, Lotte. *The Haunted Screen.* Berkeley: University of California Press, 1969.

Ellul, Jacques. *The Technological Society.* New York: Vintage Books, 1964.

Elsaesser, Thomas. *Metropolis.* London: British Film Institute, 2000.

Ewald, Paul W. *Plague Time: How Stealth Infections Cause Cancers, Heart Disease, and Other Deadly Ailments.* New York: Free Press, 2000.

Forster, E. M. *The Eternal Moment and Other Stories.* New York: Grosset and Dunlap, 1928.

Freed, Les. *The History of Computers.* Emeryville, Calif.: Ziff-Davis Press, 1995.

French, Richard D. *Antivivisection and Medical Science in Victorian Society.* Princeton, N.J.: Princeton University Press, 1975.

French, Sean. *The Terminator.* London: British Film Institute, 1996.

Fukuyama, Francis. *Our Posthuman Future: Consequences of the Biotechnology Revolution.* New York: Farrar, Straus and Giroux, 2002.

Garrett, Laurie. *The Coming Plague: Newly Emerging Diseases in a World Out of Balance.* New York: Penguin Books, 1994.

Gibson, William. *Count Zero.* New York: Ace, 1986.

———. *Mona Lisa Overdrive.* New York: Bantam, 1988.

———. *Neuromancer.* New York: Ace, 1984.

Glassy, Mark C. *The Biology of Science Fiction Cinema.* Jefferson, N.C.: McFarland and Company, 2001.

Goliszek, Andrew. *In the Name of Science: A History of Secret Programs, Medical Research, and Human Experimentation.* New York: St. Martin's Press, 2003.

Graham, Elaine L. *Representation of the Post/Human: Monsters, Aliens and Others in Popular Culture.* New Brunswick, N.J.: Rutgers University Press, 2002.

Gray, Chris Hables. *Cyborg Citizen: Politics in the Posthuman Age.* New York: Routledge, 2002.

Gray, Chris Hables, editor. *The Cyborg Handbook.* New York: Routledge, 1995.

Gresh, Lois, and Robert Weinberg. *The Computers of Star Trek.* New York: Basic Books, 1999.

Haraway, Donna. *Primate Visions: Gender, Race, and Nature in the World of Modern Science.* New York: Routledge, 1989.

Haraway, Donna J. *Simians, Cyborgs, and Women: The Reinvention of Nature.* New York: Routledge, Chapman, and Hall, 1991.

Hatt, Harold E. *Cybernetics and the Image of Man.* New York: Abingdon Press, 1968.

Hayles, N. Katherine. *How We Became Posthuman: Virtual Bodies in Cybernetics, Literature, and Informatics.* Chicago: University of Chicago Press, 1999.

Heim, Michael. *The Metaphysics of Virtual Reality.* New York: Oxford University Press, 1993.

———. *Virtual Realism.* New York: Oxford University Press, 1998.

Heinlein, Robert. *Beyond This Horizon.* New York: Signet, 1948.

———. *The Puppet Masters.* New York: Ballantine, 1951.

Herbert, Frank. *The Eyes of Heisenberg.* New York: Berkley Medallion Books, 1966.

Hillegas, Mark. *The Future as Nightmare: H. G. Wells and the Anti-Utopians.* Carbondale: Southern Illinois University Press, 1967.

Hoffmann, E. T. A. *The Sandman.* 1816; reprint, New York: Penguin, 1982.

Hunt, Linda. *Secret Agenda: The United States Government, Nazi Scientists, and Project Paperclip.* New York: St. Martin's Press, 1991.

Huxley, Aldous. *Brave New World.* 1932; reprint, New York: Bantam, 1950.

Irwin, William, editor. THE MATRIX *and Philosophy: Welcome to the Desert of the Real.* Chicago: Open Court, 2002.

Jordon, Tim. *Cyberpower: The Culture and Power of Cyberspace and the Internet.* London: Routledge, 1999.

Kerman, Judith B., editor. *Retrofitting* BLADE RUNNER: *Issues in Ridley Scott's* BLADE RUNNER *and Philip K. Dick's* DO ANDROIDS DREAM OF ELECTRIC SHEEP? Bowling Green, Ohio: Bowling Green State University Popular Press, 1991.

King, Stephen. *The Stand.* 1978; reprint, New York: Penguin Group, 1991.

Koestler, Arthur. *The Ghost in the Machine.* Chicago: Gateway, 1967.

Kracauer, Siegfried. *From Caligari to Hitler.* Princeton: Princeton University Press, 1947.

Kress, Nancy. *Beggars in Spain.* New York: Eos Books, 1993.

Kuhn, Annette, editor. *Alien Zone: Cultural Theory and Contemporary Science Fiction Cinema.* London: Verso, 1990.

Kurzweil, Ray. *The Age of Spiritual Machines.* New York: Viking, 1999.

Lifton, Robert Jay. *The Nazi Doctors: Medical Killing and the Psychology of Genocide.* New York: Basic Books, 1986.

MacLeod, Ken. *The Cassini Division.* New York: Tor, 1998.

Matheson, Richard. *I Am Legend.* Berkeley: Berkeley Medallion Books, 1954.

McAuley, Paul. *Fairyland.* New York: Avon Books, 1995.

McCaffrey, Anne. *The Ship Who Sang.* New York: Del Rey, 1969.

McCorduck, Pamela. *Machines Who Think: A Personal Inquiry into the History and Prospects of Artificial Intelligence.* New York: W. H. Freeman and Company, 1979.

McDonald, Ian. *Terminal Café.* New York: Bantam, 1994.

McKibben, Bill. *Enough: Staying Human in an Engineered Age.* New York: Times Books, 2003.

McLuhan, Marshall. *Understanding Media: The Extensions of Man.* New York: McGraw Hill, 1964.

Menzel, Peter, and Faith D'Aluisio. *Robo sapiens: Evolution of a New Species.* Cambridge, Mass.: MIT Press, 2000.

Miller, Judith, Stephen Engelberg, and William Broad. *Germs: Biological Weapons and America's Secret War.* New York: Simon and Schuster, 2001.

Minden, Michael, and Holger Bachmann, editors. *Fritz Lang's* METROPOLIS: *Cinematic Visions of Technology and Fear.* Rochester, N.Y.: Boydell and Brewer, 2000.

Minsky, Marvin. *The Society of Mind.* New York: Simon and Schuster, 1985.

Moravec, Hans. *Mind Children: The Future of Robot and Human Intelligence.* Cambridge, Mass.: Harvard University Press, 1988.

———. *Robot: Mere Machine to Transcendent Mind.* New York: Oxford University Press, 1999.

Mulhall, Douglas. *Our Molecular Future: How Nanotechnology, Robotics, Genetics, and Artificial Intelligence Will Transform Our World.* New York: Prometheus Books, 2002.

Napier, Susan J. *Anime—From AKIRA to PRINCESS MONONOKE.* New York: Palgrave, 2000.

Nelkin, Dorothy, and M. Susan Lindee. *The DNA Mystique: The Gene as a Cultural Icon.* New York: W. H. Freeman and Company, 1995.

Noble, David. *The Religion of Technology: The Divinity of Man and the Spirit of Invention.* New York: Knopf, 1997.

———. *A World without Women: The Christian Clerical Culture of Western Science.* New York: Oxford University Press, 1992.

Nottingham, Stephen F. *Eat Your Genes: How Genetically Modified Food Is Entering Our Diet.* London: Zed Books, 1998.

———. *Screening DNA: Exploring the Cinema-Genetics Interface,* http://ourworld .compuserve.com/homepages/Stephen_Nottingham/DNA1.htm.

Orwell, George. *1984.* 1949; reprint, New York: Signet, 1950.

Parker, Helen. *Biological Themes in Modern Science Fiction.* Ann Arbor: UMI Research Press, 1977.

Paul, Gregory S., and Earl D. Cox. *Beyond Humanity: CyberEvolution and Future Minds.* Rockland, Mass.: Charles River Media, 1996.

Penley, Constance, and Andrew Ross, editors. *Technoculture.* Minneapolis: University of Minnesota Press, 1991.

Perkowitz, Sidney. *Digital People: From Bionic Humans to Androids.* Washington, D.C.: Joseph Henry Press, 2004.

Piercy, Marge. *He, She, and It.* New York: Fawcett Crest, 1991.

Piller, Charles, and Keith R. Yamamoto. *Gene Wars: Military Control over the New Genetic Technologies.* New York: Beech Tree Books, 1988.

Pohl, Frederick. *Man Plus.* New York: Baen Publishing, 1976.

Preston, Richard. *The Demon in the Freezer.* New York: Random House, 2002.

———. *The Hot Zone.* New York: Anchor, 1994.

Radetsky, Peter. *Invisible Invaders: Viruses and the Scientists Who Pursue Them.* Boston: Back Bay Books, 1991.

Regis, Ed. *The Biology of Doom: The History of America's Secret Germ Warfare Project.* New York: Owl Books, 1999.

———. *Great Mambo Chicken and the Transhuman Condition: Science Slightly Over the Edge.* Reading, Mass.: Perseus Books, 1990.

———. *Nano: The Emerging Science of Nanotechnology.* Boston: Back Bay Books, 1995.

Rhodes, Richard. *Deadly Feasts: Tracking the Secrets of a Terrifying New Plague.* New York: Simon and Schuster, 1997.

Rifkin, Jeremy. *The Biotech Century: Harnessing the Gene and Remaking the World.* New York: Penguin Putnam, 1998.

Roszak, Theodore. *The Cult of Information: A Neo-Luddite Treatise on High-Tech, Ar-*

tificial Intelligence, and the True Art of Thinking. Berkeley: University of California Press, 1986.

Rucker, Rudy. *Software.* New York: Avon, 1982.

Rushing, Janice Hocker, and Thomas S. Frentz. *Projecting the Shadow: The Cyborg Hero in American Film.* Chicago: University of Chicago Press, 1995.

Rybczynski, Witold. *Taming the Tiger: The Struggle to Control Technology.* 1983; reprint, New York: Viking Penguin, 1985.

Sammon, Paul M. *Future Noir: The Making of BLADE RUNNER.* New York: Harper-Collins, 1996.

Schelde, Per. *Androids, Humanoids, and Other Science Fiction Monsters.* New York: New York University Press, 1993.

Shelley, Mary. *Frankenstein.* 1818; reprint, New York: Bantam Classics, 1981.

Silver, Lee M. *Remaking Eden: Cloning and Beyond in a Brave New World.* New York: Avon Books, 1997.

Silverberg, Robert, editor. *Beyond Control.* New York: Dell, 1972.

Skal, David. *The Monster Show: A Cultural History of Horror.* New York: Penguin Books, 1993.

Skal, David. *Screams of Reason: Mad Science and Modern Culture.* New York: W. W. Norton, 1998.

Skinner, B. F. *Walden Two.* 1948; reprint, New York: MacMillan Publishing Co., 1964.

Smith, Michael Marshall. *Spares.* New York: Bantam Books, 1996.

Springer, Claudia. *Electronic Eros.* Austin: University of Texas Press, 1996.

St. Augustine. *City of God.* New York: Modern Library, 1950.

Stephenson, Neal. *The Diamond Age, or, A Young Lady's Illustrated Primer.* New York: Bantam Books, 1995.

———. *Snow Crash.* New York: Bantam, 1992.

Sterling, Bruce, editor. *Mirrorshades: The Cyberpunk Anthology.* New York: Ace Books, 1986.

Sterling, Bruce. *Schismatrix Plus.* New York: Ace Books, 1996.

Stock, Gregory. *Metaman: The Merging of Humans and Machines into a Global Super-organism.* New York: Simon and Schuster, 1993.

———. *Redesigning Humans: Our Inevitable Genetic Future.* New York: Houghton Mifflin, 2002.

Stork, David. *HAL's Legacy: 2001's Computer as Dream and Reality.* Boston: MIT Press, 1997.

Sutin, Lawrence. *Divine Invasions: A Life of Philip K. Dick.* New York: Citadel Twilight Press, 1989.

Telotte, J. P. *A Distant Technology.* New Hampshire: Wesleyan University Press, 1999.

———. *Replications: A Robotic History of the Science Fiction Film.* Chicago: University of Illinois Press, 1995.

Tipler, Frank. *The Physics of Immortality: Modern Cosmology, God and the Resurrection of the Dead.* New York: Doubleday, 1994.

Touponce, William F. *Isaac Asimov.* Boston: Twayne Publishers, 1991.

Turney, Jon. *Frankenstein's Footsteps: Science, Genetics and Popular Culture.* New Haven: Yale University Press, 1998.

Twitchell, James B. *Dreadful Pleasures: An Anatomy of Modern Horror.* New York: Oxford University Press, 1985.

Van Vogt, A. E. *Slan.* 1940; reprint, New York: Tom Doherty Associates, 1998.

———. *The World of Null-A.* New York: Berkley, 1945.

Varley, John. *The Ophiuchi Hotline.* New York: Ace Books, 1977.

Vinge, Vernor. *True Names and the Opening of the Cyberspace Frontier.* New York: Tor, 1981.

Vonnegut, Kurt. *Player Piano.* 1952; reprint, New York: Delta Books, 1982.

Walker, Barbara. *The Woman's Encyclopedia of Myths and Secrets.* New York: Harper and Row, 1983.

Walsh, Chad. *From Utopia to Nightmare.* London: Geoffrey Blies, 1962.

Weizenbaum, Joseph. *Computer Power and Human Reason.* San Francisco: W. H. Freeman, 1976.

Wells, H. G. *The Island of Dr. Moreau.* 1896; reprint, New York: Berkeley Publishing Corporation, 1973.

———. *The Time Machine.* 1895; reprint, New York: Bantam Books, 1984.

Wheat, Leonard F. *Kubrick's 2001: A Triple Allegory.* Lanham, Md: Scarecrow Press, 2000.

Wiener, Norbert. *God and Golem, Inc.: A Comment on Certain Points Where Cybernetics Impinges on Religion.* Cambridge, Mass.: MIT Press, 1964.

———. *The Human Use of Human Beings: Cybernetics and Society.* New York: Da Capo Press, 1954.

Winner, Langdon. *Autonomous Technology: Technics-out-of-Control as a Theme in Political Thought.* Cambridge, Mass.: MIT Press, 1977.

Wolfe, Bernard. *Limbo.* New York: Ace Books, 1952.

Zamyatin, Yevgeny. *We.* Trans. Clarence Brown. 1924; reprint, New York: Penguin Books, 1993.

Zimmer, Carl. *Parasite Rex: Inside the Bizarre World of Nature's Most Dangerous Creatures.* New York: Free Press, 2000.

INDEX